James Branch Cabell and Richmond-in-Virginia

James Branch Cabell

A N D

Richmond-in-Virginia

Edgar MacDonald

University Press of Mississippi / Jackson

HOUSTON PUBLIC LIBRARY

Chronology reprinted from *James Branch Cabell: Centennial Essays,*
copyright © 1983 Louisiana State University Press. Reprinted by
permission.

Copyright © 1993 by the University Press of Mississippi
All rights reserved
Manufactured in the United States of America
96 95 94 93   4 3 2 1

The paper in this book meets the guidelines for permanence and
durability of the Committee on Production Guidelines for Book
Longevity of the Council on Library Resources.

Library of Congress Cataloging-in-Publication Data

MacDonald, Edgar E.
    James Branch Cabell and Richmond-in-Virginia / by Edgar
MacDonald.
        p.   cm.
    Includes bibliographical references (p.   ) and index.
    ISBN 0-87805-622-X (alk. paper)
    1. Cabell, James Branch, 1879–1958—Homes and haunts—
Virginia—Richmond.   2. Cabell, James Branch, 1879–1958—
Knowledge—Virginia—Richmond.   3. Authors, American—
Virginia—Richmond—Biography.   4. Authors, American—
20th century—Biography.   5. Richmond (Va.)—Social life and
customs.   6. Richmond (Va.) in literature.   I. Title.
PS3505.A153Z65   1993
813'.52—dc20
[B]   92-44966
                                                          CIP

British Library Cataloging-in-Publication data available

FOR

Richard Slatten: *Encourager*

Contents

CONTENTS

Acknowledgments

The writer of this biography first became aware of James Branch Cabell at Emmanuel Episcopal Church in Brook Hill, Virginia, just north of Richmond, where Cabell infrequently attended services. In the 1920s, students at the Parish School were drafted every year to help decorate the church with Christmas greens, and Priscilla Bradley Cabell was a friendly, colorful lady who seemed to be in charge of buildings and grounds. I was one of her youthful admirers. Her daughter Priscilla Davis was a friend of my mother, and Hopkins Davis, husband and vestryman, became my brother's godfather. One of my earliest teachers was Miss Helen Stockdell, also one of Ballard Cabell's teachers. Mr. Cabell wrote books that were somehow shocking, but how could one tell? They were deemed over the heads of most of us. Thirty years later I met Margaret Freeman Cabell, another voluble lady who had replaced Percie Cabell, and for the next quarter century was a frequent auditor of her lectures on various subjects, including her husband. I had only one serious discussion with Mr. Cabell about his work, a year before his death. This biography attempts to present him as he was seen by his contemporaries and as he saw himself in his writings. As a child, I did not consider him a remote figure, his family humanizing whatever was aloof about him. He was pretty much like my father, a quiet man who kept most of his opinions to himself in light of my mother's own flow of talk. In the writing of the biography I relived my own life in a sense, but I have tried to let Mr. Cabell tell his own story.

I am grateful to Clinton Webb and Edmund A. Rennolds, Jr., president and vice-president of the Associates of the James Branch Cabell Library, for asking me to undertake the writing of this biography. Louise Withers Ellyson and Mate Branch Converse, cousins of Cabell, were ever gracious in their support. Priscilla Harriss Cabell, the present holder of Annie Cabell's letters, kindly gave permission to publish them. I am indebted to the late Margaret Freeman Cabell and Cabell archivist John H. Whaley, Jr., for information and permission to cite from letters and manuscript materials by James Branch Cabell; to the late Mary Cary Moncure and the late Mrs. William Ronson for biographical details relative to Gabriella

ACKNOWLEDGMENTS

Moncure and for the loan of two manuscript volumes Cabell gave Gabriella and for permission to cite his letter. Virginia Page Chichester, a close friend of Cabell's stepdaughters, helped greatly with memories and sources. M. Thomas Inge, scholar and friend, was always encouraging, as was Maurice Duke of Virginia Commonwealth University. Anne Hobson Freeman willingly discussed Richmond and its avatars. Margaret Cook of the Swem Library, College of William and Mary, gave needed guidance in researching Cabell's college career and permission to quote from the Tucker-Coleman Papers. Anne Freudenberg of the Alderman Library, University of Virginia, facilitated research there. The entire staff of the James Branch Cabell Library at Virginia Commonwealth University made working there a congenial experience; I am especially indebted to the director, William Judd, and to Katherine Bachman Judd, John H. Whaley, Jr., Betsy Pittman, and a series of helpful assistants in Special Collections.

I am grateful to Mate Branch Converse for making available a memoir by James Ransom Branch as recorded by Melville C. Branch and for permission to cite as holder of the record, and for making available a letter of Martha Patteson Bowie to Martha Louise Patteson Branch and for permission to cite; to Kay J. Domine, Archivist, Swem Library, for permission to cite passages from the Faculty Minutes; to Mrs. Cassius Moncure Chichester for lending me genealogical materials; to Frederic Scott Bocock, S. B. Scott, and R. S. Scott for permission to cite the letter of Frederic William Scott; to Kenneth W. Duckett, Curator, Special Collections, Morris Library, Southern Illinois University, for making available the diary of Montgomery Evans and Hunter Stagg's letters to Evans with permission to cite as holder of the record; to the late Charlotte Nance Saylor, niece of Hunter Stagg, for permission to cite his letters held in various repositories. The letters of Carl Van Vechten are cited with the permission of his literary trustee, the late Donald Gallup; those of Hunter Stagg to Van Vechten were made available through the courtesy of Donald Schoonover, Curator of Manuscripts, Beinecke Library, Yale University; the manuscript letters of Marjorie Rawlings in the James Branch Cabell Library are cited with the kind permission of Norton S. Baskin. I am also grateful to Carmen Russell Hurff, Manuscript Curator, University of Florida Libraries, for making available Cabell letters housed there; to Betsy Pittman, Archivist, James Branch Cabell Library, to cite manuscript Ellen Glasgow letters to Cabell and for permission to cite letters of James Ransom Branch to Annie Branch Cabell contained in his 1905 Letter Book as holder of the record; to Edmund Berkeley, Jr., Curator of Manuscripts, Alderman Library, for making the letters of James Branch Cabell to Alice Serpell available; to the Curator of the Manuscripts Department, William R. Perkins Library, Duke University, for making available materials from the Henry Sydnor Harrison Papers and for allowing them to be quoted as holder for the record; to Dowson Cole, Senior Librarian, Virginia Historical Society, for making available the typescript by Mary Wingfield Scott, "James Branch Cabell and the 'Jack Scott Murder'" and for permission to cite as holder of the record; to Louise Withers Ellyson for making available a typescript by Mary Wingfield Scott, "Some Wild Branches I Have Known" and for permission to cite as holder of the record. The catalog compiled by Mary Faith Pusey and Donna L. Purvis of the James Branch Cabell Collection in the University of Virginia Library has been ever useful, and I am grateful to the staff of the Alderman for many courtesies.

Introduction

This biography of James Branch Cabell is also a "biography" of a social cosmos. Turn-of-the-century Richmond was Cabell's generating time and place. Its history, mores, and attitudes entered into his psyche. Ambivalent at heart, its neuroses, pretentions, self-mockery became the fabric of his being. Despite its mythology, Richmond grew out of a polyglot culture, a nexus between north and south, east and west. Its head was given to an industrial north, its heart to an agrarian south. Down the James, it looked eastward to a European homeland; to the west, it felt the lure of the frontier. As Peter Taylor observed, "one's memory begins not in one's own childhood but in the talk of adults around you in childhood." Cabell's life is peculiarly a drama of time and place.

Like a Gertrude Stein "novel," Richmond lives in a continuous present, unlike Virginia which lives in a continuous past. Proustian in its rituals, the city is the creation of economic forces; the Commonwealth is a philosophical concept. An uneasy commerce exists between the two, especially in the General Assembly. Terms of distinction like "aristocrat" and "plain people" have given way to "city boy" and "country boy," but the rivalries persist. Compounding the complexities of shifting allegiances are the evolving identifications of families. On both paternal and maternal sides, Cabell's Virginian ancestors became Richmonders. Ellen Glasgow, starting with *The Voice of the People* in 1900, took the shifting social roles of Virginians and Richmonders as her subject. Perversely, while steeped in Richmond's ambivalence, James Branch Cabell elected to play the Virginian, satirizing the archetype's evasions in veiled innuendo. He confessed, however, that Richmond "got at and into me when I was too young to defend myself"; as a consequence it could not ever "really seem to me grotesque."

Cabell was first employed as a newspaper reporter, and early in his career as a writer of fiction he aspired to be the social historian that Glasgow became. His eye was fixed on the novel of manners in his first extended effort, *The Eagle's Shadow* (1904), and he attempted the genre in *The Cords of Vanity* (1909) and *The Rivet in Grandfather's Neck* (1915). The novel of manners, essentially dialogue, is based on drama rather than epic, which is essentially narrative; its characters chat lightly of the social concerns of a particular time and place. At the age of seventeen, Cabell received a medal for a college paper entitled "The Comedies of William Congreve." In his library one finds *The Complete Works of Thackeray*. He turned admittedly to Dumas and the rhetorical melodrama of *The Three Musketeers*. But biography intruded in Cabell's comedies, the voices of real people spoke from behind the masks, and for his "health's comfort" he gravitated to allegory for disguise. Even so, he admitted that "the mild and provincial gossip of Richmond, as to the misdemeanors and vices and crimes of my private life, was seized upon and so very gorgeously re-embroidered as to become Neronean and nation-wide." Romance had always been the talk of drawing room and kitchen, and it became the artist's basic nourishment. He gave it a permanent structure. In mid-career Cabell rewrote all his earlier work, attempting to give life a symmetry it could only attain in art. In his study of Cabell's works, Louis Rubin concluded, "The figure of a man that he modeled and remodeled was James Branch Cabell himself, so that his collected works constitute, more than anything else, an extended essay in variously disguised autobiography." Cabell's comedies— of "Shirking," "Disenchantment," "Evasions," "Limitations"—became cosmic, but the writer's cosmos was Richmond. In his last works Cabell turned unabashedly to biography, dropping the poses, stepping out of the drama to become the Author. The drawing-room walls of his youth faded into vistas of space.

Before the Revolution, Richmond had no pretentions, socially or culturally; it was a magnet for those bent on getting ahead in an exchange of services and goods. It was early the meeting place of Scottish factors, Irish tradesmen, German artisans, and Jewish merchants. Free Negroes found work there. In 1779, fearful of British troops, the Virginians reluctantly left gracious, civilized Williamsburg for the brawling collection of riverside villages termed Richmond. They betook themselves to the hills overlooking the James and the lower "city" with its older inhabitants. Thomas Jefferson designed their new capitol and placed it on a commanding elevation. The "Virginians" are still on the hills, farther west along the river, but they return to lower Main and Cary streets to transact their business affairs. Ellen Glasgow's father walked down to the Tredegar Iron Works, situated between the canal and the river, but he walked up the hill to his handsome Greek Revival mansion on upper Main. Living and working on different levels, meeting all those diverse people, gave Richmonders perspective, a double vision that countered somewhat the restricted view-points of Virginians or southerners. The mixture gave the city many different churches, clubs, architects, cemeteries, even theaters. When the plantation owners lost their free labor, a number of Virginians married Richmonders. In Glasgow's and Cabell's youth one had to be careful how one defined them, but after a time the arbiters declared that Richmond had an English class hierarchy—old families (Virginians), old Richmonders (lawyers, physicians, clergymen), old merchants. In their works Glasgow and Cabell, and later Styron, played with these distinctions. In reality, the "best people" in Richmond have always been a heterogeneous lot, intermarriages having occurred between "old" and "new" in every decade.

When the Virginians moved from Williamsburg, the *Gazette* moved along to record their law-making. As in other commercial centers in nineteenth-century America, newspapers played an important role in Richmond, politically, culturally, and even literarily. Between 1804 and the close of the century more than one hundred fifty newspapers were founded in Richmond. While some lasted for only a few issues, the city's first great newspaper, the *Richmond Inquirer*, was a social force from 1804 to 1877. At the beginning of the twentieth century, Richmond had four dailies; its *Times-Dispatch* and *News-Leader* (merged to become the former in mid-1992) incorporated names of earlier newspapers. "Book Pages" have long been a feature of these papers, and out of them have grown book fairs and, indirectly, the Virginia Writers' Club and the *Reviewer*, both of which attracted Cabell's services. Book publishing firms flourished here at one time, and the American Booksellers Association recognizes Richmond as a prime market. Despite Glasgow's and Cabell's low opinions of the city's interest in literature, five of its writers have received the Pulitzer Prize as well as other literary awards.

When Henry James visited Richmond in the winter of 1906, he expected to find still vibrant in the air some of the tragic glamor that had been associated with the name of the capital of the Confederacy. He had envisioned a "ghost-haunted city," but to his dismay it appeared to him "simply blank and void." For James, no "references" in the romantic tradition were apparent; then he realized that "the large, sad poorness was in itself a reference." He surveyed the desolate scene and wrote mournfully of the low aesthetic level, antedating the sage of Baltimore by some years. As he wandered about the White House of the Confederacy, he mused on the sorry objects of veneration: "It was impossible . . . to imagine a community, of equal size, more disinherited of art or of letters. . . .

The social revolution had begotten neither song nor story—only, for literature, two or three biographies of soldiers, written in other countries" (*The American Scene*, 386–87).

While James composed this dirge in the solid, Edwardian comfort of the Jefferson Hotel, he seemed remarkably unaware that scarcely more than a block away on Main Street Ellen Glasgow had already published six novels, three of which were to merit prefaces for later editions—prefaces, ironically enough, compared with his own for excellence. That social revolution that James in 1906 felt was neglected and therefore so unproductive of song and story was the very soul and theme of *The Voice of the People* and *The Deliverance*. If James was ignorant of these "social histories" and their of author, Miss Glasgow was aware of Henry James. In 1906, James was also unaware of James Branch Cabell, who had enjoyed a modest success with his first attempt at a comedy of manners, *The Eagle's Shadow*, and whose short stories were appearing in respectable magazines. Though Henry James's assessment of the cultural scene in Richmond appears unflattering to the two young writers, both echoed his judgment later in their own assessments.

After their attainments were recognized, both Glasgow and Cabell commented at some length on the absence of a great literature in the South before their day. In her preface to *The Miller of Old Church*, Glasgow cited the apology of John Esten Cooke in his "Virginia Literature in the Nineteenth Century": "It may be said of it with truth that it is notable for its respect for good morals and manners; that it is nowhere offensive to delicacy or piety; or endeavors to instill a belief in what ought not to be believed." Glasgow more forthrightly suggested that the South, Virginia in particular, produced no great works because of its complacency, its blind contentment, its moral superstition—all of which resulted in a literature of evasion. Inasmuch as the region produced great men, if not great writers, she went on to suggest "that the creative art of the South was not a substitute for experience but experience itself, circumscribed and intensified." In short, the art of life was in living, not in contemplation.

In "Mr. Ritchie of Richmond," Cabell in turn cited Agnes M. Bondurant's *Poe's Richmond*: "'It was not the planters'—that is, the landed aristocracy of Virginia—'but the professional and businessmen of Richmond who were responsible for the promotion of literary culture in the city. These were the people who showed enough appreciation for Dickens and Thackeray to give them pleasant receptions.'" Mr. Thomas Ritchie was the toastmaster at the *petite souper* that some ninety of Richmond's merchants and tobacconists tendered Charles Dickens on his visit to the city. Mr. Ritchie admitted that he, a semi-retired editor of the *Richmond Enquirer*, was the only one present who might qualify as literary. He explained that "the *forte* of the Old Dominion [was] to be found in the masculine production of her statesmen . . . who have never indulged in works of imagination, in the charms of romance, or in the mere beauties of the *belles lettres*." Oratory, richly elegiac, served the literary hungers of most southerners. Cabell went on to reflect that even in his day the businessmen ran Virginia's colleges, symphonies, museum of fine arts, "while the culture of Virginia, as thus comfortably conducted, has proved to be sterile in every field of aesthetics—except only, as I have suggested elsewhere, in the superb and philanthropic romanticizing of Virginia history and in a free-spirited invention of priorities and relics" (*Let Me Lie*, 135).

If the literary tradition was oral, the great theme, infinitely embroidered during the early years of both writers, was the War. In "Almost Touching the Confederacy" and "As to Childish Matters of Long Ago," Cabell gives us two charming insights into the Richmond of his childhood. In the former essay, he marvels at the creation by his elders of the noble myth "of the Old South's perfection," of their "half-mythopoeic and half-critical frame of mind" that allowed them to talk one way upon a platform and another way "in your father's drugstore." Glasgow, in her preface to *The Battle-Ground*, also comments in some wonder on the "chanting chorus of male and female voices" that during her childhood recounted the heroic legends of the Lost Cause. Grimly realistic, she observes, "A War in which one had lost everything, even the right to own a doll with real hair, was not precisely my idea of romance." Much later, after writing *Virginia*, Glasgow recounts the visit she received from the elderly widow who reproved her for not "writing about the War": "If only I had your gifts, [the widow said,] I should devote them to proving to the world that the Confederacy was right. Of course, I know that even the best novelists are no longer so improving as they used to be; but I have always hoped that either you or Annie Cabell's son would write another *Surry of the Eagle's Nest*" (*A Certain Measure*, 84). Significantly, while both authors eschewed the historical and sentimental romance that might have appealed to the tastes of Richmonders, it was those same sentimentalists who served the two writers as the basic model for their fictional "heroes."

Both Glasgow and Cabell chose pseudonyms for Richmond. She called it Queenborough, seeing it ironically as the quintessential Virginia city and implying, one suspects, that as the seat of the Commonwealth of Virginia it was the vocal center of its demagoguery. Cabell termed it Lichfield in his fiction and elsewhere employed the hyphenated form Richmond-in-Virginia, insisting on a nuance of distinction between the two. Cabell chose a public pose of urbane distance from time and place, whereas Glasgow acknowledged that she was a product of both. With skeptical eyes she set out to record the local scene, exposing its subterfuges with irony; his subterfuge was to shift the local scene to another time and place. Richmond enters geographically into Glasgow's oeuvre; it figures psychologically in Cabell's. "I have never laid the scene of a book in Virginia," he equivocated, but his evasion was the very stuff of which Glasgow wrote. He castigated the hollow rhetoric of the Confederate apologists of his youth, but his ancestral ties rendered him powerless to break free. Cabell's early belief that "the dream is better than reality" gave way to his conviction that "the dream is the only reality." Reality is simply what one elects to believe. Facts have little to do with convictions. Neither tragic nor comic, perhaps a little of both, life is melodrama, compounded of shadowy impressions, fleeting emotions, all soon emerging as history, especially in the form of biography. Emily Clark, an unintentional social historian of the Cabell era, wrote that "Richmond means to everyone who knows it chiefly the people who live there." As Cabell's mythos expanded in the early 1920s, the writer found it convenient to retreat behind the perceived image of the bemused mage, one whose knowledge was boundless, occult. Painfully shy in large gatherings, rendered inarticulate by social converse, he was the antithesis of the James Cabell perceived by the public. He was credited with being the ultimate sophisticate but was in reality the embodiment of the domestic provincial, albeit one aware of the ironies of his position. His vaunted worldly experience was mostly fantasy, gleaned more from other writers than from lived experience. Yet he determined that his cultural heritage, Richmond-in-Virginia, embodied universal qualities and characteristics. During the writing of Jurgen in 1918, Cabell was not sure what was emerging.

In "Some Ladies and Jurgen," the short story out of which a *cause célèbre* emerged, Mencken heard a new voice in a new South. In Jurgen, Cabell sensed that he was writing more than a picaresque quest in the Fielding mode. A metempsychosis was taking place, a new author was being born. While "The Pawnbroker's Shirt," his preferred title for Jurgen, was a conscious and calculated risk to seize public attention through salacious innuendo, the author had tapped a source of psychic energy, perhaps the buried well of instinctual needs. Richmond had created its mystique out of shifting self-perceptions. Unlike Williamsburg, Richmond constantly tore down to rebuild. Significantly James Cabell had undergone palingenesis in Williamsburg, emerging as a late-Victorian poet, and now in mid-life, in Janus-like Richmond, he sensed new birth. A sophisticated mocker of local mores was replacing the chivalrous southern youth. Richmond had patronized Annie Cabell's eccentric son. Very well, he would play the Richmond game.

As James Branch Cabell broke through his own restrictive neuroses, he spoke in a new voice that was recognized everywhere as new. That recognition forced Richmond to take him more seriously. Its laughter became uneasy when laughter echoed from New York and Chicago. The new voice evoked attendant ironies. But whatever the game, whatever the price, Cabell would not crawl back into the womb. Who was the new literary mage? "Que sais-je?" Montaigne had asked and felt his quest should begin with himself. "I would present myself nude," the Frenchman decided, meaning he would hide behind none of society's prescriptive masks nor behind the protective shield of ego. The new voice from Richmond excited and puzzled the critics in their northern roosts. Through a still-powerful press, they spoke with myth-making powers. Some still heard in the new Cabell echoes of an outmoded romanticism, a few heard the new accent of post–World War I realism, and indeed it was a psychological progression beyond Howells and James. Freud was detected in Ibsen and Joyce, but Cabell's egotist presaged the rootless American antihero, his skepticism extending to all credos, even to the priestly manifestos of psychoscientists.

Figures of Earth two years later (1921) confirmed for Cabell converts that indeed a new voice was speaking in American letters. Sinclair Lewis and Scott Fitzgerald responded to that voice. Later William Faulkner, who had also inherited southern chivalry and had experienced a strangely similar psychic development, heard the mocking undertone of the Virginian's voice. Yoknapatawpha grew out of the older writer's Poictesme, and as for the interrelationship of myth and genealogy, Faulkner understood that as well as Cabell. The Bible was the one literary work known to all southerners. Cabell's later work illustrated that as old illusions are lost, new ones replace them, the result of the same demiurge that underlies all creation. The relation of writer and audience became his preoccupation just as it would for Saul Bellow, Philip Roth, Kurt Vonnegut, and others who enter the labyrinth of self. The comparatists, later the fantasists, followed Cabell into the cave. Significantly others did not, in particular the Agrarians.

As the sophisticates of the 1920s gave way to New Deal socialists, a new critical establishment supplanted the old. Emily Clark's urbane recounting of the genesis and demise of the *Reviewer* in *Innocence Abroad* (1931) was excoriated in the liberal press. Louis Kronenberger in the *New Republic* castigated it as a snobbish book about a snobbish era, "a drawing away from the real roots of American life and hence useless as a civilizing factor." As aristocratic Franklin D. Roosevelt revitalized American democracy and plebeian Adolf Hitler disinterred German nationalism, the literature of esthetics and philosophy gave way to the political treatise and the social study. *After the Genteel Tradition* in 1936 proscribed the whole Sophisticated School in a chapter entitled "The James Branch Cabell Period" by Peter Munro Jack, a proletarian with total contempt for the cosmopolites who mocked the mores of the American bourgeoisie in their mannered styles. "The Exquisites," Alfred Kazin's chapter in *On Native Grounds* (1942) spoke witheringly of "The James Branch Cabell School." "Oscar Wilde lived again," Kazin wrote. Cabell was not a real person but a legend, and Elinor Wylie was "their one tragic artist." But at least hers "was poignant fantasy, where Cabell's was merely fake."

Even those southerners attuned to Jeffersonian ideals failed to see in Cabell a fellow voyager. Like Richmonders, they instinctively mistrusted his irony. When some thirty of the South's most representative writers assembled at the University of Virginia in October 1931 for the Glasgow-inspired Southern Writers' Conference, Cabell was badgered into attending with his social-minded wife. Unlike William Faulkner, also in attendance and another recluse from public exposure, he could not revert to the bottle; he played the role expected and mistrusted, the ironic evader. Sherwood Anderson wrote that Cabell was "clever at retort, always with a streak of maliciousness." For the Nashville contingent, *Barren Ground* had established Glasgow's ties to their beloved Agrarianism, but for them Cabell remained remotely urban. M. Thomas Inge points up the irony that Davidson and others attacked Cabell with the same charge that was leveled at them—trying to escape into a romantic past. Cabell's most representative works actually illustrated the reverse, his heroes returning to an unsatisfying present, and Cabell never attempted to philosophize myth into sociology in the Agrarian or Yeatsian manner. Like Yeats, however, he did translate biography into myth. In his major phase Cabell never indulged in the magnolia mentality of the Agrarians.

When in the 1930s Cabell wished to move away from the Author of *Jurgen* to become free of readers and critics who wanted to circumscribe his personal anima mundi, just as Richmond attempted to possess his anima hominis, to employ Yeats's terms, he turned more expansively to the dream itself, of and for itself. When Cabell came to write his burlesque of the Holy Trinity, *Smirt* (1934), *Smith* (1935), *Smire* (1937), based on Joycean stream of consciousness, he entered an area that socialist critics were disinclined to explore with him. The creator who satirized the creative urge itself left no firm basis for critical declamation—except denunciation. For Cabell, if a jesting deity (or critics) decreed his role as buffoon in an anima hominis world, then he would range spaciously in the anima mundi, a world of his own invention. In that vast dreamscape, Richmonders freely intermingled with the denizens of Poictesme. Indeed, Richmonders themselves had never attempted to disentangle myth from historical fact, myths themselves being a part of history. Cabell did no more than his fellow citizens who tore down in order to rebuild. Gaiety lies in the rebuilding of things, redeeming tragedy of its temporal nature. If Joyce and Dublin had pointed the way, another Irishman anticipated the Richmonder's treatment of an elegiac past. Yeats had substituted "tragic joy" or "gaiety" in redeeming his history. In his 1907 essay "Poetry and Tradition" he wrote that "only when we are gay over a thing, and can play with it, do we show ourselves its master, and have minds clear for strength. The raging fire and the destructive sword are portions of eternity. . . . That we may be free from all the rest, sullen anger, solemn virtue, calculating anxiety, gloomy suspicion, prevaricating hope, we should be reborn in gaiety" (*Essays and Introductions*, 252). With the writing of *Hamlet Had an Uncle* (1940), Cabell restored Shakespeare's neurotic renaissance man to the healthy, active anima of historical myth. William Leigh Godschalk compared Cabell's "resolute frivolity" with Barth's "cheerful nihilism." The journey begun by Jurgen continued into areas of speculation that left once-adoring readers far behind.

While Cabell's immediate post-*Jurgen* public image served his hunger for recognition, its bemused acceptance by its author was costly. Critics wrote of his works with little knowledge of the man who created them. In an age of New Criticism in which the critic admonished one to fix his gaze solely on the work and not on its creator, ignorance of biography was not perceived as a deterrent to understanding; but for later literary historians the biographical void led to criticism that fed on other criticism, becoming increasingly hermetic. While still in mid-career and sensing a decline in literary fortunes, Cabell began to feed the myth of omniscience. James Branch Cabell chose to be reborn as Branch Cabell, the supersophisticate. Branch Cabell did not, however, explicate James Cabell: he commented at length on the works of James Branch Cabell as exemplified in the Storisende Edition, and he launched into his new phase of writing as the timeless mage. The game amused him to the end, to an increasingly indifferent readership.

In the mid-1920s, Cabell was widely accepted as the American writer most assured of immortality. There were solid reasons for the assessment. He had written four works, possibly five, that for style, craftsmanship, and content ranked with the best of the past and the then-present. They survive to this day, but as creations of fantasy, not as distillations of lived experience. His name is associated with a fecund imagination but one dissociated from any reality of time and place. The fantasists claim him as an early Tolkien, as an anomaly, one who did not conform to the stereotypes of his society. Far from being a deviate from flesh-and-blood Richmond, Cabell was an incarnation of its neuroses, pride, and divided allegiances, of its laughter and tears, of its basic humanity—that blending of cultures and ethnic diversities. The life distilled in the works of James Branch Cabell is of a unique time and place, Richmond-in-Virginia, a microcosm that reflects all time and all places.

Cabell's career spanned a remarkable transition in American, especially southern, letters. His growth and contributions to early modernism make him of significant interest to literary historians. In addition, his interpretation of the life of the mind in Richmond foreshadowed that of other southerners who followed during his lifetime. Cabell's stubborn adherence to who he was and to his vision of the creative urge may have lost him his once-acclaimed following in the Franklin Roosevelt era, but he had witnessed enough changes in the critical establishment to know that the pronouncements of critics were not the final word; their edicts too would be assigned to the apocrypha by newer critics. He placed his faith cheerfully on an ultimate assessment that would redeem his vision.

A sixteen-year-old had discovered during his sophomore year at college that he liked writing. For the next sixty-three years of his alloted time he played with words. An old man confessed that throughout his career, through all his metamorphoses, he had liked what he did—writing books, that he had never wanted to do anything else. "I have served that dream which I elected to be serving," (Let Me Lie, 286). He was admittedly, at times, "just a tiny bit envious of the Cabell of popular myth, that all defiant rake-hellion." At the end he came to agree with the 'well-born Virginian' that the art of life was in living itself. "I have liked living. . . . But, above all, I have liked writing books" (As I Remember It, 242).

Chronology

1

The Wanderer

1

Ancestral Voices

1 6 1 9 – 1 8 7 9

The name Cabell traces back to Norman French, "Caballus" being used for "horse" in Domesday Book. The Cabells were not an "old family" in Virginia terms. Dr. William Cabell (1699–1774), the immigrant, son of another Dr. William Cabell of Warminster, Wiltshire, England, did not arrive in Virginia until 1723. Once there, however, he quickly set about acquiring the endowments that conferred old-family status. He patented large landholdings in Goochland, Albemarle, and Amherst counties. Aside from his medical practice, Dr. Cabell was appointed to the offices usually associated with the head of an established family—justice, sheriff, surveyor, vestryman, coroner, militia officer. He married Elizabeth Burks of Hanover County by whom he had five children, the youngest, Nicholas, being James Branch Cabell's progenitor.

Nicholas Cabell (1750–1803) inherited land in Amherst County, was an officer in the American Revolution, and married Hannah Carrington. They had ten children, of whom the eldest, William, was the ancestor of James Branch Cabell. This William added the middle initial "H" to his name to distinguish himself from an uncle and cousins of the same name. William H. Cabell (1772–1853) was born in Cumberland County, attended Hampden-Sydney and William and Mary colleges and later studied law in Richmond, where he was licensed to practice. He married his cousin Elizabeth Cabell, by whom he had three children, and upon her death married Agnes Sarah Bell Gamble, daughter of Col. Robert Gamble. Their third child, Robert Gamble Cabell, was James Branch Cabell's grandfather. William H. Cabell had a distinguished career. He served in the Virginia Assembly, was governor of Virginia, and later became a revered judge. Upon his death in Richmond, both the Senate and the House of Delegates adjourned as a mark of respect to his memory.

Robert Gamble Cabell (1809–1889) was born in the old Gamble house in Richmond, situated on what is still known as Gamble's Hill. He attended William and Mary College for one year, the University of Virginia for three (where he was a schoolmate of Edgar Allan Poe), and studied medicine in Philadelphia. After interning a year in Baltimore, he returned to Richmond where he practiced medicine until his death at the age of eighty. He served on the Board of Aldermen of Richmond and was active in efforts to improve sanitation in older parts of the city. He married Margaret Sophia Caskie, daughter of James Caskie, a native of Scotland who was a successful merchant and banker in Richmond.

The fourth of their nine children, Robert Gamble Cabell, Jr. (1847–1922), was also raised in Richmond. He went to the Virginia Military Institute where his slightly older brother was a cadet. At the Battle of Newmarket on 15 May 1864, when the cadets of VMI were called out to defend the village from Union forces, the brothers fought side by side, William not yet nineteen, Robert not yet seventeen. William fell in battle. Robert went on to graduate with honors. He entered the Medical College of Virginia and, upon receiving his degree, was elected to the staff of the Central Lunatic Asylum. He later entered the drug business, establishing the firm of Cabell and Chelf. In later years he was the superintendent of the City Home (for the indigent) as well as the adjacent historic Shockoe Cemetery. On 14 November 1877 he married Anne Harris Branch, daughter of the deceased James Read Branch and Martha Louise Patteson Branch. As the father of James Branch Cabell, Dr. Cabell figures significantly in this biography.

James Branch Cabell's immigrant Branch ancestor arrived in Virginia commendably early, over a hundred years before the ancestor in his paternal line. Ironically, however, the Branches were not accorded "old family" status, according to the accepted Virginia definition. The early generations prospered, married respectably, and accumulated property, but they were not members of the county squirearchy that inherited high (and remunerative) office. Immigrant Christopher Branch arrived with his wife, Mary, in the *London Merchant* in the spring of 1619/20. The Virginia Company assigned them to the College Land in the Henrico area, and in 1634 Christopher registered his own land nearby. He gradually acquired land on both sides of the James just below the present city of Richmond. He was named to the House of Burgesses in the year 1629 and was appointed a justice of the peace for Henrico in 1656—both significant social accomplishments. He sired three sons, Thomas, William, and Christopher. The last, Cabell's ancestor, predeceased his father but also left three sons remembered in their grandfather's will: Christopher (III), Samuel, and Benjamin. Benjamin, born about 1665, married Tabitha Osborne by whom he had one son, another Benjamin.

This third-generation Virginian, Benjamin, great-grandson of the immigrant, took possession of a small estate in 1721 left by his father on the south side of the James. Like the first Christopher he became a man of considerable property, owning land in what became Chesterfield and Amelia counties. Prior to 1727 he married his second cousin Mary Osborne. Of their seven children, the third, Benjamin (III), was Cabell's ancestor. This Benjamin too became a man of substance, seating a plantation named Willow Hill in Chesterfield County. He was named a justice in that county in 1774 and during the Revolution served as a captain in the militia. Benjamin was twice named sheriff, a significant office in Colonial Virginia. He married Mary (Goode?) about 1755 by whom he had five children, the fourth being Thomas (born 1767) who later acquired Willow Hill from his brother Edward. In 1787 Thomas married Mary Patteson, daughter of Col. David Patteson of Chesterfield. Their union resulted in fourteen children, including another Thomas, born 23 December 1802. This man's fortunes became a major influence in Cabell's awakening social consciousness.

On reaching manhood, Thomas Branch (1802–1888) moved to Petersburg, a manufacturing and commercial center that rivaled Richmond. Establishing himself as a commission merchant and banker, he also served as a member of the Petersburg Council, as sheriff, and several times as mayor. As the Civil War approached, he was a Union man, but when he became a member of the Convention of 1861, he bowed to the desires of his fellow citizens and signed the Ordinance of Secession. On 19 October 1825 Branch married Sarah Pride Read, daughter of John Blythe Read, a native of Wales removed to Chesterfield. Their first child, Thomas Waverly Branch, died of hydrophobia in July 1831, before his fifth birthday.

The grieving parents became members of the Methodist church, and Thomas Branch played a conspicuous role in some fifty annual conferences of that denomination, his zeal extending to the Virginia Bible Society, the Magdalen Association, and Randolph-Macon College, the small sectarian school chartered in 1830 and charged with the education of young men aspiring to the ministry. Thomas Branch's zeal was rewarded by business success and numerous progeny—thirteen children by Sarah Pride Read and three by his second wife, Anne Adams Wheelright, whom he married in 1857.

Five of Thomas Branch's sons served in the Confederate forces, the three oldest as distinguished officers and the youngest, a cadet at the Virginia Military Institute, enlisting at age sixteen. The oldest living son, James Read Branch, moved his family from Petersburg to Richmond during the war. In 1871 Thomas Branch also moved to Richmond, as did his third son, John Patteson Branch, and his son-in-law Frederic R. Scott. More than likely, the move was inspired by business acumen. The financial area of Richmond had been destroyed by fire and was experiencing a regrowth advantageous to those with capital. Thomas Branch and Sons, a commodities house dealing in the purchase and resale of wheat, corn, cotton, and tobacco, had earlier established an office in the city. The Merchants National Bank was chartered there on 17 December 1870, with Thomas Branch and Major Scott, his son-in-law, as principal stockholders. Although separate institutions, the two financial establishments shared a building at 1101 East Main Street. Branch's picture appeared on all the bank's checks. Vigorous, forthright, zealous Thomas Branch may have been in the mold of earlier enterprising Richmonders, but he was not the idealized Virginia gentleman that sentimentalists memorialized in nineteenth-century romances, the true Virginian who had given his all to the cause. Money in defeated Virginia was automatically suspect. Branch coal mines in West Virginia may have served as collateral for Yankee loans, but the consensus was that somehow the Branches had profited while others had suffered.

Like other older cities that did not change too rapidly, Richmond had its distinctive criteria as to social rank. The people who were generally known fell into three classifications: old families, old citizens, and old merchants. Old families were those whose ancestors had been prominent officeholders in colonial times, tracing their forebears to the younger sons of English landed gentry; they clung to their plantations in memory or in fact, although they lived in Richmond. Old citizens were the respected professionals, lawyers, ministers, physicians, their ancestors including Scottish factors as well as pious yeomen, landholders on a smaller scale. Old merchants included the Scottish tobacconists, the few but respected Jewish shopkeepers, and other German, Irish, and Italian tradesmen and skilled workers, all of whom were addressed as Mister. There was a rapport among these three "old" categories, a mutual observance of social distinctions that made everyone comfortable, very much like British acceptance of class. The Branches of Petersburg did not conform precisely to any of Richmond's reticulated classifications. They were not "old" to Richmond in any category, yet they shared characteristics with all three groups. Outside Richmond the distinction was made between "good families," meaning old families, and the condescending "good people," meaning the pious yeomanry. With his Methodist zeal, Thomas Branch was most easily relegated to this "outside Richmond" category.

While Richmonders observed and even dissertated on inherited social distinctions, they seldom rigidly applied them in practice. Anybody one liked obviously had "good blood back there," an observation extended even to black people. Marriages took place between all three "old" classifications, and the resulting offspring took pride in laughing about their diverse lineages. Episcopalians married Presbyterians, Jews became Christians, Methodists became Episcopalians. Most of Methodist Thomas Branch's grandchildren became Episcopalians. As late as 1954 Richmond's last arbiter elegantiarum, Helena Lefroy Caperton, confessed in print how puzzling it was to her that Ellen Glasgow had received "the ever-present social climbers," although, she added gratuitously, "one of her brothers [Arthur Glasgow] had married a charming lady [Margaret Branch, granddaughter of Thomas Branch], from one of these so-called 'golden-key' families." A stunningly handsome portrait of Margaret Branch Glasgow hangs in the parish library of St. Paul's Episcopal Church.

James Read Branch (1828–1869), the second son of Thomas Branch and the oldest after the death of young Thomas Waverly, was born in Prince George County. Graduating from Randolph-Macon College in 1847 at the age of nineteen, he went into business with his father and younger brother, John Patteson Branch, in 1853 to form Thomas Branch and Sons. James Read Branch married his second cousin, Martha Louise Patteson, daughter of Dr. William Anderson Patteson on 3 December 1856. Unlike his father, James Branch was an ardent secessionist, who raised a company of infantry known as the Lee Guard and later as a captain of artillery distinguished himself at the Battle of Malvern Hill. He was promoted to lieutenant colonel and was permanently disabled in a later battle, one leg being broken in three places. In 1863 he moved his young family from Petersburg to Richmond to live with his father-in-law, Dr. Patteson. In the autumn of 1865 he established his residence in Richmond and, with his brother John and brother-in-law Frederic R. Scott, set up a banking and investment firm called Thomas Branch and Company.

James Read Branch entered politics three years later as a candidate for the Senate; the days of Reconstruction were waning and carpetbaggism tottered. Jim Crowism had not yet insinuated itself into Virginia politics, and Colonel Branch earnestly endeavored to reunite the Negro and Caucasian races. As a gesture of gratitude to the black men of Richmond who had supported Gilbert Walker for Governor over Gideon Wells, the carpetbag nominee, Colonel Branch arranged a barbecue on 2 July 1869 on Vauxhall Island in the James River between Richmond and Manchester. A suspension bridge some fifty feet in length and about five feet wide connected Vauxhall with the adjacent Kitchen Island. Hearing that some black political supporters had not been allowed to cross the bridge for want of tickets, the Colonel advanced halfway across the bridge to signal their admission. The resulting rush onto the bridge made its supports give way, and it fell into the river. Colonel Branch received a severe concussion, and debris held him under the water. Dead at forty-one, he left five orphans, the oldest twelve and the youngest three. His widow survived him thirty-nine years. For her last twenty-nine, she was a vital force in the perceptions of her Cabell grandson, named for the dead hero.

The young namesake, James Branch Cabell, was close to his aunts, uncle, and cousins. The oldest child of James and Martha Patteson Branch was Sarah Read Branch, born 9 October 1857; she married George Brockenborough McAdams and had two children, Thomas and Louise. The second child was Anne Harris Branch, Cabell's mother; born 31 December 1859, she was named for her grandmother Anne Harris, wife of Dr. Patteson. A third daughter, born 4 July 1861, was Elizabeth Halstead Branch, who married Walter Russell Bowie and had two children, Walter and Martha. The fourth child and only son was James Ransom Branch, born 14 December 1863. This uncle had a varied and colorful career as banker, horse-breeder, theater impresario, city councilman, colonel in the National Guard, and secretary of the American Bankers' Association. By his first wife, Mary Lilian Hubbell, he had three children: James (whose tragic early death deeply embittered Cabell), Mary, and Allan. Colonel Branch had another son named James by his second wife, Mary Warren.

Mary Cooke Branch, the fifth child of James and Martha Branch, was born 16 September 1866. A beautiful child, she developed into an extraordinarily intelligent woman who, like her husband, Beverley Bland Munford, had a significant influence on Cabell. The Munfords had two children, May and Beverley.

The marriage of Anne Harris Branch to Dr. Robert G. Cabell, Jr., was front-page news. The Richmond *Dispatch* for 15 November 1877 placed its account just after the weather of the wedding day:

BRILLIANT WEDDING CEREMONY AT ST. PAUL'S CHURCH LAST NIGHT.—Dr. R. G. Cabell, Jr., assistant superintendent of the Central Lunatic Asylum, and Miss Annie H. Branch, daughter of Mrs. M. L. and the late Major James R. Branch, were married at St. Paul's church last night. The pews opening on the main aisle were filled with ladies and gentlemen holding invitations to the church and reception. All were in full party dress. The other portions of the building were crowded—densely and dangerously crowded—with friends having cards for the church only. . . . From the church the wedding party went to the residence of the bride's mother, No. 101 East Franklin Street, where there was a reception from 8 1/2 to 12 o'clock. Here, as at the church, the floral decorations and offerings from friends were splendid. In many of the designs the florist displayed his ingenuity, and in all tasteful arrangement. The company well represented fashionable society of the city, and the entertainment was as agreeable to the guests as creditable to the hostess.

Anne Harris Branch, mother-to-be of James Branch Cabell, is reputed to have been beautiful, and pictures of her in girlhood support the legends. Annie, as she was called by her family, was also said to have been the most funloving and headstrong of the three oldest Branch girls. During the war, she and her siblings had lived with their maternal grandfather in Richmond. Dr. Patteson, a doting grandparent, lavished affection on this child named for his dead wife. The children were raised in the Episcopal church of Martha Patteson Branch rather than in the Methodist denomination of their paternal line; they went to nearby St. Paul's. On the death of Colonel Branch, when Annie was nine, her mother was considered the wealthiest widow in Virginia. In impoverished post–Civil War Richmond, its citizens were hungry for the legendary sumptuousness of antebellum days, and Martha Branch's parties for her daughters introduced them to the Gilded Age extravagance becoming popular in the more prosperous cities of America. Mary Cooke Branch, the youngest of the four sisters, aspired to intellectual pursuits, but Sallie, Annie, and Lizzie Branch sought amusement in society. Their attitude toward literature was later summarized by Cabell: "Books might be all very well in their place, but where was the time to read them in? Thus quoth my aunts and my mother also, in a dismissive unanimity." The Branch girls were considered good catches in Richmond for any marriage-minded young man. Annie caught the eye of Dr. Robert G. Cabell, Jr., twelve years her senior.

The Cabells, who were Presbyterian, had been raised in the doctrine that the good life is hard and anything too pleasant is suspect. Robert Cabell, Jr., and his younger brother Arthur, both physicians like their father, were considered good social catches for any young Richmond woman. Arthur, in the United States Army, had been all over the world, had lived in Europe and the Orient, and had acquired some strange tastes in furnishings. His sword in particular did not please Martha Branch, as she preferred Confederate sidearms. Robert Cabell, Jr., was all right; he had fought at New Market by the side of his older brother and had caught him dying as he fell. But not everyone in Annie's family agreed. Her Tompkins kin, related through the Pattesons, thought that "Aunt Mat" should not allow Annie to marry Dr. Robert Cabell, Jr., not that he had the reputation of his brother Arthur but that he was far too sophisticated for inexperienced and happy-natured Annie. Dr. Robert had been one of the three men-about-town who had considered themselves engaged to the belle Sallie Aylett—all at the same time. When she chose Tom Bolling, Dr. Cabell turned his eyes to another belle, and one with money, Annie Branch. At eighteen Annie was ready for marriage. Young women of her class looked upon marriage as liberation to follow their own wishes. The fact that Robert was twelve years older than Annie meant that he would probably indulge his pretty and wealthy young wife. Thomas Plummer Branch, the legal guardian of his nieces, would have to turn over their inheritances to their husbands upon marriage, but Dr. Cabell would be well aware whose money it was. If he was not well-off, the Cabells, like the Pattesons, were related to all the best people. Beautiful Lizzie Cabell, his sister, had reigned at the springs like her Aunt Lizzie Cabell, had married Albert Ritchie of Baltimore, and would produce a governor of Maryland. Of the three oldest Branch girls, Annie could be said to have made the best match as far as family connections were concerned.

2

Reflections in the Mirror

1880–1889

The early childhood of James Branch Cabell was interwoven with the fantasy that only children of affluent Victorian families could ever know. When he was born on 14 April 1879 at 101 East Franklin Street, his parents were living on the third floor of his grandmother Branch's house, following a Richmond custom that newlyweds would live with a parent or parents until the children arrived. This house was later razed to make way for the Richmond Public Library at First and Franklin streets. It amused a mature Cabell to observe that he had been born on the second floor (approximately) of the public library. He remembered his grandmother's establishment as a plantation within the city:

> It is pleasing (and yet wistfully depressing also) to remember the days of her affluence when Grandmother owned the big house at First and Franklin Streets, where the Richmond Public Library now stands. Her rambling three-storied mansion and its grounds then occupied about half of the block, with a hedged flower garden, having also a few smallish fruit trees in it, to the front and the east; and with an enormous catalpa tree—surrounded by a circular wooden bench, I remember—and a substantial stable in the rear, as well as a smoke house and a sort of storage hall with several rooms up over top of it for the servants to live in. There were two horses and two cows and a small

vegetable garden and some large grape trellises all back there too, in Grand-mother's so very big back yard. (*As I Remember It*, 145)

The dynamic Martha Louise Patteson Branch ruled her domain with aplomb, her person taking on mythic qualities in the awakening percep-tions of her eldest grandchild. "She was handsome, too, with the dark and clear-cut somewhat Spanish features of all the Pattesons." Her house was a contained universe of family and civic activities. "And besides that, she gave heaps of parties, and she had what people called tableaus and sometimes whole plays in her back parlor which you were allowed to sit up to." For the wedding reception of his aunt Sallie Branch on 6 Novem-ber 1878, the mansion was transformed into a floral bower into which the elect crowded. James Cabell was nineteen months old when his aunt Elizabeth Branch married Walter Bowie on 16 November 1881. He played an active role in this wedding spectacle, which too made front-page news for its lavishness: "Along with the members of the family were two little nephews of the bride—Thomas McAdams and James Cabell—the former dressed in white lace over blue, the latter in red plush and Duch-esse lace."

As babies began to arrive, Martha Branch was the attendant good fairy:

> On week days every morning Grandmother would ride down town, in her big carriage with her two horses pulling it, to the Sixth Street Market and buy everything she needed. Then Jackson, that fat and sort of solemn-looking colored man who was her coachman, and in a real fine uniform with nice shiny buttons to it, would drive the meat and the vegetables and the eggs, and whatever else there was, back to the house in the carriage while Grand-mother walked home. She did not have to walk but seven blocks, yet it most always took her right much time to walk them, because she would have to stop on the street and talk to such lots of her friends, or maybe she would go into this or the other cousin's house just for a little visit, or perhaps to look at the new baby. In those days nearly every one of the married ladies had a new baby every two years. And in those days nobody was ever in any special hurry about anything, anyhow. So Grandmother would very often not get home until almost two o'clock and barely in time for her dinner. (*As I Remember It*, 146)

The babies being born within the circle of Martha Branch's special at-tention were the brothers and cousins of the oldest grandchild, James Branch Cabell. Thomas Branch McAdams arrived 12 November 1879, a scant seven months after James. A brother, a third Robert Gamble Cabell, made his appearance on 27 April 1881, followed by another cousin, Walter Russell Bowie, on 8 October 1882. Brother John, named for a paternal uncle by marriage, John Lottier, was born 27 February 1883. Martha Patteson Bowie arrived on 29 July 1884, and another female cousin, Louise Brockenborough McAdams, on 25 October 1885. Next came James Robinson Branch (23 July 1886) and Mary Cooke Branch (21 December 1887), the children of young James Cabell's maternal uncle. Mary Cooke Branch Munford's children were born when James was in his teens. Three of the grandchildren born under Martha Branch's roof at 101 East Franklin were destined to attain renown in their respective professions: Thomas Branch McAdams, president of the American Bankers' Association; Walter Russell Bowie, D.D., rector of Grace Church in New York; and James Branch Cabell, man of letters.

Costume parties delighted all ages. An 1881 newspaper clipping in a Cabell scrapbook lists James dressed as a daisy at age two at the Jordan Alum, immediately adjacent to the Rockbridge Alum. The Cabells like other Virginians migrated from spring to spring, attending certain festivities sponsored by the resorts, but their favorite was the Rockbridge Alum; Cabell remained faithful to it into the 1920s long after its decline. Rockbridge Alum Springs was located in Rockbridge County, named for the great rock bridge later called Natural Bridge. The clear, cold, and odorless waters had a generally purgative effect and, in addition to stomach disorders, were credited with curing scrofula and other skin diseases. The Alum began as a summer retreat in the early 1800s; by the mid-nineteenth century it rivaled White Sulphur Springs and later Hot Springs. Refurbished in 1880, the year of James Cabell's first visit, its peak of popularity came in 1885 when a narrow gauge railroad was built from Goshen on the Virginia Central Railroad (later the Chesapeake and Ohio) five miles away. As a place removed from the workday environment of Richmond, a place dedicated to romance and illusion, it entered into his consciousness with a Wordsworthian profundity. After the demise of the hotel he continued to make pilgrimages there, and near the close of his life he observed, "I found nothing that sent my imagination soaring like that little charmed circle of buildings called Rockbridge Alum Springs."

As Perceval Reniers tells us in *The Springs of Virginia*, the Rockbridge Alum was "favored by the professional classes, the doctors and judges and professors, and socially it was always on its toes" (262). In an age of Belledom, it was patronized by Mary Triplett whose beauty engendered Richmond's last duel, by Mattie Ould whose sparkling wit ravished her admirers and was repeated in rippling waves, echoes of it detectable in Cabell's early works. "Belledom," writes Reniers, "was like a never-ending horse race; a large gallery was always crowding the rails and cheering its favorites." When Mary Triplett married Philip Haxall, whose flour mills rose on the south side of the James in Richmond, she became the guardian of younger belles, giving lavish dances and lawn parties either at the Rockbridge Alum or White Sulphur. Through the whole of the 1880s she was pointed out to James Cabell as a paragon of beauty. Mary died in 1890, but her last season at the springs had been a triumph. Mattie Ould's leave taking was the stuff of melodrama. The daring Mattie had eloped with a young northerner who lived in Richmond. From Montgomery White Sulphur they slipped away to marry in nearby Salem, scandalizing society. Judge Ould never forgave his daughter and refused to go to her deathbed; she died in childbirth. "Under the Daisies" was sung at her funeral, and her young widower was back at the springs the following August. Mattie appears in several guises in Cabell's early social comedies.

In 1880, the year James Cabell made his appearance at the springs, May Handy was noted as "one of the prettiest misses," a term for a subdebutante. A younger stepsister of Mattie Ould, May Handy emerged as a reigning belle, a role for which she had been rigorously groomed by her mother. Morning constitutionals, afternoon naps, dietary restrictions, a simplification of dress, all became components of her regimen. Her promenades down Franklin Street in Richmond were processions. She starred in northern climes—Bar Harbor, Newport, Saratoga—proof of Southern Belledom. After an extended reign, she married too quietly the wealthy but divorced James Brown Potter of New York. Another Virginian assumed her crown. This last of the great belles, Irene Langhorne, was a "natural," not a product of grooming. Though a belle, she pointed to the emergence of the new woman, who replaced limpness with vigor. She jumped her horse over tennis nets, drove her own span of horses, dressed in serviceable cottons to play tennis. When Irene Langhorne married the popular young artist Charles Dana Gibson in 1895, he transformed her into the celebrated Gibson Girl, making her the national ideal of femininity. The Richmond Times chronicled: "Miss Langhorne is one of the greatest beauties of the South and, excepting Miss May Handy, it may be said that she stands unequaled and unrivalled in her regal beauty." The year was 1895, and James Cabell, then seventeen, was a student in college. More than one Gibson Girl troops through the pages of his early works.

At the springs an impressionable child witnessed a "sport" that lived long in his memory. Since the Civil War, tournaments had become popular at the spas, an added entertainment for the entertainment hungry. Rather than armored knights dislodging one another with lance or axe, these mock medieval tourneys had competitors attempting to pick with their lances metal rings from a stationary or pivoting "arm." In "Rockbridge Alum Springs: A History of the Spa: 1790–1974," Charlotte Lou Atkins describes an event that took place on July 20, 1881, the season's major tournament. James Cabell in the arms of his nurse, Louisa Nelson, witnessed his first tournament.

"Be-plumed knights" maneuvered their gaily caparisoned steeds into the assembly area adjacent to the lower corner of the groomed lawn. Black nurses and other servants filled the windows of the Grand Hotel, straining to absorb all the action and beauty of the afternoon. The belles of the summer wore their finest afternoon dresses, freshly ironed and perfumed; and they eagerly anticipated the conclusion of the games when one of them would be chosen by the winning Knight to reign over the night's Fancy Dress ball as the Queen of Love and Beauty. When the Marshal of the tournament gave the signal to begin, the trumpet sounded; and the knights and their horses proudly strode onto the field of combat. . . . Each participant's mount was brushed to a fine sheen and adorned in its best harness and saddle. The rules were familiar to the competitors and spectators alike: he who picked off the most rings with his makeshift lance in three "tilts" or rounds would win the honor of selecting and crowning his Queen of Love and Beauty for that evening's festivities. (58–59)

While Martha Patteson Branch guided most of James Cabell's fantasy world, another presence was felt in a more subtle way. Whether in Richmond or at the Rockbridge Alum, Mrs. Louisa Nelson was ever present, tending to all the boy's physical needs and forging a lifelong psychological bond. Born about 1820 but a steady "fifty-two," she had been employed by James's parents to be his nurse. Her status as a "mammy" carried the authority of a British nanny, a being superior to other servants. She had been born a slave, but with the death of her third husband she was bequeathed a degree of economic independence a few months before James was born. She also nursed siblings Robert and John; she remained an honored and integral member of the family for the rest of her life, some twenty-five years.

Now, technically, Mrs. Louisa Nelson was a Negress; but it is not conceivable that anybody ever said so in her presence, not even after she had become very deaf. She elected instead to rank as a colored person; and her color, to be precise, was the just not golden yellow of peanut butter. As to her parents it is not remembered that Mrs. Nelson ever spoke, but her features were unmistakably Indian; her eyes had the alert black gleam of undried ink; her nose hooked slightly; her lips were thin. She too was thin; and until she had passed eighty, a ramrod would have seemed, in comparison with Mrs. Nelson, to be liquescent. Upon her flat left breast, except only when she visited Monroe Park, or during yet more stately occasions which called for an appearance in her black silk dress, she wore two or three needles with thread in them; she had wholly beautiful white crinkly hair; and she smelled very pleasantly with an indefinable odor which I can but describe as that of musk flavored with cloth.

She must have had Negro blood, but in her exterior there was not any trace of it. She most certainly had a great deal of Caucasian blood; and one imagines that every drop of it was aristocratic. Mrs. Nelson, in any case, was.

She likewise was that patron saint who performed miracles for your comfort tirelessly; and who served as an efficient mediator between you and powers which (in academic theory) were stronger than Mrs. Nelson, such as unfamiliar policemen and God and large dogs and your parents. Parents were well enough in their place, and you loved both of them; but, relatively, their place was remote; and in it they now and then were engaged, with an irresponsible graveness, by grown-up affairs in which you were not interested.

Mrs. Nelson had no such frivolous avocations. To her children (a heading under which she did not include Julia and Kizzy, or any of Kizzy's descendants, but restricted to your two brothers and you) she devoted twenty-four hours of each day—excluding only her Sunday afternoons and her Thursday evenings out. . . .

You did not mind the Sunday afternoons, when company came in or else you went out with your parents somewhere, and were allowed to be company yourself, and to let people see your raising, just as Mrs. Nelson had told you to do. But Thursday evenings were lonesome, after you had gone to bed. . . .

So you did not ever quite fall asleep until after Mrs. Nelson came in at twenty minutes after eleven. She said that you ought to have been asleep long ago. She asked if you children had been good children, and not kept everything in a swivet the first minute her back was turned. She brought you a glass of water, because you said you were sort of thirsty. That was so you could touch her. Then she got into her bed, which was next to your bed; and you went to sleep in less than no time, because everything was all right now that Mammy was back. (*Let Me Lie,* 190–92)

In later years James Cabell wrote that he had had only one grandmother and one grandfather, his Grandmother Branch and his Grandfather Cabell. His Grandmother Cabell (Margaret Sophia Caskie) and James Read Branch had died before he was born. Just as Martha Patteson Branch was a strong personality associated with a fixed abode, so too was Dr. Cabell Senior in his handsome early Victorian house on Governor Street. This house faces across the street to the rear of the Governor's Mansion in Capitol Square where this first Robert Gamble Cabell's parents had lived. Earlier Dr. Cabell had lived at 709 East Franklin Street, next door to General Lee, whom he had treated for rheumatism. Visits to Governor Street for young James were more stately occasions than those to 101 East Franklin.

On the whole, the Cabells were quieter people than the Branches. They were Presbyterians. They read books. On being told that his young grandson had a penchant for reading, Dr. Cabell recounted his boyhood days of swimming in the James River with Edgar Poe, of knowing him as a student at the university. Waving toward the works of Poe housed behind glass doors in the bookcase, Dr. Cabell advised his grandson not to read the eccentric writer until maturity would give him insight. Thereupon James, aged eight, read the complete works.

At his grandfather's house, the introspective boy was beguiled by the talk of his elders concerning the beauty and perfection of pre–Civil War Richmond. "It was confusing, the way in which your elders talked about things which no great while before you were born had happened in Richmond. —Because you lived in Richmond: and Richmond was not like Camelot. Richmond was a modern city, with sidewalks and plumbing and gas light and horse cars" (*Let Me Lie,* 146–47).

The talk was not bitter but tinged with irony, spoken "in their quiet and matter of fact and half amused voices." While the atmosphere of Richmond was elegiac during the childhood of James Cabell, the boy half-sensed that he was witnessing the creation of legend, that "the main business in life of your elders was to create a myth": "They were creating (so did you decide later), in the same instant that they lamented the Old South's extinction, an Old South which had died proudly at Appomattox without ever having been smirched by the wear and tear of existence"

(*Let Me Lie*, 153–54). As he absorbed the talk of his elders, the sensitive youngster puzzled over the disparity between the public oratory of heroic men and selfless women and the private observations of the real men and women divested of the robes of glory.

> Moreover, you noticed that your elders did not speak in the same way when they were just talking to one another in your father's drugstore, or in your mother's dining-room at Sunday night supper (when everybody ate out of the best plates, which had a different sort of bright colored bird painted upon each one of them), or when your elders were playing whist in the big and high-ceilinged pale-brown back-parlor of your grandfather's house, down upon Governor Street.
>
> Your elders, in brief, were not mad with the armies and the leaders of the armies that had invaded and seized upon the fair kingdom which really and truly belonged to General Robert E. Lee. They just kind of made fun of them. They were not even very much interested in those Yankee soldiers who had killed off a lot of your own uncles and cousins. It was only when they talked about Carpet-baggers. Carpet-baggers must have been rather like ogres, or perhaps they were churls and fell caitiffs, you decided. . . . Anyhow, whenever grown-up people talked about Carpet-baggers they would get mad as a wet hen.
>
> But that did not last for more than a little while. Pretty soon they would go back to talking, almost as if they were sitting in church instead of right here in your grandfather's back-parlor, about what a real fine place all the South used to be, and Virginia in particular. (*Let Me Lie*, 148, 157–58)

Second Presbyterian Church on Fifth Street, established in 1843, was the church attended by the Cabells. It was different from St. Paul's on East Grace Street, the church of James's Grandmother Branch. Second Presbyterian was a somber edifice, a Gothic structure from designs by Minard Lafever. Its diamond-paned windows of plain glass shed a colder light on its worshippers than did the colorful Tiffany windows of St. Paul's. In austere Second Presbyterian one sensed the presence of divine justice observing one with a critical eye. In his grandfather's church, James learned that observance of a rigid code of conduct proved one was among the elect. Even the chosen, however, were on less friendly terms with the lawgiver of the Presbyterians than with the benign deity of the Episcopalians. Both churches at the time of James Cabell's boyhood enjoyed the prestige of legendary churchmen, Dr. Moses D. Hoge at Second

Presbyterian and Dr. Charles Minnigerode at St. Paul's. Both churches had been a part of the drama of the Civil War as it was played in Richmond. Second Presbyterian lost its original windows from a nearby explosion during the evacuation of Confederate forces. Jefferson Davis and also Robert E. Lee had worshipped at St. Paul's.

When the three Cabell boys went to the springs for the summer with their mother, frequently their Grandmother Branch was a member of the party. The social columns of the Richmond papers detailed their endless rounds of parties, dances, and other pursuits to banish ennui in the mountain resorts. Names of the soberer Cabells appear rarely if at all. Those stuck in a hot and steamy Richmond were not to be forgotten, however, and James and Robert were admonished to write. From Allegheny Springs in Montgomery County, Virginia, nine-year-old James wrote on hotel stationery a letter dated "Wednesday, July, 1888":

Dear Grandpa

I am ever so much obliged to you for the knife, it is very sharp. They have germans up here every Tuesday night. I stayed up till past eleven. The waiters brought in lemon ice and all sorts of cake on trays. I stood at the door an helped myself. Mamma will not let me go bathing or up on the Mountains. She says if I go bathing I will get dronded and if I go up on the mountains a snake will bite me or I will get lost. There is a lady up here that teaches dancing lessons she charges 75¢ a day she says that she can teach anybody to dance in a day. I dont take dancing lessons because mamma says I dance better than the lady does. . . .

Your grandson

James

Annie Cabell's opinion of her son's dancing ability may have had some justification. Every well-bred Richmond child learned deportment and other social graces at one of several cotillions, dancing classes where boys and girls were taught to meet gracefully and generally to make themselves agreeable in polite society. At an early age James Cabell went to Miss Mary Thaw's, one of Richmond's two leading dancing schools. Hers was in Monticello Hall, on the south side of Broad between Sixth and Seventh where the abandoned Thalhimers department store now stands. Miss Thaw was, in the words of Beverley Munford, "a woman of position in

Richmond and one . . . that compelled the esteem of all her pupils and their parents as well."

At this time Martha Patteson Branch was active in a number of benevolent societies, most associated in some way with the late Confederacy. "She was always being put on boards to get up bazaars to help something or other that was Confederate," Cabell wrote. The Ladies Hollywood Memorial Association was a solemn duty. Indeed, "Decoration Day" enlisted the aid of Richmond school children to decorate the graves of Confederate soldiers on into this century.

> You went to her bazaars too, over at the Richmond Blues' Armory, where Grandmother bought for you, from the gentleman who made up all sorts of shiny glass things right while you were looking at him, a ship with sails and everything in a foamy little round ocean. But for your brother Robert she got two bright colored birds with long necks drinking out of a pink fountain, with the fountain part of it shaped sort of like one of those champagne glasses that Grandmother used on birthdays in the family. . . .
>
> When the Confederate Memorial Day came around, then Grandmother would take you and her next biggest grandchild, Thomas McAdams, out to Hollywood Cemetery for two or three days before it was Memorial Day, so that you could help about fixing the flags and the wreaths and the other designs and about keeping the flowers watered upon dead people's graves, who were kin to Grandmother, and in Colonel Branch's section especially. She was always right solemn about Confederate Memorial Day and about that Mr. Lincoln.
>
> She had a signed picture of the gentleman who had killed him, along with a pack of cards the gentleman had sent to Colonel Branch. Colonel Branch and Grandmother had known Mr. Booth when he was a play actor in Richmond in what people called a stock company.
>
> Well, and at first Grandmother thought Mr. Booth had done a fine thing when he shot Mr. Lincoln, but later on she decided that maybe it was a mistake, because perhaps if Mr. Lincoln had gone on living he would have been nicer and kinder to the South than those Carpetbaggers were. Mr. Lincoln had meddled with the South when he had no business to, and he was an awful tacky person. Everybody knew about how he had left five dollars for his wife upon her mantelpiece the next morning after they got married. Which simply showed you just what sort of women he was used to. But then almost all Yankees were tacky; and lots of people said Mr. Lincoln had meant well.
>
> You thought privately that five dollars was a mighty nice present, but something told you this was one of the things which grown-up people knew about, and you didn't. So you did not argue about it. And, in fact, very few

persons ever did argue with Grandmother. She was just set in her ways, and that was all there was to it. (*As I Remember It*, 149–50)

Schooling in Richmond during the 1880s and 1890s was provided mainly by genteel but impoverished ladies and gentlemen whose numerous small schools were usually in the parlors or dining rooms of private homes. Ex-Confederate officers and their daughters were favored. Although some of the ladies taught little more than social accomplishments, others aspired to inculcate in their charges a genuine love of knowledge in its more demanding forms. Several of these venerated teachers founded schools that grew into highly respected secondary schools still in existence. Two of Richmond's famous educators influenced James Cabell: Virginia Randolph Ellett, the renowned "Miss Jennie," founder of St. Catherine's, and the elder John Peyton McGuire, head of the McGuire University School from 1866 to 1906.

In the 1880s South Third Street, a fashionable residential area, boasted two highly regarded schools. Mrs. Annie Camm, daughter of Col. Raleigh Colston, conducted her school for boys at 110 South Third; among the teachers on the staff was young Virginia Randolph Ellett, who taught history, geography, and physics. Miss Ellett's own small school, located at her home on Grace between First and Second, was left in charge of her mother during the morning hours. Hurrying home from South Third, Miss Jennie, as she became known, taught her own charges, both boys and girls, in the afternoon. Her school began to grow, and in 1897 she moved it around the block to Franklin Street and limited her enrollment to girls. Boys attending Mrs. Camm's school were "graduated" at the age of fourteen and sent on to other schools offering higher instruction. At the end of South Third Street in the late 1870s and 1880s, McGuire's School was located in the historic Gamble Mansion. Designed by the noted architect Benjamin Latrobe, this house had been built in 1798–99 for Col. John Harvie, who sold it the following year to Col. Robert Gamble, James Cabell's Revolutionary ancestor. The house on Gamble's Hill passed from his heirs in 1852. In the mid-1880s, the McGuire School moved to the corner of Belvidere and Main streets, later sharing Monroe Park as a playground with Miss Jennie's when her school moved to North Laurel.

Late in life, James Cabell's first cousin, Thomas Branch McAdams, wrote him about their schooling of seventy years past. "You remember we were made to leave Miss Ellett because Mrs. Camm said she had to stop teaching boys & we then went to Mr. Archer on Cary Street. He was the type who wants to beat up 8 or 10 year boys & we went to Uncle Bowie on Park Avenue with the result we were ready for McGuire's (ahead of the boys left at Archer's)."

Another of Miss Jennie's students in her first school was John Powell, later to become internationally known as a concert pianist and composer and still later as a polemist for racial purity. When later in her career Miss Jennie spoke to her girls with such admiration of James and John, "for quite a while some of the girls thought she was referring to the famous apostles." Cabell too remembered his association with his earliest teacher. In his scrapbooks he preserved his first extant composition with the notation: "This, my first attempt at fiction, was written in the May or June of 1886, for the final exercise of Miss Ellett's School."

The Wonderful Cat

Once on a time there lived a cat that could change herself to any thing she chose. One day she was walking along by a lake she saw a swan. "O how lovely is the swan!" said she to herself, "I wish I was a swan." At that moment she found she was a swan swimming on the lake. "O how delightful it is!" cried she. She saw a turkey-Buzzard. "O how I wish I was a turkey-Buzzard"—she found that she could not swim, she was a turkey-Buzzard, she flew away.

She died—her spirit went to the evil one for she had sinned many a time.

James Branch Cabell

Evocative of literary promise, this composition written at the age of seven presents us with an interesting duality in the bird imagery, the black buzzard contrasted with the white swan. Both, however, have an underlying cat nature, mercurial and hinting at an association with Satan: "She has sinned many a time." A Presbyterian doom is pronounced on a frivolous Episcopalian.

A literary imagination was cultivated early in the boy. His Patteson grandmother as well as his Cabell uncles encouraged this bent. One still finds in Cabell's library at Virginia Commonwealth University childhood books that he treasured. Three were edited by Charles Henry Hanson and published in 1884. *The Siege of Troy and Wanderings of Ulysses* bears the autograph "James Branch Cabell" in its maturest manifestation. *Stories of the Days of King Arthur* bears Cabell's autograph as well as the inscription "James Branch Cabell/from/Uncle Landon," his father's youngest brother. *Wan-*

derings of Æneas and the Founding of Rome also has his mature signature, and its early inscription reads "James Branch Cabell/from/Uncle/Arthur/Xmas '86." James Cabell was seven, and this uncle was another of Dr. Cabell's younger brothers; Arthur, a Navy surgeon who never married, collected books dealing with demonology and erotica, many of which found their way into his nephew's library. Some sixty-three years later, the cover of *Stories of the Days of King Arthur* was accurately described in *Let Me Lie* (1947) with a citation from its preface that the work had been carefully purged of any "occasional allusions and episodes which make them unfit to be placed in the hands of juvenile readers."

Mark Twain is extensively represented in Cabell's library, and inscriptions show that his works were early reading for young James as perhaps they were for his slightly younger cousin Thomas Branch McAdams. The father of the latter, James's uncle by marriage, was obviously fond of Twain. *Mark Twain's Sketches, New and Old* (published in 1879, the year James and Thomas were born) is autographed "George B. McAdams/Oct. 29th 1880." *Life on the Mississippi*, 1883, is autographed "George B. McAdams/ #101 E. Franklin/June 1st '83." At that date the young family of Sallie Branch McAdams was still living with her mother. *A Tramp Abroad* (1880) bears the inscription "Thomas Branch McAdams/Mch 12th 1880," written by his father as Thomas was then one year old. *The Prince and the Pauper* (1882) bears the inscription "Thomas Branch McAdams/ from his father/ June 26 1882." A mature Cabell placed his bookplate in all these volumes as well as other Twain works. By age eleven, James was reading Rudyard Kipling. *Plain Tales* is autographed "James Cabell (1890)/217 S. Third/ Richmond, Virginia." Appended in his later handwriting is "James Branch Cabell/almost his first autograph."

In *As I Remember It*, Cabell pays tribute to his grandmother as "an omnivorous reader," unlike most members of her immediate family. Her preferred reading in her grandson's youth had settled on the popular romances of the day.

> She had finished with most of the standard classics of English and American literature a good while before my time; and Grandmother had dismissed them affably. Never again did she return to these time-honored volumes, during at all events the latter years of her life, but rather did she read, persistently and with zest, the novels of Miss Marie Corelli, and of Charlotte M. Braeme, and of Ouida, and of "The Duchess," and of Mary Elizabeth Braddon, and of Charlotte M. Yonge, and of Mrs. Henry Wood, and of Mrs. Forrester, and of yet many other no longer world-famous gentlewomen who,

during those far-off days, specialized in high romance and as a rule (or so at least did I, who was not familiar with their masterworks, surmise) in the upper classes of English society.

For my grandmother's demands of literature were both simple and explicit. I know because very often she sent me down to the Rosemary Library to return the three books she had finished with and to bring back three new ones.

"And try to pick out," were my instructions, "at least one love story with a duke in it."

"But why do you want a duke, Grandmother?"

"Well," she replied, and a whit wistfully, "I have known pretty much all sorts of people in my time excepting them. No, I never knew any dukes, and so of course I like to read about them."

This was logic, one felt, with a flaw in it somewhere. Yet I think otherwise today. She was but calling upon art to fulfil art's proper function, of supplementing life. Her own life had been ever busy and happy enough and duly encolored with grief and made holy by ever-abiding love. Her life had satisfied her amply. But after all, there had not been any dukes in her life.

. . . she alone of my immediate family ever read any books at all in the fields of creative writing. And so my own trend toward what is termed "escapist" fiction must have been inherited from her, says logic. (*As I Remember It*, 152–54)

While the residences of his Grandmother Branch and his Grandfather Cabell were fixed, stable, geographical poles in a slowly turning Richmond, the abodes of young James Cabell's parents were peripatetic. Like migrating birds, they moved from shelter to shelter. From his grandmother's house at 101 East Franklin Street where James was born, Dr. and Mrs. Cabell moved two-and-a-half blocks to 5 South Third Street when he was two. A year later they were at 822 West Grace, the following year at 302 West Main. In 1885 they were living at 100 East Main in what is known as the Crozet House, a handsome brick edifice built around 1814. It had been the residence of Captain Claudius Crozet, the first professionally trained engineer employed by the Commonwealth of Virginia. The Cabell's three-year residence in this house when James was six to eight must have been a congenial haven for the three young Cabells; it adjoined at the back their grandmother's little farm within the city. A block west, at 1 West Main, Mr. Francis Glasgow had established his family in a commodious Greek Revival house; among his five daughters was the introspective Eleanor, later known as Ellen, five years older than James. From the Crozet House, the Cabell family moved to 217 South Third, again for three years. South Third Street, which runs south along a ridge to Gamble's Hill overlooking the James River, remained a fashionable Richmond address until the early decades of this century. The Gamble in his grandfather's, father's, and brother's names reminded James that he was in the vicinity of ancestral territory even if his was an arrested flight. In 1892 when he was thirteen his parents moved to 918 West Grace, where they lived until James departed for college.

These frequent wanderings from house to house were somewhat atypical for established Richmond families of the period and might have been symptomatic of other discontents in the marriage of Dr. and Mrs. Cabell. After the early years of marriage, their differences of temperament became manifest and led to an eventual separation. The stability of Martha Branch's establishment at 101 East Franklin ended in 1888 when, her once-ample means exhausted, she moved to her oldest daughter's home at 305 West Franklin Street and later to 914 West Franklin. The senior Dr. Robert Gamble Cabell's death in 1889 ended the Sunday visits of the younger Cabells to Governor Street. By the time James Cabell left for college in 1894, at the age of fifteen, Richmond was his hometown, but no stately mansion suggested a permanence associated with home. A sense of impermanence is detectable in his earliest poetic efforts.

James Cabell's childhood impressions of his grandmother, his grandfather, his nurse, Louisa Nelson, and his wife come to us from his pen, after mature reflection, and all that he observed of an objective nature can be verified from other sources. The clippings and mementos he saved were constant reminders of his impressionable years. When a biographer comes to James Cabell's early impressions of his parents, no such source material is readily at hand. Brief allusions to his father's drugstore and his mother's dismissal of reading, as well as a few society notes in newspapers, constitute the record. For the most part, Cabell the adult writer saved every scrap of paper that would contribute to a future biography, one that would reveal the complete man. There can be no doubt that he manipulated the record for purposes of publicity, and perhaps vanity, but he also longed for an eventual setting straight of the record, as evidenced by the scrapbooks he so assiduously compiled in telling detail. Family material is abundant in the first two books, but the material that would give insight into Dr. Cabell and Anne Branch Cabell is found only in their obituaries. Their frequent moves during their years of cohabitation, less than twenty, may explain some absence of letters and family papers, and their eventual separation may account for losses. One also suspects a natu-

ral reticence on the part of the children of this marriage to divulge unhappy domestic divisions within the family.

The relationship of James Cabell's parents during his childhood years
was locked away in memory, but its buried presence is detectable. It likely
contributed to making an essentially shy youngster even more introspective and less inclined to exhibit his emotions openly. "Love" is not a word
employed casually in Cabell biography; he admitted it was a word never
exchanged in his marriage of thirty-six years to his first wife. In the oeuvre
it is associated with madness along with heroic exaggeration. Somehow,
early, James Cabell learned to mistrust emotions, or at least to put away
those of a painful nature. But in the catharsis of writing, the stored experience emerged in telling, if indirect, portraits of his parents. Psychological
maturity allowed the man to realize he had become his father and his
mother in understanding.

In the autumn of his career, the mature author commented in *Quiet,
Please* on the many personal traits of people he had known that found
their way into his fictive characters. He alluded, indirectly, to several
women—Gabriella Moncure, Priscilla Bradley Cabell, and to Anne Branch
Cabell, his mother:

> And lastly, the self-same gentlewoman, or at any rate some fragments of her,
> can be found surviving under a new alias from one book into another book,
> as when Marian Heleigh quits the pages of *Gallantry*, to enter *The Cords of Vanity*
> as Gillian Hardress, and a while later intrudes into *The Cream of the Jest* as Muriel
> Allardyce; or as when, most notably, that Claire Bulmer Townsend, who fig-
> ures briefly in *The Cords of Vanity* as Mr. Townsend's flibberty-gibbet young
> mother, after contributing to Patricia Stapylton throughout *The Rivet in Grand-
> father's Neck*, becomes Melior in *The High Place*, then gets into *The First Gentleman
> of America* (more or less) as Doña Antonia, and rounds off all in *There Were Two
> Pirates*, by turning into Isabel de Castro. Economy could not very well go far-
> ther. (92)

The composite portrait of Annie Cabell is that of a charming woman
whose talk could soar into flights of illogic and as quickly descend into
the reproachful. Melior in *The High Place* is a delicious confection of beauty
devoid of metaphysical concepts. If "this bright light creature's very diverting chat" does not savor of the intellect, the hero reasons that after all
"he had not married her in order to discuss philosophy." In *The First Gentleman of America* Antonia is referred to as having "the mind of a canary."
The protagonist observes, "Your logic, like the logic of all other women,

is an unanswerable and sound reason for doing whatever you may prefer to do." When the male's incomprehensible conscience results in high-minded talk, she begins "to speak with a commensurate but more cheerful lack of coherence." The civic-minded Dr. Cabell was twelve years older than his wife. While age differences were common in marriages at the time, Annie Cabell was not cast in the mold of the subservient Victorian wife. Highmindedness to her was unamusing and therefore unsociable, and talk of "higher emotions" could be construed as criticism thinly veiled. One hears the voice of Annie Cabell when Antonia observes, "'He suffers, just as you said this morning, from having too many convictions; and they upset him every now and then into being high-minded all over the place, in a way which very few other women, I am certain'—Antonia concluded, with a blending of resignation, of reproach, and of modesty—'could ever put up with'" (208).

As Cabell's career retreated into the golden haze of serenity, his parents emerged more wholly from the pages of *There Were Two Pirates*.

> Just as my father knew everything which had been printed in books, so did my mother know everything else. My mother was beautiful. She had brown eyes and brown hair which crinkled, but there was gold in them too. My mother was the most beautiful person in the world, as well as the most useful, because whatever you needed, you went to her and asked for it, and then she gave it to you.
>
> It was in this way that I thought about my parents, as being all-perfect and all-powerful; and I regarded them also as being perpetual. It did not ever occur to me that my parents might become older or change at all. (32)

Dr. Cabell's participation in the Battle of New Market when he was not yet seventeen,—the battle in which his brother William was killed, colored the cast of his mind. His profession dealt with the soberer side of life. His church saw life as a testing. He analyzed the quality of life dispassionately. The social contract, as he perceived it, was essentially a pact between a gentleman and his God. In human relationships, propriety and good manners were called for.

> In brief, my father was wholly selfish and, in consequence, wholly charming. He made himself agreeable to everybody, because he disliked to associate with people and with women especially, who were not in a complacent frame of mind. But I do not think that he cared deeply about any person,

during the time I knew him, except only his dead Provençal poets. [For "dead Provençal poets" read "dead Confederate heroes."]

To my mother, for example, he was far more than courteous. He agreed she was right about everything. He told her incessantly how well she was looking today, and how very becoming was her hat, or her gown, or her mantilla, or something else she was wearing. He protested, as if in real dismay, whenever she had brushed back her crinkly brown hair so that it did not cover the tops of her ears, because, he said, this made her somewhat less beautiful.

He did not call her Juanita, but darling; and I remember how the tall, thin, handsome, but vaguely languid man always arose from his chair when she came into the room, as well as what a ceremony he would make of arranging my mother's chair for her in our dining-room at every meal. It was all quite as if he were her lover instead of her husband. But at bottom, I now believe, he looked upon her as being a highly useful person who attended to his housekeeping, and so enabled him to go on with his writing in comfort.

I did not think about my father in any vein so critical during the time that he and my mother and I were happy together. I knew then that my father was the most learned person in the whole world. And I liked him, too; for even though he did not spoil me quite so actively as did my mother, yet toward me he exhibited a never-failing, grave courtesy; and he addressed me, almost always, as if I were his equal image.

I did not suspect that, for a father, this was unusual. I knew only that, in addition to his having read everything which had ever been printed in any book, my father was interesting to listen to when he talked about his Provençal poets. (*There Were Two Pirates*, 78–79)

Another biographical detail may be gleaned from this work. Although the child-hero is descended from "once famous" families, he remembers "we were poor." "Poor" in this sense carries the implication of genteel poverty, endemic in the post–Civil War South: "We did not worry concerning this circumstance. Neither one of my parents, I am certain, ever thought about money except as a thing which, when you had it, you spent. If you lacked it, you had only to sign a paper . . . or to sell some of the furniture with worm holes in it, or some of my mother's jewelry, or a piece of my father's land; for then, at once, without any least trouble, you again had money" (73).

If young James Cabell was aware that there were times of affluence and times of financial drought, he must have become aware that his Branch and Scott cousins had money in a stable fashion. As his first cousin Walter Russell Bowie, another "poor" cousin, would observe, the Branches and their in-laws were now among the "economic royalists" of Richmond. Consequently they married well and augmented their positions; "they took for granted a social order in which privilege and control would remain with them" (*Sunrise in the South*, 127). It had demonstrably not remained with the dynamic Martha Patteson Branch:

> I have spoken thus far of the days of her affluence alone as my first childhood observed them, howsoever briefly; for by the time I was ten or thereabouts Grandmother had spent cheerily almost the last penny of Colonel Branch's money, just somehow. Nobody ever knew quite how, and least of all did she. The once largest fortune in Virginia lasted her, though, for near twenty magnanimous years, throughout which economy and my grandmother remained total strangers, and profuseness and generosity stayed her hourly companions. To anybody who was in trouble, I mean, but in particular to anyone who was blood kin to her, or to any public cause of which she approved, she immediately and with eagerness gave whatever was needed— or to be wholly accurate, whatsoever was asked for—as befitted a Patteson. To do that was her code. The resultant, the inevitable, poverty and the twenty years of dependence upon her nearer relatives, of whom but yesterday she had been the free-handed patroness, and the disappearance of her bodily health—all which followed—she faced not one whit less cheerily. (*As I Remember It*, 150–51)

When Dr. R. G. Cabell, Jr., married at the age of thirty, he was an assistant in the local insane asylum. His circumstances were modest compared to those of his wife's family. Later with the aid of Branch money, he was able to establish himself in the pharmaceutical business. By the mid-1880s, advertisements began to appear: "Ro. G. Cabell, Jr., Apothecary, Cor. 3rd & Main Sts., (Child's Old Stand)." By 1888 the business was listed as "R. G. Cabell & Co"; associated with him were T. W. Chelf and Clarence R. Shryer. The 1892 city directory reflected a further expansion of the firm to "Cabell and Chelf, 106 N. Pine, between Franklin and Grace, branch of R. G. Cabell & Co., Druggists and Apothecaries." The new location was the west end of Richmond, in the city's traditional path of growth. Trains to the north, Ashland and Washington, left from the nearby Elba Station at Pine and Broad streets, a modest structure that locals dubbed "Elbow Station." But three-story houses had been built along Grace and Franklin streets almost to Richmond College, just beyond Harrison Street where Grace ended at Ryland. The family of Sallie Branch McAdams and their impoverished pensioner, Martha Louise Branch, was established at 914 West Franklin Street, a handsome graystone house now part of the campus of Virginia Commonwealth University. The family of Elizabeth Branch Bowie lived nearby at 913 Park Avenue, and Dr. and Mrs. Cabell occupied a spacious house at 918 West Grace, a short two blocks from the new store on Pine.

Black servants were cheap and even families with modest means had cooks, house servants, wash-women, and frequently stable help. Economy was rarely observed in most households of the older families, who continued a style associated with pre–Civil War plantation living. Frugality could be applauded in matters of dress but never in hospitality, especially at the table. If Martha Branch's prodigal style lasted twenty years before it gave out, whatever affluence Dr. Cabell attained as a druggist was of much briefer duration.

The money that Annie Cabell and her sisters inherited, upon marriage, from their father's estate caused considerable strife within the family. Col. James Read Branch had left a sizable fortune that had been invested in the best securities, held by the Richmond firm of Thomas Branch and Sons. In his will, Colonel Branch had named his younger brother, Major Thomas Plummer Branch, to be legal guardian of his children. A veteran of the battles of Fredericksburg and Sharpsburg and a former prisoner of war, Major Branch moved to Augusta, Georgia, after the war and established another Branch Sons and Company with his younger brother Melville. Because he was living in Georgia, Thomas left control of James Read Branch's securities to the discretion of officers of Thomas Branch and sons: the brother and brothers-in-law living close to the nieces. As guardian, Thomas P. Branch made an accounting on 15 January 1881, turning over $20,556.54 to each of the two older daughters, who had married, and to Elizabeth, who planned to marry later that year. The sum that Annie received, if prudently invested, could have provided financial security for her young family.

On 18 December 1883, however, a suit was instituted in the Chancery Court of Richmond in the name of Dr. Robert Cabell and his wife. G. B. McAdams, husband of Sallie Branch, among others, provided depositions, all of which were taken by Elizabeth Branch's husband, attorney W. R. Bowie. The suit named as defendants the officers of Thomas Branch and Company: Thomas Branch, John P. Branch, Frederic R. Scott, Thomas P. Branch, and George A. Cunningham (husband of Emily Read Branch); they were charged with trading the assets of the heirs for the benefit of the firm. John P. Branch was alleged to have "verbally and in writing urged and directed" conversions of securities which the plaintiffs deemed "improper and unauthorized," and Thomas P. Branch was accused of purchasing rail stock at exorbitant prices and of investing in "worthless land in Georgia." The lengthy replies spanned a number of years. The case carried overtones of *Jarndyce v. Jarnydyce* in Dickens's *Bleak House*, but no wrongdoing was proved.

One irony of the case was the plaintiffs' involving Martha Louise Branch in the suit on grounds that she had been a surety for the guardian. The redoubtable lady stated in her deposition that she was not conversant with the management of her husband's estate. Having disbursed her own share with a lavish hand, she had left financial matters to those who understood them. And doubtless Martha Branch's oldest grandchild was equally unconversant with these grave financial matters, if he was even aware of them. Indeed his parents did not appear to understand, he realized later. To what extent an impressionable child would sense the resultant stresses in his parent's marriage is conjectural. But money, or the lack of it, intruded into his consciousness with growing insistence. Not until his own marriage in 1913 at the age of thirty-four did he settle again into the relative financial security he had known in the first decade of his life.

3

The Emerging Chrysalis
1890–1894

The Richmond in which James Cabell was growing up paid its public respects to the Lost Cause, ennobling its garrulous relics and raising monuments to its dead heroes, but the city's industrial heart tore down the center of what had been Confederate Richmond. Antebellum mansions bespeaking their southern heritage gave way to rows of narrow houses in a ubiquitous late-Victorian style. Commerce moved up from lower Main Street to invade the crown once known as Shockoe Hill. From there it moved westward into the best residential area. More houses gave way to stores, churches, hospitals, modern hotels, their architecture indistinguishable from that of any growing northern or western metropolis. The antiquarians lamented the old city's cultural loss, but even they invested in its commercial growth. James Cabell witnessed an older city falling to a progress as ruthless as any war and the rise of a new city in what had been country fields. In 1888 at age nine, he boarded the first electric streetcars in Richmond. That same year, the legendary colossus, his great-grandfather Thomas Branch, died on 15 November, his death blazoned in all the papers as the passing of an institution that had survived the war unscathed. 'The Dispossessed Garden,' to use Lewis Simpson's felicitous phrase for the South's lost pastoral dream, became the major theme of

Ellen Glasgow's oeuvre. In her work, Richmond is simply the seat of dis-possessed Virginians. While Cabell would not subscribe to agrarian con-cepts, lost illusions became the central motif in his works. For a child of the city, the constantly shifting environment with its changing perspec-tives layered reality with irreality; in his perceptions oddly angled mirrors shifted surface illusions.

In a dying-renewing Richmond, James Cabell could hear time's winged chariot hurrying near. The legendary Dr. Minnigerode lay down his pas-toral staff at St. Paul's in 1889; St. Luke's Hospital would rise at the corner of Grace and Harrison, site of a creek filled in. Death entered the family again and took Grandfather Cabell, that childhood companion of Poe. The senior Dr. Cabell's will was written 16 November 1889 and probated a week later. It named his sons Dr. Robert Cabell, Jr., and Henry Landon Cabell as co-executors. The seven heirs, four sons and three daughters, were to share equally in the estate consisting of 221 Governor Street and other property. A provision in the will stipulated that Landon was to be trustee for his sister Agnes Bell (Cabell) Lottier so that her property would not be subject to the debts of her husband. James's youngest brother had been named John Lottier after that gentleman, but the once-close relationship had deteriorated. Agnes Lottier lived with her family, and the Governor Street mansion continued as the residence of several of the heirs. From time to time the Cabell heirs sold off other pieces of the estate, but they clung to the family home.

On 20 September 1890 when James was eleven, his parents bought their first property, 918 West Grace Street between Shafer and Harrison, a house only twenty feet wide but rising three stories over a high English basement. A steep flight of steps rose to a narrow veranda, where to the right of the entrance two tall, large-paned windows reached from floor to ceiling. The deed to the property was recorded in the name of Annie B. Cabell, wife of Dr. R. G. Cabell, Jr.; she paid $7,000 in cash. Cash sales for real estate were most unusual at that time in Richmond, and one can assume that the seller, William G. Stokes and wife, had convinced Annie Cabell, if not her husband, that a sale on those terms meant an advantage. It may have been a good investment as a residence, but it did not offer a ready return on capital. A little over a year later, on 21 January 1891, Annie Branch Cabell and husband agreed to sell this property; the sale did not go through, however, and they continued to live there. Annie may have regretted tying up so much cash in this house, especially when there were threats of hard times ahead and ready money would increase in value.

The Grace Street residence was only a step away from the McAdams residence at 914 West Franklin, where James Cabell's beloved grandmother now lived. Sallie Branch McAdams, the oldest of Martha Patteson Branch's children, had taken in her strong-willed mother when she became destitute. Sallie's businessman husband was prospering. George Brockenborough McAdams had come to Richmond an orphan, but through industry, acumen, and falling in love with an heiress of means, he had established his family in security. He had left Richmond College at the age of seventeen to go into the insurance business in which he prospered. After his marriage he became the senior partner in McAdams and Berry, one of Richmond's better clothiers. George B. McAdams, the fatherless boy from Florida, gradually became the stable influence in the larger family of James Cabell's aunts, uncles, and cousins on his mother's side. The friendly orphan "adopted" a larger family, perhaps in part because he was not a Confederate, bonded to ghostly comrades. When Cabell met Priscilla Bradley Shepherd many years later, she confided that she had worked as a typist on Main Street, "just across from McAdams & Berry": "She remembered my uncle by marriage, Mr. McAdams, very well, because he was one of the most handsome men that anybody ever saw anywhere; and he nearly always wore a light gray suit of clothes, with a red flower on the lapel of it." (As I Remember It, 14.)

McAdams showed particular concern for the declining fortunes of Lizzie Bowie, sister of his wife and Annie Cabell. After business reverses, lawyer Walter Russell Bowie became ill and was unable to work for the last seven years of his life. In the later 1880s, the support of their family fell upon his wife. Lizzie Bowie took in fancy work and kept boarders to make ends meet. She borrowed from her uncle John P. Branch in order to keep up the payments on her husband's life-insurance policy and she pledged her diamond earrings for a bank loan. When Walter Bowie died on 14 November 1894, Lizzie was left with a twelve-year-old son and a ten-year-old daughter to support. The $10,000 life insurance policy had claims against it, and George McAdams as guardian of the two orphans claimed two-thirds of the remainder as their inheritance. On 27 April 1895 Elizabeth H. Bowie contracted to buy the furnishings of "The Franklyn," a boardinghouse at the corner of Second and Franklin streets on the opposite end of the block where she had been raised in affluence at 101 East Franklin, the birthplace of her children. With the furniture, Elizabeth Bowie inherited some of the boarders, and she retained "The Franklyn" name. It soon became "home" for James Cabell.

James Ransom Branch, Annie Cabell's only male sibling, unlike many of his fellow Virginians, was liberated by the flux of post–Civil War change. Vital, amorous, curious, he savored life hugely. Born in Petersburg in 1863, he grew up wandering around Reconstruction Richmond, frequently leaving home for days. His schooling included samplings of McGuire's, McCabe's, General Ransom's (for whom he was named), Colonel Carter's, and Richmond College. In 1884 at age eighteen, he entered the Merchants Bank. At twenty-one he raised thoroughbred horses and cattle. Then he became an impresario for a chain of theaters in Virginia and North Carolina, including Richmond and Norfolk. He returned to the Merchants Bank in 1890 and, through ingenuity, innovative approaches, and social aplomb expanded the out-of-town accounts of the bank so that it became the largest between Baltimore and New Orleans. He was appointed a National Bank Examiner and was an active member of the Richmond City Council. He served in the National Guard and in the U.S. Volunteer Infantry in which he was a colonel during the Spanish-American War. Upon his appointment as secretary of the American Bankers' Association in 1895, he became a resident of New York City.

Jim Branch was a garrulous raconteur, who delighted in telling stories of his own youth to his young nephews. James Cabell heard legendary stories about patriarch Thomas Branch's tremendous girth, his weight over 250 pounds, and his evangelical zeal of which his grandsons made fun. The dark days of the war and Reconstruction were recalled as times of high adventure. According to Jim, his mother, Martha Patteson Branch, had been holding him in her arms in the backyard of their Petersburg house when one of Grant's bombs fell unexploded into the yard. A fifteen-year-old black boy had picked it up and dropped it into a bucket of water. Because Grant had given up trying to take Richmond, that city was safer than Petersburg under siege; so Jim's mother hitched up the wagon, put straw in it, and drove her family to her father's home in Richmond. A year later when Richmond was being evacuated and many buildings were being fired, Jim's mother took the black boy and a wheelbarrow and got three loads of goods, mostly cloth, from Thomas Branch and Company. The salvaged goods later sold for $5,000 in gold, according to Jim, and the same cash started Thomas Branch and Company on its phenomenal road to recovery. He remembered his father, James Read Branch, back from the fighting, starting up the business again in the basement of a building down on Main Street next to the old O. H. Berry Company. Through enterprise, hustle, and business acumen, the Richmond branch of the company did so well that the Petersburg office was closed. Jim revered Confederate heroes as well as any other southerner, but business was sort of war too. One had to rally the troops and launch surprise attacks in the big corporate meetings. War, politics, business were all part of the game of life.

When Jim Branch was twenty-one, he was engaged and equally devoted to three lovely girls, one in Petersburg, one in Richmond, and one in Baltimore. He married the latter, Mary Lilian Hubball, in Richmond, on 28 October 1885. They got along at first, but Jim admitted that both were headstrong and there were many disputes. Jim had three children by his first wife. James Robinson Branch, born 23 July 1886, developed into a fine, manly boy and a good athlete. His tragic death on 7 November 1905 at the U.S. Naval Academy after an unequal boxing match created international discussion. James Cabell, his first cousin, was profoundly moved; he had turned down an appointment to Annapolis. Jim Branch named his daughter, born 21 December 1897, for his youngest sister, Mary Cooke Branch. Another son, Allan Talbott Branch, was born 20 February 1890 but died of heat prostration at a funeral in Charlottesville less than five months later. By his second wife, Mary Warren, Jim had another son named James. Cabell dedicated two books to this uncle.

If James Ransom Branch was the splendid rake in the family, Annie Cabell's youngest sister was the jewel. Mary Cooke Branch, some eight years younger, was a beauty like Annie. Martha Patteson Branch had a full-length portrait of this youngest child painted in a white dancing dress with a blue sash. In its huge gilt frame the portrait graced 101 East Franklin during the days of luxury, and then 914 West Franklin in the days of Martha Branch's decline. It now hangs in a corridor of Mary Munford School in Richmond's west end. Unlike her three sisters, Mary Cooke Branch was studious. Like her mother she read and respected the past, but only the nobler aspects; she did not sentimentalize, and as her nephew wrote, "she could never be at rest in any small intellectual or spiritual space." She felt conflicting loyalties, to others and to her own need to free herself intellectually. Like her brother Jim, she welcomed a New South, not as the arena of a great arm-wrestling economic competition but as the home of an open society freeing all people to expand their horizons. Mary Cooke Branch passionately longed to go to college, an idea adamantly opposed by her mother. For Martha Patteson and other Richmond matrons, "there might be women's colleges somewhere, but they could be disposed of as 'only a Yankee notion.'" Herself a strongly opinionated

woman, Mat Branch shared the local abhorrence of strong-minded females, meaning those with scholarly interests or any interests outside
family and church. Mary Cooke Branch's "college" developed out of two
extraordinary friendships. Confederate General Logan, a family friend, encouraged her reading of serious scholarly works, such as Mill's *System of
Logic* and Spencer's *First Principles.* Then in 1887, at the age of twenty-two,
she met Mary Safford, called Mae, of New York, a widely traveled woman
four years older and one with superior intellectual endowments. Their
friendship flowered into a lifelong devotion.

At an age when other Richmond girls sought eligible males for courtship and marriage, Mary Cooke Branch stood aloof and indifferent and
caught the attention of one of the most eligible. Beverley Bland Munford,
a brilliant young lawyer, fell in love with her, but he had to press his suit
for seven long years. He finally won her by encouraging her endeavors to
be socially active in the best sense. Theirs was a marriage of true minds,
and their nurturing influence on nephews and nieces was significant.

Beverley Bland Munford, born in 1856 in Richmond, spent his early
childhood in Williamsburg at his home Tazewell Hall, formerly the home
of Edmund Randolph, first attorney general of the United States. Munford
entered William and Mary College when he was fifteen and studied there
four years. Unable to afford law school, he read law with his brother-in-
law, Judge James Dodridge Coles, of Chatham in Pittsylvania County. After
establishing himself as a country lawyer and entering politics, he moved
to Richmond in 1887. An able politician, he became an active legislator.
Graced with a distinguished Virginia ancestry, he entertained liberal out-
looks, a combination rarely found in the commonwealth since the days
of Jefferson. When he and Mary Cooke Branch married in 1893, they first
lived in a house on Laurel Street overlooking Monroe Park where the
present Grace and Holy Trinity Church stands. He encouraged his wife in
her efforts with other forward-looking Richmond ladies to establish the
Woman's Club. The greater number of Richmond females sniffed along
with their spouses. Why would ladies want to meet outside their own
homes? As they rightly suspected, this club was not formed for social
entertainment in the conventional sense. It was intended to foster intellectual pleasures, and almost a hundred years later it still exists as a forum
to stimulate its members' minds. Mary Branch Munford and her husband
championed two causes in Virginia: "the public school system, which
touched the great body of Virginia boys and girls" and "a fairer chance for
the weakest and most disadvantaged class in the community, the Negro

people." When Lizzie Bowie's husband died in 1894, the year after the marriage of Mary Cooke Branch and Beverley Bland Munford, they took in Mary's nephew Russell Bowie to live with them on Laurel Street, leaving Lizzie free to run her boardinghouse on Franklin Street. The education of young Martha Patteson Bowie also became the Munfords' concern. The education of two young minds was a congenial pursuit for the Munfords.

The year 1893 was a pivotal one in the affairs of the parents of James Cabell. Dr. Cabell's business appeared to be flourishing. There were prominent advertisements for his two drugstores, and he was listed in the 1893–94 city directory as president of the "Chester Clay wkng co." *The Elite Social Directory* for 1893 informed social Richmond that Dr. Cabell, along with his brothers, was a member of the Richmond German and that Mrs. Cabell's "at home day" at 918 West Grace was Thursday. Annie Cabell was thirty-five, her husband forty-seven. She was still an attractive woman, indeed still considered beautiful. Her open nature made her disregard the more rigid strictures of Richmond society. Presbyterian Calvinism was still a meaningful part of Richmond's social fabric, but Annie Cabell, freed from Branch Methodism by Patteson Episcopalianism, dared to smoke cigarettes and drink cocktails (not yet christened such) before other ladies freely confessed to those pleasures. Among her other pleasures was agreeable company, and a favorite in that category was her amusing, man-about-town first cousin John Walker Scott, only one year older than she and never loath to have a drink with a charming woman.

The sad old days of Reconstruction were over, and Richmond's regained prosperity was to be crowned with a splendid new hotel, the Jefferson. Planned as early as 1888, it began to materialize 1 May 1893, between Franklin and Main streets on Jefferson. But as summer approached, debates on the weakness of the national currency accompanied a financial panic. Gold was scarce, and the 16 to 1 parity of gold and silver for the dollar was questioned. Runs on banks led to the failure of many. Business in Richmond, as elsewhere, came to a standstill. The New York stock market fluctuated erratically so that "securities" became an ironic misnomer; liquidation was the order of the day. Local papers discussed "The Silver Question" and "Bimetallists," and financiers everywhere called for the repeal of the Sherman Act which required the coinage of a certain amount of silver. In July the clothing firm of McAdams and Berry advertised that merchandise on sale was limited to payment in silver. The 30 July Richmond *Dispatch* headlined the opening of the Chicago World's

Fair in a week's time, as well as the letter by Major James H. Dooley to President Cleveland attributing the panic to the Sherman Act. The same issue chronicled activities at the Virginia resorts: at the Rockbridge Alum Springs "Mrs. Dr. R. G. Cabell established herself as a hostess in a beautiful progressive euchre party at the Grand on Wednesday night."

The President called a special session of Congress on 7 August, and after prolonged debate the Sherman Act was repealed. Old Dominion Day was celebrated at the fair on 10 August with a reproduction of Mount Vernon as Virginia's exhibit, and on the speaker's platform along with General Fitzhugh Lee and Senator John W. Daniel was Mrs. Caskie Cabell (Nannie Enders), wife of Dr. Cabell's oldest brother. On the same day at the Rockbridge Alum, "Mrs. R. G. Cabell Wednesday morning assisted by Mesdames Lottier, Stokes, and Boykin Wright honored her Georgia friends with an exquisite lunch with champagne." Also on the 10th, Mr. John P. Branch, just returned from Europe where his wife and oldest son wandered from spa to spa in search of her health, expressed his optimism that the economy would improve with the repeal of the Sherman Act. That day, however, "the banks stopped paying out money except in small amounts and began paying in script," leading to further panic. People no longer trusted banks; they kept their money at home and purchased only essentials.

Evidently pressed for ready cash to meet his business obligations, on 14 November 1893, Dr. Cabell conveyed by deed his one-seventh interest in his father's estate to his wife for $1,400. The principal asset of the estate was 221 Governor Street, still occupied by Dr. Cabell's siblings. Dr. Cabell had turned to his wife in the belief that his inheritance would remain in the family and that the eventual settlement of the estate would more than cover what was essentially a loan.

On the 22 August, the Cabells attended the wedding of Mary Cooke Branch to Beverley Bland Munford. In contrast to her three older sisters who had elaborate weddings at St. Paul's, the bride elected to be married at the Franklin Street home of the McAdamses where she lived. While commenting on the beauty of the arrangements, the reporter for the *Dispatch* observed, "The ceremony was marked by unusual simplicity, but the arrangements and decorations were of the most chaste and exquisite order." The Honorable Claude A. Swanson, then a member of Congress, later governor of Virginia and secretary of the Navy, was the best man; Mae Safford of New York was maid of honor; and Mr. John P. Branch gave away the bride. "Three little nieces and a nephew of the bride held the ribbons as the cortege entered. They were little Misses Mattie Bowie, Louise McAdams, Mary Cooke Branch, and Master John Cabell." The reception following the ceremony included old families, new economic royalists, and the politically elite, the latter headed by Governor and Mrs. P. W. McKinney. Beverley Bland Munford, liberal-minded but politically astute, would begin to play an influential role in the affairs of James Cabell.

Despite hard times in Richmond, getting worse rather than better as 1893 drew to a close, Annie Cabell continued to enjoy a seemingly carefree life of social pleasures. The *Beau Monde* for 7 January 1893 reported that she had attended the Christmas German held in the new Masonic Temple at Adams and Broad. This affair had been graced with two of the celebrated belles of the day, indeed the last two associated with Richmond, May Handy, the future Mrs. James Brown Potter of New York, and Irene Langhorne, who went on to marry the young New York artist Charles Dana Gibson and be immortalized as the "Gibson Girl." Younger Langhornes were in the wings ready to take their turns in the international spotlight, in particular Nannie, a student of Miss Jennie's, the same age as James Cabell. The homely ring of "Nannie" later gave way to Nancy, Lady Astor, who became the first woman elected to the House of Commons. Commenting on the irony of calling the last decade of the nineteenth century "gay," Virginius Dabney observed, "On the other hand, the nineties were marked by the serious financial panic and depression of 1893, which caused suffering, unemployment and bankruptcies in Richmond for years." The famous Haxall-Crenshaw flour mills went into receivership, and other established firms that had survived the war failed.

On 24 January 1894, Dr. and Mrs. Cabell had their signatures notarized on the deed granting her sole title to his paternal inheritance, notably his share of the Governor Street house. On the 26th, a mortgage was placed on 918 West Grace, one note for $2,500 and another for $2,000; the holders of the notes were W. Brydon Tennant and Landon Cabell. The deed of trust was notarized by Dr. and Mrs. Cabell on the 27th and recorded in the Court of Chancery on 5 February. The Richmond City Directory has the Cabells still living on Grace, in the mortgaged house, that year.

On 14 April 1894 James Cabell turned fifteen. His secondary education was drawing to a close, and he was ready for college. Late in life he wrote that he had attended four different private schools in Richmond, the last of which was McGuire's. At this time, however, he had not settled on a career, though there was no question that he would have to support himself. Later evidence indicates he may have given thought to service in the

Navy or the diplomatic corps and may even have considered teaching. Unlike his brother Robert and cousin Thomas McAdams, he was disinclined to follow a career in banking or business. His paternal grandfather, Dr. Robert G. Cabell, Sr., had attended William and Mary his freshman year (1828–29) but had graduated from the University of Virginia. His maternal grandfather, James Read Branch, graduated from Randolph-Macon College (1844–47). Virginia Military Institute, the alma mater of Dr. Robert Cabell, Jr., would be John Cabell's choice, but a more introspective James was not drawn to the rigors of a military regimen. His Cabell heritage should have suggested the University of Virginia, but its social style may have been thought too lively for a fifteen-year-old or too expensive for the hard times. In 1894, despite its historic past, William and Mary was a small, provincial college dedicated to preparing male students for careers in public teaching; most of its students came from the rural middle classes. But James Cabell's newly acquired uncle, charming Beverley Bland Munford, had fond memories of the quiet school; he was on the Board of Trustees and he may have paid the studious James's tuition, given the straits in which the boy's father found himself.

Whatever financial difficulties existed for the Cabell family, the summer of 1894 again found Annie Cabell and her three boys up at cool, congenial Rockbridge Alum Springs. James was developing into a handsome youth and, while still reticent, showing an awakening interest in female companionship. He was attracted to Alice Serpell of Norfolk who was also at the springs with her mother, three sisters, and brother. Alice Serpell and James Cabell passed the time agreeably reading novels aloud, making candy, having suppers together, and dancing under the benign gazes of their elders. As a young beauty with charm, Alice attracted the attention of other youths, particularly "Kinny" Kinsolving, the son of an ecclesiastical family. Prudent enough not to play favorites at her age, Alice Serpell annoyed a jealous James Cabell to the point that the two did not speak for four days. At the end of the summer, however, they agreed to correspond.

Back in hot, humid Richmond, Dr. Cabell was evidently feeling the pressure of creditors. Perhaps his two brothers, Landon and Arthur, feared that their residence in the family home at 221 Governor Street was in peril of an attachment for debt owing to the one-seventh interest now owned by Annie Cabell. On 5 July a deed was drawn up selling R. G. and Annie Cabell's equity to Landon and Arthur Cabell for "the sum of five dollars." This instrument was sent to Rockbridge County for Annie Cabell's signature, and although she held a deed of trust on the same property from her husband, she signed on 2 August. Annie Cabell was caught in a whirl of social distraction, entertaining, being entertained, and making excursions to other nearby resorts. The Richmond *Dispatch* for 22 July reported that one of the more novel entertainments had been given the previous Wednesday by Mrs. Cabell in her cottage on Baltimore Row. Guests had thrilled to a "Spiritualistic Seance" that included mediums, fortunes told, ghost stories recounted, a party that lasted until dawn. The same paper's correspondent announced that "everybody is interested in the approaching encampment of the First Virginia Regiment, under command of the gallant Colonel James Branch, of Richmond." Later in August, Colonel Jim invited some thirty guests to supper at the encampment, an affair catered by "Forrester of Richmond" with "champagne and other wines in abundance."

Back in Richmond, on 11 September, Annie Cabell took her deed of trust on the Governor Street property to the Merchants Bank where her brother Jim accepted it as collateral to secure a loan of $1,100. In the Chancery Court records James Ransom Branch is named as trustee for the bank. Did the borrower realize that she had signed a deed conveying the same property to her two brothers-in-law on 22 August? Did Dr. Cabell know she was borrowing on the earlier deed of trust he had given her? One also wonders how he had sold to his brothers the property he had already conveyed to his wife. Her "dower right" signature had been required in the sale to his brothers, but in the later borrowing on the same property his "courtesy right" signature had not been required, perhaps the instrument itself being deemed to abrogate that right. Then a further complication occurred. A week later, on 18 September, Dr. Cabell had his signature notarized on the 5 July deed to his brothers and it was recorded. Though for the past several years Dr. Cabell had been a director of the Merchants Bank, he was probably not privy to all its business transactions. Was Jim Branch the type to lend his sister money without informing her husband? One of Jim's earlier escapades may be illustrative. Using bank business as an excuse he had talked Thomas P. Branch into letting him go to New York for new accounts when a horse race was really his goal. There he placed $100 of bank money on Troubadour at 7 to 1. True, his brother-in-law George McAdams was also in New York, near delirium from a spree, and had agreed to lend Jim the money if Troubadour lost. Fortunately Jim won $700 by risking the bank money. George McAdams won $70 by risking $10 of his own money. No doubt Jim warned Annie that there would be trouble if she did not meet the payments on the loan. It was a risk, but he had returned George McAdams home safely to his family. Jim liked Dr. Cabell. Moreover, Annie may have reminded her brother that *her* money had purchased the deed of trust on Governor Street.

A fifteen-year-old boy preparing to leave for college had other concerns than the financial dealings of his parents. Though his mother may have talked freely of these matters in his hearing, one doubts that he understood their ramifications anymore than she did. Dr. Cabell probably felt divided between loyalty to his brothers and their family interests and his obligations to his immediate family. A gentleman of his temperament did not discuss business matters of a stressful nature with a teenaged son. James Cabell was leaving home in a more significant way than in his excursions with family and friends to the springs. Williamsburg was only fifty miles away, but it represented a psychological distancing from Richmond. In a place where time had stopped, he would learn to know who he was. He would call that place "the Garden Between Dawn and Sunrise."

Ellen Glasgow, who may have observed Richmond more objectively than James Cabell, gave a telling summary of their time and place during their childhood years. In an overview of his work written in 1930, she commented on the phenomenon that in the South of their youth southerners abhorred solitude and silence. Anyone who expressed the desire to be alone was thought neurotic and therefore in need of company. Cabell wrote of himself as one "who was born taciturn" and as a result was thought strange. As Glasgow remembered him "in boyhood, he appeared shy, reserved, over-sensitive, with a face of tempered melancholy, and with the manners of the Victorian age." She went on to observe of Richmond:

> In this transitional period, it is true, the old culture was dying, and the new industrialism was only beginning to prepare the ground for its ultimate triumph. Much was lost of the past, but the little that was left continued to be picturesque; and in Richmond, where the charm of the village still lingered, the little James, peculiar only in his spells of silence, encountered the usual perils of infancy. As he grew up, the world was changing without violence. In his youth, the familiar welcome still awaited one in country houses. The gardens on James River, though untended and fast running to seed, were en-

chanting places in which to play games or make love. Even in Richmond, where assembled law-makers were already dismantling the scene for democracy, the established social order had not surrendered unconditionally to its Chamber of Commerce. (*Sat Rev of Lit.*, 7 June 1930)

In a Richmond where all was transient, James Cabell observed that the roles played by members of his own family seemed assigned by irrational forces. The glittering surfaces of society were only projections of egos unwilling to let the underlying anguish of loss rise to public view, smiling masks held to cover fear, grief, and disillusionment. Confessional passages in the highly autobiographical *Cords of Vanity* (1909) touch on his boyhood:

> I was always proud of my handsome mother, but without any aspirations, however theoretical, toward intimacy: and her periods of conscientious, if vague, affection, when she recollected its propriety, I endured with consolatory apprehension of the ensuing and agreeable era of untrammelled negligence (12).
>
> I fancy that at bottom I was lonely without suspecting it. . . . I was accounted an odd boy; given to reading and to secretive ways, and, they record, to long silences throughout which my lips would move, shaping noiselessly the words they never articulated; and it was not until my career at King's College [William and Mary] that I may be said to have pretended to intimacy with anybody (13).

4

Severing the Cords

1894–1895

Demands for public schools were being forced on a reluctant Virginia legislature, but Beverley Bland Munford was in the vanguard of legislators sponsoring public education. To the question of where the teachers would come from, the response was an appropriation of $10,000 annually to the closed college in Williamsburg on the condition that it train male teachers. Each county and city would be entitled to send one pupil tuition-free to be trained as an instructor. All these students were to pledge that they would teach two years after leaving college. Minimum age for entrance was fifteen, and a total of 128 nominees were eligible for free tuition.

Restored Williamsburg and reglorified William and Mary have obliterated the town and college that James Cabell came to in October 1894. When the capital of Virginia was transferred from Williamsburg to Richmond in 1779, Mr. Jefferson's university in Charlottesville replaced the colonial college as the school for gentlemen. William and Mary had closed during the war, and it closed again in 1881 for lack of patronage. Through appeals to the Virginia General Assembly, it won a modicum of state support, opening again in the fall of 1888 as the College of William and Mary and State Normal College of Virginia for Males.

When James Cabell arrived for the 1894–95 session five years after the reopening of the college, 113 young males were pledged to teach and 43 were not. His name was not among the pledged. Total expenses for a non-pledged student for the nine-month term amounted to $161. The free tuition allowed a young man to obtain an education in very lean times, and it assured him a teaching position upon completion of his studies. The geographical distribution of the appointments assured a largely rural student body, drawn for the most part from the middle-class yeomanry, a class that was on the rise in post–Civil War Virginia.

The fall semester of 1894 began on 4 October. Cabell's reference in a letter, written soon after his arrival, to "this hole I am now inhabiting" makes it appear that he was lodged in one of the four college dormitories—one a primitive structure devoid of plumbing or a name and designated simply as "Rear Dormitory." New classes were taught on three levels, junior, intermediate, and senior. Most of the students were striving for a Licentiate of Instruction, a two-year degree comparable to today's Associate degree from a junior college. A Bachelor of Arts degree required three diplomas, usually after four years of study. Diplomas from six of the schools (departments), with the exception of Pedagogy or Education, earned a Master's degree. The ratio of degrees earned to the number of enrolling students was low. Since the curriculum was structured on three levels, fourth-year students were termed "Graduates in Schools." Tuition on this level was free, and these students frequently served as instructors for the normal-school classes. James Cabell, along with his entering classmates, was probably instructed by upperclassmen during his first year in college.

Cabell's educational background was superior to that of his rural classmates, and his social background had exposed him to a wider culture and a far more sophisticated world of style. Classroom attire at such colleges as William and Mary was the ubiquitous dark Sunday-best suit, usually ill-fitting and inhibiting. The cut of young Mr. Cabell's clothes set him apart, and the cane and yellow gloves marked him as someone outside the experience of his rustic counterparts. His city refinements earned him the sobriquet of "Sister," a cause for hurt resentment but also for secret pride in his social superiority. While his classmates went to their Baptist, Methodist, and Presbyterian churches on Sunday, he attended services at Bruton Parish Church and joined the choir.

Soon after James Cabell arrived in Williamsburg, he received a letter from Alice Serpell, the girl from Norfolk whom he had met at the Alum.

His reply is dated only "Saturday," probably 20 October, and it reflects a college freshman's initial loneliness away from familiar faces.

My Dear Alice,

I received your letter on Monday and have not read it often since then—only nine or ten times I believe. So you have been to New York and returned while I have been to Richmond. I saw the Exposition and did not enjoy it very much as I have seen mostly the same things several times before. O if you had only been there as I hoped—do you know the Foot Ball Team plays Norfolk on the tenth and it is barely possible I may come down with them. And see you? Really it seems almost too good to be true. When I read your letter for the first time and saw you had met Mr. Kinsolving I positively dropped it on the floor but then I read a little further—and smiled most contentedly. Really I am frightfully jealous—though I don't see why I should be—of Kinney at least. Though when one comes to think of it he did have his good points but of course I was not in a position to appreciate them as he was "me hated rival" as they say in melodramas. Dont refuse me a photo-graph—you cant imagine how much I want it. You say the only one you have is horrid—well I make you a proposition. Send me one and if I think it is ugly or horrid I promise to return it by the next mail. Of course it doesnt do the subject justice—no photograph could—but I want something to remind me of you continually. Think of it I have nothing but a small lock of hair which you want me to throw out of the window—and of course I am very liable to follow your orders. So dont forget but send me a picture and in exchange I will give you Miss Rankins or Daisie Yarbroughs address or in fact anything that I have. So you are reading "Trilby" aloud. Do you know what that re-called to me? Why the happy days when we read "Peter's Wife" together. I never enjoyed any book so much in my life—even if Kinsolving was around most of the time. Do you remember that night you took supper with me? I like to think how furious he must have been. Well I have used up the paper and it is late so goodby.

James Branch Cabell

P. S. Dont forget the picture

The novel Peter's Wife read at the Rockbridge Alum Springs was a work just out in three volumes. George DuMaurier's sensational best seller Trilby was also published in 1894, and James Cabell's copy has some inter-esting annotations. At the top of the flyleaf in his college handwriting is "Trillby—Graduate of William & Mary." Next below is his autograph "James Branch Cabell" in its later form. In the middle of the page he scrawled in pencil: "Property/of/James Cabell." At the bottom of the page appears the notation, "This book went through the college of William and Mary in the year 1894–95 A.D./presented by F.L.C." *Trilby* gave the world's dictionaries a new entry, "Svengali," a maleficent hypnotist, one who attempts to persuade or force another to do his bidding. Maidens of the day shivered deliciously at the thought, and doubtless young males entertained fantasies of possessing such powers.

The college freshman's education concerning the female psyche took a small step forward with the receipt of Alice's reply four days later.

Thursday Night [25th]

My Dear Alice,

I received your letter Wednesday, have puzzled over it ever since, and yet I cant understand what's the matter. Why the tone of your epistle is so cold that it positively threw me into a chill. Can it be that I begged you for a photograph of yourself? Well if you dont care enough for me to let me have your picture, I suppose I must submit in sorrow but dont let us quarrel about it. Why it makes me shudder even now to think how unhappy I was when we used to disagree last Summer. You have great influence over me, Alice—dont use it to make me unhappy. So dont get mad—and to prove it write me a long friendly letter—all about yourself and what you are doing for these are the subjects that I am most interested in. You dont encourage me much in my idea of coming to Norfolk—prophesying certain defeat and not even saying you would be glad to see me—but nevertheless I intend to persist for I would give ever so much just to look at you and hear you speak. So you are reading books with *several* parties—I cant help hoping that they are all girls. For myself I have just begun "Trilby"—what wouldn't I give if you were here to read it with me? So good by

[The bottom of this letter is cut off. It is postmarked the 29th, the following Monday.]

James did not accompany the football team to Norfolk on Saturday, 10 November, for a game that was to be played against the Norfolk YMCA. Perhaps as a result he received the long letter he ardently desired from Alice Serpell.

November 20

My Dear Alice,

It is needless to say how pleased I was to get your letter and how flattered I was at your being disappointed on not seeing me. Your letter shows vast improvement—the one before was short and frappe while the last was longer and like your own sweet self. Some how your letters are not answers to mine—they are friendly and kind but that is all. Alice you know I care more for you than any one and so remember this when you write. I am glad you remember when we made candy last summer for it was certainly [The end of this letter is missing.]

Encouraged by the friendly tone of her last letter James determined to make an excursion to Norfolk during the Thanksgiving holiday to see her. The Serpells then lived at 38 Duke Street, in a fashionable section called Ghent.

Wednesday 5 December

My Dear Alice,

And so I have seen you once more—really when I think of it it all seems like a dream. I had ever so many things I wanted to say to you but some how I never got a chance. I admit I was sorry to see Selim Myers—I like him very well but still—still I didn't want him that night. As usual you looked at him all the time—but I have got accustomed to that now and managed to console myself with the candy. You never looked better in your life than on that night—my first thought on seeing you was "How beautiful she is." And you were very sweet and kind—until Selim came and then I was promptly forgotten. What is it you see in him—he is rather handsome and dances well but that is all. Where I—but modesty forbids me to finish. Well I staid in Richmond until Tuesday and had rather a good time but am now again in Williamsburg. I wish you could see this hole I am now inhabiting. I want you to come up on some of the excursions in the spring and see the place and the queer menagerie of students. I know they would all fall in love with you—and according to Kinsolving you would flirt with them and I should of course be desperately jealous—which would be quite like old times. Well goodby and remember you owe me a long letter for I dont count that little note I found in Richmond.

James Branch Cabell

The young lover had the good fortune to encounter Alice at a party in Richmond over the Christmas holiday. In an undated letter postmarked 25 January 1895, he wrote:

My Dear Alice,

What in creation means this unearthly silence? I have heard nothing of you since that most delightful night in Richmond, and I wrote to you shortly afterwards. Do write immediately and by the way be sure and address Williamsburg, *Virginia*, for I have lost several letters because that was not attended to. Tell me about *yourself*—a subject which interests me. Did you enjoy Christmas? I had rather a pleasant time in Richmond though it seemed almost too wildly gay after Williamsburg. And now I am back again and doomed to six months more in this horrible tread-mill and my only consolation is to think of you. Last Thanksgiving you were prettier than I ever saw you—which is the greatest compliment I can possibly pay you. I had a thousand things to say to you but I never got a chance some how. It is barely possible that I may be in Norfolk on Sunday, but any way be sure and write to me as soon as you can.

James Branch Cabell

Apparently Alice Serpell never addressed her young lover again. He wrote three more importuning letters. Perhaps her interests were fixed elsewhere, or she did not care for the tone of his letters. Being called a flirt by a jealous friend may have been sufficient to cool the friendship on her side, or Richmond gossip about the separation of James's parents may have reached her parents in Norfolk.

Like many another young man undecided as to vocation, especially in uncertain financial times, James Cabell considered military service as providing education and career. Sometime during the fall of 1894 he applied for an appointment to the U.S. Naval Academy. Such a suggestion could well have come from Col. James Ransom Branch, whose own son received an appointment some years later. Another uncle, Dr. Arthur Cabell, was a Navy surgeon, and Beverley Munford, his uncle by marriage, had the political associations to assure an appointment for a well-qualified student. Despite his matriculation at William and Mary, Cabell does not seem to have seriously considered teaching as a career. Annie Cabell had exposed her son to a style of living above the expectations of his classmates at William and Mary.

The college that James Cabell attended was chaired by seven professors, dubbed "the seven wise men" by the students. Each professor headed a school, and three of them incorporated multiple disciplines. Lyon G. Tyler, M.A., president of the college, taught moral science, political economy, and civil government, a division that today would be called social sciences. John Leslie Hall, Ph.D. (Johns Hopkins), taught English and history. Charles Edward Bishop, Ph.D. (Leipzig), taught Greek, French, and German. Bishop's course load was four classes in Greek, two in French, and two in German; he lectured over twenty hours a week. The college magazine complained in December 1895, during Cabell's second year, that the professors—especially Bishop—were overworked and had little time for scholarship.

Lyon Gardner Tyler (1853–1935), president of the college, had assumed office on its reopening in 1888. Son of John Tyler, eighteenth President of the United States, he was a graduate of the University of Virginia, had practiced as a Richmond attorney, and had been a member of the Virginia House of Delegates. There he had helped push the bill to reestablish William and Mary as a state normal school, a project shared by Beverley Munford, who served as a college trustee. Tyler was scholarly by nature. As a "liberal" he was an active reformer interested in public education, temperance, and women's suffrage, but as a "conservative" he was an ardent defender of Virginia's tradition of an elite leadership. He established the *William and Mary Quarterly Historical Papers* in 1892 and continued as its editor during his tenure as president. Upon his retirement, he founded *Tyler's Quarterly Historical and Genealogical Magazine*, which he edited until his death in 1935. James Cabell and Lyon Tyler were to become well aware of each other.

It has been suggested that Cabell was inhibited intellectually at William and Mary, but a case can be made that the reverse is true. William L. Godshalk observed that at William and Mary "Cabell did not neglect his studies, and each year saw him gain several Certificates of Distinction: his freshman year in Greek and French; his sophomore year in English, Greek and French; his junior year in English, mathematics, Latin, Greek, and German; his senior year in 'Moral Science, Political Economy, and Civil Government' and in history. We have record of Cabell's taking courses and distinguishing himself in every area of study offered at William and Mary except 'Natural Science' and 'Pedagogy.' The diversity of his studies suggests the width of both Cabell's interests and his abilities, which, in turn, are reflected in his later writings. However, as his Certificates of Distinction and his later novels indicate, Cabell's forte was languages, and his most influential professor, Charles Edward Bishop, who helped introduce him to the glories of ancient Greece and medieval France" (4).

There is no denying that the significant friendships James Cabell established early in Williamsburg were with people older than he. One, Schuyler Otis Bland of Sassafras, Virginia, had entered William and Mary as a "free tuition" student when the college reopened in 1888 and had been among the very first to receive its Licentiate of Instruction in 1890. Having fulfilled his pledge to teach, he returned to take upper-level classes in preparation for his goal of becoming a lawyer. Because of his strong scholarship, he was named an instructor in English and history in the 1895–96 term. He participated in oratory, debates, and amateur theatricals. Otis

Bland was seven years older than James Cabell, and their friendship was based on social ties and similar interests; Bland was later Cabell's confidant during a period of great stress.

The college librarian when Cabell matriculated was Charles Washington Coleman. A published poet, he had recently been appointed to expand the hours of the library and to guide student reading. Coleman was a thirty-two-year-old bachelor who lived with his mother, Mrs. Cynthia Beverley Tucker Coleman, in the historic Tayloe House. Related to some of the illustrious families in Virginia, Coleman recognized a social peer in young Cabell, and he found the youth highly receptive to his suggestions in matters of reading. Cabell later credited Coleman along with Professor Bishop for his abiding interest in classical, medieval French, and Provençal literature, all lasting influences on his later work. It was most likely at Coleman's suggestion that Cabell moved into the Coleman home.

Cynthia Coleman (1832–1908) was a dynamic personality, in the mold of Martha Patteson Branch. Her husband, Dr. Charles Washington Coleman, died the month before James Cabell matriculated, and, like other gentlewomen in reduced circumstances, she opened her house to certain carefully selected paying guests. Her family consisted of three sons, Charles, George, and Nathaniel, and one living daughter, Elizabeth. Her two youngest sons had recently attended William and Mary, where their grandfather, Nathaniel Beverley Tucker, had been an eminent professor of law. In her youth Mrs. Coleman had been Williamsburg's "peerless queen of society," and now her daughter Elizabeth was one of the college belles. Upon the death of her youngest child, Catherine, in 1884, Mrs. Coleman channeled her grief into the Catherine Memorial Society, dedicated to the restoration of historic sites, in particular Bruton Parish Church and its graveyard. Along with Mary Jeffrey Galt of Norfolk and some Richmond friends, Cynthia Coleman founded the Association for the Preservation of Virginia Antiquities (APVA) primarily to secure the remains of the Jamestown church ruins. As James M. Lundgren points out, they based their efforts on a new civil religion: patriotism was God-given, and "Jamestown, Williamsburg, and other patriotic sites became 'holy ground.'" The fervor of these dedicated patriots was not lost on an impressionable James Cabell, and in time the forces of Manuel the Redeemer would sweep the invaders from Philistia out of his land of pure romance. Equally important in Cabell's development, Mrs. Coleman was passionately fond of genealogy. With her interest in genealogy and her son's in poetry, James Cabell never lacked for lively lectures in the historic house into which he had moved. The Colemans also drew him into the social life of the town, another change he found congenial as he had little in common with an essentially athletic-minded student body.

The family of Dr. James Dunlop Moncure, head of Eastern Lunatic Asylum in Williamsburg, also had Richmond ties. Dr. Moncure had earlier been associated with the Central Asylum, the institution where Dr. Cabell had been an assistant when he married Annie Branch. On the death of his first wife Dr. Moncure had remarried, but living with his new family was another daughter, Gabriella, four years older than James Cabell. At his fifth birthday party given by his grandmother at 101 East Franklin, Ella Moncure had played the role of Mother Goose watching over her son Jack, young James Cabell. After a ten-year lapse, their meeting again in a quaint, bucolic setting was a cause for reassessment in their relationship. There could be no thought of marriage between the two. Archness, whimsy, irony was called for. Over the next three years, in an increasingly congenial Williamsburg, James Cabell and Gabriella Moncure shared a relationship that had a lasting impact on both their lives.

In March 1895 James Cabell heard that his application to the Naval Academy was being favorably considered. The Honorable Tazewell Ellett, congressman for the Third Virginia District, had nominated him for one of the coveted appointments that led to a commission as an officer and a career in the Navy. The young man was ambivalent in his feelings. He had discovered his talent for verse and his facility for writing in general. Meter and rime were growing in fascination for him. His earliest extant poem, "On Meter," is dated April 1895 and is in the predictable vein of sixteen.

> There's a meter for poetry, a meter for gas,
> And a meter for measure of stone;
> But O how much sweeter, than each other meter,
> To meet her by moonlight alone.

Spring made Williamsburg appear a more congenial place than it had seemed in a lonely fall and a bleak winter.

The young poet did not have a literary outlet for his talents at that time. The college magazine had expired with the January issue, for lack of patronage and funds. As was common then in most colleges, the administration required all students to participate in one of two (or more) competing literary societies for weekly readings, oratory, and debate; members of both societies at William and Mary, the Philomathean and the Phoenix, were supposed to contribute essays, poetry, and fiction to the *William and Mary College Monthly*. The magazine also served in a limited way as a forum for college news. In the spring of 1895 the literary societies petitioned the Board of Visitors for support of the defunct magazine; given the hard times and the low economic level of the student body, the board's assistance was needed if the college was to have such a publication. This appeal was approved and resulted in the revival of the *Monthly* the following fall.

When Cabell penned his poem on meter in April, the young lady in Norfolk, his companion of the previous summer, was on his mind. Though apparently unsuccessful in this affair, he wrote her once again, on Friday the 13th of April, the eve of his sixteenth birthday.

Dear Alice,

Though indeed I have no right to address you so after your long silence yet tonight I fell to thinking of you and thought that I must write one more letter to you. What is the matter? I saw you last Thanksgiving and thought that I had never seen you prettier or kinder. Since then I have written two letters and received no answer. (torn) proud—you (torn) mean so much to me that I now write to you for the third time to find the reason of your silence. Do you remember when we quarreled last year and did not speak? Well I have told you how miserable I was then and I have felt exactly the same way since Thanksgiving only instead of four days it has lasted four months. Alice you dont know how fond I am of you—I have every letter that I ever received from you and that lock of hair is on the table now—all that I have left to remind me of you. Think of these things and write to me—your letters mean so much to me.

As ever

J.B.C.

Alice Serpell's seeming indifference to James Cabell's entreaties played a significant role in his later work. "Divine discontent," he philosophized, spurs the artist. Alice's popularity grew in social circles, and she became a belle at the Rockbridge Alum. She alone of the four Gainsborough Serpell daughters married and married well. Her chosen was Dr. Edward Carrington Stanard Taliaferro, an alumnus of William and Mary and a slightly older contemporary of James Cabell.

On 13 May 1895, the freshman from Richmond attended the Jamestown Celebration, sponsored jointly by the college and the APVA. Mrs. Coleman and President Tyler were both in attendance, and a feature of the program was the recitation of "Westward Ho" by Charles Washington

Coleman, a patriotic poem extolling the civilization that had crossed the Atlantic to be planted at Jamestown and had since extended to the Pacific. Both the Richmond *Dispatch* and the *Times* printed the poem in full, the latter referring to Coleman as a "poetic genius." Such recognition thrilled a just-turned-sixteen impressionable esthete. While the poem was in the filiopietistic vein of oratory James Cabell had been raised on, it had a broader concept of the hero, an Anglo-American younger and more universal, than the gray Confederate veteran extolled on most public occasions within the boy's experience.

Other subtle psychological changes were at work. The influence of those associated with the APVA Cabell encountered in Williamsburg would go far to induce a child of commercial Richmond into posing as an aristocratic Virginian. His industrious forebears were as qualified as other Virginians to claims of public service, the essential qualifier in the absence of inherited titles. He doubtless realized that his pose would alienate him from the majority of his peers at college, but they had their games and he had his. He could not have foreseen the long-term consequences, the flowering of an alter-ego that would later overshadow the hidden self, and still later a public pose that would be exploited for publicity purposes, especially during the post–World War I period of literary sophistication. Gabriella Moncure may have even seen the Coleman-bred influence of the APVA as pernicious, leading a shy youngster away from the natural to the artificial. What was amusing on the stage hardly constituted meaningful human intercourse. Miss Moncure would play on that stage with Mrs. Tyler, Mr. Coleman, and Master Cabell, and she would see a faun play the fop. One of Cabell's favorite professors, John Leslie Hall was a frequent APVA lecturer, and he too spoke on Jamestown Day in 1895. His elitist sentiment extended back to eighth-century Anglo-Saxon mythology, not just to the Civil War.

On the 17th of May James Cabell received an official notification to report to the Naval Academy on 2 September for the requisite examination of his qualifications. He was asked to acknowledge receipt of the Navy Department notice and to send his birth records. Cabell was certainly qualified scholastically. His reply may lie buried in navy files, but apparently he passed up this opportunity to become a cadet with an assured career upon graduation.

At this decision-making time the student must have been aware of the growing malaise in his parents' relationship. While they played the obligatory roles of a harmonious couple in social circles, the domestic tensions within the family were growing. Much of the summer of 1895 Annie Cabell continued to act the part of the carefree socialite at Rockbridge Alum Springs. The Richmond *Times* reported in July that she was established in her cottage on South Carolina Row. On Tuesday the 15th she entertained at a champagne supper; on the following Saturday she attended a ball dressed in black satin. On Sunday, 28 July, the *Times* announced, "It is with regret that we learn that Mrs. Robert G. Cabell will leave on Monday for Bath Beach, New York. She will be greatly missed until her return the middle of August." The Sunday, 18 August issue of the *Times* reported that Dr. Cabell was at Rockbridge Alum with his two sisters, Mrs. Boykin Wright and Mrs. John Lottier. Dr. and Mrs. Cabell attended a German on the 21st. Annie was still at the springs early in September.

The public image of harmony in the marriage of Dr. and Mrs. Cabell was a social front dictated by the prevailing codes of the day. Sometime during this year a confrontation took place that resulted in a permanent parting of the ways. Annie Cabell did not seek a divorce until twelve years later, but in those papers she stated in the language of divorce proceedings: "At the time he was very angry and it was willful desertion and he has not lived with me since, nor has he contributed anything to my support." While financial strains on the marriage doubtless played their part, Annie Cabell's social behavior was probably the deciding factor in the separation. The term "lover" was applied to her cousin John Scott in Richmond gossip. Margaret Freeman, born in 1893 and only two years old when the separation occurred, opined late in life that Arthur Cabell told his brother Robert that Annie was talked about in social circles in a way intolerable for any Victorian husband. Margaret's speculation was that only a close family member could divulge such information, indeed deeming it a brother's duty, and that as a bachelor, a navy officer, and a Richmond man-about-town, Arthur Cabell was the logical bearer of the titillating gossip. Dr. Cabell may have realized that his wife's indiscretions were the actions of a woman willful in her pursuit of pleasure, one perhaps blinded by a degree of innocence. Innocence in a girl might be overlooked by an indulgent husband, but it seemed out of place in a woman approaching middle-age. Robert Cabell, no prude but raised in the Presbyterian church, found his position as compromised husband, even if only in talk, intolerable.

The Cabells are not listed in the 1895–96 Richmond City Directory, nor do they appear in the 1895 Virginia Personal Property Tax Records. Dr. Cabell left Richmond, not to reappear for more than ten years. Annie

Cabell and her sons moved to 113 East Franklin Street, the boardinghouse of her widowed sister, Lizzie Bowie. Whatever Annie Cabell's emotional state may have been, and whatever may have been known by intimates, she elected to be known as Mrs. Robert Cabell, shunning any public acknowledgment that she had been abandoned by her husband. Dr. Cabell's absence as a husband employed out of town supported her subterfuge; when his name reappeared in the 1899 city directory, she had him living at 113 East Franklin, although other documents prove this untrue. Annie Cabell's pose as a woman still protected by the bonds of matrimony was not entirely a fiction, and whatever her status might be, reasoned most Richmonders, she was after all widely connected with the best people.

The summer of 1895 could hardly have been a happy one for James Cabell, even at sixteen. A growing sense of impermanence must have suffused his thought. The springs were always a place of fantasy, and the house in Richmond that now sheltered the fatherless family stood at the opposite end of the block on which he had been born. At 113 East Franklin, his aunt's struggle to support herself and his mother's financial concerns were in depressing contrast to the luxury they had all known at the 101 address in the days of Martha Patteson Branch's affluence a scant few years before. Even the wealthy members of Cabell's family were seeing changes. Colonel Scott and his son Fred pulled out of Thomas Branch and Sons to start the brokerage firm of Scott and Stringfellow, precipitating a crisis in the older firm. The colorful James Ransom Branch would soon take his family to New York to live, and Cabell's handsome, intelligent young cousin James Robinson Branch would leave. But Louisa Nelson remained constant in the background. In the wanderings from house to house, in the slow disintegration of his family, her presence was a dark, protective spirit.

5

Palingenesis

1895–1898

When James Cabell returned to Williamsburg in the fall of 1895, he and Otis Bland were the last to sign the matriculation register on 5 October. Also entering William and Mary that semester was James's cousin, Mayo Cabell of Richmond, son of Paul Carrington Cabell of Amherst. The place that had seemed exile the year before was now more congenial than Richmond, where so much was in flux within his family. In "Fairhaven," the name he would give Williamsburg, he was being accepted as a personality outside the sphere of his mother's jurisdiction, and he felt a sense of awakening to identity and vocation.

The neophyte poet and essayist was a part of the team that planned the resurrection of the college literary magazine. It appeared in November. Among the assistant editors named were S. Otis Bland and James Branch Cabell, representing the Philomathean Society. They were also named fraternity representatives, Bland for Kappa Alpha and Cabell for Alpha Sigma Alpha. Charles Coleman represented Phi Beta Kappa. The editor, Plummer F. Jones, called for a first-class college magazine. "We have a hundred and sixty students at college now," he remarked, "some of whom, we know, have literary tastes." Jones proclaimed the serious intent of his publication: "We expect to express ourself fearlessly." James

Cabell was named editor for "Exchanges," reviews of the literary magazines of other schools. In this debut issue, he assessed those for Hollins, Vassar, Yale, Davidson, Wake Forest, Bowdoin, and Western Maryland, generous in praise for all except the latter. Reviews of the publications of other schools would follow for a two-year span. Though the reviewer may have grown weary toward the end of his editorship, it exposed him to the work of his peers in more prestigious schools.

With the appearance of the December 1895 issue of the *William and Mary College Monthly*, the literary career of James Branch Cabell was launched. His essay, "The Comedies of William Congreve," is attributed to Clarence Ashley Bell, a punning pseudonym; a poem, "The Blind Desire," is credited to Charles A. Ballance, another pen name; two "Pastels," prose poems entitled "The Dreamer" and "Babette," are also signed by Ballance. All these works of the college sophomore found their way into the later publications of the mature writer. The Congreve essay has an especially interesting history. Among six volumes of Congreve's works extant in Cabell's library, the earliest is dated 1697 and is autographed "Property of/James Branch Cabell." Another volume is entitled *William Congreve*, [n.d.] Unexpurgated Edition, with two autographs: "James Branch Cabell/ William & Mary College/Williamsburg, Virginia" and "James Branch Cabell/1894," the latter in the distinctive hand he developed in his sophomore year. Later in the school year the magazine announced that Charles Coleman was offering a medal for the best contribution to the publication during the year, and the Congreve essay won. The award was noted in the Richmond *Times* as deserving special attention, its author being "Master James Branch Cabell, of this city, who has just reached his seventeenth year." A revised version of the essay was published in 1901 in the *International*, with extensive reviews following in the Richmond *News* and the Richmond *Times*, and it was further revised in 1919 for inclusion in *Beyond Life*, the mature writer's credo.

The January 1896 issue of the *Monthly* contained a single poem by James Cabell. Dated September in manuscript, "A Ballad of Ye Hungrie Maydde" is in the sophomoric vein of "On Meter." It recounts the rivalry of two suitors for the favor of a maydenne "clad in a sad sweet smile—Also a necklace." After the rival males kill each other, the maiden thriftily cooks and eats them. The facetious tone of these poems was soon abandoned, however; while the succeeding poems of Ballance and Bell, later credited to Townsend, retain a youthful ardor, they develop into serious expressions of growing love. In form the poems are derivative, showing multiple influences; Swinburne, Browning, Keats become increasingly evident. In their inspiration, one can detect the intellectual stimulation of Charles Coleman and the emotional stimulation of Gabriella Moncure. In contrast to James Cabell's burgeoning literary output, few other students were producing anything worthy of the magazine. The editor lamented in the January issue that the publication was appreciated elsewhere but not on its own campus. Defending the school, he admitted that certain students were sensitive to "the scathing epithet of 'normal school'" applied to William and Mary, but he went on to observe that above that level, degrees were difficult to obtain, that only two baccalaureate degrees had been awarded the previous June.

While James Cabell's name does not appear as a participant in the forensic events of the literary societies, his attendance is likely. On 11 January, the Philomathean Society entertained the public in the old chapel with his friend Otis Bland as Orator of the Evening. Fleet W. Cox, president of the society presided. In a later reminiscence disguised as a short story, the Gabriella Moncure character says to the protagonist, "I was thinking of those Saturday nights when your name was up for an oration or a debate before the Eclectics [Philomatheans], and you would stay away and pay the fine rather than brave an audience." He never overcame the reluctance to speak as himself, a trait that carried over into his writing. Speaking in the guise of another, however, gave his voice release, and in that same January he stood before an audience; on the 15th, Otis Bland and James Cabell made their debuts as actors.

The Virginia Comedians, a local amateur group, presented two short plays that day in Cameron Hall, which at that time was used extensively for civic and social functions. The hall was part of Eastern Asylum, headed by Dr. James Dunlop Moncure, Gabriella's father. The first offering of the evening was *Withered Leaves*, a comedy in two acts by F. W. Broughton, published in 1894 by French. The cast amusingly parallels that in the real-life drama of young Cabell's development. Playing Sir Conyer Conyers was Dr. Charles Bishop, professor of Greek, French, and German. Tom Conyers, his son, was played by Charles Coleman. Mr. J. B. Cabell played Arthur Middleton, and Mr. S. O. Bland, Cecil Vane. Mrs. Tyler, the president's wife, portrayed Lady Conyers, and Miss Moncure was May Rivers. A play of intrigue about flirts and dangerous young men, the climax has Sir Conyers getting "jolly volcanic." The afterpiece was *Bluebeard*, a burlesque in three scenes by E. C. Nugent, dating from 1870. Playing the two principal roles were Mons. Nameloc (Coleman spelled backwards) as

Bluebeard and Mlle. Le Bac (Cabell) as Bluebeard's wife Fatima. The piece is in jogtrot riming couplets employing multiple puns, interspersed with songs. With young Cabell in ludicrous drag, it must have been dreadful.

The following month, James Cabell had shocking news from home. Death had snatched away his uncle by marriage, the charming, outgoing George McAdams. He had dropped dead while watching a parade in front of his home on Franklin Street. It was as if death was a jester in a farce. Richmond was the scene for that type of drama. It was different in Williamsburg. There, reality never quite intruded, and the poet continued to spin out his dreams. To the February issue of the *Monthly*, the budding author had contributed a fable entitled "Ignis Fatui" and two poems, "Aphrodite," dated the previous month in his notebook, and "Ye Lyttle Rhyme," also dated January. The latter poem, a rondeau, had one of its two rimes built on the name Gabrielle in manuscript but omitted in courtly fashion in print. Replacing "Gabrielle" was "Ye College Belle," a term that may have disguised the beloved but could hardly have flattered her sensibilities. The March issue again complained of the lack of student support, observing that it was impossible to publish a college literary magazine without contributions from its students. That lack, however, was a growing stimulation for the one who was contributing. The March issue also reported that the resurrected chapter of Phi Beta Kappa had met on 18 March and that Col. William Lamb of Norfolk, president of Alpha chapter, had introduced Mr. C. W. Coleman, "poet Laureate" of Virginia, who recited his poem on the King of Misrule. The chapel had been graced by the beauty and fashion of the Old Capital attending in evening dress.

April found the Virginia Comedians again in Cameron Hall. *Withered Leaves* was repeated on 7 April, with two substitutions in the original cast. J. E. Harris replaced Professor Bishop as Sir Conyer Conyers, and Elizabeth Coleman replaced Gabriella Moncure as May Rivers. The afterpiece on this occasion was a farce by J. M. Morton entitled *Box and Cox* with Mr. J. B. Cabell as John Box, a journeyman printer, and Mr. C. W. Coleman as James Cox, a journeyman hatter. Miss Coleman played Mrs. Bouncer. On 16 April, the Comedians presented *My Uncle's Will*, a "comedietta" in one act by S. Theyre Smith. Playing Charles Cashmore of the navy was Coleman, with James Cabell as Mr. Barker and Mrs. Tyler as Miss Florence Marigold. A farce in one act followed—*A Needless Stratagem* by Thomas J. Williams. Again Coleman and his sister were in the cast, with James Cabell playing Otway Sheridan Brown and James Dunlop Moncure playing a gardener. By nature shy and reserved, James Cabell was testing his verbal wings in public. Coleman's coaching seems obvious in these amateur performances where no director is listed. Noteworthy also is the fact that they were not college productions; young Cabell was associating with a society older than his peers, and this venture into theatrical activity set him somewhat apart in the eyes of the less sophisticated student body.

The literature of the theater was already known to the neophyte actor. Congreve and Wycherley were in his personal library, and that spring Professor Hall had organized a special Shakespeare class. Despite the requirement of "essays suitable for the College magazine," the course proved popular. The *Monthly* observed that it was "the most agreeable and fascinating of all the studies that our college affords." Professor John Leslie Hall was in the linguistic avant garde of his time, eschewing Latin syntax as a basis for English grammar and employing instead an analytical approach, emphasizing the study of Anglo-Saxon and the history of the language. The college catalogue carried a full-page advertisement of Hall's translation of *Beowulf* into modern English verse, published by D. C. Heath of Boston. The influence of James Cabell's philological studies while at William and Mary manifested itself later in multiple paraphrases sprinkled throughout his major work. A "Chaucerian" quotation appears on the title page of *Jurgen*. The comedies of Shakespeare set the tone of many of the earliest short stories. As a writer, Cabell was essentially a verbalist rather than a visualist. A student avid for new ideas in this springtime of his intellectual development, young James Cabell was in striking contrast to the athletically minded students frequently mentioned in the faculty minutes. Much of his social time was spent listening to Coleman talk and reading his poetic endeavors to Gabriella Moncure.

Charles Washington Coleman's study, in a wing of the Tayloe House, overlooked a back lawn and trees. The room was filled with books and pictures of writers and actresses. Stopping by on the way to his own room, the sixteen-year-old was enchanted by the talk of the older man. He had never heard words used so charmingly to convey ideas in a socratic monologue, devoid of cant. In Richmond, he had been raised on the orotundities of piety and politics, but pulpit and platform had their dogmas to sell. Words for the sake of words, an enchantment for orator and auditor, the term *belles lettres* took on meaning; the didactic made way for the artistic, the pedant for the poet.

There were no material promptings for young James Cabell to turn author:

> Authorship was not esteemed in the Virginia of my boyhood, and in fact, for all practical purposes, authorship was unknown there. Upon but two flesh-and-blood writers had the eyes of my adolescence rested; and none, in so far as I knew, thought of these two as being, primarily, writers. One was Amélie Rives, whose first novels were then being read furtively in Richmond, with shocked zest, as really not at all the sort of thing which you might expect from an unmarried girl, and as, in brief, books which the well-bred must blandly ignore when such books were published by a Rives of Albemarle,— and the other was Thomas Nelson Page, who, in Richmond, was esteemed and made much of on the ground that, apart from being "one of the real Pages," he had married considerable money in taking his second wife.
>
> A bit later, to be sure, when I was at college, I heard that the youngest Glasgow girl had published a book, but by that time my business in life was fixed, nor did I remember clearly which one of the five was Ellen. (*Special Delivery*, 50–51)

Authorship, he later realized, was not a consciously made decision; it was more a matter of awakening to a need, a compulsion, an undefined urge. Everyone fantasizes, he perceived, but the writer stood a better chance of giving his reveries validity. Indeed, writing as an exercise was perhaps the only way to give structure to personality. I think, therefore I exist; I write, therefore I create a persona: "For there was never any doubt in my mind, after my sixteenth year or thereabouts, that I would 'become a writer.' And yet there was never any definite notion, I am sure, what form this writing was to take. There was, most certainly, no stimulating delusion that writers were rewarded with affluence or high esteem" (*Special Delivery*, 49–50). In his later ruminations concerning his genesis as a writer, Cabell does not tell us and perhaps would have rejected the idea that it was a part of an awakening sexual drive. Some twenty years after the fact, he attributed it to a habit he picked up in writing for the *William and Mary College Monthly*: "So it seemed natural to write for the magazine—in fact, obligatory, because we were always short of material. Thus, I unavoidably got into the habit of 'writing': and this habit, contracted like that of cigarette-smoking in impressionable years, has of course clung to me. The whole sequence of events, on looking back, seems really to have left me no personal choice"("Cabell").

James Cabell's perceptions of himself and his family were greatly influenced at this time by a work published in late 1895. Alexander Brown's monumental *The Cabells and Their Kin: A Memorial Volume of History, Biography, and Genealogy* traced the Cabell family of Virginia from the Norman invasion to the generation of Dr. Robert Cabell, Jr. James and his two brothers were included in the list of descendants of Dr. William Cabell, the immigrant. James Cabell's awakening interest in genealogy was being abetted by Mrs. Coleman, his landlady, and by her son Charles. Moreover, part one of Brown's work ("The Cabells and Their Kin in England") paralleled the college sophomore's studies in Old English and Old French. The tome associated his ancestors with the days of knighthood, a period of history that stimulated his imagination to a far greater extent than any contemporary history of his native area. The work also appeared at an opportune time to assuage psychological wounds from his father's failed business and his parents' separation. Dr. Brown's preface, with its ringing exhortation to honor our forefathers by rescuing their memory and making it "our sacred duty" to resist "the effacing fingers of destruction and decay," fell on attentive ears.

Cabell copied excerpts from the work into his manuscript books of poetic endeavors, two of which he presented to Gabriella Moncure as offerings of a despairing love.

The Richmond social columns for the summer of 1896 contained no social activities for Annie Cabell and her seventeen-year-old son. Instead, the dispatches from Rockbridge Alum were filled with news of the "brilliant Miss Serpell." Mr. Gainsborough Serpell led a german. Another young woman's name, Miss Norvell Harrison, entered the lists; she won prizes at games, and her brother Henry led germans. They were there as part of the family of Professor Caskie Harrison of Brooklyn, cousins of young James Cabell who later entered into the personal drama of his life. In September, Mrs. Lottier and Mrs. Boykin Wright, sisters-in-law of Annie Cabell, were a part of the festivities at the Alum. Young James Cabell's poetry written that summer contained seascapes, and Annie Cabell may have sought entirely new surroundings for her summer hegira. Wherever they were, her son was retreating into a world of poetic fantasy.

The Matriculation Book at William and Mary has James Cabell signing in on 1 October 1896, but the signature is in the eccentric hand of Charles Coleman, a style he employed only for signatures. Whether the student was in Williamsburg or not is a matter for speculation. Another cause for mild speculation is the disappearance from college publications of Alpha Sigma Alpha, a fraternity associated with James Cabell's name the previous year. It may have merged with the local chapter (Alpha Zeta) of the Kappa Alpha order, as Cabell later claimed that he was a member of the latter fraternity from his freshman year. In the fall of 1896, he replaced Otis Bland as the KA representative on the *Monthly*. James Cabell's association with Kappa Alpha came when he was at an age to take seriously the pieties of the society. Founded at Washington College, now Washington and Lee, in 1865, it looked upon its members as an "Order of Knighthood": "Its essential teaching was that members should cherish the Southern ideal of character—that of the chivalrous warrior of Christ, the Knight who loves God and country, honors and protects pure womanhood, practices courtesy and magnanimity of spirit and prefers self-respect to ill-gotten wealth. Something might thus be saved from the wreck of material interests and political rights caused by the Civil War" (*History of the K. A. Fraternity*, 3). William and Mary received its charter for Alpha Zeta chapter in January 1890. Otis Bland was one of the six charter members. The rituals of brotherhood emerged later in the writer's major work. The Order of the Silver Stallion, "rampant in all members," had its genesis in Williamsburg, not in Poictesme.

On his return to college in the fall of 1896, James Cabell continued as editor of "Exchanges." The November issue of the *Monthly* contained the poem he had written about his mother, here misspelled "A Minature," credited to Charles A. Ballance. Ballance contributed "Christopher Marlowe—Poet and Dramatist" to the December issue, as well as the previous summer's "A Ballad of the Celestial Kingdom." The poet at this time was also writing love lyrics, many too personal to publish because they were addressed to Gabriella Moncure. He recorded these verses in bound notebooks in a small, almost hieroglyphic hand, one that became his signature in a wider, psychological sense. Perhaps it evolved as a paper-saving device, or one intended for his eyes only, bespeaking delicacy of spirit, personal thought, a sheltering of the interior anima from the casual observer. Then, as he came to think of the poet as his truer identity, this hand emerged, gradually replacing the schoolboy script nearly indistinguishable from that of other well-schooled youths. The sometimes difficult-to-read poetic hieroglyphics became the man himself. His letters to Alice Serpell in his freshman year were in the schoolboy script; the poems addressed to Gabriella Moncure were in the delicate print mode.

In January of the new year, James Cabell participated with other townspeople in a "library tea" given for charity by Mrs. Tyler at the home of the president. Charades were acted out with tableaux from forty popular books. The guests were to name the titles, and winners were awarded prizes. Young Cabell enacted the *Seven Seas*, Kipling's latest volume of verse. The writer was an early favorite of his and remained so into maturity. That same January, Charles A. Ballance contributed "A Rondeau," a poem in praise of his Ladye's Eyes, to the *Monthly*. The new year ushered in the young poet's most prolific period. Almost every fleeting thought flowered into a poem. He addressed the months, Theocritus, Congreve, Beowulf, Ballplayers, Thanatos, Horace, the game of poker, Keats. In February, he wrote "Ballad of Burdens" bewailing the rigors of mathematics and Greek and advising his professors that they were trying to fill another Williamsburg institution, the asylum. "A Ballad of Beowulf," which appeared in the May issue of the college magazine, was doubtless a tribute to Professor Hall whose modern rendering of that poem had been widely adopted by other colleges. One can only conclude that it was a happy spring in the life of a young man successful in his studies, romantically involved with a young lady, and secure in his friendships. He had turned eighteen in April, and the future appeared a shining expanse before him.

The dispatches from the Rockbridge Alum during the summer of 1897 made no mention of Annie Cabell or of her sons. Peripheral evidence places James and John in one of the country boardinghouses that flowered in the summer for the less social and less affluent. Escape from Richmond's red-brick ovens was considered a matter of survival in July and August, and almost any lodging outside the city was deemed adequate for a retreat. Norvell Harrison too was sojourning in this lesser resort. Annie Cabell may have journeyed north for her therapeutic sea baths, and some of her son's poetry suggests he may have joined her at a seaside resort for part of the summer. Engrossed in his poetry, place probably mattered little to him.

As James Cabell entered his senior year at William and Mary in the fall of 1897, he gave promise of becoming one of its most distinguished students; but certain academic and social patterns emerged that led to unforeseen results later in the year. Relinquishing the editorship of "Exchanges," he had become Dr. Bishop's assistant. Writing in the third person some twenty years later, he said of himself: "During his last two sessions at William and Mary he was instructor in French and Greek, and established for himself a post-graduate course in early French literature. The course was unique, in that there were no recitations and no tests: the French professor selected and loaned the books, young Cabell read them, and on Friday afternoons the two talked them over. In this way everything of weight in Provençal and Old French, down to the complete plays of Molière, was gone through before the boy was nineteen: and the fruitage of this "course" matured a deal later" ("Cabell").

James Cabell's senior year was notably more social, in ways that today would bear the term "elitist" and which doubtless gave rise to envy in the largely poor student body. "Social Notes" crept into the *Monthly*. On 16 October, Mrs. Dr. Van Garrett entertained fraternity members at a reception honoring a younger sister from Louisiana. There were only two social fraternities on the campus by then, and they were both small. Among the Kappa Alphas attending the Garrett party were E. B. Travis, T. J. Stubbs, R. M. Hughes, J. B. Cabell, Page Marsden, and John Porterfield. Consciously social in an Old South tradition, the Kappa Alphas became the subject of titillating gossip over the next several months.

It was increasingly apparent that James Cabell's contributions to the college magazine, urbanely sophisticated, showed a casual disregard for the mores of a provincial village. In the November 1897 issue of the *Monthly*, in an article on Dickens entitled "A Defence of an Obsolete Author," the young writer declared, "Life is a series of false values. Art attempts to remedy this. It may be defined as an expurgated edition of Nature." The following issue contained "On Telling the Truth," an essay in which the young author expanded his artistic credo, as Godshalk observes, concluding that "if we assiduously cultivate our powers of exaggeration, perhaps we, too, shall obtain the Paradise of Liars." The artist gives us visions of beauty and harmony unrealized in a real world, transporting us to metaphysical realms, a place where "no one will speak the truth . . . , and we shall all be perfectly happy." Such ideas may have charmed the esthetes, the literary "Wilde-eyed young men," but they can hardly have won the approval, if they were understood, of the earnest young men in the YMCA, the most active social organization on campus. The December issue also contained "A Summer Scene," a bit of innuendo about a young lady caught in a compromising situation; though deftly handled, it was surely thought risqué by the late Victorians of Williamsburg. In the same issue, "Charles Antrim Ballance" paid Charles Coleman the compliment of imitation: the poem "Phyllida's Letter" bears the annotation "Writ att her Majesty's Roial College of William and Mary," the superscript appended to Coleman's "*Alma Mater*," which is a tribute to the college's two-hundredth anniversary.

It was common knowledge among readers of the *William and Mary College Monthly* at this time that James Cabell of Richmond was the prolific contributor of the best, if most disturbing, essays and poetry, yet his real name had never been appended to any of them. "Charles Antrim Ballance" contributed "Black Spirits and White" to the February 1898 issue. The subject was witchcraft, "almost exclusively prevalent among women." What was a good Christian to think? The essay had Lilith, a witch, as Adam's first wife, one who supposedly became well known in medieval demonology. Young Mr. Cabell had to be sort of weird. He was good looking, and he associated exclusively with the best people, but a person never knew what someone like that was thinking.

The social notes in the February issue of the *Monthly* contained fulsome details of two fraternity parties that took place in January. "One of the most delightful social events of the season was a tea given on January eighteenth by Messrs. Hughes and Cabell at the Klondyke rooms in honor of the Kappa Alpha Fraternity. The long drawing room was handsomely decorated with the fraternity colors, old gold and crimson, cut flowers and potted plants, and the faint glow from the pretty lamps added to the scene." Young ladies received with the hosts, and the wives of professors chaperoned. Among the guests were Elizabeth Coleman and her brothers Charles and George. Among the students named were E. B. Travis, J. T. Porterfield, B. P. Marsden, and W. V. Mason, all to figure in a later drama. After the tea a german was given at Cameron Hall. As the evening wore on, the festivities, in the usual fraternity tradition, were said to have grown bacchanalian: "the figures were beautifully led by Mr. Chas. Washington Coleman, and the exquisite brilliancy of the scene reflected 'lines of dazzling light' as the couples moved with ease and grace in Kaleidoscopic succession. The pleasure of the dance was carried far into the 'wee sma' hours' of the morning." Among the "stags" at this festivity was J. B. Cabell, although a KA.

James Cabell contributed "La Thébiade of Racine" to the March *Monthly*, fruit of his solo seminar with Bishop. Like almost all of the young author's literary essays written in college, it was incorporated into his later artistic polemics. Significantly, no poems in young Cabell's verse-notebooks were dated March of this year, a silence probably indicative of growing emotional stress.

About this time rumors were circulating in Williamsburg that certain young men carried their pleasures into forbidden realms. The trial of Oscar Wilde a scant three years before branded as a pervert almost anyone considered an esthete. Nothing, however, in any contemporary record spells out the exact nature of the rumors, nor does the term "homosexual" appear in any of the evidence touching on this period. Professor Godshalk's assessment of this phase of James Cabell's education was thought accurate by Margaret Freeman Cabell, who may or may not have discussed the episode with her husband when he was in his seventies.

Cabell's last months at the College were darkened by what has been called a "scandal," but what was in actuality a series of vicious rumors. The origins and details of these rumors are, by their very nature, impossible to trace with any degree of accuracy. It has been conjectured that they grew out of a party given by Cabell "in honor of the Kappa Alpha fraternity" and followed by a dance on January 8, 1898. The *Monthly* described it as "one of the most delightful social events of the season" (VII, 153–154). How did the rumors begin? It has been suggested that everyone at this gala event ended the evening too inebriated to recall what, or if anything, had happened. But about the same time, Charles Coleman fell from "a ladder, while arranging some books in the up-stairs apartment of the library" (*Monthly*, VII, 296–297), breaking his leg; he was seriously shaken. His name was added to the rumors. Ellen Glasgow, who was in Williamsburg in the spring of 1898 and who knew James Cabell, suggests that the rumors had something to do with homosexuality; but her source, as she says, was mere rumor: "The leading middle-age intellectual of the village, or so I was told, and had exercised a pernicious influence over some of the students." (8)

At a regular meeting of the faculty on 31 March, the subject of the rumors came up. One can only assume that a faculty member broached the subject, but no names are mentioned in the faculty minutes. A matter that might well have been brushed aside at the University of Virginia as unworthy of faculty consideration was a cause of concern at the Williamsburg institution, the State Normal Male College of Virginia, subsisting on charity from Baptist and Methodist legislators. The faculty determined to call a special meeting the following day. On April Fools' Day they assembled. "Whereas certain rumors have reached this body concerning certain practices alleged to have been in existence between students and certain college officers tending to the detriment of the College," they resolved to investigate "as soon as circumstances permit." The matter might have rested there, the qualifying clause indicating that the faculty foresaw the difficulty in obtaining substantive evidence for such sensitive rumors. The resolution might have been intended not so much as a call for action as a warning to rumormongers to desist. The faculty was forced to take action, however, before they were ready or before the rumors subsided. Hearing that the faculty had passed a resolution, three victims of the rumors demanded immediate public exoneration. Eugene B. Travis, James B. Cabell, and William V. Mason, Jr., were indignant that the faculty would appear to give credence to rumors by discussing them in an officially called meeting. Thus the faculty met again on 6 April at 9 P.M. and "after some discussion" agreed to start the inquiry. They met the next three successive days, hearing testimony from students. Godshalk writes: "The campus was in an incendiary condition, and, at one point on Friday, April 8, the students were near riot state in the Chapel, protesting that the faculty was persecuting fellow students while not considering its own dirty linen. Apparently, the rumor-victims were getting the support of their fellow students. Hearing of the student gathering, the faculty sent Professor Stubbs to quiet them. He assured them that the faculty was acting in all fairness; the students cooled down" (9).

On 9 April, Benjamin Page Marsden wrote from Norfolk withdrawing from college. He was a KA and another implicated in the rumors. A weary faculty met again on Monday the 11th at 8 P.M. After reviewing their labors they opined "that no evidence has been adduced before it sufficient to warrant a finding against Eugene B. Travis, James B. Cabell and William V. Mason, Jr." At the meeting a letter written the same day was entered into the minutes:

Williamsburg April 11th 1898

Gentlemen of the Faculty,

Actuated by sincere love of the College, and in view of the present widely-spread rumors, whose presence we cannot but feel must necessarily make our present stay at Williamsburg neither pleasant, nor profitable, we hereby have the honor of presenting our resignations as students of William and Mary, and of desiring that our names be removed from her roll. At the same time we desire most emphatically to deny the truth of these reports and to pronounce them absolutely and totally without foundation.

With best wishes for the future welfare of the College, we remain

Yours most respectfully

James Branch Cabell
Eugene B. Travis
W. V. Mason

The resignations were accepted. In the light of the young men's wounded honor, one could have hoped that the president might have consulted their families as to the withdrawals. His failure to act met with criticism. John T. Porterfield, another student who was implicated in the gossip and confessed to participating in some unspecified activity, resigned as president of the Philomathean Society as well as an instructor for the coming year.

The faculty minutes that exonerated the students also referred to the college librarian, perhaps because the student petition of 7 April in support of the student victims had implicated him. Coleman's name had frequently surfaced in the investigation, and the faculty felt that two statements should be entered into the minutes, perhaps as a legal precaution. First, it acknowledged that as a body it had no legal right to investigate a fellow member, and second, that no evidence had been "adduced before it sufficient to warrant a finding against him." Shortly before the investigation of the rumors, Coleman had fallen from a ladder in the college library and had broken his leg. When he heard that his colleagues determined to look into the rumors, the fact that his name would be discussed behind closed doors was galling to his pride. His nerves were shattered as well as his leg. His physician, Dr. James Dunlop Moncure, father of Gabriella, was a specialist in mental stress. In the light of Coleman's anguish, he advised flight. The poet wrote his poet friend, H. M. Alden, editor of *Harper's Magazine*, to find lodging for him and his sister, Elizabeth Coleman. Then unfortunately he took an action that was interpreted by the gossipmongers as an admission of guilt: he resigned as librarian. Coleman and his sister left for New York City like many another wounded southerner seeking anonymity. Alden had found them accommodations in a boardinghouse for five dollars per week. Mrs. Coleman left for a visit to Richmond, where she stayed a block from the boardinghouse run by Elizabeth Bowie.

Having returned home, James was informed that his wounded pride had blinded him to the consequences of his withdrawal from college three months before he was to graduate. He and his mother consulted Beverley Bland Munford, who convinced the young man that in order to counter the implications of his withdrawal and to save his academic degree, his return to Williamsburg was imperative. Munford, a trustee, could not personally intervene, but he obtained the services of William C. Preston, a Richmond lawyer. Preston wrote President Tyler requesting a transcript of the investigation. In reply, Tyler stated that no recorder had taken minutes of the hearing and that any attempt to reconstruct the testimony from memory would be impossible. He reminded Preston that the hearing had produced no evidence worthy of bringing charges against anyone. As quoted in the faculty minutes, James Cabell wrote a second letter to the faculty:

Richmond, Virginia
April 23, 1898

. . . This letter [of April 11] was written without the knowledge of my parents and without conference with any of my friends except Mr. S. O. Bland a former student and Mr. Lyon G. Tyler, President of the College. Both of these assured me that they did not believe me guilty of the bad conduct indicative in the rumors above referred to. Since my withdrawal, however, from the college and after conference with my parents and other friends, I am convinced that notwithstanding the protestation of innocence contained in my letter of resignation and the circumstances under which it was written yet the Public is liable to construe and has construed this action on my part as a virtual confession of the truth of the rumors referred to. . . . . I respectfully suggest that I be permitted to withdraw my resignation and be reinstated as a student of the College. I also ask that in view of the fact that my resignation, together with the findings of the Faculty, was read before the body of students in the Chapel, in like manner, the purport of this communication be announced by you in the same place. . . .

The faculty met at the president's house to consider this and other requests for reconsideration of student resignations. James Cabell's letter was acted on favorably. A letter was read from William Virginius Mason, Sr., inquiring into his son's withdrawal on the advice of Otis Bland, a matter referred by the faculty to the Executive Committee. Eugene B. Travis also requested readmission and graduated in June. The minutes record a testy exchange of communication between the father of John T. Porterfield and Tyler, the former having come from Charles Town, West Virginia, to Williamsburg where he had been informed by a "citizen" that his son was being persecuted by the faculty. Doubtless the faculty felt it had been entangled with the Hydra and had ended up looking provincial and bigoted in its attempt to allay the rumors. It deferred further decisions to the Executive Committee, which met in May, and reassured the faculty that it had acted wisely in the opinion of the committee.

James Cabell's return to Williamsburg found him isolated from those who had seemed most congenial before the hearing. The Colemans gone, he lodged elsewhere for the remaining two months in the semester. For reasons unknown, Gabriella Moncure determined it best not to see her young friend, who had just turned nineteen. At twenty-three she may have lacked the sophistication to brave the gossip of the local inhabitants of the town. Every action seemed to be misinterpreted, and she may have felt defensive about her close relationship with the central subject. As a result, James Cabell spent lonely afternoons and sleepless nights while he waited for the escape graduation would bring.

In May of that year Ellen Glasgow, six years Cabell's senior and already a published writer, visited Williamsburg with her sister Cary. She intended to use the colonial capital as the setting for her third novel. Her assessment of the scandal gives us a contemporary perspective. Cabell remembered their meeting as the first in which he spoke to her, "among circumstances such as she depicted with a reasonable accurateness." The Glasgow sisters were lodged at the Colonial Inn, along with "several famous gossips of the 'best families.'" They were told that the college was split by a scandal "of that peculiar nature" associated with Oscar Wilde.

What had happened, as I gathered, however inaccurately, from the cheerful gossips, was simply this. The leading middle-aged intellectual of the village, or so I was told, had exercised a pernicious influence over some of the students, and the faculty of the College, uniting with certain people of importance, had banished him forever from Williamsburg. But, instead of stopping here, they had attempted to root out and exterminate every trace of the scandal, and condemned, without proper investigation, every student who had even a literary association with the supreme offender. A number of students, and a number may include any figure, would be dismissed from the College because they had been seen in unfavorable company. Among them—I am relating merely what I was told—was the most brilliant youth in the student body. His name was James Branch Cabell, and he was to receive his diploma in the spring. Hearing this, his mother had come from Richmond with an attorney, and in the end the College had been obliged to withdraw its charges. Mrs. Cabell, who had been a beauty in her youth, was now staying at the Inn, and the attorney, after a triumphant dismissal of the case, had left town a few hours before I arrived. But there was not a shred of evidence to connect James in any way with the scandal, or with the Author of Evil. There was, indeed, not anything more compromising than a shared preference for *belles-lettres*. (*Woman Within*, 131–32)

Then after a paragraph on the mob spirit, the French Revolution, and the gossips of Williamsburg, Glasgow continued her account:

But sheep are not the only creatures that run together. More from shyness than from intellectual exclusiveness, James was drawn into a small circle; yet he had not been intimate enough with this circle to have it tighten in his defense. For weeks before the Commencement, he lived utterly alone in the College center, and the acquaintances he passed in the street had fallen into an abstracted habit of sky-gazing. In those weeks my sister and I longed to approach him, but we were doubtful whether he would wish to be spoken to by persons he did not remember. Every afternoon he would sit, alone, on the porch of a tavern across the street, while Cary and I were reading on the porch of the Inn. Then, at last, one afternoon we did walk across the green to the tavern porch, and I recall still how grave, inscrutable and disdainful he appeared, while groups of students and citizens of the town passed by in the street. He had, even then, that air of legendary remoteness, as if he lived in a perpetual escape from actuality. I was young enough to feel that he was a romantic figure, innocent but persecuted, and I admired his aristocratic detachment, the fine, thin modeling of his features, and the enigmatic quality of his expression. (133–34)

Such were the public perceptions. While the faculty investigation was intended to dispel the rumors, the result had been to give them credence. Although the Executive Committee of the trustees commended the faculty for its zeal, no one had emerged from the hearing unscathed. The trivial had escalated into the sensational, honorable people had been maligned, and nothing was solved. No one can be held totally blameless, but whatever indiscretions were committed were hardly worth the anguish inflicted on a number of people. The world was no longer a friendly place for a sensitive young man. The lie had been believed and truth was suspect. Security fell away and life revealed itself as a bitter comedy. Godshalk suggests that part of Coleman's fall from public esteem in Williamsburg may be attributed to his moving away from religious orthodoxy, from rituals to a freer search for spiritual values. His friend H. M. Alden had traveled that path a generation earlier. James Cabell's awakening agnosticism was accelerated by his trial during the last months in college; he sank deeper into disillusion and perhaps into blasphemy. The disintegration of his college relationships liberated him from an alma mater sentimentality, if not from sentiment itself. Disintegrating family relationships had severed the umbilical cord to Richmond four years earlier.

James Branch Cabell received his baccalaureate degree on 23 June 1898.

For the next thirty years Cabell debated the meaning of his experiences in Fairhaven. It had a dreamlike quality that defied rational analysis. Richmond had demanded social masks, as had Rockbridge Alum Springs. Had he erred in Williamsburg in not wearing an appropriate mask, or in not wearing any? Neither chivalry nor gallantry had won the day, but there was yet the artistic approach to life to be reckoned with. Something yet might be wrested from the confused images of ecstasy and despair.

6

Charles Washington Coleman
and Gabriella Brooke Moncure
1862–1955

The psychological metamorphosis that James Cabell underwent while a student at William and Mary can be attributed only in part to the college itself. Beginning with his second year there, body and spirit were awakened by two friends who had a lasting influence on his life. While Dr. Robert Cabell and Anne Harris Branch gave physical life to James Branch Cabell, Charles Washington Coleman and Gabriella Brooke Moncure were more truly the parents of the literary figure who emerged in the first two decades of the twentieth century. Coleman put the pen in his hand and Moncure gave him the inspiration. Both deserve their chapter in any biography of Cabell.

Charles Coleman was born in Richmond on 22 November 1862, the son of Dr. Charles W. Coleman and Cynthia Beverly Tucker, both of distinguished Virginia ancestry. After the war, the Tayloe House in Williamsburg became the home of the Coleman family, with its three sons and one daughter. Charles attended the University of Virginia, where he earned Phi Beta Kappa honors and joined the social fraternity of Pi Kappa Alpha. Though he studied law, he gave his heart to poetry. With gratifying frequency his poems were accepted by the better popular magazines such as *Harper's*, *Century*, and *Atlantic Monthly*. In 1942, ten years after his death, a brother and sister published a volume of his verse bearing the title, *In His Own Country*. Coleman's work reflects his wide reading, from the classical poets to the French symbolists.

The title poem, "In His Own Country," is a self-portrait in the style of Browning, summing up man and poet.

"Can you, good sir, not tell me aught of him?
     He lived once hereabouts."
           "Yes, I recall
   An idle fellow of his name—was slim
   Right fair of person, some thought, but not tall
   Leaning to woman in the face and voice
   Except for *something*. Yet some spoke him well
   Some—women mostly—loved him. But my choice
   Would be for brawnier sort. To buy and sell
   And hold the world at reck'ning takes strong limb
   Such he had not. Was he you speak of now
   He whom I speak of?"
         "Doubtless"
         "Anyhow
   I knew but this one of that name; and him
   Not well."
     "But still you knew him?"
         "Yes and no—
   Granting the passing speech can make it so.
   To hold himself aloof—indifferent
   (Old blood, you know, his family were proud)—
   Not caring if he pleased or not the crowd—
   Conceited—that to most his manner meant.
   Others, 'tis true, bespoke him courteous,
   Less self-bound than the world, of heart more true.—
   Each to his thinking:—it ne'er struck me thus."

"Made he no verses then?"
       "I do not know—
   "Ah, yes—some lines about a woman's hair—
   No more than that, I think. His grave is there."

February 29, 1888

With the resurrection of William and Mary College in 1888, the library was open only two hours a day. The name of Charles Coleman first appeared in the 1893–94 catalogue as librarian, and the following year prospective students were informed that the library would be "open to students several hours every day of the week, with Mr. C. W. Coleman, the well-known Virginia poet, to aid students in their reading and researches." Although Phi Beta Kappa, the first Greek letter fraternity in the United States, was founded at William and Mary in 1776, its Alpha chapter had expired. Coleman was instrumental in reviving Alpha in 1893, and he became its secretary.

Charles Coleman was sociable by nature, loving talk of parties and family affairs, sharing his mother's passion for genealogy. He thrilled to the performances of great actresses such as Maud Adams and Ellen Terry; he sent them flowers, corresponded. He attended the german in Richmond and led the intricate figures in Williamsburg. Beauty in any form intoxicated him, but better than any drink was guiding the reading of a young acolyte. For a man of his nature, life was largely lived vicariously.

Coleman's tutelage of James Cabell began in earnest in the fall of 1895, tutelage that released an outpouring of poetic endeavor from the youth. James had proved proficient in Greek, and Coleman saw in him the Greek youth Antinous beloved by the Roman emperor Hadrian. In a poem entitled "A Reed Call (Antinous of the Capitol)," published in Harper's Bazaar, 13 June 1896, the speaker calls not to a living being but to the deified boy who drowned himself in order to add his remaining years to the emperor's. The speaker of the poem, a voice poetically ambiguous, lays in the hollow of the hand "a stranded shell," a metaphor of the poet's lyre. The deified youth will, like Apollo, move the elements in song. Young James Cabell will make the music that Coleman could only dream of making, will mold two lives into one span of song.

In later life Cabell readily acknowledged his indebtedness to Coleman, both in his work and in personal interviews. The older man had heightened his appreciation of classical, medieval, and Provençal poetic forms as well as the seductive rhythms and impassioned imagery of the Pre-Raphaelites. Coleman entered into the Cabell oeuvre under the guise of John Charteris, something of a philanderer in The Eagle's Shadow, The Cords of Vanity, and The Rivet in Grandfather's Neck, and as the principal spokesman in Beyond Life wherein the author expounded on his literary credo. Charles Coleman's friendship, his ready response to a youth's first poetic endeavors, had determined Cabell's vocation, and the mature writer remembered that older friend with respect and affection the rest of his life.

Coleman's feeling for his protégé is perhaps best expressed in the poem "Bloom-Time." Written in the spring of 1898, James Cabell's last semester in "Fairhaven," it made its appearance in Harper's, ironically in the sad April when all their happy times together ended in humiliating debates about their relationship. The poem concludes:

> Had you passed me all unseeing
> In the May-time of your being,
> I'd not say these rhymes of mine
> Had been fewer by one line,
> That my heart had gone unsung
> All the blooming ways among,
> Had you passed by me unseeing
> In the love-time of your being.
>   Only, had you never come,
>   Just one heart-beat were unstirred,
>   Just one chord had waited dumb,
>   One song failed to find its word.

In Charles Coleman's fall from the ladder in the library at William and Mary, more than a leg was broken. Like a character in a Tennessee Williams play, his dreams had been shattered. At thirty-six he wrote no more poetry reflective of the child-spirit he had been. James Cabell inspired one more poem, and the entry of the United States into World War I prompted a belated effort. In spirit, if not in act, he had placed his pen in the hand of young Cabell.

Early in 1899 Coleman became associated with the Library of Congress, where he remained until his death in 1932. Aged seventy, he was at the time assistant superintendent of the reading rooms, having come full circle in his appointed task "to aid students in their reading and researches." Daniel C. Mearns, reference librarian of the Library of Congress, wrote in a memorial that Coleman was "one possessed of gentle dignity, rich experience, broad interests, discriminating taste, unusual and abiding friendships, and a profound concern for the welfare of others. His spirit was not only sensitive, but generous and kind and healing."

In 1923, when Cabell saw clearly what he had been attempting to do in his earlier work, that portion he would term "the Biography," he put together a pastiche of book reviews and essays entitled *Straws and Prayer-books* (1924). The object of the work was to present the author's artistic credo and to claim a unity of vision for all his work. Charteris, Coleman's persona, opens the dissertation: "'But this is grossly unfair!' John Charteris complained. 'All these long years you have been promising to write a book about me. And now it seems, I am to remain forever a minor character.'"

But in reality he got more than his book. His attitudes, fancies, ambivalence, mockery inform almost everything from the pen of his acolyte. He is in large degree the co-author of the eighteen-volume Storisende Edition of the Works of James Branch Cabell. The latter equivocated about the "authorship" of his output for the first thirty years of his career, attributing various works to Nicolas de Caen, Robert Etheridge Townsend, and Richard Fentnor Harrowby. Horvendile the whimsical Author intrudes as a deus-ex-machina into the story at odd moments. Like Svengali in the novel Cabell read during his freshman year, the hypnotist who made Trilby sing beautifully, John Charteris—alias Charles Coleman—guided the pen of James Cabell in trying to make him write beautifully. The inspiration came from Gabriella Moncure.

The second child of Capt. James Dunlop Moncure and Anne Patteson McCaw, Gabriella Brooke Moncure was born 7 March 1875, four years before James Cabell. Her father, a physician specializing in mental and nervous diseases, was elected head of the Eastern Lunatic Asylum in Williamsburg in 1884. His wife having died in 1882, Captain Moncure remarried in 1889 when Gabriella was fourteen; her stepmother was only five years older. They lived in the superintendent's house on the hospital grounds, then located on Francis Street, one of the three thoroughfares in Williamsburg. A younger sister remembered Cabell as a frequent guest on Francis Street.

In his French studies James Cabell read courtly romances in which medieval pages were allowed to serve as youthful courtiers to noble ladies, ladies who tempered ardor into chivalrous expressions of love, so that the lover learned to extract from the transitory moment an enduring poem to immortalize his lady. Gabriella Moncure had been bred in the tradition of the game. She was nobly born, and the boy had been entrusted to her care as a child. He would prove adept as a troubadour. She, alternately defensive and receptive, was increasingly aware of the ironies of the relationship.

Cabell dedicated his second "novel," The Cords of Vanity (1909), to Gabriella and acknowledged that the character Bettie Hamlyn was modeled on her during their three-and-a-half-year association in Williamsburg. While Cords is a weakly structured work, an episodic reworking of six previously published short stories and some thinly disguised biography, the character Bettie Hamlyn gives it a semblance of unity, a unity that doubtless reflects the central position Gabriella held in Cabell's thought at that time. The cad-hero is named Townsend, Cabell's punning alias for his youthful persona. After referring to his frivolous mother, Townsend observes, "It was not until my career at King's College that I may be said to have pretended to intimacy with anybody . . . and at my graduation I carried little of moment from the place save many memories of Bettie Hamlyn." In the passage following this observation, Townsend-Cabell gives a portrait of Gabriella Moncure that accords with the memories of those who knew her. She was not reputed a beauty in the fashion of her day, but she is remembered for her wit. "Her enemies deny that she is good-looking, but even her friends concede her picturesqueness and her knowledge of it. Her penetration, indeed, is not to be despised; she has even grasped the fact that all men are not necessarily fools in spite of the fashion in which they talk to women." Townsend comments on her critical nature and adds that "when driven by impertinences into a corner she conceals her real opinion by voicing it quite honestly, as if she were joking. Thereupon you credit her with the employment of irony and even with being open to reason." At the end of the passage, the author observes: "Four years, in fine, we spent to every purpose together, and they were wholly happy years. To record them would be desecration."

But Cabell does record them. Townsend-Cabell assigns a number of pseudonyms to his various loves in the novel and tells us that Heart o' My Heart was his favored appellation for Elizabeth Hamlyn. Here Cabell plays with the French origin of the name Moncure—mon coeur or "my heart." Townsend is presented as a youthful poet, one who writes solely for the pleasure of reading his poems aloud to Bettie Hamlyn. If we keep in mind the four-year difference in age between Gabriella and James, the following scene from Cords gives us an insight into their relationship at that time.

"Dear boy," said Bettie, when I had made an end of reading, "and are you very miserable?"

Her fingers were interlocked behind her small black head; and the sympathy with which she regarded me was tenderly flavored with amusement.

This much I noticed as I glanced upward from my manuscript, and mustered a Spartan smile. "If misery loves company, then I am the least unhappy soul alive. For I don't want anybody but just you, and I believe I never will."

"Oh—? But I don't count. Or, rather, I have always counted your affairs, so that I know precisely what it all amounts to."

"Sum total?"

"A lot of imitation emotions." She added hastily: "Oh, quite a good imitation, dear; you are smooth enough to see to that. Why, I remember once—when you read me that first sonnet, sitting all hunched up on the little stool, and pretending you didn't know I knew who you meant me to know it was for, and ending with a really very effective, breathless sob,—and caught my hand and pressed it to your forehead for a moment—Why, that time I was thoroughly rattled and almost believed I was falling for you."

She shrugged. "And if I had been younger—!" she said, half regretfully, for at this time Bettie was very nearly twenty-two (31).

And James Cabell was eighteen. The novel ends with Townsend ambiguously engaged to Bettie Hamlyn, fiction here compensating for the painful parting between Gabriella and James that really took place. The refrain in the last pages is, "I must tell Bettie everything." *Cords* was an attempt to convey to Gabriella, across time and space, James Cabell's conception of the irrational forces that separated them.

The last months at William and Mary, in contrast to the first three-and-a-half years, were a time of intense emotional stress; readmission did not reestablish the former easy social relationships that had drawn a boy out of his innate shyness. In particular, his shame and his fear of further linking Gabriella's name with his own discredited standing in Williamsburg effectively ended their relationship. Her life was soon to be drastically altered, and what might have been a brief separation with a happy reconciliation was denied by other complicating circumstances in both their lives. Some months after he graduated from college, James Cabell sent Gabriella two notebooks of poems that he had read to her in happier days, with a passionate avowal of his love for her.

As well as recording a young man's despairing and serious attachment to one woman, these notebooks constitute a record of his intellectual growth. They are, in effect, a diary of Cabell's inner life during the three-year period of 1895–98. His themes, as they were to be developed in his major work, are stated here in embryonic form, awaiting a mature craftsman to give them voice. They record the swiftness of his intellectual development, from the insouciance of the adolescent, through the despair of love unconsummated, to an acceptance of art as the timeless record of all emotion.

In these notebooks James Cabell copied poems that had been written earlier, but with very few exceptions he carefully recorded the date of composition of each poem. Thus while the poems follow a chronological sequence, occasionally a poem written in one month will precede a poem written the previous month. "Hymn to Aphrodite," January 1896, shows a student's close study of Algernon Charles Swinburne's rhythmic patterns and shimmering surfaces; its refrain, "Hear us, Aphrodite,—hear us, mother of mine," echoes the repetitive devices in much of Swinburne's poetry. This poem is James Cabell's earliest reference to the love goddess, the woman of pleasure, in his theme of triune woman as a reflection of man's three basic attitudes toward life: the chivalric, the gallant, the artistic. One can see the writer working toward this concept in a poem entitled "Sonnet—January 1896," in which the lover sees all these conceptual loves embodied in one real woman and ends with the plea: "Bend, O beloved, to my waiting breast / And whisper, "Love, I know you love me best." When Cabell read this poem to her, Gabriella evasively asked for another proof, a poem that was specifically about her. His response was a poem entitled "Gabrielle," January 1896, in which the first verse states his obligation to write to order. The poem continues:

> Which shall it be—ye villanelle,
> Ye epigram, rondeau, rondelle,
>   Ballade, or sonnette—each is highte
>   Ye lyttle rhyme?
>
> Yet none will aid my hapless plighte;
> Ye lyttle rhymes are shorte and slighte;
>   Ye Epic's length alone can telle
>   Ye manie charms of Gabrielle.
> It is in vaine—I cannot write
>   Ye lyttle rhyme.

A revised version appeared in the college magazine omitting her name, and Cabell later included this poem in *From the Hidden Way*, changing "Gabrielle" to "Florimel" in the tradition of pastoral poetry. While this effort was slight, it safely made love a game in which the lady maintained control of the poet's ardor. An approving note to the young lover resulted in another poem, "Your Letter Came," which was spontaneous and charmingly free of the affectations Cabell found so irresistible in his courtly models:

> Your letter came—before me lay
> An Exercise with long array
>   Of foreign words, whose verbs despise
>   The proper tense and wax in size
> As Nouns with Prepositions play.
>
> The Grammar spread its dreary sway
> Till all the world seemed old and gray,
>   And while I cursed that Exercise
>   Your letter came.

And then—the book was cast away,
For skies were bright, and life was gay;
    I saw again your laughing eyes,
    I heard your musical replies,—
It was a very pleasant day
        Your letter came.

The form of this poem was one the young writer favored, a variation of the rondel. At first glance, it appears to be a sonnet, but then one notes the extra line, occasioned by repeating the first line as a refrain in the middle and at the end.

In *The Cords of Vanity*, Bettie Hamlyn's obvious dislike of Charteris reflects the distrust Gabriella felt for the influence that Charles Coleman had on Cabell's poetic endeavors. Cabell's penchant for the rondeau and rondel, with their structures limited to two rhymes, gave his poetry a tinkling effect; it lacked a sonority that bespoke seriousness. Much of Coleman's poetry reflected the influence of Swinburne. Gabriella could not approve of Swinburne's "paganism," nor could she warm to his affected diction and veiled archness. In an effort to win his lady over to an admiration for Swinburne, Cabell gave her a treasured volume from his collection, *Laus Veneris* (In Praise of Love). Whatever her reservations may have been, this volume remained with her until her death. In exchange for the Swinburne, Gabriella gave Cabell a volume of Browning's poetry that she had received as a graduation present four years earlier. The influence of Browning, along with a deeper probing into human relationships, becomes apparent in certain of Cabell's poems. In "After Thoughts," April 1896, Cabell debates the implications of a kiss Gabriella gave him upon his seventeenth birthday: "the sun above / Reeled in the sky—for I found you human." Ideal love and earthly desire had trembled in the balance; the latter triumphed and the former "fled with the shadows in bitter fear."

The struggle within the young poet to reconcile his chivalrous and gallant natures resulted in his longest poetic endeavor to date, a poem in four parts covering eight manuscript pages. The hero with whom the poet identified was the Roman who relinquished the world for love. Oddly though, "Antony," dated April 1896, has as its hero a Christian tortured by his passion for a pagan Cleopatra. The psychological implications here are obvious; not having great worldly honor to lose, the young Cabell's "honor" was his inbred Victorian concept of purity. Cabell made significant revisions in this poem two years later, altering its affirmation of God's power to a serious questioning of divine justice. But in April 1896, the young poet, in his struggle with the precepts of the church, soon relinquished an ascetic Christ and returned to his more satisfying *carpe diem* verses. Significantly the next poem was entitled "The Poete Tunes Hys Lyre." In May, Cabell further revealed his growing respect for literature as a serious voice rather than as an outlet for youthful effusions. In "To My Verses" he wrote:

> Ah, had we but the power—then you and I
> Should sing together notes so pure and high
> That no man but must listen nor pass by.

This verse is quoted in part in the introductory poem, "At Outset," in *From the Hidden Way*, a hidden acknowledgment to the "co-author" of all these rhymes.

Facing a summer's separation from Gabriella as the school year drew to a close, he wrote "A Rondeau," in May 1896, with the refrain "Will you forget?" In June he confessed that all his fantasy loves were centered in her:

> Should she devine that I in all my lays
> But feebly fashioned forth some varied phase
>   Of love for her beneath a fabeled name
>   Have written every word to win her fame
> And found no strength to sing save in her praise—
>
> Ah, then the glance of pity that repays
> The years of waiting—and—perchance she says,
>   *For thy reward what guerdon wilt thou claim—*
>   Should she devine.

When Cabell revised this poem for publication years later, he changed the refrain to "Had she devined," implying that their lives would have resulted in union rather than separation.

That same summer he wrote "A Ballad of the Celestial Kingdom," a poem that appeared in the *Monthly* and was later included both in *The Cords of Vanity* and in the second edition of *From the Hidden Way*. This tinkling bit of chinoiserie with its overtones of a child's verse probably reflects the influence of Charles Coleman. Bettie Hamlyn's outburst against Charteris in *Cords* comes to mind here: "'I hate that wizened man,' she presently volunteered, 'more bitterly than I do any person on earth. For it was he who taught you to adopt infancy as a profession. He robbed me. And Setebos permitted it'" (310). Many critics have commented on Cabell's allowing a sophomoric whimsy to intrude in passages where it seemed inappropriate.

Three poems written in July contain sea imagery, one entitled "Sea Scapes" appearing later in *The Hidden Way*. A sonnet apostrophizing John Singer Sargent's *The Israelites Led in Captivity* gives evidence that Cabell may have spent the summer abroad in 1896. It was followed by a sonnet to Molière. That fall, poems addressed to Alpha Zeta fraternity, to shadows, to Ares God of War, and to Solitude alternated with love lyrics. In a truncated villanelle he offered an apology "Toe Hys Mystresse" for "ye Villainous Verses" he had written wherein he addressed her under multiple pseudonyms "inn Lover's guise." December found him writing "A Ballad of My Lady's Service," a poem of four pages highly autobiographical in nature. In response to Cabell's seeking love through poetry, his lady says, "Serve me with deeds." A personification of Disbelief witnesses their discussion, but the poet swears that "none shall love thee in so pure a wise" until his death. In the final line she asks, "Who is this woman that he worships thus?" His last poem of the year was "A Christmas Message," written to Gabriella. He sends her

> The simple words of my heart's repeating,
> The old, old words that I still must tell,
> *I love you dear*—'tis my only greeting
> To Gabrielle.

The year 1897 was perhaps the happiest of Cabell's life, and he filled a hundred manuscript pages with verses. Almost every fleeting thought flowered into a poem. He addressed the months, Theocritus, Congreve, Beowulf, ballplayers, Thanatos, Horace, the game of poker, Keats. In February, the poet wrote "Ballad of Burdens" bewailing the rigors of mathematics and Greek, advising his professors that they were trying to fill another Williamsburg institution, the asylum. In April he was again singing, "Heart of my heart, I am thine alway" and imagining himself Shelley: "Has she / Forgotten I lie at the heart of the sea?" He addressed Gabriella as Sylvia, Stella, Ettarre, Chloris, Phyllis, Heart's Desire, all names he applied to the fantasy women in his later work. As the year drew to a close, however, overtones of melancholy intruded, engendered apparently by Cabell's jealousy of Gabriella's other friends. Poems entitled "The Passing of Chloris," "Twilight" and "The Dream Mistress" spoke of parting. The closing lines of the latter poem, written in December 1897, proved an ironic prophecy: "I shall not lose my hold on Chloris' heart / So long as I keep friends with Jack o' Dreams."

In the new year four poems are dated January 1898, including an effective paraphrase of Verlaine's "Chanson d'Automne":

> The long low sobbing of the violin,
>> Sad as the stillness of an Autumn day
>> When wistful Summer lingers on her way
> A little while, speaks of the Might-have-been.

Then occurred the event that altered Cabell's perceptions of life profoundly, the fraternity party that gave rise to the exaggerated rumors concerning its festivities, and the resulting faculty investigation.

Only one poem is dated February—"The Last Lover," a poem of twelve stanzas covering three manuscript pages. The Lady Alice receives a lover risen from the grave. She speaks:

> "For I, besought by many a knight
>> And many a lusty squire,
> Turning from all in sick dispite,
>> Not having my desire,
>
> Finding nought good to sight nor touch,
>> Weary of words man saith,
> I that have loved life over-much,
>> Take for my lover, Death."

In his shame James did not see Gabriella, and in separation he became her aching alter ego. As the dead lover, he turned for his model to Poe, a poet he had read as a child and whom he later declared the first American literary genius.

There are no poems recorded for March that year. One April poem, "Sonnet, à Rebours," appears in the verse diary; the title suggests his looking backward as well as a sense of regret for the turn of events:

> The shadows of the shameful time
> Around all last year's memories climb;
>> And all old things that were to me
>> More dear than life, take wing and flee.

In May Cabell transcribed a poem entitled "Une Nuit Blanche" wherein he recorded his sleepless nights, lying in "the shadow of an unknown shame." Abandoned by friends, in the poem he cries out, "Ah God, thou knowest what I am." While the young poet admits that "thirsting lips were set to kiss, / My throat made lax as one that sings," he obviously feels that his transgressions have not deserved the ostracism he suffers.

But God too, like human friends, is mute: "He answers not! He hath not heard."

James Cabell's last month in college inspired four poems, all touching on his separation from Gabriella Moncure. The first is a rondel built on the contrast of joyful nature and unhappy lover. The second, a longer poem of three ten-line verses, is addressed to Dorothy, who reappears much later in *Jurgen* as Dorothy-the-Desired. In this poem he laments that she sees him dishonored: "My love is her shame / And I stain what I strive for and praise." If she could only know him truly, rather than turn away she would love him. It concludes:

> Though all men have trust in me, still
> My heart hath its fill
>   Of all bitterness, seeing I know
> That you never will.

The next poem, a sonnet, starts with the cry "Could I but come!—Sweete, I am bound in *Hell*." The fourth, also a sonnet, is entitled "A Leavetaking" and is again addressed to Dorothy.

> I shall not e'er repeat
> My rhymes to her, nor e'er bend to meet
> Her lips this side of Eternity;
>   Farewell, my sweet.

This is the last poem addressed directly to Gabriella Moncure in the manuscript notebook, although two fragments and a long poem of twelve pages follow. James Cabell's graduation on 23 June 1898 was a happy occasion for others, but for him it was a time of intense despair.

The first fragment of two manuscript pages that continue the verse diary starts, "What should I hold them—a god?" The nature of Christ's divinity is debated, and a disillusioned James Cabell appears to reject the godhead of Christ in exalting his humanity—his rage, his pride, his fear. For a reader in 1898, the poem may have approached blasphemy in its fusion of spiritual and physical love: "We have but love for the man; / The man that Magdalen loved." Gabriella Moncure too suffered, as we shall see, but when she read this poem she was not prepared to follow into the anguish of religious doubt—at that moment. Two leaves constituting four manuscript pages are torn from the notebook. Although the emotions that led Gabriella to this act can only be surmised, she may have reacted to an implication that she had not responded with humanity to the poet's human weakness. With the ending missing, we cannot know the date of this poem, but the following fragment—a poem in French—is dated July. Written in the style of Ronsard, the fragment has as its refrain "Le Temps Jadis" (Yesteryear). James Cabell's sense of time passing, never to be re-captured, is underlined.

At this bitter time, the lover began rewriting "Antony," his last offering in the notebooks. This long, tortured poem is perhaps more properly a study for the clinical psychologist, with its disturbing metaphors and symbolism. One can readily understand that the bereft lover empathized with Antony; his world too had been lost for love. In the first of four parts Antony, a Christian doing penance for an unholy love, awakens just before dawn and is visited by the ghost, a very sensual ghost, of the dead lover. If she can force her tongue between his clenched teeth, his soul will be lost. Part two is an impassioned plea to God to save him from this vision brought back to test his will anew. Part three starts by describing the beloved's beauty and her pride in her dominion over the lover whose soul slept during the supremacy of passion. But Cabell-lover remembers he serves "the great pale Christ"; he scourges himself and is pardoned. Assured of Heaven, he awaits death tranquilly. Then he asks a fatal question: "It is well with me; / O woman that I loved, how is it with thee?" He can envision her in no other place but Hell, and then a new blasphemy enters his thinking:

> When I am sped
> To the fair courts of Heaven and art among
> The blessed saints, how shall I bend my tongue
> To worship him that damn'd thee? shall I be
> Happy in Heaven, and through eternity
> Hear thy voice call in agony to God
> And he not hearken, dear?

The fourth section of the poem contains even more ambivalence. The first thirty lines apostrophize Lust, "masker of all temporal things," a god in whose service the poet has made his poems. Then comes a twelve-line lyric with implications that the poet's service had its rewards despite the cost:

> Grieve not for memory of past delight,
> My sweet, and take no sorrow for the night,
> Now we have garner'd all the joy thereof.

And whosoever made us—be his name
Jove or Jehovah—shall we blame
  Our Maker that he also hath made Love?

For He that made the faltering soul of man,
That fashion'd all things after His own plan,
  Disclosing nothing of the ends there-of,

Made Love; and if Love prove victorious,
Who made Love strong? And if Love conquer us,
  How shall he dare to blame us, that made Love?

Back in the persona of Antony-Cabell, the poet rejects the lyric's premise that because God does not disclose his own nature (his ends) he may not be in a tenable position to judge man's. But again the voice in the poem shifts, and again the youthful lover questions the purpose of Lust. "I know not. Yet I trust / God sees the meaning clearly." "Trust" is used ironically here, for the poem further narrows the distinction between God who created the world and the god of Lust. The poem concludes with a statement and question: "God is God. Can God do wrong?"

This poem carries a number of implications. Because Cabell's essential communication with Gabriella Moncure during their three-and-a-half-year intimacy had been through poetry, only the rhetoric of poetry could express what an outwardly shy youth could never say in person. The poem's length and its shifting voices indicate a new effort to call into service a poetry capable of sustaining a deeper thought, a deeper passion than the light lyrics of happier days. If it does not succeed as poetry, it does succeed as a record of a psychological state and of a growth in artistic ambition. The conflict in the poem between love of the ideal and physical passion conveys with sensitivity the direction James Cabell's feeling for Gabriella Moncure had taken from 1895 to 1898, from chivalry to gallantry, from the desire to worship to the desire to possess. Other seminal ideas in the poem, observable in his later work, are apparent. First, lust as the procreator of life is thereby also the creator of art. This belief leads to his third attitude toward life, after the chivalrous and the gallant: the artistic, life or experience as the raw material of art. Second, any act of creation can be construed as sin because it invades the domain of God, who claims universal copyrights. Third, if man is imperfect, his nature divided, the cause may lie with God, who gives and withholds at the same time. At best, such seeming irrationality appears unjust; at worst, inartistic. These ideas reach their fruition in The High Place (1923), whose hero observes: "Gods and devils are poor creatures when compared to man. They live with knowledge. But man finds heart to live without any knowledge or surety anywhere, and yet not go mad. And I wonder now could any god endure the testing which all men endure?"

"Antony" is dated December 1898, five months after the previous poem. It marked the conclusion of an important stage of the writer's development and fixed, when he was not yet twenty, the direction his major work would take—its philosophy, its forms, its themes. When Cabell determined to send these two manuscript books of poems to Gabriella, it was more than an acknowledgment of what she meant to him; a new man was speaking, in part her creation. It told her he acknowledged his fate, and it announced his resolution, like Romeo's, to defy the stars. The following letter accompanied the poems:

> Dear, since I love you above all women on earth, it is not fitting that my gifts to you should be of little value. And so I send you these two books. It seems a gift of little worth, these books of halting rhymes, pilfered from Swinburne and Austin Dobson. But you, who have seen these verses in the making, you know better. There is nothing of my life for the past three years that is not set down there-in. All of me is there.
>
> And so it is fitting that you should have the books. For my life in this time has been yours—yours, yours, all yours. We are no longer two persons. You will remember in reading not only, *The boy who has written this is mine,* but *This boy is I.* And the verses? Ah, there is no one of them, good, bad, or indifferent, that would ever have been written save for you. Take them, dear. For the verses are yours not mine.

At this unhappy time, other events were conspiring to effect a permanent parting of the two friends. The separation of Cabell's parents left his mother in an awkward position in Richmond society, and the murder of her first cousin, her reputed lover, in 1901 was a further deterrent. In November 1898, Gabriella's father died, leaving a young widow with children. Gabriella, twenty-three, had to make a life for herself. She turned to art. Her father had studied medicine in Paris; she would go there to study painting. But the winter in Paris brought on pneumonia, and she was warned that continued residence might lead to tuberculosis. She returned to the United States to be watched over by her physician uncle, Walter D. McCaw, a bachelor serving in the Army Medical Corps. While recovering, she kept house for her uncle, moving with him to various army posts, and she continued her art studies. A clue to her feelings for James Cabell is a notation in the volume of Swinburne he had given her in Williamsburg; over the poem "Rococo" she wrote the word "seperation."

While the physical separation of the lovers lengthened into years, the years did not diminish Gabriella Moncure's influence on the maturing writer. In "Love-Letters of Falstaff" (Harper's Monthly, March 1902), the aged knight burns "Toe Hys Mistresse" (November 1896) and "Cupid Invaded Hell" (February 1897), two of the poems in the notebooks. "When You Are Very Old," a paraphrase of Ronsard dated July 1898 in the manuscript, became the theme of "The Conspiracy of Arnaye" (Harper's, June 1903). The August issue of that year contained "The Castle of Content," grown out of the poem of the same title dated December 1895. "Rustling Leaves of the Willow-Tree," dated October 1897, appeared in "The Story of Adhelmar" (Harper's, April 1904). The following year all these stories reappeared in The Line of Love. At the end of The Cords of Vanity (1909), dedicated to Gabrielle, the hero determines to return to Bettie Hamlyn, for she is in a sense the collaborator who will make him the writer he aspires to be. Knowing friends still predicted that James Cabell and Gabriella Moncure would be reunited. In The Soul of Melicent (1913), the chivalrous Perion wins his way back to his lady after multiple foes and events separate them. At their moment of reunion, no longer young, Perion falls to his knees: "Their love had flouted Time and Fate." But in the same year, at the age of thirty-four, Cabell proposed to Mrs. Shepherd, a widow with five children and a healthy inheritance from her husband. She had dark hair and eyes and was four-and-a-half years older than her suitor. When Gabriella learned of the impending nuptials, she took out Cabell's avowal of love for her and wrote across it: "Oh Absalom my son my son! September 1913."

In 1916, Cabell published many of the poems he had written for Gabriella Moncure under the title From the Hidden Way. The following year saw the publication of his first critical success, The Cream of the Jest, wherein the writer Kennaston leads a dual life; during the day he lives in a real world with his pedestrian wife, but nightly he escapes into a dreamworld, lured there by Ettarre, the eternal witch-woman. When Kennaston touches Ettarre, however, the dream vanishes, and he awakens again in his mundane surroundings. Cabell had become his wife's seventh physical child, but he remained under Gabriella Moncure's enchantment.

In Jurgen (1919), Cabell again played with the idea of having a second chance to alter the course of his life. During his chivalrous stage, Jurgen composes a "sirvente" for Guenevere. It takes the form of a sonnet, its fourteen lines falling into an octave and sestet, but every line ends with the word "love." Because the poem is presented as prose, some readers are unaware they are reading verse. This poem appears in the notebooks as "A Word With Cupid," dated September 1897. While *Jurgen* brought notoriety to Cabell, it brought a hidden message to Gabriella. In his next work, *Figures of Earth* (1921), Cabell carried the game further. Alerted by the preface in the Storisende Edition, Warren A. McNeill analyzed in his *Cabellian Harmonics* (1929) the "fifteen passages of contrapuntal prose to be found in *Figures of Earth*." McNeill suspected quite rightly that Cabell had transcribed actual poems in many cases. Concerning a passage beginning "I cry the elegy," however, he made the mistake of opining, "It seems improbable that Mr. Cabell had any verse form in mind when he wrote this and the two succeeding paragraphs, but that they were carefully planned according to his idea of prose counterpoint seems equally evident." Cabell had in truth incorporated another poem written in July 1897. McNeill analyzes the skillful blending of verse and prose in the passage beginning "Yes but the long low sobbing of the Violin." Three other observations should be made: the poem is a paraphrase of Verlaine's "Chanson d'Automne," Cabell wrote it in January 1898, and its reworking in *Figures of Earth* is intensely autobiographical. Only Gabriella Moncure could know the import of what Cabell said in this passage.

Priscilla Bradley Cabell became the prototype for all the real, the domestic, women; Gabriella Moncure was the genesis of all the fantasy women. In *Figures of Earth* the former is embodied in Manuel's wife, Niafer. Cabell tells us in the preface that the germ of this work came to him in his study when he saw his wife and child through the window. What if he were to open the window to find that wife and child were but images in the glass and that the window really looked into the twilight world of the sweet-scented past? Gabriella plays multiple roles in this work, but most significant in psychological terms is Suskind, an anagram for "unkiss'd." At the end of this autobiographical allegory, Manuel invades the twilight world of Suskind to kill her. "She is my heart's delight," Manuel says, "my heart" echoing once again *Moncure*. But Manuel cannot survive the death of Suskind; they are one heart. The work ended, as numerous Cabell students have observed, where it began. Most of his works are circular, a quest that returns to its starting point. In the writing of *Figures of Earth*, Cabell made a profound discovery: all his work was biographical. It was really a Biography with a capital B.

The year after the publication of *Figures of Earth*, Cabell started writing *The High Place*, in many respects his best work. He at last understood fully the psychological and artistic implications of his love for Gabriella Moncure, and his firmness of purpose shone through this autobiographical allegory. Significantly it incorporated no previously published short stories, nor did Cabell indulge in his usual deception of attributing the work to another author. The hero's father advises his son that the great law of life is, "thou shalt not offend against the notions of thy neighbor," doubtless echoing the advice of Dr. Cabell, a Presbyterian, to his sons. Melior is modeled on "Mr. Townsend's mother," a pseudonym for Anne Branch Cabell. Priscilla Cabell plays no significant role in this comedy of disenchantment, but Gabriella Moncure enters the drama in two significant guises. She is the fairy Mélusine who guides all the dreaming of the young hero and who determines all the conditions for the operation of the machinery. She is also the clear-seeing half sister, Marie-Claire, an adept at necromancy; "in their shared youth these two had not been strangers." Cabell gave Marie-Claire the physical attributes of Gabriella, in particular her intensely dark eyes with extraordinarily thick lashes, her gaze giving him "the illogical feeling that, where he was, Marie-Claire saw some one else, or, to be exact, saw some one a slight distance behind him." Marie-Claire also has another of Gabriella's features, apparent in old photographs: "Her neck remained wonderful: it was still the only woman's neck familiar to Florian that really justified comparison with a swan's neck by its unusual length and roundness and flexibility. But her head was too small for that superb neck." Chapter 24 of this work contained many messages for the woman in Cabell's youth. "Marie-Claire alone knew that this fourth Duke of Puysange was still the boy who had loved her; and her blind gazing seemed always to penetrate the disguise." Upon its completion, Cabell was more pleased with *The High Place* than with any of his other works. It had a well-defined plot, it had symmetry, it was the type of work he had intended writing all along.

Cabell was ever ready to tell his readers what they should see in his work; it was time to tell them that he really was an epic romancer of no small order. He made the announcement in *Straws and Prayer Books*, assuring the 1924 reader that the Biography was really begun in 1901 with his first story. Of course, he would have to rewrite all his earlier works to make them conform to his projected perfection. A scoffing Coleman-Charteris assures him his efforts will be futile, and the Storisende Edition (1927–30) bore out the judgment. He had been bound to a dream impossible to attain. At the end of *Figures of Earth*, Manuel had symbolically killed Suskind (Gabriella). Now he would have to kill the author of the Storisende Edition. He announced the demise of James Branch Cabell and wrote under the name of Branch Cabell for the next sixteen years. But having killed the lover of Gabriella Moncure, he appeared to have lost his direction. Branch Cabell was a bitter, ironic commentator.

For Gabriella too the years spent in Williamsburg with young Cabell were doubtless a sweet-scented April twilight. Time was an irreversible distance. She had a bush social life on the army bases where her uncle was stationed. Here she was called Gabrielle, rhyming with *villanelle*, rather than by her schoolgirl Gabriella. With World War I, General McCaw, then Assistant-Surgeon A.M.C., acquired a house on Nineteenth Street in Washington, and Gabrielle began to spend her summers in Woodstock, New York, congenial for its mountain freshness and its artists' colony. She bought a house there, and when General McCaw retired, they made it their permanent home. Her brother William, also a career army officer, brought his family to live close by. Her young sister-in-law found her nature generous and her conversation sparkling. With age Gabrielle's wit became a little sharper, but her words were softened with a wry smile and an understanding gaze. When she died on 6 June 1955, she was buried according to her wishes in the Artists' Cemetery in Woodstock.

In *Let Me Lie* (1947) James Cabell accepted his Virginia heritage and returned from his self-imposed exile, changing places with Branch Cabell. The following year saw three previously published stories appear as *The Witch-Woman: A Trilogy About Her*. Ettarre the elusive continued to trouble an aging Cabell with her haunting music. Widowed and remarried to a competent, no-nonsense second wife, Cabell wrote an affectionate appreciation of Priscilla Bradley Cabell, his first wife. "She meant more to me than did all the books in the world," he concluded in *As I Remember It* (1955). A grieving and remorseful husband wrote those lines. Bettie Hamlyn, Mélusine, Marie-Claire, Ettarre smiled with compassion, but when the lines appeared in print Gabriella was dead and Cabell had written his last book.

7

Exile

1 8 9 8 – 1 9 0 0

Released from the last bitter days in Williamsburg, James Cabell returned to Richmond fallen from grace. The formerly happy haunt of the Rockbridge Alum was again avoided for less familiar scenes. The Richmond *Times* for Sunday, 10 July 1898, announced that Mrs. Robert G. Cabell and Mr. James Branch Cabell were visiting friends in Massachusetts. Again Alice Serpell reigned at the rounds of pleasure at the Alum. Cabell's poems at this time make it clear that he spent a retrospective summer on the beach. Doubtless sea baths had been prescribed for Annie's "nervous" condition.

Back home in the fall, the ex-student was faced with the problem of finding a job. Without money of his own, he was still dependent on his mother's support. His aunt's boardinghouse at 113 East Franklin was again home. He later wrote of this period in the airy, detached style that he affected for his youthful persona: "After graduation came a brief session as copy-holder for the *Richmond (Va.) Times*. Cabell had decided to 'write': and the first available employment in connection with a newspaper, which appeared the natural avenue to 'writing,' was not to write at all, but to assist in correcting proofsheets. It was the best they offered, just then" ("Cabell"). The young man's proofreading duties did not infringe on social time, but then his social life was not the round of pleasures he had known in happier days. The subject of scandalous gossip and without means, he found time on his hands. The copyreader was obviously the author of an item that appeared in the Richmond *Times* for 2 October 1898: "Mr. James Branch Cabell has, during his vacation, been engaged in getting up pedigrees, purely as a means of utilizing his time. In this connection he painted, simply as a diversion, the coat of arms of the Branch family. . . . It was pronounced worthy of a professional, and, young as Mr. Cabell is, establishes the fact that his talent as an artist is of a very unusual kind, well worth the practical interest of any friend able to direct it into a remunerative channel."

A Virginian's solace in any time of adversity is contemplation of his pedigree. The stability of the past calms the turbulence of the present and restores one's faith in his self-worth. His father's family having been memorialized with the publication of *The Cabells and Their Kin*, James Branch Cabell had set out on a ten-year genealogical journey to ennoble his mother's family. One gathers that the young man's appeal for commissions was too veiled to result in directing his "unusual" talent into a remunerative channel.

The questing youth had to find more lucrative employment, and the proving ground for talent was New York; it also offered a refuge from the critical eyes and furtive snickers of fellow Richmonders. In January of the new year he left for New York, having secured a place with the *New York Herald*. Cabell continued his account of this period:

He was soon in charge of the old Herald Harlem Office, at 125th Street, where he remained for two years. "There were only two of us, reportorially speaking," Cabell records, "and we were supposed to 'cover' pretty much everything that happened north of Eighty-fifth Street after ten o'clock in the evening, with a general responsibility as to the suburbs. That constituted a tolerably large order. And as a rule, there was no time to write the 'story.' You telephoned it to the Main-Office, from Harlem or Port Chester or Mamaroneck or wherever you happened to be, and somebody else did the writing quickly enough to get the facts twisted and catch the first edition. So I had very little practice at actual writing, except in the Society Page that we ill-fated two compiled every week for the *Sunday Herald*. But I was thrown with all sorts and conditions, from prisoners to archbishops, and including coroners and caterers and 'prominent club-women.' Then, in the summer months, I 'covered' the western half of Long Island, for both the *Herald* and the *Evening Telegram*, and wrote some eight columns of 'society stuff' every week, besides attending to any news story that might crop up in my territory. All in all, these were two busy years. ("Cabell")

At seventy, Cabell elaborated on this period to a Richmond reporter. "While on the *Herald* he reported a wedding so strikingly that his journalistic triumph earned him a post in Harlem as columnist under the heading 'Colored Society News.'" One wonders if the recollection is totally accurate, for in 1900 Harlem had not become a black enclave. Preserved in a scrapbook is a style manual for the novice reporter. "Never use the word 'on' for 'in' a street. For instance, the old Herald office is *in* Broadway, not *on* Broadway." "Never use the word 'coaches' for 'cars.'" In a later work Cabell referred to "the virtually village-like New York in which as a newspaper reporter I had passed some three more or less glamorous years." Time had expanded the length of his stay and the glamour. Lodged at 125 West 45th Street in Manhattan, the young reporter felt lonely in exile from family and friends. Few northerners pronounced his name correctly, making it Cáy-bel or Cay-bél.

In nearby Brooklyn lived a family of distant cousins, the Harrisons. Professor Caskie Harrison, who ran a Latin school, was related through Cabell's grandmother, Margaret Sophia Caskie, who had married Dr. Robert Gamble Cabell. John Caskie, one of the two Scottish brothers who had settled in Richmond, married Martha Jane Norvell of that city. This family was related to Theodore Roosevelt, a fact of which he was aware. In the household was Henry Sydnor Harrison, a year younger than James Cabell, whose later career as a writer rivaled his cousin's; Norvell Harrison, who had been a recent belle at Rockbridge Alum Springs; and a younger sibling, who was later killed in World War I. James Cabell had met Miss Harrison two summers previously at a boardinghouse in Virginia. He wrote her a letter in March 1899 reintroducing himself and asking whether he could "call some evening after dinner."

Cousin Norvell was delighted at the prospect of a gentleman caller. Cousinship was a bond, not a deterrent, for one of Virginian ancestry. She had played the Southern Belle at the Rockbridge Alum, and expected Cousin James to be an experienced player in the rituals of belledom; his very own mother essayed the role. They both knew he was not a good matrimonial prospect at this time, but he would of course play the suitor. No strong physical attraction was necessary, just a sense of how the game was played. Brooklyn was no fantasy setting in lofty mountains, and newsmaking on a metropolitan daily was not a venue for flights of romantic fancy; but a front parlor and sparkling repartee could overcome these deficiencies. In time the ironies of her situation might intrude into her fantasies, but not before the play began. For Cabell, it would be the continuation of a game begun with Alice Serpell at the Alum and perfected with Gabriella Moncure in Williamsburg. As the writer confessed in his seventies, one never thought of these women as bed-partners. Keeping one's thoughts pure paid off in other ways. But both cousins were eager to play in a romantic comedy. Upon receiving James Cabell's letter, Norvell Harrison replied the same day.

Receiving a prompt response, Cabell wrote two days later. Prophetically, the letter is headed with a quotation from *As You Like It*, spoken by Jaques: "And each man in his time plays many parts." The relationship between the two cousins resulted in a later short story entitled "Afternoon in Arden"; both were conscious of playing roles.

The game that Norvell Harrison and James Branch Cabell played over the next several months was primarily a drawing-room comedy. As the daughter of a pedagogue, the sister of a future best-selling writer, and a young woman who would espouse the suffrage movement, Norvell too had read Laura Jean Libbey, Anthony Hope, and other popular fiction writers. Both she and Cabell knew the comedies of Shakespeare, and both had been players in the comediettas extemporized at the Rockbridge Alum Springs. The course of their relationship can be gleaned from Cabell's parting epistles and from two of his earliest stories. The following letter and "Exhibit" provide insight into the author's emotional self-debate. Both are written on the stationery of The Edgemere on Long Island, which may have been his base for his summer coverage of the western half of Long Island for the *Herald*. The letter as it exists today opens with no salutation, and the lengthy dashes and points of suspension are in the original:

> It is a difficult matter to write to you again. It must result in explanations and they always befog any matter hopelessly. However, I am about to attempt the impossible and in several pages of indecipherable hieroglyphics to say what is, I think, the conclusion of the whole matter between us——In the first place, let us begin where we left off, with our parting in Remsin Street. . . . After leaving you I went home in company with an Emotion which remained with me some time and whose name I have not yet discovered. I will not, at this late date, attempt to settle what it was. Only it urged me to the writing of a letter, or, rather, several letters, and it is these letters that I purpose to discuss. First, let me call your attention to Exhibit A——An epistle

in this style would, I think, have enabled us to close the incident with a pleasant man-and-woman-of-the-world feeling, and at our future meetings to have
discussed the things in which we were interested, dealt in allusions rather
than statements and, in fine, to have given a creditable adaptation of any one
of the *Dolly Dialogues*. And so I was tempted to send it——But on the other
hand, there was another equally attractive course—a letter resembling the
one I have marked Exhibit B—— It is, you see, in the style of Kipling and
enables me to retire with a broken heart—and, truly, I know of no article
possessing greater dramatic possibilities. While a little florid it would still have
formed a harmonious ending—— I pass over the other courses I might have
taken. A letter beginning *Dear Miss Harrison* and *thanking you for a pleasant flirtation*
was, of course, too crude to be thought of. A few years ago, I would certainly
have assured you that *my faith in woman has been destroyed* and have hinted that
your conduct had driven me to a prolonged course of hopeless dissipation. I
have known this to be very effective, though personally, I think, *You don't love
me and therefore I am going to the Devil* is poor reasoning. However, Swinburne
made a very good poem out of it in *The Triumph of Time* and I plead guilty to
having employed it myself on former occasions. . . . You see, in short, that I
could have done an infinite number of dramatic things. But I am doing none
of these. Instead I am frankly showing you my hand—partly, because I want
to and, partly, because it is in any game the most difficult maneuver to meet.
Even truth lies at the bottom of a well, you know, *and not infrequently in other places*.
And now I am telling you the truth in so open a manner that the chances are
ten to one you will suspect me of attempting some deception. Be it as you
will - - - The drawback to any of these methods was, I found after delibera-
tion, that each ended the coming of any more letters. There was the rub. I
wished for them, you see, remembering what they had meant in the past
year. It was because I was- - -and am- - -what you call in love. And here
another explanation is necessary. I am in love with Phyllida, not with Miss
Norvell Harrison,- with the person who wrote the letters, not with the girl I
knew two years since, and, certainly not with the girl I saw a month or so
ago. I have erected an ideal which I want to worship without bothering over
whether it exists or not. That is, really, immaterial. There is an axiom I made
some years since- - -when I was older than I am- - -which runs like this: *The
poet's love is like his hat in that any rack will do to hang it on*. . . . I have invented
Phyllida—with your kind assistance—and with her I am in love. With you,
Miss Norvell Harrison, I have no concern, for I really know nothing about
you. If we were thrown together for any length of time, I would certainly, if
you gave me the opportunity, make love to you. This, however, would, I
fancy, be the case with any attractive girl. At any rate, it would hardly be a
desirable thing, I think, and in defence of my position I introduce Exhibit C,
part of a letter writen some years ago to her who figures in the Black Books

under the name of Chloris—— The cases are not quite similar, of course, but the exhibit goes to prove my point, namely, that this love-making—between boys and girls—while it enables one to make the most of life does not quite get the best out of it. It is beautiful—at the beginning—but the end—well! confess that the conclusion is humiliating, at best. You love like mad, you dream dreams and in what does it result. Sometimes, in verses one may sell to a publisher, but rarely. And never more than that, so far as I know. And here I bring to your notice Exhibit D, as a specimen of the beginning, . . . But . . . but . . . I do not think it ever lasts. . . . And a woman—forgive me, but I am about to be cynical in my boyish fashion—a woman, I think, always on hearing the words I *love you* mentally adds *only* and *forever* or some other word that insignificant as it is, somehow quite alters the sense of the remark. So you may have your own opinion on the subject. I only offer mine as an opinion, not as a fact, and you are free to accept it or not as you will—— So then the conclusion, argued out logically, is that this playing at love making is hardly worth while for us. We do not know each other as we are but only as we have played at being. . . . But the letters—the dear letters! They attract me more for we are both at our best on paper. They are too good to lose. And so, I say, let the letters continue. For in that line there is much for us to do. There are many dramas—tragedies, comedies, what you will—to be played between Phyllida and Little Willy. But none, I think, between Norvell Harrison and

James Branch Cabell

August the seventh

Exhibit A

It is exceedingly crude, I admit, to say I *told you so* and yet, under the circumstances, I cannot refrain from it. For behold, Phyllida and Little Willy have met in nervousness and parted in boredom. . . . Both a trifle flurried, we discussed Shakespere and the musical glasses, and grew secretly irritated with one another. The situation was grotesquely impossible. Here was an absolute stranger cast for the opposite part in the teacup comedy that had run for several months. How could one act creditably with such unreliable support? It was out of the question, and in sheer desperation we set to tearing down the Arcadian scenery and showing the naked scantling behind. Your verses, you admitted, were copied from old magazines—mine, I confessed, were taken from a collection I have made, which with a few alterations will afford something suitable for any occasion. And so it went on—now, at the bottom of our hearts, we both, I fear, acted out the little comedy before upon the same boards, or, at least, under the same management. But to stop thus in the midst of the performance—to destroy utterly the dramatic illusion—

admit that it was grossly inartistic. The pastoral was running so smoothly, too. At almost a moment's notice the dainty combination of sentiment and cynicism could have been worked out to a regretful parting scene, the curtain have fallen on a wellarranged picture, and, rubbing the rouge from our cheeks and pocketing the rouge pot for future use, we could have slipped out of the stagedoor, each representing a Buried Past. That would have been the proper end—and, now, we have bungled it beyond hope of repair. Well! let us forget, as far as possible, our mistake. Let us remember only the opening scenes of the comedy, or, rather, take the last letters beginning *Dear Cousin* for the Epilogue. It makes not a bad ending. —Or, stay. We will end it in verse, as comedies of sentiment should end, and I, with your permission, will speak the last word—a privilege I rarely enjoy—something in this fashion.

> So, it is over. Touch hands. Goodbye.
>   For you the future is nowise dim;
> For me there are other loves, and I
>   Will forget you now that you go to him.
>
> And we shall laugh in the after times
>   At two young people we knew, no doubt,
> Who scribbled each other such woeful rhymes
>   And played a comical tragedy out.
>
> We shall not die of it. We shall be
>   Contented and healed of the passing smart;
> And yet, if you had been true to me—
>   Ah, God! I had loved you so, sweetheart.

Admit that I have saved the play. And so *exeunt omnes* and put out the lights.

J.B.C.

In Exhibit B, Cabell stresses the importance of "the letters. They brought the Boy every thing he needed—comprehension, sympathy and, at last, comfort and strength when he was sorely in need of them. So the Boy announced to himself that he had made a discovery. *I have found, he said, the great white love that poets have dreamed of. I love this woman and she, I think, loves me. God has made us for one another, and by the help of her love I will be pure and clean and conquer this foul thing that else had been too strong for me.* You have doubtless perceived by this that the Boy was something of a Fool—He perceived it himself in due time. For the Girl liked him and was amused by him. So she had added him to her collection of Boys." Having declared his foolishness, Cabell concludes with a generous comment: "But one thing puzzles him. It is this. The Girl's love—which never existed— caused him to do the only thing he has ever done in his life. It led him, safe and unafraid, through Hell itself. And now the Boy is wondering what credit is due the Girl in the matter."

In the cover letter to Norvell Harrison, Cabell refers to four "Exhibits," but only two are found in the manuscripts at Duke University. With these papers, however, is a manuscript poem in Cabell's hand. "A Rondel to my Mistress" is a bit of juvenilia beginning and ending with the line, "Seeing your picture has never come"; it was probably addressed originally to Alice Serpell, whom James Cabell importuned for a picture when he was a freshman in college. Frank Durham, who analyzed this material in a *Mississippi Quarterly* article, sees in the Exhibits "two definite and conscious exercises in literary style with a possible third and the knowledge of a fourth, now lost. But in none has Cabell found his medium. It is the covering letter that is of the greatest interest."

In this letter Professor Durham sees the young writer "striving for an image of himself, the image of its creator that his later style was to project." One sees him groping toward a fulfillment in art, compensating for a less-than-satisfactory treatment of the ego in real life. Professor Durham's summation of the Norvell Harrison episode echoes that of later socialist critics who found Cabell's work lacking in moral fiber: "For in this fragment of an almost adolescent affair, one sees a Bookish young Southerner to whom style is more important than emotion, illusion more satisfying than reality, a platitude modishly clothed more desirable than a fresh truth laid bare, a polished irreverence more pleasing than a simple faith, and a romantic cynicism more comforting than a romantic ideal."

Cabell was clearly a spectator as well as a participant in his dealings with Norvell Harrison. As an exercise the affair strengthened his lateral vision. A newspaper reporter had watched a story being created. Whatever else he learned, he gleaned at least two short stories from the extemporized playlet, and Norvell Harrison too utilized the material in at least one of her stories.

"Afternoon in Arden" appeared in the July 1902 *Smart Set*. It incorporates Exhibit B and much of the cover letter given above. The Girl is called Rosalind and the Boy embodies Jaques, the cynic in *As You Like It*. This story gives us a further glimpse into the affair. The following passages are from the 1909 *Cords of Vanity*, which incorporated the story:

> "Oh, yes! I forgot to say that the man was poor—also that the girl had a great deal of common sense and no less than three long-headed aunts. And so the girl talked to the man in a common-sense fashion—and after that she was never at home."
>
> "Never?" said Rosalind.

"Only that time they talked about the weather," said I. "So the man fell out of bed just about then, and woke up and came to his sober senses."

"He did it very easily," said Rosalind, almost as in resentment.

"The novelty of the process attracted him," I pleaded. "So he said—in a perfectly sensible way—that he had known all along that it was only a dainty game they were playing—a game in which there were no stakes. That was a lie." . . .

"She had known all along that the man was but half in earnest—believe me, a girl always knows that, even if she may not admit it to herself—and she had known that a love affair meant to him material for a sonnet or so, and a well-turned letter or two, and nothing more. For he was of the kind of man that never quite grows up. He was coming to her, pleased, interested, and a little eager—in love with the idea of loving her—willing to meet her half-way, and very willing to follow her the rest of the way—if she could draw him. And *what* was she to do? Could she accept his gracefully insulting semblance of a love she knew he did not feel?" . . .

Rosalind flushed somewhat. "And so," said she, "she exercised her common-sense, and was nervous, and said foolish things about new plays, and the probability of rain—to keep from saying still more foolish things about herself; and refused to talk personalities; and let him go, with the knowledge that he would not come back. Then she went to her room, and had a good cry. Now," she added, after a pause, "you understand."

"I do not," I said firmly, "understand a lot of things." (196–200)

Norvell Harrison's short story "Misunderstanding" appeared in the April 1903 issue of *Harper's Magazine*. It has two males corresponding, each in the mistaken belief that the other is a girl through a confusion of first names. Doubtless Miss Harrison herself had been addressed as a male with her first name, given in this instance as Corvell Harrison. After the inevitable meeting of the two males and the resulting disillusionment, the hero continues to treasure the letters from his "female" correspondent as incorporating an ideal of sentiments unexpressed in ordinary relationships. The point of the story could hardly be missed by James Cabell, echoing as it did Exhibit B written to Miss Harrison three years earlier: "With the Boy the letters began to mean more and more. They said many things that he had thought, many things that he could not say without being misunderstood." "Misunderstanding" is a peculiarly modern story, suggesting that the extroverted, logical male suppresses an intuitive heart in daily social intercourse, one that could more truly bond him to a female than conventional mores allow.

In the game that Norvell Harrison and James Cabell played, she at times must have grown weary of her role as Southern Belle, the tireless entertainer—arch, coquettish, presenting a façade of constant gaiety. As Southern Suitor, he had been obliged to play nothing more strenuous than silent admirer, no chore for an inhibited young man. The ordained ritual left him free to record, to compare Miss Harrison's performance with that of Alice Serpell and of Gabriella Moncure, and to compose in his mind what replies he should have made if he had been verbal. The value of their meetings, aside from social solace for a lonely young man, had been the exchange of letters they provoked. Letters, especially those that gave the appearance of spontaneity, required literary imagination. On the whole, from the viewpoint of the male, the relationship had been fruitful, providing entertainment, stimulation, education into the feminine mystique, and a portfolio of fine thoughts. Moreover, he was still safely unattached. Gabriella had not been replaced in his dreaming. Indeed, could real women compete with dream women?

New York without the stimulation of visits to Brooklyn was again a lonely place for young Cabell. As the year 1900 waned, his thoughts turned to home. His job on the Herald precluded writing of a literary nature, and the conviction that he wanted to be a creative writer was growing stronger. A job in Richmond would allow him to enjoy a family relationship with his grandmother, mother and brothers, and there he might find time to embark on a literary career. Moreover, he could again observe the Southern Belle on her native territory; Miss Harrison, a transplanted variety, had—he almost suspected—grown tired of playing in a comedietta that had so little substance. It was up to him to make the fleeting thought into timeless art.

The Magus

8

Murder in Rue Franklin

1901

Robert G. Cabell III, younger than James by two years, graduated from Richmond High School in 1897 and at age sixteen went to work as a clerk in the Merchants National Bank. Allied with his Branch cousins, Robert Cabell later rose in the financial world and in time handled the business affairs of his older brother. In the fall of 1897, John Lottier Cabell, youngest of the Cabell brothers, enrolled in Virginia Military Institute where their father had distinguished himself. John too proved an exceptional student and became an instructor at the institute upon graduation in 1901. In 1898, Robert Cabell was the first of Annie Cabell's immediate family to reenter the Richmond City Directory. His domicile was given as that of Elizabeth Bowie at 113 East Franklin. The following year Robert was again listed with "Jr." added to his name. For the first time in five years the name of Doctor Cabell reentered the directory, also at 113, his occupation listed as "In spr Ins Co Bds." Other records prove that at this time Doctor Cabell was actually living in North Carolina. In 1900 he and son Robert were listed in the directory as living at 106 West Main Street, the "Jefferson Flats," also the residence of Elizabeth Bowie. Directories for 1901 and 1903 list James Branch Cabell and Robert Cabell as domiciled with Dr. R. G. Cabell at 511 West Franklin Street along with Elizabeth Bowie.

Annie Cabell was maintaining the fiction that her husband was a Richmond resident and that the family remained united. On his return from New York, James Cabell called 511 West Franklin home. It was the setting for his first literary acceptance as a writer and figured in another personal drama that had a bearing on his later work.

Cabell returned from New York in late 1900. In his 1917 biographical sketch, he continued writing of this period in his third-person voice.

> Then came the return to his birthplace, Richmond, in Virginia, as a member of the staff of the old *Richmond News*. Cabell now "covered" the doings of architects and builders, of the various fraternal organizations, of all the Federal Government offices, and especially of the police-court. It was in the police-court, he asserts, that he learned to write real stories; and probably he could nowhere have found a field more opulent in material. The Richmond police-court has for the last twenty-nine years been conducted by Justice John J. Crutchfield, a noted "character" throughout the South, as famed for his trenchant observations as for his profoundly informal administration of justice as he sees it irrespective of any existent statute laws. Cabell sat in the little "press pen" at Judge Crutchfield's feet, six mornings in every week, and wrote allegedly humorous or pathetic stories of such cases as came before the court. The follies and the crimes, the whims and the sufferings of humanity—white, black, and intermediately shaded—were unveiled there, hour after hour, in multifarious parade, and were dealt with summarily, but in the main with understanding and sympathy. "It was life quintes sentialized, and condensed into a matinée," as Cabell put it, later; and contemplation thereof afforded the young reporter the opportunity to write daily some three or four thousand words, in which he handled nearly every conceivable happening to, and combination of, human beings. Thus it was that he learned how to approximate the telling of a story in its most generally appealing form, by a daily effort toward, and a daily falling-short of, success at doing it.

The reporter saved many of his news stories, pasting clippings into scrapbooks. The *Herald* style manual had stipulated that reporters were to suggest heads and subheads for their stories, and apparently the new reporter for the Richmond *News* was allowed large leeway in this matter. Alliteration and rime were frequently employed: "Watch Awakens/Woe and Warrant." "Her Trousseau/The Cause of Woe." The *News* was indulgent enough to allow the following: "Chicken and Corn/Cause the Calamity"; "William Roane is Too Fond/of Pone"; "Doesn't Scowl At A Fowl"; "Squire Graves Hears His Tale and/Lodges Him in the Richmond/Jail."

When news was scarce, Cabell interviewed a loquacious gentleman by the name of Theodore, "Monarch of Capitol Square," who expounded readily on any subject—police-court justice Crutchfield; the Jefferson Hotel, both before and after the fire of 29 March 1901; the weather; the dangers of work. Cabell also contributed fillers, an activity known as "paragraphing" in the newspaper parlance of the day. He authored a feature headed "Pointed Paragraphs," aphorisms about male-female relationships, and one called "Maxims For The/Girl in Love/by Max O'Rell." Max wrote longer observations on the sexes as well, a forerunner of today's advice columns. Cabell's longer fillers were sometimes termed "Fables," each ending with a moral. One fable, for example, takes place at a seedy Virginia resort: Susie beats Albert in sporting events, whereupon he proposes to clinging vine Grace. "MORAL: The Gymnasium Girl does not always have the strongest Pull." Some vignettes, not termed fables, ended with a "MORAL" and bore the notation "Copyright 1901, by Robert Howard Russell." Some of the fables were really short stories. Paragraphers were notorious borrowers, and James Cabell's thoughts were turning to the writing of magazine fiction. Certainly he is the author of "The Vampire/A Hair-Raising Horror Story From/Virginia/As Told by Hastings."

> The story that follows is not mine. It was told me by Hastings, the "star reporter" of the Day, after the imbibing of many curious mixed drinks, as we sat in the Harlem office one night . . . .
> "When the city editor of the Day sent me to Williamsburg, in Virginia, for a Sunday story on the place and 'the next oldest college in the United States,' I was rather glad to get out of town for a few days."

While staying at a decidedly seedy Colonial Inn in Williamsburg, the teller of the tale is invited to spend a few days in the country house of a college acquaintance. The mother of his host is a southern gentlewoman who has become a vampire; her victim is another guest, and his death is reported as a suicide in the Richmond papers. While Poe is the inspiration for the story, with its ironic detachment and pointed symbolism, it can be seen as foreshadowing the later Southern Gothic school.

Newspaper work was a challenging postgraduate school for the young writer, but he was by nature a reticent person. His emotions were concealed from others, expressed only in writing, introspectively, and writing to him was essentially rewriting, a refining of the expression of emotion. Throughout his career a drive to repolish remained with him, and newspaper work did not allow this indulgence. It was the antithesis of what he desired to write: "All this was grinding work. A newspaper-man in a smallish metropolis must be 'on his job' just twenty-four hours to the day, neither more nor less. Cabell decided to enter the more reposeful field of magazine-work, and at twenty-two made his first attempt at fiction writing. He built three short stories, which were mailed, on the same day, with fine catholicity, to the *Argosy*, the *Smart Set*, and *Harper's Magazine*. All three were accepted: and on the strength of this he relinquished newspaper work forever." ("Cabell")

Elsewhere Cabell wrote that he sent out five short stories and that three were accepted. He remained proud of this record the rest of his life. Encouraged, he gave himself to writing the type of fiction that magazines of the day sought. Turn-of-the-century readers devoured the inconsequential pap that now is fed to today's television addicts. Some of the "better" magazines aspired to present fiction of value, "wholesome," family oriented. Cabell took as his models Anthony Hope, Maurice Hewlett, Justus Miles Forman. Popular magazines eschewed realism; moreover, the young reporter's encounters with the realities of daily living had not inspired his muse to dwell on social ills. Instead, he turned in memory to the repartee of Gabriella Moncure in Williamsburg and to a lesser degree of Norvell Harrison in Brooklyn for inspiration. His early stories were essentially short plays, consisting primarily of dialogue, their genesis the poems written under the guidance of Charles Coleman and read to "Gabrielle" in a sweet-scented twilight. Just as Gabriella had played multiple, variously named women, the poet assumed various guises as the lover in these dramatic projections of poems. Frequently the hero bursts into song, his lyrics those of the youthful lover. "Love Letters of Falstaff," published by *Harper's* in March 1902, makes Sir John the author of two of James Cabell's college poems, "Have Pity Stella" and "Cupid Invaded Hell." The seven stories composing *The Line of Love* (1905) all contain poems written for Gabriella.

But while James Cabell translated his happy memories into the saleable stuff of magazine fiction, transforming once happy poets into unhappy heroes, fate again ordained that he should play a more dramatic role. Still employed as a reporter but writing the stories that would mean release, late one night in November 1900 he was working at the dining room table of 511 West Franklin Street. His mother and aunt had retired for the evening. One block away at the Commonwealth Club a man sat drinking with friends, while outside two brothers awaited a confrontation that proved fatal.

The fifth child of patriarch Thomas Branch of Petersburg was Sarah

Frances Branch. She married an Irishman, Frederic R. Scott. The parents of six sons and three daughters, they too after the war moved from Petersburg to Richmond. These offspring were the first cousins of Anne Branch Cabell, and the Scott family lived in a commodious house two blocks west on Franklin, opposite Monroe Park. Their first child, born 19 January 1858, was John Walker Scott, whom a niece called John *Waverley* Scott. He attended the University of Virginia, ostensibly to study law, but his interests appeared to be in engineering. His niece, Mary Wingfield Scott, wrote: "In Charlottesville John fell in with a wild crowd, one being George Fawcett, later a well-known actor. If John ever got his degree, he never used it: he drank. When the family home was being emptied, I read a number of letters from him, apparently from a 'cure' in New York State. They are the letters of a complaining dyspeptic." John Scott also attended Harvard University and traveled widely. In Virginia, he spent much of his time at Donegal, an estate in Albemarle that his father had bought in the 1800s. His brothers found various pursuits there, horses, hunting, but of the oldest a retainer observed, "Mis'r John, he de only gemmun o' de lot; he don' do nuthin'." In his forty-fourth year he began to give some thought to settling down to the practice of law, and he rented an office with that view in mind. His younger brothers were already a part of the financial structure that Branch industry was rebuilding. His brother Frederic William Scott was a successful stockbroker and was regarded as the head of the Scott family after the death of their father, a father who had taken the precaution of leaving his eldest son's share of the estate in trust.

John Scott frequently stopped by to commiserate with his cousin Annie Cabell, living as she did halfway between his family's house and the Commonwealth Club. Of Cabell's mother, Miss Scott wrote: "I got the impression that she was a 'gay lady' which was about as far as my Mother would have gone in moral censure, but could have been said if she smoked, let alone was divorced. Quite recently [1975] I have talked to someone who saw her frequently but whom I may not quote by name. She says that Cousin Annie was perfectly beautiful, that she was frequently hospitalized, and that she drank."

On Wednesday afternoon, 13 November 1901, John Scott went riding at the Deep Run Hunt Club. He dined with his family in their mansion at 712 West Franklin Street, later called on a young lady, and then proceeded to the Commonwealth Club at 401 West Franklin, some four short blocks from the Scott residence. He left the Commonwealth at 1:45 a.m. on the 14th, after ascertaining from a friend that he was in walking condition. He walked west, past the residence of his cousin Annie Cabell, 511 West Franklin, where her widowed sister Lizzie Bowie lived on the third floor. Young James Cabell was there, recently returned from working in New York and now employed as a reporter for the Richmond News. Scott passed the iron gate of 515, the residence of Major E. T. D. Myers, president and general superintendent of the Richmond, Fredericksburg and Potomac Railway, on the corner of Belvidere and Franklin streets.

Suddenly screams awakened many in the neighborhood. A trail of blood marked John Scott's passage back to the gate of 515 and up to Major Myers's house. Neighbors heard him pounding on the front door and crying out for admittance. Charles N. Lacy, cycling west on Franklin, heard the screams as he passed the Jefferson Hotel four blocks away; he heard the knocking on the door as he passed 515. He circled back, but as the knocking had ceased, he continued on his way home. Though the corner was brightly lighted, he had seen no one.

Mrs. Preston, Major Myers's daughter, whose room was over the front door, heard the screams and the knocking. In great agitation she hurried to awaken her father, who was asleep in the back of the house. Major Myers partially dressed himself and finally opened the door. He saw a man whom he took to be drunk lying in the shadows of his porch. Major Myers telephoned the police, who soon arrived and found the victim still in a semiconscious condition. A letter in his pocket revealed his identity, and Major Myers advised that he should be taken to the Retreat for the Sick Hospital. There doctors determined that his skull had been fractured, the weapon possibly a cane with a heavy projecting knob. Nothing could be done for Scott, and he died within a few hours. That afternoon the Richmond News headlined the fact that the victim had been "Robbed and Slain."

The murder created a sensation in Richmond, and the four daily newspapers chronicled every detail as well as the mysteries surrounding the event. The Richmond Dispatch on 15 November speculated that the victim might have been struck by a passing engine of the R. F. & P. Railway, whose tracks then ran down Belvidere Street from Elba Station on Broad Street to the warehouse area in lower Richmond. Another speculation was that in an inebriated condition Scott had fallen, striking his head on the iron fence or granite coping surrounding the Myers' yard. They further speculated that Scott might have been attacked elsewhere and placed on Major Myers's porch. The News reported the same day that personal malice was also believed to be a motive. On the 16th, the Dispatch announced that the family of the slain man believed the robbery theory, claiming a wallet and watch were missing. The police held to the series-of-falls theory or to the revenge motive. A large and valuable gold ring had been left intact, and the pockets of the victim had remained untouched. Further, they observed, a cane was not the weapon of a footpad. A growing antagonism between the police and the Scotts is detectable in the news accounts. Questioned on the family's cooperation, "Mr. George Scott stated that the family had no desire to hold back from the public any information or facts which might come to their knowledge."

On Monday the 18th, the *News* optimistically headlined "Mystery Seems Clearing Up." At approximately the time of the murder, a resident of Main Street, a block south of Franklin, had seen a man of the gentleman class in a light overcoat hurrying south on Henry Street from Franklin. He had paused uncertainly on the corner of Henry and Main, and the witness had noted the fine cut of the overcoat. The *News* further revealed that the Scott family had employed a detective from the Pinkerton Agency, a tight-lipped sleuth named Krewson who was promptly dubbed "Gruesome" by the local police. Another detail was that Mrs. Cabell of 511 had read very late on the night of the murder and had heard the cries. The *Dispatch* for the 19th reported that the accident and robbery motives had been abandoned. It added significantly: "The most interesting development of last night's investigation was the fact, repeated by several residents of Franklin Street near the scene of the tragedy, that a number of the ladies who were awakened by the noise in the street in front of the Myers' house know a great deal more of what really transpired than they have told the police or the reporters."

All the rumors of arrests referred to "a very important person," "a well-known citizen," or "a society man." A grand jury was summoned and the inquest was held on 19 and 20 November. Mrs. William L. Royal and her sister Mrs. John Enders, of 504 West Franklin, had heard two men talking loudly but could distinguish nothing they said. Mrs. C. E. Borden of 514 had heard terrible language. Major Myers affirmed that he still believed it was a case of intoxication, that when he had called Fred Scott in the morning the latter asked if his brother had been drinking. The attending physicians testified that Scott had been drinking. Mrs. Elizabeth Bowie of 511 had heard the cry for help and had gone to the room of her sister Mrs. Cabell on the second floor. Mrs. Cabell was awake. "The two went to the rear to the room of Mr. James Branch Cabell. He was in the dining-room, and they went down stairs. Mr. Cabell went out on the porch, but heard or saw nothing." Mrs. Cabell corroborated her sister's account in her stand before the grand jury. The coroner's inquest determined that Scott's death was murder. The Scotts gave Krewson three more private detectives.

On the 21st, the *Dispatch* reported that the motive now accepted was revenge for violating "the sanctity of a home." Certain letters were being investigated. Two female victims of John Scott were mentioned in the rumors, one married, one not. The *News* headlined "Wild Rumors of a Confession." On the revenge motive it reported: "One of these has an injured husband as a suspect and the other concerns a supposed rivalry between the deceased and a former friend in a love affair that would not be considered creditable to either." The *Dispatch* underlined the fact that the person closest to the dispute and murder had been unavailable for the inquest; Mrs. Preston, very nervous, had been sent to Washington for her health. Further, Major Myers admitted he had not encouraged his daughter to talk of what she might have heard in her agitated state. It appeared that Major Myers had closed ranks with the Scotts.

The papers for the 22d discredited the story that Scott had lost a wallet. Mr. Lilburn Myers testified that his sister Mrs. Preston had heard nothing of importance. The "Man in the light overcoat" held center stage in the "talk of the town." The *Dispatch* added significantly: "In the continual rumor of yesterday concerning the one man singled out by the amateur theorists and gossips, a great deal of harm has probably been done. It was almost equal to charging him outright with murder, so persistent was the story that he was the guilty man and the confessed murderer. It was impossible for any of his friends to fail to hear this rumor, and they were, of course, sorry and indignant that his name should have been used so freely. The police finally declared that he was not the man being looked for and that as far as they knew, he knew nothing of the tragedy." Reacting to the growing accusations on the part of the reading public that facts were being withheld, the *Dispatch* protested that of the four papers it had printed the fullest and most accurate accounts. Both the press and the police came to the obvious conclusion that the Pinkerton Agency was receiving cooperation from the Scott family that was denied them.

The news accounts of the 22d were the last substantial coverage the murder was to receive. Considering this fact, two items are of significance. The *Dispatch* reported that "the Pinkerton man was closeted with Mr. Fred Scott for over an hour yesterday, and it is possible that a favorable report was secured by the latter, although nothing positive or presaging an early arrest was made known." It also noted that "Mr. Scott seemed more cheerful yesterday than on any day since the tragic death of his brother." According to the *News*, "Mr. Fred Scott stated that no woman entered the case as a cause. He denied a rumor that he would allow the case to continue as a mystery rather than divulge the name of some woman should it come up." Brief notices of a lack of new developments appeared for a few days. Wednesday the 27th saw Krewson, the private detective, return to Philadelphia, ostensibly for Thanksgiving. No further news of the case of any kind appeared in the Richmond papers. In less than two weeks after the murder, the rumors and speculation still at fever pitch, silence gave credence to whatever one wished to believe.

On the whole, the news accounts seemed to substantiate the gossip that James Cabell was the murderer of John Scott. Rumor would have it that he had returned from New York and discovered the liaison between his mother and Scott. Knowing Scott's routine of remaining at the Commonwealth Club until closing time, Cabell had waited until he passed in front of 511 West Franklin. After accosting Scott he had walked a few steps westward with the intention of thrashing him with his cane, but in the heat of anger he had gone too far. When Scott fled back to Major Myers's house, Cabell had followed him to the gate; but realizing that the neighbors were now awakened, he hurried on east the short distance to Henry Street. Cabell had not dared enter his own house by the front. Turning south, he walked swiftly to the corner of Main and Henry. Here he was observed. Returning up Henry to the alley between Franklin and Main, he had slipped into his house by a rear door. So the account went. At the inquest his mother and aunt had testified to finding him in the dining room and not in his bed. Only a near neighbor could have escaped the scene of the murder so easily. Witnesses had an unobstructed view of Franklin and Belvidere streets; no one had crossed them immediately after the screams. Thus Richmond construed the evidence.

The findings of the Pinkerton Agency were never revealed to the Richmond police, and for the latter the case was never solved. Ellen Glasgow wrote: "At last, however, the truth was reluctantly divulged. . . . It was revealed that the erring cousin had been struck down, in front of Cabell's house, by the brother of a country girl who had been seduced. Morality was avenged, for it was generally thought that the family of the seducer had benevolently aided the slayer to escape" (*Woman Within*, 135). Here Glasgow intimates that the Scotts "reluctantly divulged" the findings of the private detectives. If so, it must have been a very private revelation, for there was no public accounting. Further, her version has one brother as the avenger of the seduced country girl. Other verbal accounts reported two, and as will be seen, Cabell appeared to corroborate the story of dual avengers. "But this was divulged accurately or inaccurately, years later," Glasgow went on to observe, "and during all those years James was living as a hermit, burning his kerosene lamp in patience, and sleeping in his third-story room until sunset."

James Cabell did not learn of the precise role assigned him in this new scandal until nine years later. Biographical details seeded in his fiction make it appear that he was aware of being credited with murder before he learned of the slander against his mother. Perhaps he thought at the time that proximity to the crime and the old Williamsburg gossip would naturally accord him a role in public speculation. His mother could observe with one of his characters in *The Cords of Vanity*: "People talk of course, but it is only on the stage they ever drive you out into the snowstorm. Besides, they don't talk to me." Cabell was absorbed in his writing during this period, and Townsend in *Cords* most likely echoes his attitude toward the gossip: "I did not greatly care what Lichfield said one way or the other. I was too deeply engrossed; first, in correcting the final proofs of *Afield*, my second book . . . ; secondly, in the remunerative and uninteresting task of writing for *Woman's Weekly* five 'wholesome love-stories with a dash of humor'" (157).

The Alchemist

1902−1909

On the surface, James Cabell was indifferent to Richmond gossip. He did not go out in society or meet people under conditions where they would confide to him the part he was accorded. Moreover, he had reversed night and day, escaping into an in-between world where he created the social order, one that he determined to make real for others in his writing. As he worked on his stories through the spring of 1902, he resolved that he would return to the Rockbridge Alum Springs for the summer. He and his brother John would not retreat to a country boardinghouse just to escape the heat. He would again observe society in that most carefree setting, that swirling stage where the masks were changed daily in a ritual denial of pain and stress. He and John could receive cheap board as young bachelors, and he could earn pocket money by writing social dispatches for the local papers.

By July the Richmond Sunday papers were full of resort news, and the 12 July report from the Alum to the *Dispatch* had Mr. James Branch Cabell participating in every round of pleasure. A few days later Professor John L. Cabell of the Virginia Military Institute, as well as "Mrs. M. L. Branch [sometimes Mrs. James Branch] and Mrs. Elizabeth Branch Bowie of Richmond," joined the festivities. In the special to the *News* on 7 August, "Mrs. M. L. Branch, Mrs. E. H. Bowie and maid of Richmond" are among favored celebrants, possibly owing to the generosity of Colonel Jim Branch, the son and brother upon whom fortune was smiling. Coaching parties to and from other nearby resorts—Warm Springs, the Rockbridge Baths, the Hotel Alleghaney—were popular, and John Cabell was admired for his skill in driving the coach through Goshen Pass and returning late at night with horns blaring.

The year 1902 saw the publication of seven stories by James Branch Cabell: "An Amateur Ghost" in the February *Argosy*; "Love Letters of Falstaff" in the March *Harper's*, "As Played Before His Highness," "Afternoon in Arden," "In the Summer of St. Martin," "As the Coming of Dawn," and "An Invocation of Helen" in the March, July, August, September, and October issues of *Smart Set*. The goal of *Smart Set* was "to appeal to the literate section of New York society and authentically reflect, in fiction and articles, the interests, tastes, codes, and activities of that society." Considered indecorous and immoral by the older guardians of literary taste, the *Smart Set* sought fiction by new and unknown writers, fresh, daring, and alive. It attracted an atheneum of "discoveries" who soon became the popular authors of the day. Among other writers it discovered was one who signed his stories O. Henry. Twenty-two-year-old James Cabell could be justifiably proud of a letter dated 20 September 1902 from Marvin Dana of the *Smart Set* editorial office announcing an increase in its usual rates for his stories and requesting a "novelette of from twenty-five to thirty-five thousand words." In Richmond, the *Times, Dispatch,* and *News* were trumpeting the appearance of each story by the local author; the *Times* announced that "Mr. Cabell is at present hard at work on a novelette which he has been engaged to write."

The *Smart Set* stories elicited a response from Justus Miles Forman (1875–1915), another young writer who was appearing in popular magazines and whose romance *Garden of Lies* had just been published in book form.

My dear Mr. Cabell—

It is no habit of mine to inflict my enthusiasms or my critiques upon the various writer-people whose work interests me but the fact that we are, in a way, fellow workmen—in contributing largely, both, to one periodical,—and the fact that your work has so easily attained qualities for which I have long striven quite in vain, these things have lead me to the desire for telling you how tremendously I have been enjoying your Smart Set contributions and how truly I have—among many, I am sure—appreciated the points you constantly make and which are quite beyond the ordinary writer. I read, this summer in London, your 'Summer of St. Martin' with a rare enthusiasm. I would give much to have done it myself, very much. Everyone who does his work before the public eye has more than enough unintelligent matinee-girl gush, but appreciation from one's neighbor workman is rarer, and, I fancy, rather more valued—to me at least. It is only on this ground that I have attempted to tell you of the pleasure your tales have afforded me—May there be many more as good—

Very sincerely yours,

Justus Miles Forman
New York
October the third—'02

Before Cabell responded, he was careful to read *Garden of Lies*. His flattering letter to Forman was received just as the latter "was en train to write" (23 January 1903) praising Cabell's latest story, "Heart of Gold," in the February *Smart Set* and observing that "we become a mutual admiration society of two." Forman exhorted Cabell, five years his junior, to "write a book! Don't bury yourself in the back files of a magazine. It really is burial."

Many of the early *Smart Set* stories incorporated biography. The young author altered settings, supplied commentary, polished prose. In "Afternoon in Arden" the hero is writing "As the Coming of Dawn," another consideration of the Norvell Harrison episode. "It was—oh, just about her. It tried to tell how greatly he loved her. It tried—well, it failed of course, because it isn't within the power of any writer to express what the man felt for that girl." In the *Smart Set* story entitled "As the Coming of Dawn," the hero-writer meets "Marian Winwood" at the Green Chalybeate (read Rockbridge Alum) who inspires his muse. Unknown to him, however, she too is a writer and uses him for her source material. The male reads her version of their summer idyll with "augmenting irritation."

Here was my great and comely idea transmuted into a rather clever melodrama . . . .

"And to cap it all, she has assigned her hero every pretty speech I ever made to her! I honestly believe the rogue took shorthand jottings on her cuffs. *There is a land where lovers may meet face to face, and heart to heart, and mouth to mouth*—why, that's the note I wrote to her on the day she wasn't feeling well!"

. . . Naturally I put the entire affair into a short story. And—though even to myself it seems incredible—Miss Winwood wrote me a very indignant letter within three days of the tale's appearance.

The niece of Norvell Harrison observed that the latter did not regard her cousin James "highly as an author or a relative and pitched out a lot of his synthetic-love missives." In 1902, on the death of Professor Harrison, Norvell moved to Richmond with her mother and younger brother, but Cabell made no attempt to renew the blighted friendship that had flowered in Brooklyn. In 1904 her brother Henry Sydnor Harrison also moved to Richmond, where he began to review books for the *Times-Dispatch*. Unlike James Cabell, young Harrison was a gregarious, charming man on friendly terms with the best people in town. As a newspaper writer he advanced rapidly.

Richmond readers were quick to pick up the autobiographical references seeded in the stories of the increasingly popular magazine writer. In "The Shadowy Past," written in 1902 and published in the January 1903 *Smart Set*, the young author gave a contemporary portrait of his mother. In the Social and Personal column of the Richmond *Times*, the reporter quoted from the story at length:

> Ah! who shall ever write the tragedy of a frivolous woman's middle-age—the middle-age of the pitiful butter-fly woman, whose life is all made up of worldly things, and whose mind can't because of its very nature, reach to anything higher? Middle-age strips her of everything—the admiration, the flattery, the shallow merriment—all the little things that her little mind longs for, and other women take her place, in spite of her futile, pitiful efforts to remain young. And the world goes on as before, and there is a whispering in the winter garden and the young people steal off for wholly superfluous glasses of water, and the men give her duty dances, and she is old, ha! so old, under the rouge and inane smiles and dainty fripperies that caricature lost youth.

When Cabell incorporated this story into *The Rivet in Grandfather's Neck* a few years later, he softened the personal portrait of Annie Cabell into the more universal metaphor of the Southern Belle: "Ah, who will write the tragedy of us women who were 'famous Southern beauties' once? We were queens of men while our youth lasted, and diarists still prattle charmingly concerning us. But nothing was expected of us save to be beautiful and to condescend to be made much of, and that is our tragedy. For very few things, my dear, are more pitiable than the middle-age of the pitiful butterfly woman" (*The Rivet in Grandfather's Neck*, 181).

It was a theme that would be expanded by other Richmond authors, particularly Ellen Glasgow, Mary Johnston, and Henry Sydnor Harrison, but Cabell's affections were too involved to treat the belle clinically or at length. Further, her role as victim or victimizer was uncomfortably akin to the role of the poet who played a large part in the creation of the legend. His own assumed persona of poet excused him from conventional social responsibilities, and he could treat the two roles—belle and poet—only at a safe remove, comically.

These early stories were seen by Richmonders as society sketches, and each appearance was heralded in the local press with encouraging headlines such as "Success for Mr. Cabell" (*News*). His prolific output continued into 1903, and in New York the weekly *Town Topics*, an early precursor of the *New Yorker*, accorded the Richmond author favorable recognition. January saw the publication of "The Shadowy Past" in *Smart Set*; February, "Heart of Gold" in *Smart Set*; May, "In Ursula's Garden" in *Harper's*. In June the novella commissioned by *Smart Set* was published. "The Husbands' Comedy," the lead story, was widely advertised in other major publications. *Town Topics* singled it out for praise in "'The Smart Set' and Its New School of Fiction," opining that in invention and style the new school was peculiarly Gallic. The young author must have felt that success was assured when the Richmond papers expressed reservations. The *News-Leader* deplored, "There is not a single wholesome character drawn," and admonished, "Try again, Mr. Cabell, and infuse some womanly virtue in your leading lady." The *Times-Dispatch* faintly praised its "modernity" but associated it with "bathos" and a "lack of right feeling and real sentiment." But Cabell had subscribed to a clipping service and was gratified to find that newspapers across the nation praised the story, most of them borrowing the phrase, "The story is strikingly distinctive and clever." All professed to admire an underlying pathos. This was the recognition that James Cabell longed for, and he determined to write an even longer work; length determined success. Thus he started writing *The Eagle's Shadow*. When the *Times-Dispatch* learned of the admiring reception of "The Husbands' Comedy" outside Richmond, it reassessed its earlier criticism, concluding that "the story is strikingly distinctive and clever as fiction may be. It is full of humor that is delicious; but, too, there is very genuine human feeling in these pages, and an underlying pathos."

Again Justus Miles Forman responded charmingly. Writing from London on 17 July he explained his lateness: "I read the tale with great interest and enjoyment while rolling up the Adriatic toward Trieste in a Hungarian bumboat having stolen the magazine from a drunken Englishman in Malta. I was very curious, being as you know, a constant though unwilling enthusiast over your shorter tales and was much annoyed to find that you took the jump without appreciable effort. I see nothing for it but for me to insult you grossly in some manner. In that event you would have to call me out and one of us would shortly cease to impede the others' progress. Meanwhile—as I think I urged you once before—write a novel."

June 1903 also saw the appearance of "The Conspiracy of Arnaye" in *Harper's*. "The Story of Stella" appeared in the August *Smart Set*, "The Castle of Content" in the August *Harper's*, and "Old Capulet's Daughter" in the September *Smart Set*. The Richmond *Times-Dispatch*, possibly chagrined by its misjudgment of "The Husbands' Comedy," accorded him an extensive interview entitled "Mr. Cabell and His Work," hailing "a new star in the South's literary firmament." In the interview Cabell discusses his family and educational background, his reading preferences, and his work to date. He was then at work upon a novel, but he worked slowly, "never accomplishing more than 500 words at a sitting." He was judged "a keen observer and analyst of human nature. His 'characters are suggested by types deeply studied, while his plots are invariably drawn from actual happenings.'" We are told that "the author, for the sake of uninterrupted quiet, has acquired the habit of writing at night, often remaining at his desk until daylight, and spending the hours of the forenoon in sleep." In June the *Times-Dispatch* published a large photograph of Cabell with the announcement of the new story in *Harper's*. It also gave biographical details: "Mr. Cabell for some years has been living quietly with his mother, Mrs. Robert G. Cabell, on West Franklin Street, thoroughly engaged in fulfilling the demands made upon him by his publishers. It is possible he may go abroad this winter to remain a year, but that matter has not been fully decided, with reference to his literary engagements. The most important work which Mr. Cabell now has on hand is a book to be made up of a cycle of love stories, beginning with the twelfth century and coming down to modern days." The cycle of love stories resulted in *The Line of Love* two years later, and perhaps a case can be made that the projected range of the stories is the germinal idea of the extended Biography of the Life of Manuel. Cabell would carry the idea back to 1901, but hindsight refreshed his memory in that 1923 revelation. Certainly Justus Miles Forman had helped seed Cabell's decision to gather his short stories into book form. The former's admonition not to get buried in back files of magazines had made the younger writer give thought to retrieving his stories. One way would be to present these minor works as parts of larger cycles, sufficiently broad to cover their diversity. An epic theme was needed to unify them.

Meanwhile, Cabell *filius* had become a nocturnal creature in a house that saw the comings and goings of his mother, his Aunt Lizzie, his old nurse, Louisa Nelson, his brother Robert, and his studious first cousin, Walter Russell Bowie, now twenty-one and destined to become a noted clergyman and author of inspirational biographies. Dr. Cabell was also listed as living at 511 West Franklin, Annie Cabell sustaining this public fiction. John Cabell, "Teacher," was given as a resident, but he was there only on holidays. James Branch Cabell was designated "Bookkeeper," suggesting he may have supplemented his income from writing by keeping books a few hours a day. The following year this ménage moved to a newer house on the 1500 block of Grove Avenue. Another three-story house, less Victorian in character, it still stands, its broad front porch overlooking a block-long terrace of houses known as Old Dominion Row.

While Cabell wrote his stories under the lamp over the dining room table at 1509 Grove Avenue, upstairs Louisa Nelson lay dying. At age eighty-four the black woman who had been born in slavery reverted to her childhood memories. The children she had raised faded from a present that had no reality, those whom she had nursed now nursing her. When she died on 7 February 1904, obituaries of her passing appeared in all the Richmond papers. James, Robert, and John, with three of their cousins, were her pallbearers. A tribute by Annie Cabell praised her life of service:

> For a quarter of a century she had lived in the family of Mrs. Robert G. Cabell and it had been her greatest joy to bring up her three children—James Branch Cabell, now an author, Robert G. Cabell of Thomas Branch and Company, and John Lawrence [sic] Cabell, a professor in the Virginia Military Institute—from the day of their birth to manhood: all three being glad to testify that whatever success they have attained in life was due largely to their dear mammy's counsel and example. To her, her boys were perfect and whatever they were, they were the result of that good woman's precept and example: since to them she offered her best, and her best were the finest qualities of her race, patience, sobriety, unfailing kindness and a desire to serve God. (Scrapbook 3, Cabell Special Collection)

The year 1904 was to see the Richmond author, who turned twenty-five on 14 April, receive nationwide notice in the press. Unlike magazine stories, books exposed a writer to reviews. *The Eagle's Shadow* accomplished what the young writer sought: recognition that would vindicate him in the eyes of Richmond and Williamsburg society. His mother too sought rehabilitation through her son's success by marketing the manuscript of the novel. James Cabell had made a name as a writer of magazine fiction, but he was unknown to the larger publishing houses. Annie Cabell knew Walter Hines Page, a graduate of Randolph-Macon College where her father had gone to school. Page, a native of North Carolina, had gone on to Johns Hopkins and had established himself as a journalist, a spokesman for a new South. He was editor of the *Atlantic Monthly* and, in 1899, was a co-partner in the establishment of Doubleday, Page and Company. In the literary memoirs of Isaac Marcosson, we have a contemporary glimpse of Annie Cabell as her son's agent:

> One morning after I had been a member of the Doubleday, Page organization for several years, an aristocratic looking woman arrived at the front office and asked to see Page. She did not belie her appearance because she was Mrs. Ann Branch Cabell, one of the elite in Richmond, Virginia, society. As she passed my desk I saw that she held what was obviously a manuscript under her arm.
>
> Page saw her immediately and after fifteen minutes had passed sent word for me to come into his office. There I met Mrs. Cabell. The manuscript she brought was *The Eagle's Shadow*, the first book by her son, James Branch Cabell.
>
> After Page and I read the story the firm decided to publish it. *The Eagle's Shadow* was rather thin but it showed the promise that Cabell later fulfilled. His controversial book *Jurgen* was the talk of the country directly it hit the book stores and remained the subject of varied discussion for a considerable time.
>
> Cabell was adored by his mother. For years he lived almost like a recluse in the top floor of the family residence in Richmond. He was pale and shy and would not even venture forth to buy cigarettes which were purchased for him by his mother who attended to all his other wants. (*Before I Forget: A Pilgrimage to the Past*, 528–29)

Henry W. Lanier, an editor at Doubleday, Page, wrote Cabell on 3 March 1904, saying he found the story delightful and offering to publish it. He agreed to pay a royalty of ten percent and to purchase the serial rights for seven hundred dollars. He asked for a reply by return mail. Cabell telegraphed acceptance and wrote that night.

An abridged version of *The Eagle's Shadow* appeared in the *Saturday Evening Post*, 6 August to 30 September. Doubleday, Page issued the work on 4 October, bound in red with gold lettering, illustrated by Will Grefe and decorated by Blanche Ostertag. It was dedicated to "M.L.P.B.," Cabell's Branch grandmother. Widely advertised, the novel was reviewed by every newspaper in the country that published literary news. Its reception was generally favorable. Margaret Hugonin, the heroine of *The Eagle's Shadow*, hostess to a house party in the country, has thirty-two chapters devoted to her beauty, charm, wilfulness, wealth, the latter sought by several suitors, but love overcomes greed, and a desk with secret drawers serves as the *deus ex machina* to set things right. *Town Topics* gave this debut novel a tolerant, bemused assessment, but the reviewer confessed, "I should have more enjoyed reading this pleasant little romance if Mr. Cabell had not begun with the intention of being terse as Maurice Hewlett and reconsidering in favor of the modish epigrams of Robert Hichens." The *Congregationalist-Boston* gave it a one-sentence review: "A comedy well suited to the theatrical stage, in which sentiment and satire are both occasionally overdrawn, but with such genuine descriptions of character and such wholesome humor that one lays down the volume after reading it as he would rise from an amusing play." The reviews in the Richmond papers were highly gratifying, the *Times-Dispatch* comparing the young author to Thomas Nelson Page, Ellen Glasgow, and Amélie Rives, and the *News-Leader* comparing him to Thackeray. Many reviews were accompanied by photographs of a rather pudgy young man, one who apparently ate the substantial meals of the day without a corresponding amount of exercise.

An added bonus of publicity for *The Eagle's Shadow* came in the form of a letter from a moralist critic to the *New York Times Book Review*. "Old Fashioned" of St. Louis (18 November) objected to the heroine's use of profanity. She had screamed "Damn you!" in a moment of stress, believing her lover dead. Profanity was "the mark of a degraded mind, an ineradicable evil." On the 28th "E.H.B." wrote in agreement: the heroine was "a light-headed shrew." These carpings inspired an agreeable number of letters in defense of a "modern" heroine, one from "M.L.P.B.," the novel's dedicatee. Grandmother Branch compared Mr. Cabell with Dickens and opined that the young writer's genius bid "fair to make a great name." Her letter is dated "New York, December 18." Another letter dated "New York, December 20" and signed "Young Virginian" may have been from another of her brilliant grandchildren, James Robinson Branch, a student at the Naval Academy. "Young Virginian" wrote, "Mr. Cabell's book seems to me to be the most promising first book by any American author in many a day." Joining in the defense was Richard B. Glaenzer, soon to make his own name in the literary world; he and Cabell began a friendly correspondence that continued over the years. Cabell's early admirer, Justus Miles Forman, wrote on 4 October, thanking his rival for a presentation copy: "Let me have more as delightful." Despite the relative success of Cabell's first novel, however, only 2,871 copies were sold, not quite covering the expenses of production and advertising.

Earlier H. M. Alden, the venerable editor of Harper and Brothers, had taken kindly to the suggestion that a book should be made of the stories that had appeared in *Harper's Monthly*. Alden wrote on 24 March, "We take much pleasure in sending to you herewith the proofs you asked for in your last letter." Thus before Doubleday, Page published *The Eagle's Shadow*, the manuscript of *The Line of Love* was in the office of Harper and Brothers, a few stylistic flourishes having been made to the previously published stories. The production of the book did not take place until the following year, careful attention being given to the esthetic appearance of the physical product. *The Line of Love* finally made its appearance in September 1905, designed as a Christmas gift book. Fancifully decorated, it had illustrations in color by Howard Pyle, and Cabell dedicated it to R.G.C. Thus his first two books honored the two grandparents he had known.

In May 1905, when Jim Branch heard from Sallie McAdams that their sister Annie Cabell was planning a trip to France for the summer, he wrote Annie on the 27th: "I have no desire to make comment on your expenditures or way of living, but judging from what I have seen, would imagine that at odd times you could chip in with the rest of us" (Letter Book, 34). Jim, Sallie, and Mary were all contributing to their mother's support; Lizzie could not afford to, and Annie indulged herself. In an effort to extract support from her separated and now jobless husband, Annie asked Jim to get Dr. Cabell a job as an insurance health inspector. Jim replied that those positions were being phased out, but he offered his brother-in-law a job in West Virginia selling coal on a commission or for a salary of seventy-five dollars a month. Even Annie felt that the offer was demeaning, and Jim wrote her in Paris on 30 August: "Dr. Cabell is no longer a young man, and as he has a bad affliction on one side of his face on account of his eye, it will be difficult to get him a good position." (LB, 368). Whatever hopes frivolous Annie had for an improvement in her family fortunes had to come from her sons. Robert and John were gainfully employed, but James was getting only a pittance from his stories. Like his father, he too needed a job—or a good marriage. Of course Annie was proud that James was being noticed as a writer.

The year 1905 also saw more stories appear in magazines: "Sweet Adelais" in the March *Harper's*, "Simon's Hour" in the April *Ainslee's*, "The Rhyme to Porringer" in the 15 April *Collier's Weekly*, "April's Message" in the May *Ainslee's*, and "The Fox-Brush" in the August *Harper's*. The story in *Collier's* was the result of Cabell's entering its 1905 short story contest, where his submission had placed thirteenth in an acceptance of stories;

he was paid two hundred dollars, the highest sum he had ever received for a story. "Simon's Hour" prompted more praise from Forman but with a reservation: "So fine a tale I have not met in a very long time. But why, *why in Ainslee's?* How it would have shone in *Harper's!*" (24 March). Forman added that he was off for his annual six months in Europe, doubtless arousing some longing in the Richmond-bound younger author. Forman later drowned with the sinking of the *Titanic* in 1912.

Tragedy again struck in Cabell's family. On 7 November 1905, his first cousin, James Robinson Branch, died at the Naval Academy as the result of brutal beating by a heavier, stronger midshipman. The hearing that followed created wide discussion in the world press. As the penman for the family, James was urged to express its corporate outrage for the judicial process that exonerated the murderer. Cabell's scathing indictment of court and culprit was entitled "That Opera Bouffe Court Martial" and was probably published at the urging of his distraught uncle who had written the secretary of the navy as well as his friend Theodore Roosevelt. On 26 December, Cabell wrote James Ransom Branch:

My dear Uncle Jim,

This is to thank you for the "Naval History," which I shall prize not only for its integral value but more especially on account of its former owner, James Robinson Branch. The "Sword" book I shall forward you tomorrow or next day with cordial appreciation of the loan. It has been to me quite tremendously useful—apropos, I have a story in the January *Harper's* in which you ought to take a proprietary interest, since it contains an excellent fight pilfered almost word for word from your book. And the long story I am just finishing has two fights therein, each due to the collaboration of you and Mr. Hutton.

If it were my part to offer you a word of advice, I would suggest that in writing to Grandmother you had best not allude to James in any manner. It is not my part, but I do it, nevertheless. She is now so feeble as it is possible for any human being to be and yet live. Your letters prostrate her. She loves you, at a moderate computation, about ten times as much as she does any of her other children and any realization of your present unhappiness brings her, in sober earnest, within an inch or two of death. I know, for I have seen her afterward.

Please do not regard this as a piece of impertinence on my part, for it is prompted solely by love for her. And I believe that you, too, love her, since you must if you are human.

Neither in Richmond nor now did I offer you any of the commonplaces of consolation in regard to James' murder. People talk smugly of the "designs of mysterious Providence," but the same Providence endowed one with consideration, and as long as I consider the affair the more brutal and uncalled for it appears to me. If I am wrong, it is a defect rather than a fault. In any event, I cannot offer you, nor do I pretend to offer you, any consolation, but I do extend my most cordial sympathy.

Cabell dedicated his next book, *Gallantry*, to the young victim.

James Cabell's interest in genealogy, first stimulated by the Colemans in Williamsburg, continued unabated, and at this time it was directed toward his mother's Branch ancestry. He was publishing genealogical notes in the Richmond papers. A national revival of interest in America's colonial history was being manifested in architecture and patriotic societies. John Patteson Branch, one of Richmond's wealthiest bankers, whose mansion at 1 West Franklin had been altered from its 1840 chastity into a Victorian pile, encouraged his great-nephew in his research, agreeing to underwrite a projected family history. The records of Henrico and Chesterfield counties, home for the Branches from the earliest days, had survived the ravages of war and were close by. Apparently of yeoman stock, the progenitor Christopher had arrived commendably early, thereby qualifying his descendants for membership in the most prestigious lineage societies that proliferated in the twentieth century.

Indirectly another family connection entered into the Richmond author's literary career at this point. Theodore Roosevelt visited Richmond in October 1905 and was handsomely received. The president confided to Thomas Nelson Page that he had a grand time. The great man had a tie with Richmond. Elizabeth Caskie, daughter of John Caskie of the city, had been the first wife of James Bulloch, uncle of Mr. Roosevelt. The president's aunt, Miss Annie Bulloch, had visited the Caskies before the war, although she was no blood kin, being a child of a second marriage. The Bullochs and the Caskies had remained close, and Cabell's grandmother was a Caskie. Sometime during Mr. Roosevelt's visit to Richmond the young writer's name was mentioned, and a few days later a suitably inscribed copy of *The Line of Love* was forwarded to the vacationing president. A typed letter marked "Personal" arrived from St. Augustine, Florida, on 21 October 1905.

My dear Mr. Cabell:

I have just received the really beautiful volume, and I value it not only for its own sake and for its setting, but for the kindly words of the donor. I have already read and greatly liked most of the stories; and I shall go through the whole book as soon as I get in a place where I shall be certain that there will be no danger of the railroad dust hurting it!

If you are a kinsman of Martha Bulloch you are a kinsman of mine. If you come to Washington pray let me know. It would be such a pleasure to meet you.

Sincerely yours,

/s/ Theodore Roosevelt

Most likely with urging from his mother, James Cabell decided he would be passing through Washington in the near future. Not many young authors could boast of being read by the president of the United States. On 3 February, a telegram arrived at 1509 Grove Avenue from the White House: "Letter received can you lunch with the President, Tuesday at one thirty. Please advise if you accept. Wm. Loeb, Jr., Secy." The President's kind words for the stories in *The Line of Love* had been duly leaked to the press, and Cabell's luncheon became chapter 15 in *The Cream of the Jest*. Kennaston, one of Cabell's mid-career personas, contributed little to the luncheon table chat, "rather ill-at-ease among these men of action."

> "It has been a very great pleasure to meet you, Mr. Kennaston," quoth the personnage, wringing Kennaston's hand.
>
> Kennaston suitably gave him to understand that they shared ecstacy in common. But all the while Kennaston was, really, thinking that here before him, half-revealed, shone the world-famous teeth portrayed by cartoonists in the morning-paper everyday, everywhere. Yes, they were remarkable teeth—immaculate, mormoreal and massive—and they were so close-set that Kennaston was now smitten with an idiotic desire to ask their owner if the personnage could get dental floss between them. (81–82)

Cabell knew that he really should make the most of his fortuitous contact with the great man. While his genealogical research passed the time agreeably and his discoveries soothed wounded vanities, as a pastime it was even less remunerative than short-story writing. None of it produced an income commensurate with his tastes and social background. His mother, ever conscious of reduced circumstances, urged her oldest son to seek other employment, perhaps a position that would allow him sufficient freedom to pursue literary endeavors. Not only did Thomas Nelson Page have the forethought to marry money, but he also had an eye on a diplomatic post. Service in a foreign country was a respectable sinecure, she argued, and James's proficiency in foreign languages would qualify him admirably, aside from his being a gentleman. Annie Cabell had met the well-placed; though her social standing might be impaired in little old Richmond, she could still be the fashionable lady in less provincial society. She had gotten her son's novel published; she would get him a diplomatic appointment. He might meet an heiress abroad. He seemed more interested in writing about females than in meeting them; a diplomatic post entailed a necessary amount of social activity.

Through Annie Cabell's efforts, James Branch Cabell, Jr. [sic], heard from the State Department the following year. He was invited to take an examination in July and, upon passing, would be assigned a post. An alarmed young man, comfortably ensconced in the maternal bower, wrote asking where and how much. In a letter dated 20 July 1906, Robert Bacon, acting secretary of state, responded: "In reply to your letter of the 17th instant, I have to inform you that it is our intention to send you as Secretary of Legation to Athens, or some South American post of the same grade, the salaries of each of which have been fixed by Congress at $2,000. The examination would embrace about ten questions on the principles of International Law and a like number in diplomatic usage. If selected for Athens you would be required to make a written translation into English of an extract in modern Greek or French of an English extract. If sent to a South American country the translation would be from Spanish or French into English and vice versa." James Cabell's linguistic studies made him admirably qualified, but not even the July heat in Richmond would lead him to cut the umbilical cord. His reply was prompt, for on White House stationery dated "Oyster Bay, N.Y., July 24, 1906," he heard from William Loeb, Jr., secretary to the president: "The President requests me to acknowledge the receipt of your letter of the 23rd instant and to say he is very sorry you could not afford to take that position. As soon as your mother wrote me he began to look about for a position he thought you could take. Unfortunately, in the diplomatic service, from the highest to the lowest, the salaries are invariably inadequate, and usually disproportionally so, especially in the higher positions. It was a very real pleasure to the President to offer you the position, and he is only sorry you could not take it."

Cabell's 1906 bibliography consisted of six magazine stories: "The Sestina" in the January Harper's, "The Casual Honeymoon" in the May Ainslee's, "Actors All" in the May Appleton's, "The Housewife" in the August Harper's, "The Scapegoats" in the September Appleton's, and "The Tenson" in the December Harper's. All were republished in book form, for Cabell was determined to prevent their being buried. Doubtless Annie Cabell was again acting as her son's agent when she called at the editorial offices of Doubleday, Page in May or June. Walter Hines Page wrote Cabell on 8 June: "We were disappointed not to see you up in New York when we expected you, and we hope you will repair that omission before long. I have felt great regret—and, indeed somewhat ashamed of myself—that I was able to pay your mother no attention when she was here. This editorial life is a slave life."

In the 1906 Richmond City Directory, Dr. Cabell's name was dropped as a resident with his family at 1509 Grove Avenue, and Annie had become officially Mrs. A. B. Cabell. She had seen one of the city's leading lawyers to institute a legal separation. Dr. Cabell returned to Richmond about this time and became a resident at 619 East Franklin in quarters leased by a brother. Annie Cabell could no longer maintain the public fiction that the bonds of matrimony held firm. She testified on 19 March 1907 that Dr. Cabell had not lived with her for over ten years. Her sister Elizabeth Bowie, who had lived with her for twelve years, and nephew Thomas B. McAdams testified to the desertion. The divorce was entered into the court records on 21 March 1907. All was accomplished so quietly that even some family members were unaware that a legal separation had taken place.

At about the time his mother was granted a divorce, Cabell decided he would take his revenge on Richmond society by satirizing it in a "novel" that would expose its multiple hypocrisies. The hero of the novel is Townsend, a writer who exemplifies the philandering cad that gossip made of the reticent Cabell. Its setting, Lichfield, is clearly Richmond. Begun early in 1907 and published two years later, *The Cords of Vanity* followed its author's penchant for reworking previously published short stories, resulting in a very episodic novel. The romantic fluff of popular magazine fiction is bound together by a protagonist of Cabell's age who speaks in the first person. Much of the cement is thinly disguised autobiography, but the young man's sentimentalism keeps interfering with his irony. In the middle of the novel he observes: "When I began to scribble these haphazard memories I had designed to be very droll concerning the provincialism of Lichfield; for, as every inhabitant of the place will tell you, it is 'quite hopelessly provincial,'—and this is odd, seeing that, as investigation will assure you, the city is exclusively inhabited by self-confessed cosmopolitans. I had meant to depict Fairhaven [Williamsburg], too, in the broad style of *Cranford,* say" (106). He goes on to confess, indeed touchingly, that "Lichfield, and Fairhaven also, got at and into me when I was too young to defend myself. Therefore Lichfield and Fairhaven cannot ever, really, seem to me grotesque" (*The Cords of Vanity* [Storisende ed.], 166).

Only three stories appeared in periodicals in 1907: "In the Second April," "The Navarese," and "The Rat-Trap," in the April and May, September, and December issues of *Harper's*. Much of Cabell's writing time was given to editing another collection of *Harper's* stories that appeared under the title of *Gallantry* in October and to preparing his genealogical research on the Branch family for the printer. Handsomely designed and produced, *Branchiana* traced the ancestry of patriarch Thomas Branch to his immigrant ancestor, Christopher, and chronicled Thomas Branch's numerous and, on the whole, successful progeny. It made its appearance on 10 October, the same day as *Gallantry*, and was dedicated to John Patteson Branch, "the first to suggest its compilation and the most eminent living member of the family which it commemorates." While the Branch line qualified for "First Family" designation, it lacked an illustrious figure venerated by family memory, and the Branches seemed to fall into that middle category of respectable and pious good people, the counterpart of the "old citizens" in Richmond. To counter the gossip concerning current Branch peccadillos, "The Compiler's Foreword" is a virtuous advertising of Branch marital fidelity. Implying that the noble connections of many illustrious families were frequently the result of extralegal bed-play, the compiler notes that "the authentic forebearer of this family was merely an honest and God-fearing yeoman whose reputation is not attestedly enhanced by even the tiniest infraction of the Decalogue" (9). Only 147 numbered and signed copies of *Branchiana* were issued in the first printing, and only 30 copies in a slightly later edition. John P. Branch presented them to family and friends. The Richmond *Dispatch* for 20 October praised the work's accuracy, good taste, and style. The St. Louis *Republic* observed that despite being a genealogical work its "description of daily life among the earlier settlers [is] particularly vivid and felicitous." For *Branchiana* Cabell received two hundred fifty dollars from his uncle, somewhat less than he would have received from two stories sold to *Harper's*. But then the work salved his self-esteem, and his mother shared in the distinction of ancient lineage revealed.

Gallantry, also published by Harper and Brothers, was designed in the ornate style of *The Line of Love* and was intended to be a Christmas gift book. Commercial success for the new collection of stories was, however, denied by a financial panic that closed banks in the latter part of October

1907. Cash was hoarded and interest rates rose to 125 percent. While Cabell was piecing together *Gallantry*, he was contemplating another collection of *Harper's* stories, on a medieval theme, to be called *Chivalry*. He tells us in the "Author's Note" to the Storisende Edition of this title that again an outside force influenced the direction of his literary endeavors:

> The stories appeared in *Harper's Monthly* Magazine at irregular intervals between August 1905 and April 1907, the more thanks to the then lately perfected method of reproducing paintings in full color. For they were stories which the then famous artist Howard Pyle, at that time under an annual contract with Harper & Brothers, could more or less illustrate with brightly tinted pictures. . . .
> . . . So, after finishing the two illustrations which were to accompany *The Story of the Scabbard*, Howard Pyle sought relief from our joint paymasters, and explained to them, in the April of 1907: "I am now at the height of my powers. . . . I do not think it is right for me to spend so great a part of my time in manufacturing drawings for magazine stories which I cannot regard as having any really solid or permanent literary value."

Cabell confesses that under the gentle persuasion of H. M. Alden, he was honoring all the sacred taboos associated with good taste in a prudish era and "learning, without knowing it, just what regrettable veracities had to be gingerly skirted or ignored or lied about. . . . But, as it happened, in the very last nick of occasion, Howard Pyle requested that for the future he be given some other author to illustrate; and he thus deprived me of my six-year-old market, but he decisively preserved me from becoming an esteemed contributor to the best-thought-of American magazines of the Rooseveltian era." Cabell still placed stories with *Harper's* but with dwindling frequency.

As he spun his fantasies into the brightly illustrated stories in the better magazines, time was transforming his Grandmother Branch from the dynamic matriarch into an ancient seeress, garrulously talking of a past that was ever present. Toward the end of 1906, she disappeared from public view. Her life ended on 23 April 1908, on the eve of her seventy-seventh birthday, and a week after James Cabell turned twenty-nine. "Well, and it was then," Cabell wrote, "that forthwith I got the notion of the dear heaven of Jurgen's grandmother, into which the rejuvenated pawnbroker was to climb upon Jacob's Ladder." The many good works of Martha Patteson Branch were chronicled in Richmond's two daily newspapers, and in the custom of the day, her funeral took place in her home with burial in Hollywood Cemetery. Four of her grandsons were pallbearers along with four other relations. James and Robert Cabell were among them, and doubtless John would have been too, but he was employed in Waterbury, Connecticut.

Another family sorrow was contributing to the gloom of this period for James Cabell. Beverley Munford, the brilliant and civic-minded husband of Cabell's youngest aunt, was terminally ill with tuberculosis. His mother had died of the disease, and a life of hard work had weakened his fragile constitution. The Munfords had sojourned in Colorado Springs in 1901 and had gone to Arizona in 1906. Returning to Virginia in 1907, they rented a house first in Albemarle County and then on Hermitage Road, outside Richmond's soft-coal smoke. For the next two years, Munford devoted his time to writing *Virginia's Attitude to Slavery and Secession*, published in 1909 and favorably received. Beverley Munford continued to be a counselor to family and friends, just as he had been to young James Cabell at college. While his name continued at the head of his prestigious law firm, he took no profits from the firm because of his absence. Mary Branch Munford's stoic courage impressed her nephew, and Munford's life of service filtered into Cabell's chivalrous tales.

In his notebook of literary accounts, James Cabell wrote: "*September 23rd 1908—Nadir*," underlined in triple with blue and red ink. Perhaps he assessed the year as a low point in that he published only three stories, all in *Harper's*: "The Choices" (March), "The Scabbard" (May), and "The Ultimate Master" (November). But in the same year he placed two other stories and contracted for the publication of *The Cords of Vanity* with Doubleday, Page. In addition, his notebook shows him conceiving of other works that led into his major phase as a writer. He groups six published and unpublished stories into the nucleus of a "novel" entitled *Blood* that became *The Rivet in Grandfather's Neck* (1915). He projects a series of tales concerning the love affairs of Henry VIII. He plans two more collections of published stories in book form. He envisions a romance centered on the fairy Melusine and her husband Hugh de Lusignan, an idea that later grew into the Manuel cycle. "To make a series of embroideries upon history, all the main characters being actual and familiar personages," led to the eventual writing of *The Cream of the Jest*, which also incorporated his note "to make a series of monologues by the participants."

The career of the thirty-year-old author soon took a turn upward, the year 1909 seeing the publication of two books and four stories. *The Cords of Vanity*, published on 11 March by Doubleday, Page, absorbed six of his previously published stories. Inasmuch as all had a young lover approximately the same age as their author, the hero was a consistent personality; but because each story had, in theory, a different heroine, no one of whom detained the hero's wanderings, he was of necessity a philanderer, significantly named Townsend. Widely advertised, *Cords* was also widely reviewed and commented on. The Omaha *News* for 23 May observed, "There isn't much of a story: it is almost entirely dialogue . . . chuck full of epigrams and puns and fanciful turns of speech and wit." The more extended reviews consisted of quoted excerpts, and a large number of reviewers termed the work "tedious" and "guiltless of plot." To a modern reader's eye, it also appears guiltless of characterization. The multiple heroines bear different names and coloring, but all emerge as the prototype of the talkative female, the stock magazine heroine of the day. Elizabeth Hamlin is clearly modeled on Gabriella Moncure in physical appearance, and all the female characters had their genesis in her: collectively they represent "the woman we have all loved and lost and still dream of." The hero is accused of adopting infancy as a profession, a charge leveled by Gabriella in Williamsburg.

Cabell was not termed a salacious writer until the appearance of *Jurgen* in 1919, but *Cords* foreshadowed his later reputation. During his correspondence the previous summer with Henry W. Lanier of Doubleday, Page, Cabell expressed the desire to have this work serialized before publication in book form, just as *The Eagle's Shadow* had been. Lanier forwarded to Cabell a response he had received from R. H. Dana of the Frank A. Munsey publications. The philandering cad-hero of *Cords* drew Dana's ironic admiration, but with a reservation: "Really, Brother Lanier, do you think a family magazine ought to lay this book upon its counter? It might do in the obscurity of one's chamber (a gentlemen's chamber) but for the centre-table—IMPOSSIBLE. It will make a great book, and it will sell. But I am afraid of it for serial" (21 August 1908).

Richmonders were titillated by the biographical tidbits seeded in *Cords*. Though exemplifying the cad, Townsend deplores the decline of romance and a race of heroic men (for example, Col. James Read Branch, C.S.A.). Yellow journalism now records our vices, he remarks, but "in real life our peccadillos dwindle into dreary vistas of divorce cases and the police court." Townsend's uncle observes, "Blow, bugle, blow, and set the Wilde echoes flying!" And Cabell affects the style of that author:

"Blanche and I were just talking of you, Mr. Townsend."
"I trust you had not entirely stripped me of my reputation?"

"Surely, that is the very last of your possessions any reasonable person might covet?" (93–94)

Undisguised autobiography comes to the surface:

Depend upon it, Lichfield knew a deal more concerning my escapades than I did. That I was "deplorably wild" was generally agreed, and a reasonable number of seductions and murders and sexual aberrations was, no doubt, accredited to me.

But I was a Townsend [Cabell], and Lichfield had been case-hardened to Townsendian vagaries since Colonial days; and, besides, I had written a book which had been talked about; and, as an afterthought, I was reputed not to be an absolute pauper, if only because my father had taken the precaution, customary with the Townsends, to marry a woman with enough money to gild the bonds of matrimony. For Lichfield, luckily, was not aware how near my pleasure-loving parents had come, between them, to spending the last cent of this once ample fortune. (157–58)

For Bulmer throughout the novel read Branch. Townsend's mother is clearly Cabell's mother, and her witticism "James and I just live downstairs in the two lower stories and ostracize the third floor" is given to Mrs. Townsend. The character of Stella Musgrave too appears to be modeled on a younger Anne Branch Cabell, and her description of her Methodist grandfather is patently a portrait of Thomas Branch of Petersburg. The psychoanalysts will note that Cabell kills off both Stella and Townsend's mother. Among other biographical touches too numerous to detail here, we may note that one of the indulgent ladies observes to Townsend, "You would only be whipped by some real man, and probably shot," and Charteris, likewise a philanderer, is shot by an avenging husband.

One of the few favorable reviews of *Cords* came from the normally acerbic pen of H. L. Mencken. Writing in the June *Smart Set*, he allowed that there was "a certain flimsiness in the plan" of the work, but because of its originality and humor it stood "head and shoulders above the common run of department store fiction." Cabell possessed "the talent of a true craftsman." The seeds were sown for a later literary friendship when Mencken hailed the Richmond writer as an iconoclast who rebelled against the stultifying mores of middle-class America. Cabell probably sent the venerable William Dean Howells a copy of *Cords* along with a note, for he received a letter from Howells dated 5 November thanking the younger man for his praise.

Cabell received an advance of $145.50 for *Cords.* He was so pleased with his income for the year 1909 that he recorded the sum in a notebook. It was a record $1,311.60, in complete contrast to the "nadir" of the previous year. "The Satraps" was published by *Harper's* in April and included in *Chivalry* issued later in the year. "The Second Chance" was sold to *Harper's* for $150 and appeared in the October issue. *Red Book* purchased "A Fordyce of Westbrook" for $200 and published it in July. "His Relics" was bought for $150 and appeared in the November *Ainslee's. Harper's* acquired "The Soul of Mervisaunt" for $200 but did not publish it until April 1911. *Chivalry,* another collection of *Harper's* stories, was published 21 October and brought in $380.22 in royalties by the end of the year. Sales of *Gallantry,* the crash victim of 1907, added another $17.93 for the banner year of 1909.

Chivalry was designed as another Christmas gift book, bound in red and green, with twelve full-page color illustrations. Most were by Howard Pyle, although his name does not appear on the title page. The works of two other artists are included, owing to the defection of Pyle from the ranks of Cabell admirers. Cabell had wanted to call the collection *Dizain des Reines,* but his editors objected. In a foreword termed a "Precautional," the author attributed the ten stories to a fourteenth-century monk, Nicolas de Caen. An early Cabell named Nicolas had lived in Caen, and the game of attribution gave these stories a remove to enhance their early Renaissance settings. Gullible reviewers fell for the ruse, but a few astute historians and fellow hoaxers saw through it. Exposed, Cabell, who was ever alert to the possibilities of publicity, announced his discovered deception to the press. *Chivalry* received extended advertising and publicity; it pleased the genteel tastes of the late Victorians. Its sales brought Cabell the best royalties he had received to date.

Cabell dedicated *Chivalry* to his mother, soon to turn fifty. Below her name was appended the dedication in French: "Therefore to you madame—most excellent and noble lady, to whom I love to owe both loyalty and love—I dedicate this book." In *Cords,* Cabell had referred to his mother as a "silly, pretty woman," which had affronted sensitive reviewers. There he had presented truth in the guise of fiction. In the dedication and in the prologue of *Chivalry,* he assumed the public stance. His mother's trials in the courts of Richmond society were elevated to royal forbearance on her part: "You alone, I think, of all persons living have learned, as you have settled by so many instances, to rise above mortality in such a testing, and unfailingly to merit by your conduct the plaudits and the adoration of our otherwise dissentient world. You have sat often in this same high chair of Chance; and, in so doing, have both graced and hallowed it. Yet I forbear to speak of this, simply because I dare not seem to couple your well-known perfection with any imperfect encomium."

In January 1910, Cabell's cousin Henry Sydnor Harrison resigned as chief editorial writer for the *Times-Dispatch* and turned his efforts exclusively to literature. In that year his first novel, *Captivating Mary Carstairs*, appeared under the pen name Henry Second; by the time of its publication, he had already completed a second novel, *Queed*, which appeared the following year. *Queed* became a national best-seller, and with its Richmond setting, it awakened large numbers of Richmonders to a literary consciousness. It was certainly more to their tastes than Mr. Cabell's unpleasant *The Cords of Vanity*. The *Nation* compared it favorably to the work of Mark Twain, and the New York *Times* termed the work "altogether an unusual performance in both its interest and ability."

Though Mencken termed Harrison "a merchant of mush," Harrison may have interpreted the contemporary social scene more accurately than Cabell. The heroine of *Queed* is obviously Harrison's ideal of the "new Southern woman," a sympathetic interpreter of the past but one who works for a better future. A descendant of slave-owning aristocracy, she earns her own living. She is sentimental but also democratic in her outlook, and she lives in a healthy present. She is a heroine worthy of the respect of Mary Johnston and Ellen Glasgow, two other Richmond authors who had gained national reputations. Harrison supported the Equal Suffrage League, formed in 1909 at One West Main Street, home of Cary and Ellen Glasgow. Norvell Harrison attended meetings led by Lila Meade Valentine and Mary Johnston. While James Cabell did not attend such meetings, he read about them, and he heard querulous voices ask why his heroines could not be so relevant as his cousin's. Females in his fiction were simply clichés of the outmoded Southern Belle. He became increasingly defensive on this point and later claimed that he depicted all women from the viewpoint of a specific, admittedly chauvinistic, male.

10

The Skeleton in the Closet

1910–1912

John Cabell, four years younger than James, graduated from Virginia Military Institute with a degree in civil engineering. After serving as an instructor there for two years, he was employed in 1904 by the United States Gas Improvement Company and was stationed in various parts of the country. He never returned to Richmond to live. Robert Gamble Cabell III, two years younger than his brother James, was succeeding as a banker and stockbroker in the Branch enterprises of his cousins. Robert wooed and won the affections of Maude Morgan, a young lady of wealth whose family came from North Carolina but had lived in Richmond and New York. Twelve days before the wedding on 24 February 1910, James Cabell wrote his future sister-in-law a strangely worded letter: "I am sincerely desirous of writing you the very nicest sort of note, and my one obstacle is that I cannot think of anything to say in it. You see, if you were not, to all intent, an entire stranger, and the circumstances were not—well! what they undeniably *are*—it would be so much easier." He continued in this awkward vein, professing affection for his brother and expressing the desire to serve his wife.

The tone of the letter to Maude Morgan reflected a peculiar embarrassment. A strange request had been made to the reticent author, who seldom ventured into society. He was asked to provide a signed affidavit that he was not the murderer of John Scott, the man who Richmond gossips had assured the Morgans was his mother's lover. Annie Cabell had to make the painful confession to her incredulous son that he was indeed suspect in the social circles that mattered. Her cousin Fred Scott, brother of the murdered man, alone could attest to the fact that James was not the culprit, but Mr. Scott's private investigation into the matter had never been divulged. The Cabells knew that a signed statement from Scott should reassure anyone legitimately interested as to James Cabell's innocence. Robert could show it to his apprehensive new wife and in-laws, and the statement could be saved to allay the fears of James's and John's future brides.

Fred Scott was in New York on business when both mother and son wrote him on 1 March. Annie Cabell then departed for Atlantic City, ostensibly for her health but possibly to escape supervision of her addiction to alcohol. Her letter assured Scott that "no one of us care for any publicity—just justification." She appealed to his parental instincts and family pride: "As a man and with your own children you must recognize our request in this matter since anything hidden must reflect on your issue the light is beneficial to us all—and remember your mother was my father's sister." Cabell sent the following letter:

> 1509 Grove Avenue
> Richmond, Virginia

My dear Cousin Fred,

I have recently discovered that for the last eight years the rumor has been circulated and commonly accepted as the truth—both in Richmond and elsewhere—that it was I who in the November of 1901 murdered your brother John Scott.

You will readily conceive that such reports, however idiotic, become a serious matter when a sufficiency of scandalmongers has been found to disseminate them. This has, unluckily, been done, and the fact is my excuse for troubling you.

I am given to understand that the investigation you set afoot—eight years ago—eventually revealed the murderer, but that—for reasons with which I have no concern—it was decided to drop the matter. In a phrase, I am told that you know who the murderer was, and—in that event—can positively testify it was not I.

If so, it is my right to ask you to do as much. If so, I am requesting you to sign a statement that you absolutely know that I was not concerned in the affair. There is no necessity of straying into any byway as to who the guilty person was and so on, no thought upon my part of making such a paper public, and in fine there need be no re-opening of the matter such as would be commonly unpleasant for both you and me. . . . I ask for such a paper simply in order to be able always to demolish this idiotic charge in dealing with people who are, or may become hereafter, my immediate associates. As far as idle rumors go, I must confess to a lack of both the aspiration and the ability to deal with them.

I think you will concede, upon reflection, that what I ask is nothing more than justice.

Anticipating the favor of a reply, I remain

> Faithfully yours,
>
> James Branch Cabell
> *March 1st 1910*

Neither letter was received by Mr. Scott in New York; both were forwarded to his Richmond office. Apparently Annie's letter, addressed simply to "Mr. Scott," had been mistakenly opened by another, and Fred Scott decided to talk the matter over with his business partner, Blair Stringfellow. Scott wrote Annie in Atlantic City, and Stringfellow telephoned James simply to say that Scott was writing. Scott's letter, on business stationery, is dated 9 March 1910:

Dear Annie

Your letter of March 1st was received by me here after my return from New York where your letter was sent.

In the investigation which I made of the facts and circumstances attending the death of my brother John nothing developed that connected any member of your family with the affair. I trust however that nothing may be done to revive the discussion of a matter which must be painful in the last degree to all interested and which had better be ignored if it cannot be forgotten as I presume it has been.

> Yours truly,
>
> Fred W. Scott

Under the impression from Mr. Stringfellow's call that Scott had also written him in a letter addressed to Atlantic City, Cabell again wrote Scott a letter that was hand-delivered to 810 Park Avenue, the Scott residence.

He enclosed the following typed statement that he wished Scott to sign and promised that the statement would not be made public.

Mr. James Branch Cabell,
1509 Grove Avenue,
Richmond, Virginia

My dear James,

Having heard of certain rumors which connect your name with the death of my brother John W. Scott, I desire, in justice to you, to state that, in the thorough investigation which I made of all the facts and circumstances attending this occurrence, no reason was developed for supposing you could have any motive for, or could have played any part whatsoever in, the bringing about of this event.

I remain,
Yours truly,

March 21st, 1910

Mr. Scott elected not to sign this letter, probably feeling that his letter to Annie absolving James was sufficient. The correspondence remained in his business files until after his death; a son passed it on to Robert Cabell III many years later. Hearing nothing from Fred Scott, James Cabell wrote again on 10 April, addressing his cousin formally in a typed letter. "When Mr. Stringfellow telephoned me at your request," he explained, "I understood him to say that you had written a letter to my mother and another letter to me, both of which were addressed to Atlantic City. I now deduce that you wrote to my mother only." He assured Scott that he had been motivated "by no wish to stir up a discussion as to the circumstances of your brother's death so long as any other course was open to me. I merely asked of you a personal and explicit guarantee that there was no reason for believing me to be concerned in the affair. And I still fail to see wherein such a request can seem exorbitant."

Apparently Fred Scott asked Annie Cabell whether she had received his letter to her addressed to Atlantic City, one in which he had exonerated James of any complicity in the murder of his brother. Annie replied that she had forwarded the letter to James; "then there was the misunderstanding through Blair Stringfellow." Her letter chastized Scott: "Had you done as I first suggested had a quiet conversation with us realize our position you would have seen it was the wisest plan and in no way disagreeable to either party. . . . Both Uncle John and Mr. Munford consider James entirely correct in his plain and courteous request of you. . . . The matter has been very more far reaching than you can possibly imagine and one that only perfect frankness can eliminate."

As a result of this appeal, a copy of the Scott letter of 9 March was entrusted to Robert Cabell, the bridegroom whose new in-laws had prompted the exchange. Fred Scott made a fine distinction: a personal note to the mother of the aggrieved son was a private matter between relatives; a formal statement to James Cabell could be regarded as a document intended for public scrutiny. Mother and son were well aware of the difference. In reality they both wanted exoneration in the court of public opinion. Annie Cabell fired a final charge. She mailed it to her cousin's office and marked it *Personal*:

June third

My dear Fred

Robert has handed me the amended copy of your letter addressed to me which was first sent to Atlantic City—for which please accept my thanks. Inasmuch as Major Stringfellow drew up the same and it is not as emphatic a denial of the very disagreeable accusations as I desire I am very frank to say knowing all the facts in the case I shall not hesitate to discuss the matter with any of my friends or relatives who have my interest at heart. I consider it is only fair to write you this.

Faithfully yours

Anne Branch Cabell

The bad blood engendered between the Scotts and the aggrieved mother and son endured the rest of her short life and the remaining forty-eight years of James Branch Cabell's. His animus rose to the surface in numerous instances in his work, but not until the major phase of his writing was over and after the catharsis of many years did he refer openly to this episode in his life. In his most confessional sketches written later in life, he never could bring himself to write of Annie Cabell; the emotional umbilical cord was never severed.

Underlying the emotions of mother and son at this time was the death of Beverley Bland Munford on 31 May 1910. The man who had sacrificed his health in noble causes, especially in nourishing the welfare of those less fortunate, was a shining foil to the man who protected a dead profligate at the expense of a relative's reputation. Munford's death inspired Cabell to write a sonnet in tribute. After the funeral in Hollywood Cemetery, he walked around to 503 East Grace Street and handed the poem to his aunt, Mary Branch Munford. Some fifty years later, lines from this poem were carved on Cabell's sarcophagus.

> Today unfearingly, in Paradise
> And near the inmost court of Heaven's house,
> A gentleman to God lifts those brave eyes
> Which yesterday made life more brave for us.

A respite from family unhappiness came in the form of a trip abroad in the summer of 1910. James Ransom Branch was interested in having the ancestry of Christopher Branch, the immigrant, traced in England. Colorful Jim Branch himself epitomized the American tycoons who were lords of banking and industry. He subsidized a leisurely summer of research in British archives for his maligned, scholarly nephew. A newspaper account reports that Cabell spent "several months last summer near Abingdon-on-Thames, England, collecting and verifying facts concerning his ancestors there, in the British Museum, the New Record Office [Public Record Office?] and other centres of information." His difficulties in conducting research were later detailed in *Special Delivery*: the suspicions associated with an American who wished to see parish records, the ecclesiastical bureaucracy, the indifference of the American Embassy. "Passports were not obligatory in those days; and I had none: and nobody had ever heard of me at the Embassy," he wrote. Finally, "as a reward for knowing a well-to-do woman who lived in Berkeley Square," he obtained a reader's ticket in the British Museum Library. He was not allowed to copy records at the Probate Registry in Somerset House but was permitted to "procure official copies of all the wills I required, at eight pence the folio page." The results of Cabell's British labors were presented under the title *Branch of Abingdon* two years later. *Branchiana* had prompted numerous inquiries from Branches scattered west and south, and Cabell's scrapbooks contain a large correspondence related to family matters. Responding to these letters was time consuming and unremunerative, but Cabell's interest in genealogy must have compensated. The only significant payment for his research time came from his two maternal uncles. Rather remarkably, 1910 records no stories written or published. Cabell's creative energies were given to putting together the volume which appeared later as *The Rivet in Grandfather's Neck* but was more significantly entitled *Blood* at this time. "Bad Blood" would have been more appropriate, as an aggrieved Cabell intended its opening pages to touch brazenly on the Scott murder and his mother's divorce. A pastiche on the order of the disliked *Cords of Vanity*, it underwent a series of rejections before finding a publisher five years later. Like *Cords*, it too had its secret message to Gabriella Moncure, here the sestet of a sonnet before the final section, "Imprimis":

> I was. I am. I will be. Eh, no doubt
> For some sufficient cause, I drift, defer,
> Equivocate, dream, hazard, grow more stout,
> Age, am no longer Love's idolater,—
> And yet I could and would not live without
> Your faith that heartens and your doubts which spur.

With Robert Cabell and his bride living at the Chesterfield Apartments and John Cabell living in Savannah, Annie and James Cabell found the three-story house at 1509 Grove Avenue too large for their reduced household. Elizabeth Bowie, so long an integral part of the family, was now residing with her daughter and son-in-law at the Berkeley, a new apartment building at Harrison and Franklin streets. Apartment living was becoming fashionable in Richmond. Retainers like Louisa Nelson were being replaced with part-time help, and central heat freed one from the constant care of coal grates in chilly rooms. Annie and James Cabell moved to a spacious apartment called the Nelmar at 1811 Park Avenue, one block from the Lee Monument. Fifty-one-year-old Annie, once so beautiful and popular, had bouts of hypochondria, and family and friends sought to keep her amused and out of hospitals. Except for summers at resorts, James's social life in Richmond bore little resemblance to that of the debonair protagonists of his contemporary stories.

In the summer of 1911, Cabell again traveled to Europe to do further research on his forebears, the Cabells in France and the Branches in England. His mail was addressed in care of Humphreys and Glasgow on Victoria Street in London, a firm still in existence. Arthur Glasgow, Ellen's older brother, had married Margaret Branch, the youngest daughter of John Patteson Branch and therefore Annie's first cousin. The Arthur Glasgows consorted with the wealthy and titled in London, and Cabell acknowledged that doors had been opened for him in his genealogical search. His letters trace the course of his travels that summer. He sent a picture postcard of the Tuileries in Paris to his mother in July. Writing friends in Paris, Cabell said he had had a good channel crossing; the weather was warm. In early August his mail addressed to London was forwarded to High Street in Oxford. He bought and annotated a number of postcards of scenes in Abingdon-on-Thames, ostensibly the ancestral home of the Virginia Branches. James Ransom Branch, patron of the trip, many years later named his Palm Beach estate Abingdon. Back in London, Cabell wrote his mother a card: "Will have to sail as arranged, if only for pecuniary reasons. Have had the loveliest time—and, oh, I am so proud of your pedigree! The C— aren't in it in comparison. James." On 14 August James wrote brother Robert: "Am sailing on the nineteenth. Since there are no accommodations available in the flat shall probably go direct to Natural Bridge." On the card Robert wrote: "Suppose this means the Philadelphia which is American Line." In September Cabell's correspondence is addressed to 1813 Park, next door to the Nelmar.

From the zero level of publications for 1910, Cabell's publishing record for the next four years remained low in comparison with his record for the years when he was the star of *Harper's*, with a story appearing in nearly every issue. Three of his stories were published in 1911: "The Soul of Mervisaunt" in the April *Harper's*, "Prince Fribble's Burial" in the May *Red Book*, and "Concerning David Jogram" in the November *Harper's*. The first blossomed into *The Soul of Melicent* (1913), the second was rechristened "A Princess of Grub Street" and included in *The Certain Hour* (1916). *Branch of Abingdon*, privately published, appeared in January 1912. The only other publication that year was "The Dream," in the San Francisco *Argonaut* (23 November); it was later included in *The Certain Hour* and retitled "The Lady of All Our Dreams." On 1 May 1912, Cabell wrote an agent that he had five stories he would sell to anyone for any price.

In "The Dream," a middle-aged Cabell returns to Williamsburg as a finals speaker at William and Mary. He looks out into the audience and sees himself and Gabriella Moncure, now christened Pauline Romeyne. Charteris-Cabell and Pauline-Gabriella meet in the moonlight by the statue of Lord Botetourt. "'I wonder,' said Pauline, with that small plaintive voice which Charteris so poignantly remembered, 'whether it is always like this? Oh, do the Overlords of Life and Death *always* provide some obstacle to prevent what all of us have known in youth was possible from ever coming true?'" At midnight the former lovers part. "You will not ever quite forget me, Jack," she says, and then confesses that she still loves him: "Yes, even when you went away and there were no letters, and the days were long." He admits that he has given himself wholly to serving the dream that she awakened. "I might not dare to dissipate my energies by taking part in the drama I was attempting to re-write, because I must so jealously conserve all the force that was in me for the perfection of my lovelier version." Just when the possibility appears imminent that the two lovers can be rapturously rejoined, the illusion disappears. Gabriella under many guises weaves in and out of Cabell's writing as the untouchable woman who deprived in the moment that she gave.

During 1913 "Balthazar's Daughter" appeared in the May *Smart Set* and was also incorporated into *The Certain Hour*. *The Soul of Melicent* was published in September by the Frederick A. Stokes Company. An expansion of the *Harper's* story, it also absorbed "The Ultimate Master," a 1908 entry in the same journal. In December the Richmond writer expounded in a letter to the Boston *Herald*, "Author Discusses Public with Non Literary Taste"; it was incorporated into the "Auctorial Introduction" of *The Certain Hour*.

The Soul of Melicent is stretched to 216 pages by the insertion of colored illustrations by Howard Pyle, introductory poems to each part, an afterword, a pseudo-scholarly bibliography, and widely spaced type. It is a modern medieval romance that incorporates fantasies inspired by Gabriella Moncure. In one of her guises she is the fairy Melusine whom Perion, the hero, has loved in his youth. In their meeting, he confesses: "That I once loved you is a truth which neither of us, I think, may ever quite forget, I alone know how utterly I loved you—no, it was not I who loved you but a boy that is dead now. . . . the years are as a mist between the heart of that dead boy and me, so that I may no longer see the boy's heart clearly." Cabell dedicated *The Soul of Melicent* to his aunt Sarah Read McAdams. Widowed early, she had given a home to her mother, Cabell's grandmother, another Melusine who had guided a boy's fantasies. The book was widely reviewed, generally in favorable terms. Never again did Cabell write in so purely a romantic style. Irony and intrusive satire began to infect the romantic excursions. Accused early of being a poseur, even by Gabriella, the hero-author was increasingly subjected to critical analysis, his works becoming a mirror in which to view the emerging self.

During this period, a pause between ebb and flow in his career, Cabell was feeling the necessity of marriage and taking stock of who he truly was. The critiques of *Cords*, his most aptly named work, doubtless played their part; its irresponsible protagonist was a metaphor of vacillation. The reviewers of *Soul* admired the hero's steadfastness in the pursuit of an ideal. Both heroes were projections of the author's own persona. Indeed, Cabell perceived that while multiple protagonists wore various guises, all were facets of one ambivalent heart and mind. They spoke to him mockingly in his own voice. In the notebooks his younger self continued

to scribble poems; the more mature writer began to outline essays—
projected prefaces, justifications of the younger writer's flaws, comments
on the composite and imperfect portrait of the central I.

On page 86 of one notebook, he jotted suggestions for future works.
On the same page, he started a poem.

> In the beginning the Gods made man, and fashioned
> the sky and the sea,
> And the earth's fair face for man's dwelling place,
> and this was the Gods' decree:—
>
> "Lo, We have given to man a mind: he discerneth
> folly and sin;
> He is swift to deride the world outside, and
> blind to the world within:—"

The poem continues on the next page, where his income for 1909 is also
recorded. The poem concludes on page 88.

> So this is the song of the double-souled,
> the wail of the two in one,
> Of the wearied eyes that still behold
> the fruit ere the seed be sown,
> And derive affright for the nearing
> night from the light of the noontide sun.

This poem was included in *From the Hidden Way*, published in 1916. Also
on notebook page 88, Cabell projected another collection of stories with
the intended title of *Authority*; each story would deal with the love affairs
of an author. On the same page the creator of all these fictional authors
begins an apology. As a writer, he says, he simply desires to write perfectly
of beautiful happenings. Then a remarkable admission creeps into the
confession. At no time in his career did Cabell extol his time or environment, and as a result of not being topical in his concerns he was dismissed
by later critics as socially irrelevant. In his notebook he admits that "the
work of any man of letters is, almost always, a congenial product of his
day and environment. . . . Nor is the rationality of that axiom far to seek;
for any man of genuine literary genius, since he possesses a temperament
whose susceptibilities are of wider area than those of any other, is inevi-
tably of all people the one most likely affected by his surroundings. And
it is he, in consequence, who of all people most faithfully exhibits the
impress of his times and his time's tendencies, not merely in his writ-

ings—where it conceivably might be just predetermined affectation—but in his personality." In this self-analysis, Cabell was echoing the critical dictums of the English Romantic poets, in particular those of Shelley who compared the poet to a sensitive plant that responded to external stimuli. These ideas may have been half-remembered as the introspective author discovered their verity for himself.

This essay is followed by another poem addressed to the tillers in the field of rime. The young expend their time heedlessly, not as an allotted span for accomplishment. Cabell was arriving at his thesis, expressed often in later years, that only the young man properly essays poetry. The mature artist turns to prose as his proper craft. He realized, of course, that one carries the discipline learned in the earlier craft over into the later medium. On page 92 of the notebook, he outlined two significant works, one looking forward and one backward. "*Toward Essays (with revisions and considerable additions)*" would list his college essays on literature along with "A Modern Author (*unwritten*)" and other already published reflections on literature. This sketchy beginning of *Beyond Life* (1919) was followed in the notebook by "*Toward Letters*—nothing save the general plan." Cabell then devoted considerable space to arranging all his poems, from college days to the present, into a farewell offering to the spirits that had guided his youth—Beverley Bland Munford, the chivalrous man, and Gabriella Moncure, the lady of all our dreams.

One was dead, she yet lived. While reunion with Gabriella was still a possibility, it was hardly plausible. She would not recognize in him the boy she had known, nor would the woman approaching forty resemble the youthful wraith who troubled him nightly. Common sense told him that fantasy and reality were the opposite poles of an axis on which the world turned. Gabriella could only live in the shadows of his mind as he in hers. Though alive, she joined the beloved spirits—his grandmother, his black nurse, his gallant cousin killed at Annapolis, his chivalrous uncle. Gabriella was not really fading into oblivion; she was being accorded her proper recognition, in the inviolable regions of the heart, and the change would be reflected in his work. The grand design of that work had not yet clearly revealed itself, but it was essentially biography.

Where did biography end and fiction begin? And where did fiction end and life emerge? Sometimes, for the creator, they were indistinguishable. The exalted moments of life were fusions of fiction and reality. For nearly twelve years he had endeavored to translate those moments into the timelessness of art. Had he succeeded? There had been some small recognition, a few intelligent commendations for craftsmanship, but the mass of reviews filling his scrapbooks mindlessly repeated publisher's advertising slogans. Plot rehashes and clichés trivialized what had seemed so brave and beautiful in the small hours of the morning. Certainly there had been insignificant recognition in a monetary sense. He was hardly able to support himself, far less another. It was a sobering reflection. As he gazed into the mirror, the figure who gazed back disturbed him—the clinical scrutiny, the half-smile of mockery, the unrecognizable features. Surely, out of sight, a raven perched over the door.

He closed his eyes, sat back. It was time for more seasoned work: allegories of man, epic journeys of the spirit, probings into the alchemy of creation. His tinkling verses, his filigree stories had celebrated love, honored death, evoked tears and smiles. Marlowe, Goethe pointed the way. Shakespeare had married an older woman, sired a family, and invested money; indeed he had left a handsome estate and a legacy for posterity. Young James Cabell had borrowed Sir John Falstaff for his first *Harper's* story. Like the aging knight in that story, he would figuratively burn his love letters to Gabriella Moncure. He would publish them. Freed and gaily bedight, a no longer young man would reappear in the haunts of society, those matrimonial marts so beloved by Annie Cabell.

11

A Brown Woman

1912–1916

In *As I Remember It*, Cabell makes meeting Mrs. Shepherd at the Rockbridge Alum Springs more casual than it probably was. "Mrs. A. Branch Cabell" was also estivating there in 1912. After years of being a wandering exile to other resorts, she had returned to the scenes of her belledom, and her son was again the society reporter for the Richmond papers. Featured in his dispatches were the activities of Mrs. Emmett A. Shepherd and two of her older daughters. Widowed now for two years, Mrs. Shepherd entertained frequently, having been left a handsome estate by her late husband, a lumberman. She lived just north of Richmond at Dumbarton, in a large frame house with her five children. Richmond readers of social news were informed by the correspondent that Mrs. Shepherd especially enjoyed motor excursions to nearby resorts, and that the Misses Priscilla and Grace Shepherd were the belles of the season. The correspondent was never shy about reporting the participation of "James Branch Cabell, the Richmond author," in the activities. The costume balls, supper parties, and card parties by Mrs. Shepherd were reminiscent of Annie Cabell's lavish entertainments given twenty years earlier.

A social note of interest appeared in a dispatch dated 3 August of that summer:

"Automobile parties continue popular and especially enjoyable. One being given on Monday by Mrs. A. Branch Cabell, of Richmond, in honor of Miss Grace Shepherd, of Dumbarton. The trip was to the Hot Springs where the party lunched at the Daniel Boone Cabin, returning to the Alum in time for supper."

Grace and Priscilla Shepherd were too young to be ready for marriage, but in a few years they would be catches for an improvident fortune seeker, just as Annie Branch herself had been. Socially, a Cabell would be a catch for a Shepherd. Annie Cabell understood these things better than anyone, and so did her three boys. Robert had assured his future through marriage, John was engaged to marry well in Savannah, and James, a dangerous thirty-three, knew that he would be a fool not to strike while he still had some looks left. Indeed, he was old enough to consider matrimony with the wealthy widow herself.

James was not averse to the security of a comfortable marriage, and since passion played so small a role in his consideration, he saw the reasonableness of his mother's suggestions for marriage. But he was through with the badinage of young lovers, the inconsequential chit-chat of shallow perceptions. His eyes were drawn not to the Shepherd girls but to their mother, four-and-a-half years older than he, about the age of Gabriella. True, as a Richmond paper would observe, she was "possessed of a large fortune in her own right," but subtler forces may have led James across the lawn to meet her:

> She was sitting alone upon the trellised porch of the fifth cottage from the hotel, to the right hand side of me. I remember how, at that not inconsiderable distance, I noted the free and proud poise of her head when you saw it thus in profile. I remember how I walked across the lawn, through the prolonged shadows of sunset, in order to talk with her.
>
> I do not know what moved me to do this. I can recall only that it seemed natural, and in some vague sense it seemed inevitable, for me to be going to this woman, about whom I knew nothing at all except that she was a Mrs. Somebody-or-Other Shepherd from Somewhere. . . .
>
> What trifles we may have talked about until it was time to go in to supper at the hotel I do not recollect. But I know nowadays that, during this talk upon her cottage porch facing the sunset, I became fond of her. I began to regard her with affection. . . .
>
> As to what was her first sentiment toward me I was never told by the one person who knew anything about it. I think, though, it was curiosity. She had been forewarned by the legends of my native city, as she admitted later, that in addition to being the writer of some highfaluting books nobody ever thought of wasting any time on (when I might have kept a perfectly good

newspaper job except for my complete worthlessness), I was likewise a murderer spared only so as to prevent a family scandal, as well as being a sexual
pervert, a seducer of womanhood at large, a sponger upon my well-to-do
relatives, an habitual drunkard, and a practitioner of I, at this distance in time,
forget just what other misdemeanors. Richmond was never over gentle with
my repute. (*As I Remember It*, 3–5)

Thus somewhat airily did James Branch Cabell, the Richmond author,
depict his meeting with the woman who became his wife the following
year. In his "dispassionate" appraisal "of this slender and brown-haired
and dark-eyed woman," he noted characteristics other than her "pretti-
ness"; he observed her self-assurance, her delight in the company of others, her acceptance of people simply as people. Indeed, her unconcern
for the restrictive mores of Richmond society, or perhaps her ignorance
of them, recalled the innocence of Annie Cabell in earlier days. She really
needed someone to protect her. While this woman's talk was not teas-
ingly romantic or remotely literary, its casual intimacy awakened in him
the contentment he had felt as a young poet at the feet of Gabriella. If
marriage with this brown-eyed woman would not exactly be reunion
with the weaver of spells, it would have symbolic logic. An aging poet
could start anew with a woman who was the same age and bore a beguil-
ing resemblance to his earlier love. He was faithful to the type. No
younger enchantress had troubled his heart.

As Cabell grew fond of Priscilla Bradley Shepherd and the practicality of
marrying a woman of means impressed itself, he debated the implications
in his work, that extended diary of his inner life. The first of the two
stories he wrote at this time was "The Dream," published in late November 1912. This allegorical goodbye to Gabriella Moncure refers to her replacement, jarringly, as was usually the case when Cabell allowed reality
to enter his fantasies. When the lovers in the story confess that neither
has married, Pauline-Gabriella questions the response of Charteris-Cabell,
who in turn wonders, "Now, how in heaven's name, could a cloistered
Fairhaven have surmised his intention of proposing on the first convenient opportunity to handsome, well-to-do Anne Willoughby?"

Continuing in this autobiographical vein, the author—"weary of loneliness" and disheartened by his parodies of the Dream—confesses to
disillusionment.

Having said farewell to past associations, the Richmond author then
started "A Brown Woman," his first of many stories inspired by Priscilla
Bradley. Mrs. Shepherd is metamorphosed into a shepherdess, beloved
by a world-weary, grubbing poet, oddly Mr. Alexander Pope. In his breast,

love replaces the desire to write beautifully of beautiful happenings, even if it means a step down in the social scale. A storm ensues, paralleling the interior turmoil; lightning strikes, killing the beloved and her rustic swain. The poet returns to his writing, philosophically. Transient life is simply the raw material of art.

Contemplating marriage, even to one who would be able to support him, meant that James Cabell needed money for the actual event—clothes, rings, honoraria, wedding trip. In 1903 he was listed in the Richmond City Directory as "bookkeeper"; and now nine years later, necessity had led him to accept a somewhat similar position with his Uncle Jim's business in West Virginia. James Ransom Branch had financed the writing of *Branch of Abingdon*, which appeared early in 1912. A colorful baron of the Gilded Age, Uncle Jim had coal-mining interests in the remote fastness of Branchland, West Virginia. Isolation from all civilized society was no deterrent for a man like Cabell who flowered socially only in the summer, and he could save his money there. Cabell later referred to having worked in the coal mines, a myth accepted by the gullible. The winter of 1912–13, however, must have been a lonely time in Branchland, situated on the Guyandot River in rugged mountains. There he corresponded with reviewers and readers who liked his work, and he sent out his unsold manuscripts to various publishers. In January 1913, he put the finishing touches to a collection of stories he then called "At a Certain Hour." At this time he destroyed "a well-nigh completed novel," one beginning in Abingdon, England, where he researched the Branch lines in 1911, and ending "at Natural Bridge in Virginia." This work incorporated legends concerning Pocahontas and satirized the myths compounded by her soi-disant real-life descendants, the Bollings and the Randolphs. He then turned to a modern romance appropriate to his mountain isolation, *The Strength of the Hills*. It had as its hero "George Bulmer who appears, not very importantly, in the *Cords of Vanity*, as Mr. Townsend's uncle." His employer, James Ransom Branch, was the model for this character. "In the background of the comedy was a most regrettable story of embezzlement and incest; Dame Venus herself, that lady of the hollow hill [who was now resident among hills less completely hollow, in that they were merely tunneled for coal mining] figured in the story." Uncle Jim may have supplied the plot, but this endeavor too was destroyed the following year.

When youngest sibling, John Cabell, married Anna Elizabeth Bell of Savannah on 22 April 1913, James did not go. Robert Cabell was his

younger brother's best man, and Mrs. Anne Branch Cabell was in attendance. Social events usually relieved her spells of hypochondria. May
saw the appearance in *Smart Set* of a short story, "Balthazar's Daughter,"
penned in the high, melodramatic style of earlier stories; hero and heroine renounce power and wealth for love. Before the lovers turn into the
forest, they gaze out over the civilization they are leaving behind. "It is a
very rich and lovely land," says the hero, "this kingdom which a half hour
since lay in the hollow of my hand." James Cabell himself had not re-
nounced the comforts of affluence, but he had determined to enter the
forest. Like Siegfried and other mythic heroes, he would draw the sword
Nothung ("Need") and become a man. That sword, symbol of phallus
and honor, as wielded by Jurgen, redeems the creator of a literary kingdom. From the fairy tales of childhood, which deal simplistically and optimistically with problems of growth, James Cabell moved into the darker
area of myth, in the main pessimistic and reflecting adult psychology.

In the summer of 1913 Mrs. A. Branch Cabell and her oldest son were
again at the Rockbridge Alum Springs, as were Mrs. Emmett A. Shepherd
and her daughters Priscilla and Grace and her niece Louise Shepherd.
Grace Shepherd entertained the VMI cadets whose summer school was
held at the resort; sixty guests were seated in bowers on the lawn. When
the cadets gave a german for the young ladies, Louise Shepherd was chosen to lead. Also in residence was a sister of Irene and Nancy Langhorne,
Mrs. Moncure Perkins, who referred to herself as "Mrs. Obscure Perkins."
Everyone noted Mr. Cabell's friendship with the vivacious widow, Mrs.
Shepherd.

The publication of *The Soul of Melicent* in September gave the Richmond
author's self-esteem a boost. Back in Branchland, he sent out complimentary copies to all who had given him a kind word. This work was an old-
fashioned romance, safe enough to send to the venerable editor of *Harper's.* Though H. M. Alden had caviled at episodes in the stories published
by his own firm, he was still an eminence in the publishing world, one
who could wave a magic pen over Cabell's moribund career.

The year 1913 was a remarkable one in Virginia letters. Ellen Glasgow's
Virginia, Mary Johnston's *Hagar,* and Henry Harrison's *V. V.'s Eyes* all treated
the Southern Belle with philosophical and critical scrutiny. Was she the
victim or the victimizer? She was both, all three authors agreed. Harrison's
heroine in particular could have been modeled on Annie Cabell. Also
living in Richmond was another writer (and another Cabell cousin) who
published in 1913. Unlike the feminists, Ellen Wilkins Tompkins, known

as Nellie, catalogued the old-fashioned virtues of self-sacrifice and the power of dreams. *The Egotistical I*, published by Dutton, occupied a middle ground between Cabell's outright romanticism and the realism of Johnston, Glasgow, and Harrison. She autographed his copy "For James Branch Cabell—/my literary adviser/from Ellen Wilkins Tompkins."

When the engagement of James Branch Cabell and Priscilla Shepherd was announced in the Richmond *Times-Dispatch*, the article featured a large portrait of the thirty-four-year-old bridegroom-to-be rather than the future bride. Headed "Richmond Author to Marry," it detailed Cabell's ancestry and literary career. Both the New York *Times* and New York *Herald* noted the approaching nuptials (24 October); the *Times* gave the bride the place of honor: "Mrs. E. A. Shepherd to Wed Novelist." The accounts of the wedding in the Richmond papers accorded the bride equal social recognition. In one, the pen of the bridegroom is apparent: "She was Priscilla Bradley, daughter of William Joseph Bradley, of the old and distinguished family of that name of Charles City County. Everybody in Richmond, and probably every visitor there, knows her handsome residence, Dumbarton, just outside the city, where she dispenses so much of the royal hospitality for which the chatelaines of the South are famous, and which she can do so well, as her beauty and agreeable personal qualities are aided, if that were possible, by a large fortune in her own right."

The *News-Leader* for 8 November 1913 reported the nuptials under the large heading of "Society" with the subheading "Wedding of Mrs. Shepherd, of Dumbarton, to James Branch Cabell Took Place Today":

> A wedding of the greatest interest to society took place this morning at 11:30 o'clock, when Mrs. Priscilla Bradley Shepherd, widow of the late Emmett Albin Shepherd, and daughter of William Joseph Bradley, of Charles City County, became the wife of James Branch Cabell, the well-known writer of this city. The wedding was quietly celebrated owing to a recent bereavement in the bridegroom's family, and was witnessed only by the immediate relatives and a few intimate friends. The Rev. Ernest E. Osgood, assisted by the Rev. Walter Russell Bowie, officiated, and the ceremony took place at the bride's home in Dumbarton, near this city.
>
> Mrs. Shepherd wore a handsome brown traveling costume, and her only ornament was a necklace of topazes formerly owned by the bridegroom's ancestress, the wife of Lieutenant Pride, of the Third Virginia Line in the Revolution. The matron of honor was the bride's sister, Mrs. Edgar B. Walters, of Garden City, L.I. Robert Gamble Cabell, III, attended the bridegroom as best man, and the other attendants included Beverley B. Munford and Miss Priscilla Shepherd of Garden City, L.I.

A special train leaving Elba at 10:35 conveyed the RICHMOND guests to the wedding. The wedding journey will include a motor tour of the Northern states, and Mr. and Mrs. Cabell will be at home after Dec. 1 at Dumbarton.

Even before marriage, Cabell had started recreating the public perception of Mrs. Shepherd, shifting it from her secretarial days and her middle-class first marriage to a more genteel emphasis on her plantation roots in Charles City County. Once installed in his second-floor study at Dumbarton, he began research into his wife's ancestry, intent on transforming her from "not anybody in particular" in Richmond into a Virginian with first-family roots. "I am not denying that Richmond—in 1913, I mean, of course—was snobbish; nor that, more or less anyhow, I was a by-product of Richmond," he wrote. The first half of *As I Remember It* (1955) recounts his happy labors in his wife's transformation. The more immediate results were *The Majors and Their Marriages* (1915), discreetly sent to all the arbiters of social rank in the commonwealth. Cabell also began to work on his wife's diction, that other criterion of family background. Her speech, rife with the homely colloquialisms endemic to the South, he would claim to be uniquely that "spoken in Charles City County since 1619." This exaggeration for her clichéd idioms may have been his psychological approach in persuading her to adopt a choice of metaphors more in keeping with her position as Mrs. James Branch Cabell. A new being of poise, speaking a genteel diction, emerged to the delight of her new husband. He was quite conscious of his role as Pygmalion, the necromancer. It would be pleasant to report that Cabell's transformation was wholly successful. Those who got to know Percie Cabell and her maternal ways grew to love her, but there were critical Richmonders who averred that she used her new husband to advance her daughters' social position. Her unconcern for literary matters affronted a few, and her democratic ways with everyone earned her sniffs from the neurotically snobbish. Ellen Glasgow termed her "kind, tolerant, civilized"; Emily Clark called her "common."

Cabell's marriage and his removal to Dumbarton meant a drastic change in his living arrangements. While he was allotted the triple-windowed room over the front door as his retreat, he could hear the sounds of an active family below.

I have contended also that when I married an extremely strong-willed widow with five children, for four of whom a continual argufying (as Charles City termed it) was their pet diversion, I ought to have been awarded the Carnegie medal for bravery. . . .

Now of these five children, the oldest one—born upon West Avenue, and called Isabelle, which was after Mr. Shepherd's mother of course, and she really was just the brightest baby that you ever saw anywhere—had been stricken, when barely three years old, with infantile paralysis. After which she developed into girlhood as a witless and inarticulate fragment of wreckage, unable to move the lower half of her body. And, in consequence, Isabelle had to be fed and tended by her Negro nurse, large, blatant, large-voiced Martha Cousins, who intended to be made simply a door mat of by no white folks anywhere so long as she was able to walk straight out of this house.

Never at any time after my wife's second marriage, it may be added, did Martha Cousins consent to speak of or to address my wife except as Mrs. Shepherd. And never during my earthly existence have I been hated so actively, or so wholly without concealment, as by Martha Cousins during the years that followed my marriage.

But otherwise, I believe, I fitted smoothly enough into the extensive family circle which I had acquired overnight; and my four other stepchildren—from a perplexed unease as to the so very many dreadful things which Martha Cousins predicted, volubly and without any cessation, I was going to do to them right off when once that crazy mother of theirs had simply killed herself by marrying me—the children, I repeat, passed from a reserved suspicion into tolerance, and thence, I think, into a fair amount of affection. That was my wife's doing, I know, for she managed everyone of us—even Martha Cousins, almost—forthrightly, with tact, blandly, unswervingly. (*As I Remember It*, 17–18)

With Cabell busy tracing his wife's pedigree, in 1914 he had his lowest publication record since 1901. One article was his sole output: "On the Mercifulness of Being Vital," published in the Richmond *News-Leader* in May. In debating whether style or subject most interested a reader of modern fiction, the essayist revealed that his wife would choose the latter, preferring stories about automobile trips; "she is an ardent automobilist." Besides making over his wife's appearance and social graces, the mythmaker waved his wand over their "anonymous house." Old portraits, antiques, bric-a-brac replaced the furniture-store decor. "Our stage setting, in brief, became notable." Long hours were given to painting colorful, elaborate multiquartered coats of arms of his wife's ancestry, which he hung over the mantelpiece in the large, square entrance hall. This room had been made into the equivalent of a nobleman's medieval hall, wherein all the trophies of a glorious past were displayed. "So then did I create Priscilla Bradley Cabell, along with Dumbarton Grange."

In July 1914 Mr. and Mrs. James Branch Cabell were in their own cottage on Kentucky Row at the Rockbridge Alum Springs. They gave a dansant at the Casino in honor of their daughter Virginia Shepherd and entertained Richmond friends at a swimming pool party followed by a luncheon. Mr. and Mrs. Cabell were among the few who had their own automobiles at the resort. The driver of the sports roadster was always the efficient Mrs. Cabell; her writer-husband never touched the wheel, though he did learn to open and close the garage door. The last week in July, the newlyweds were invited to spend a week at the White Sulphur visiting the venerable John P. Branch. On 9 October 1910, the Richmond *Times-Dispatch* had given Branch an extensive encomium on his eightieth birthday, calling him "one of the foremost citizens of Richmond." He doubtless approved of the friendly, efficient woman his great-nephew had married. That her first husband had been a successful lumberman was no social stigma in his eyes. On their return to the Alum, the Cabells were hosts to the VMI cadets. When the cadets entertained the guests at the resort, Mrs. Cabell was asked by the resplendent marshall to lead the dance with him. Also at that dance was a young lady of twenty from Richmond, Margaret Freeman, who was escorted by Thomas Branch Scott, Jr. One wonders if Priscilla Cabell met the woman who would become the second Mrs. James Branch Cabell thirty-six years later. Antipathy for Scott cousins may have prevented James Cabell from meeting his young cousin's date.

While Cabell decorated, did genealogical research, and integrated himself into his wife's family, he also attempted to clean out his files of unsold manuscripts. Entries in his notebook are quoted verbatim below. Ever mindful of Forman's admonition concerning the ephemeral fame associated with magazine fiction, he was determined to see all his short stories in book form.

"*At a Certain Hour*"—finished January 1913; rejected by Frederick A. Stokes Company January 1914; rejected by Charles Scribners' Sons April 1914; rejected by Harper and Brothers, May, 1914; rejected by Mitchell Kennerley May, 1914; rejected by Houghton Mifflin Company June, 1914; rejected by Henry Holt and Company, July 1914; rejected by Dodd, Mead and Company August 1914; rejected by John Lane Company September 1914; by J. B. Lippincott Company, October 1914; by G. P. Putnam Sons November 1914; by the Macmillan Company December 1914; accepted by McBride, Nast and Company March 1915; published 4 November 1916.

Cabell was likewise determined to see his college poetry issued in a bound volume, even if he had to pay for it. This early work, associated with Gabriella Moncure, was close to his heart, and it was a part of the biography. It represented his awakening into the dream world that had absorbed him ever since their parting. If Descartes could say "I think therefore I am," he could say with equal assurance "I dream therefore I exist"—but only if every phase of the dream was published.

"*Echoes from the Hidden Way*"—finished 1913; Richard Badger Company offered to publish it for $465.00, October 1913; Moffat, Yard and Company for $285.00 March 1914; rejected by Harper and Brothers April 1914—as previously by Stokes Company and Putnam Company—on any royalty basis; by Houghton-Mifflin Company May 1914; by John Lane Company May 1914; by Mitchell Kennerley August 1914; by Sherman, French and Company, October 1914; by Seymour, Daughaday and Company April 1915; accepted by Robert M. McBride and Company April 1916; published 18 November 1916.

Cabell had finished the work published under the title *The Rivet in Grandfather's Neck* in 1911. The protagonist in this work, Colonel Rudolph Musgrave, is an unlikely hero, a genealogist; but as Cabell observed, life imitates art, and he found himself in the amusing position of Colonel Musgrave in elevating his wife's social position. Cabell's scrapbooks contain letters of rejection for this rambling, unfocused work. Because it too contained a large amount of diffused biography, however, Cabell felt that it had to be published. The notebook records that *The Rivet in Grandfather's Neck* was "rejected by Charles Scribner's Sons July 1914; by the Century Company August 1914; by Doubleday, Page and Company September 1914; by Houghton Mifflin Company October 1914; by George H. Doran Company January 1915; by Bobbs-Merrill Company April 1915; accepted by McBride, Nast and Company June 1915; published by Robert M. McBride and Company 13 October 1915."

A few yards east of Cabell's study at Dumbarton Grange, the trains of the Richmond, Fredericksburg and Potomac Railway thundered past. Only commuter trains stopped where east-west Dumbarton Road crossed the tracks. Express trains hurtling north snatched with an iron hook mailbags that hung from "a sort of gibbet beside the track." As old manuscripts wended their way north and returned, a new manuscript was emerging in the confines of the triple-windowed study. The prosaic rituals of domestic life with his wife and stepchildren were tinged with irreality, contrasting strangely, indeed disturbingly, with the more real intensity of his dreaming. Something that had been buried within was forcing its way into his conscious perceptions. The life of illusion was more dynamic than pallid reality. His previous urge to capture a lost dream inspired by Gabriella Moncure was perhaps doomed to failure. You could not touch a dream without destroying it. On the other hand, an analysis of the demiurge that underlay creation might bear fruit. Reality was itself an illusion. By juxtaposing passages of mundane reality with those inspired by the demiurge, he could demonstrate which was the more dynamic, which in truth had led human beings out of the primitive world of primates into civilization. Begun in 1913, this manuscript grew through 1914. With the arrival of 1915, it too began to make pilgrimages to the north. Also rejected at first, it became, in the words of its author, "the most potent of all my books in its influence upon my career as a writer."

Each of the notebook citations above are brief résumés of Cabell's career: he at long last found his publisher, his dogged perseverance resulting in a meeting with the editor he would term "co-author," the collaborator who would spank his moribund works into life. He had passed through a vale of rejection by those who had looked favorably on his work in the past and also by others, the prestigious and the less so. On his carefully maintained list of publishing houses, he had arrived at the name McBride, Nast and Company. On 2 January 1915, he wrote an autograph letter:

Gentlemen:

I am today submitting via parcel post what to cursory inspection looks like a volume of short stories. I do not think it is a volume of short stories, for reasons I have stated at some length in the book's "Auctorial Introduction." Still, knowing that collected short stories are to publishers anathema marantha, I am offering, as a possible makeweight toward this book's acceptance, a speedy option upon a long modern novel. I would suggest, in passing, that possibly some of these stories—Nos. 1, 3, 4, 6, 7, or 8—might be available for the new *Lippincott's*. But at all events I would be pleased to hear if this proposition in any way interests you—and am

> Yours faithfully
> James Branch Cabell

While Cabell awaited a response to this letter, a matter of more immediate concern dominated his thoughts. His mother's health took a turn for the worse. This time it went beyond hypochondria. Annie Cabell was then living in the Shenandoah, a six-story apartment building on the corner of Allen and Grace streets in Richmond. Annie's illness necessitated bed-care and supervision. After the death of her husband, Mary Munford had returned to living in the beautiful Abram Warwick House at 503 East Grace Street, built in 1834, "the first real Greek Revival mansion built in Richmond." Mary Munford had her sister brought there in order to care for her. Annie Cabell died at the Warwick House on Sunday, 14 February 1915, at 7:50 in the evening. The funeral was held at the Munford home with her nephew Russell Bowie officiating, and she was interred in Hollywood Cemetery next to her parents. The obituaries in the *Times-Dispatch* and the *News-Leader* were brief, listing her three sons, three sisters, and brother as survivors. No mention was made of Dr. Cabell, then superintendent of the City Home. Her funeral took place at noon. At 3:30 Mrs. James H. Dooley entertained at cards at Maymont, Mrs. Archer Anderson was at home at 103 West Franklin from 4:00 to 7:00, and the Woman's Club held its February Card Tournament at 8:15 in the evening.

Annie Cabell was dead at the age of fifty-six. Her oldest son knew that people did not die of broken hearts, but he also knew that a happy, child-like spirit had been saddened in her later years. Like many neurotics, Annie Cabell had centered her unhappiness on another person, not on her husband but on her cousin Fred Scott. He had held the key to her social redemption in Richmond; he had refused, however, to reveal the identity and motive of his brother's murderer. John Scott had been killed for philandering with another woman, not her. It was true that she smoked, and as her son James would observe, "no virtuous woman smoked." She had also been frivolous, but belles had always been forgiven that shortcoming. And though she had divorced her husband, he had abandoned her. She had been less hypocritical in her pleasures than most women in her position. Now the bright, light child-woman's most diverting chat was stilled, and the silence underscored her oldest son's own sense of lost youth. His hair was thinning; a waist-line uncurbed by exercise was expanding.

Outwardly stoic, inwardly in turmoil, the son felt guilt that he had been critical of his mother. Even now it was impossible to consider her objectively; head and heart would always be divided. She entered into the oeuvre at a remove. His Grandmother Branch, his Grandfather Cabell, Gabriella Moncure, and Charles Coleman could freely enter and speak in their own voices. But Annie, a lady of joys and sorrows, of annoying and endearing imperfections, harbored griefs expressed and inexpressible; she was a character in a Glasgow novel, the Southern Belle, victim and victimizer. Her son, however, could not read her like a novel. What she felt, he felt. Pain, unreasoned empathy, cannot be objectified. Later, in

Annie's clearest projection, in *The High Place*, Melior gives birth to her child, figuratively James Branch Cabell, but she is immediately transported back to the high place where beauty and holiness abide, safe from disillusioning contact with reality.

The following month Cabell's novelist cousin was reacclaimed Richmond's very own Henry James. Although Henry Sydnor Harrison's fourth novel, *Angela's Business*, was a feminist tract in the guise of fiction, its comedy of manners was played out in a setting recognizable to local readers. Like Mrs. James Cabell out at Dumbarton, Angela Flowers drives her roadster down Washington Street (Franklin) and Center (Main). The hero is writing a great new novel on the emancipated woman, and he gradually learns to distinguish between the natural woman, Mary Wing, independent and self-supporting, and the woman who pretends to be feminine, Angela Flowers, whose "business" is getting herself married. Angela as the "Womanly Woman," a term burlesqued by Ellen Glasgow in *The Miller of Old Church* (1911), is a choice creation; she totally rejects the idea of work outside the home, for that would unsex her: "In short, how to get money without working for it. That truly, was the great question confronting every nice girl, every womanly woman." It was also a problem for some men, and Cabell had solved it in the same manner as Angela, with marriage.

Then Cabell received a reply to his letter of 2 January to McBride, Nast and Company. The response to this letter was encouraging enough to lure the reclusive author to New York. On 15 April 1915, his thirty-seventh birthday, he visited the McBride editorial offices on Sixteenth Street, bearing in his portfolio the manuscripts of four works: *The Rivet in Grandfather's Neck*, *The Certain Hour*, *From the Hidden Way*, and *In the Flesh*. The young man who greeted him was Guy Holt and their rapport was immediate, each finding in the other an alter ego. The Cabell-Holt collaboration lasted over a fruitful ten-year span.

> Holt was throughout this period the literary editor of the publishing firm of Robert M. McBride & Company; and when I first heard from him, in the April of 1915, he had but newly turned twenty-three. This youthfulness may well have accounted for the enthusiasm with which he then accepted an oddly entitled novel, *The Rivet in Grandfather's Neck*, after that story had been rejected by I know not how many publishers beyond the fact that they in numerousness exceeded thirteen.
>
> I met him in that same April; and we, as they say, took to each other at once. (*As I Remember It*, 184–85)

Like Cabell, Holt had been something of a scholarly wunderkind, but he had not chosen a reclusive role in life. Boston born, he had attended public schools in New York, had taken classes at Columbia College, and had entered the publishing business at seventeen. After five years with Doubleday, Page & Company, "he edited two magazines, first *Lippincott's* and then *McBride's*. He was in charge of the book, editorial, and sales departments at McBride's from 1917 to 1926."

Not since his college days had Cabell enjoyed such an uninhibited exchange of literary ideas. Charles Washington Coleman had been reincarnated in Guy Holt, and Charteris, the garrulous literary persona who intrudes into Cabell's works, echoes the esthetics of all three men. But Holt was the needed antidote to Coleman's escapism. While James Branch Cabell spun his dreams into the stuff of literature, as Dorothy Scura underlines in her essay "Cabell and Holt":

> Holt was a pragmatic, active man who understood "the whole Art of the Book" from composition to manufacture, promotion, and distribution. Too, Holt possessed an instinctive sensitivity to literature as well as editorial talent, critical and creative. He was described in a high tribute as having the faculty for never "mistaking literature for merchandise, or the even more common publisher's error of mistaking merchandise for literature." The intelligent, sensitive, and energetic Holt was just the editor the obscure Virginia writer needed. Their mutual love of writing gave them common ground for a profound relationship, but their differences made them a compatible team. (41)

While Cabell rejoiced in his encouraging new relationship with an understanding editor, opening the prospect of renewed life in his faltering career, he was also feeling a growing sense of personal renewal. His wife was pregnant. This baby was symbolic of the future. An unhappy past had died with Annie Cabell; a psychological cord had been cut. His child would redeem his manhood. His stepchildren addressed him as "Mr. Cabell," but with the birth of a half-brother named Cabell, perhaps his acceptance as a paternal presence would become complete.

The Cabell-Shepherd ménage repaired to cool Rockbridge Springs in July 1915 but returned to Dumbarton on the 23rd. With their mother soon to give birth to her sixth child, the Shepherds were sent to summer camps and to visit with their aunt in Long Island, Grace Bradley Walters, married to a wealthy businessman, Edgar B. Walters. The house at Dumbarton, a large frame structure, was at least a cooler place than Richmond to live. A wide deep porch extended across the front with a porte-cochere on the west and a screened side porch on the east. Out of the eyes of society, Percie Cabell could wear the loose maternity dresses dictated by the heat and her advanced pregnancy. Even so, she did not give up all social intercourse. In *As I Remember It*, Cabell wrote of the sudden arrival of the baby in the early morning hours of 23 August after an evening spent at a neighbor's with his wife driving the car.

Ever conscious of the social importance of names, James Branch Cabell had determined to name the new arrival Ballard Hartwell, thus honoring two of the distinguished lines he had discovered in his wife's lineage. Although the night of the birth had been spent in nervous anxiety, summoning doctor and nurse and attending mother and child, when day came the new father dispatched telegrams and wrote notes to family and friends. Ballard Hartwell Cabell would heal all family divisions, beginning with grandfather Dr. Robert G. Cabell, Jr. That hitherto remote gentleman was among the first to arrive at Dumbarton to pay his respects to mother and child. Annie Cabell's garrulous banker brother, James Ransom Branch, came with his wife. The new babe slept in an ancestral cradle. In a note penned 22 December 1904, Martha Patteson Branch had decreed that the cradle in which all her children had slept was to become the property of her oldest grandson upon the birth of his first child. It had been in the keeping of Mary Branch Munford, whose own two babes had had their turns as occupants.

Ballard Hartwell Cabell was christened 11 December in Emmanuel Episcopal Church, Brook Hill, by the rector, the Reverend Ernest Earle Osgood. It was the Shepherds' church; Mr. Shepherd was buried in its cemetery, and Cabell had officially become a member in his quest for civic approval. Ballard's sponsors in baptism were his Presbyterian grandfather, Dr. Cabell; his uncle Robert G. Cabell III; his great-aunt Lillian Branch, wife of James Ransom Branch; and his half-sister Priscilla Shepherd. Three great-aunts were in attendance: Bell Cabell Lottier, Nannie Enders Cabell, and Sallie Branch McAdams, the latter accompanied by a young granddaughter, Louise Withers.

The year 1915 also recorded a resurgence in Cabell's literary production. "Vitality in Vogue," appeared in the *Sewanee Review* in January; it was later incorporated into *The Certain Hour*. The ideas expressed in this essay were developed more fully in *Beyond Life*, but here Cabell was already attacking the realists in fiction: "First-class art never reproduces its surroundings," and "Modernity of scene, of course, is almost always fatal to the permanent worth of fictitious narrative." This from an admirer of Dickens. Then the newspapers full of war news from Europe turned his thoughts to another war in which his father and grandfather had fought. "Aprilis Gesta," a sonnet, appeared in the Richmond *News-Leader* on 3 April and in the Richmond *Times-Dispatch* on 30 May. Another war-inspired poem appeared in the August *Poetry* as "Post Annos"; in *From the Hidden Way* it is called "One End of Love." In this latter poem a French Crusader returns from thirty years of fighting the heathen to meet an old love; her son has gone to fight the English at Calais. France and England, Cabell and Branch, love and death—it was a recurring pattern.

Then the McBride Company accepted Cabell's proposal to publish the stories in *The Certain Hour* first in periodicals. Five of the stories appeared in 1915: "Belhs Cavaliers," "Judith's Creed," and "A Brown Woman" in the June, July, and August issues of *Lippincott's*; "Pro Honoria" and "The Irresistible Ogle" in the September and October issues of *McBride's Magazine*.

The Rivet in Grandfather's Neck was published by McBride on 13 October. Although this title incorporated five previously published stories, militating against any cohesion, Cabell had intended saying something in the work. On a note card he had jotted ideas he wanted to embody in what he intended as a novel of manners: "older society," "famous beauties," "the mulattoes," "mulattress as Nemesis (?unknowingly)," "portraits of their ancestors must be about them, as actually present." McBride gave *Rivet* extensive advertising, and its title page designation of "A Comedy of Limitations" gave reviewers their clue. It was a novel of "the New South"; it was a satire of "the Old South." Cabell gave the place of honor in his scrapbook to the review from the *Morning Union* (Springfield, Mass.), 15 October 1915, which proclaimed in bold type "JAMES BRANCH CABELL WRITES HIS BEST BOOK." In a publication announcement, the Richmond *News-Leader* proclaimed in equally bold type "James Branch Cabell Breaks His Literary Silence With Love Song," referring to the dedicatory sonnet to Priscilla Bradley Cabell. The New York *Times* complimented the substance of the novel but had reservations about the morals of the characters. The work, it said, was "one that does not yield up its significance upon a single reading" (28 November). The *Nation* for 18 November, in a review headed "Romantic Realisms," was complimentary about what Cabell had attempted: "He fain would dissect your old-fashioned Southern gentleman—and then put him together again, turn him inside out, and yet keep him a hero, shatter illusion and retain partiality—in short, he proposes in one and the same book to exercise the acumen of an Ellen Glasgow and indulge the sentiments of a Thomas Nelson Page."

Patriarch Thomas Branch (1802-1880), with second wife Anne Adams Wheelright, twenty-five years his junior. He had thirteen children by his first wife and three by his second. He was James Branch Cabell's great-grandfather through the patriarch's second son, James Read Branch (1828-1869) for whom Cabell was named. *Courtesy Cabell Library and Maurice Duke*

Right: Anne Harris Branch (1859-1915), Cabell's mother, as a girl in mourning for her father. On the back of a copy of this photograph she wrote: "Most beautiful of all Branches." *Courtesy Cabell Library and Maurice Duke*

Below: Martha Louise Patteson Branch (1831-1908), James Branch Cabell's redoubtable grandmother, in the days of her affluent widowhood during the 1870s. *Courtesy Cabell Library and Maurice Duke*

Left: Robert Gamble Cabell, Jr. (1847-1923), father of James Branch Cabell. *Courtesy Priscilla Harriss Cabell and Maurice Duke*

Below: 101 East Franklin Street, Richmond, Virginia, in the late `20s. The house of Cabell's grandmother, Martha Patteson Branch, where he was born on the 3rd floor, 14 April 1879. At one time the grounds of this house occupied half a city block. Now the Richmond Public Library occupies almost the entire block. *Courtesy Cabell Library and Maurice Duke*

Right: James Branch Cabell, age four years and five months, 28 September 1883. His next birthday party, on 14 April 1884, was at his grandmother's where he was dressed as Jack, the son of Mother Goose, the latter played by young Miss Gabriella Moncure.
Courtesy Cabell Library

Below: Louisa Nelson, the Cabell nurse for James, Robert, and John Cabell, taken in the early 1890s.
Courtesy Cabell Library and Maurice Duke

Left: John and Robert Cabell, younger brothers of James, in a photograph probably taken at the same time as Louisa Nelson's. *Courtesy Cabell Library and Maurice Duke*

Below: Gabriella Brooke Moncure, seated second from right, with a group of her classmates at Miss Gussie Daniel's School, 1891. *Courtesy Valentine Museum, Richmond*

Right: James Branch Cabell
in 1893, photographed in
Chicago at the World's Fair.
This is the youth who
entered William and Mary
the following year at fifteen.
Courtesy Cabell Library

James Branch Cabell (standing second from right) as a sophomore (late 1895) at
William and Mary in a photograph of members of the Kappa Alpha Order. His
older mentor-friend Otis Bland stands at far right. *Courtesy Virginia Historical
Society*

Above: Charles Washington Coleman (1862-1932) in a drawing dated 1910, when he was forty-eight, twelve years after his and Cabell's parting in Williamsburg. *Courtesy Maurice Duke*

Left: James Branch Cabell (circa 1906), author of *The Eagle's Shadow* and short stories in the better popular magazines. *Courtesy Cabell Library*

Right: Priscilla Bradley Shepherd
(Mrs. Emmet A. Shepherd), later
Cabell. *Courtesy Virginia
Historical Society*

Dumbarton Grange, the Shepherd house a few miles north of Richmond.
Cabell lived here from the day of his marriage, 8 November 1913, to Priscilla
Bradley Shepherd until their move to Monument Avenue in Richmond in 1925.
The triple-framed window over the front door lighted Cabell's study and figures
in his work. *Courtesy Cabell Library*

Three generations of Cabells (1915): Dr. Robert G. Cabell, Jr., James Branch Cabell, and Ballard Hartwell Cabell. *Courtesy Cabell Library and Maurice Duke*

Left: Guy Holt (1892-1934), Cabell's editor. The year 1915 was pivotal for James Branch Cabell; his mother died; his son was born; and he met Guy Holt who influenced all his subsequent work. *Courtesy Cabell Library and Maurice Duke*
Right: Hugh Walpole (1884-1941), popular English writer and early champion of Cabell. Their friendship cooled in later years. *Courtesy Cabell Library and Maurice Duke*

Left: Burtin Rasco (1892-1957), newspaperman, whose championship of Cabell helped launch the major recognition of his work in 1917. They remained friends until death. *Courtesy Cabell Library and Maurice Duke*
Right: Henry Mencken (1892-1957), another early champion of Cabell, whose praise of "Some Ladies and Jurgen," published in *Smart Set*, led to its expansion into *Jurgen*. They too remained friends until death. *Courtesy Cabell Library and Maurice Duke*

Elinor Wylie (1885-1928), whose *Jennifer Lorn* (1923) made her the darling of the "James Branch Cabell School." *Courtesy Cabell Library and Maurice Duke*

Left: Joseph Hergesheimer (1880-1954), popular writer and close Cabell friend during the latter's major phase. *Courtesy Cabell Library and Maurice Duke*
Right: Carl Van Vechten (1880-1964), popular writer, later photographer, the sybarite of the "James Branch Cabell School," whose friendship lasted till death. *Courtesy Cabell Library and Maurice Duke*

"The James Branch Cabell School." Here Cabell holds court on Halloween, 1923, in West Chester, Pennsylvania. He is seated center in dark suit. Dorothy Hergesheimer is seated to his right, Phoebe Gilkyson on his left. Seated at far right are Blanche and Alfred Knopf, and seated at far left is Priscilla Cabell with Joseph Hergesheimer to her left. *Courtesy Cabell Library*

Above: Hunter Taylor Stagg (1895-1960) in the early 1920s. The Cabell-Stagg friendship remained firm through the years. *Courtesy Charlotte Nance Saylor and Maurice Duke*

Left: Margaret Freeman (1893-1983) in the 1920s, from a pastel, artist unknown. Urged on by James Branch Cabell, Hunter Stagg proposed to Margaret, but she declined. At age seventy, Cabell, urged on by Marjorie Rawlings, himself proposed. He was accepted, after Margaret consulted with Hunter Stagg. *Courtesy Cabell Library*

Ellen Glasgow (1873-1945)
from a miniature painted in
the 1920s. This photographic
copy was presented to Cabell
in 1926. Their friendship
flowered in mid-career but
was subject to strains at the
end. *Courtesy Cabell Library
and Maurice Duke*

Left: Marjorie Rawlings (1896-1953), whose late-blooming friendship with
Cabell was a joy for both although his star was setting and hers was in the
ascendant. Their correspondence was as uninhibited as any Cabell ever
enjoyed. *Courtesy Cabell Library and Maurice Duke*
Right: Emily Clark (1893-1953). *Courtesy Charlotte Nance Saylor and Maurice
Duke*

James Branch Cabell and Margaret Freeman on their wedding day, 19 June 1950, exiting from Emmanuel Episcopal Church, Richmond. *Courtesy Richmond Newspapers*

3201 Monument Avenue, where Cabell lived from 1925 and where he died on 5 May 1958. *Courtesy Maurice Duke*

Having missed the "cleverness" of *The Cords of Vanity* noticed by out-of-state reviewers, this time the critic for the *News-Leader* played safe and delayed its review of *Rivet*. Its headline read "James Branch Cabell's Vogue Spreads As Critics Praise Merit of His Work." A letter from the reviewer, Jeffrey G. A. Montague, dated 13 December, accompanied the review:

Dear Mr. Cabell:

Here is the long-deferred book notice of The Rivet. Bell tells me he has sold out and English (at Bell's) today said he had a fresh shipment on the way to meet the demand. I hope this will inspire even larger buying—the test of success!

Never mind about your works not appealing to a tremendous audience in Richmond; there are those who consider you superior to any other Virginia novelist,—and time will tell it to the mob who prefer the horticultural authors.

Jeffrey Montague saw what other reviewers could not, that "the whole story is strongly suggestive of this old Confederate city." He went on to observe: "Mr. Cabell is a Richmonder, and, whereas, as Goethe said, 'A man's writings are his autobiography,' it is just possible that, all unconsciously to him, there has slipped off the point of his pen some of the tradition, gossip and atmosphere he absorbed in this city." Then in the guise of presenting an example of Cabell's style, the reviewer cited a long passage from the opening pages of the work that touch on the "Pendomer" divorce and "the notorious Scott Musgrave murder." Montague classified Cabell as a realist, not "that term for literal exposition" but one who described "reality of life in its accustomed phases among 'the people you know.'" Richmonders of the day could clearly see that Patricia Stapleton was modeled on Annie Cabell and that her grandfather was a paraphrase of patriarch Thomas Branch. Then chapter 4 of part 4 was a shameless burlesque of *Branchiana*, which could hardly have pleased his Branch cousins, and the references to the John Scott murder further alienated his older Scott cousins. Mary Wingfield Scott, writing many years later, observed that "meanwhile all the talk about *The Rivet in Grandfather's Neck* came in, my cousin and contemporary Frederica Campbell was not allowed to go to a party at the Cabell's so I knew there was a family feud but the subject was never mentioned."

That Colonel Rudolph Musgrave admitted to himself that he lived on his wife's money was not lost on Richmond readers—like father, like son. Then there was the admission in the novel that certain ladies in Richmond society drank, like two in the author's very own family. "It was through Virginia that Miss Agatha furtively procured intoxicants." True to the author's notes, in the novel the "mulattress" Virginia plays Nemesis, the goddess of retributive justice. Musgraves who end up in her ministering hands are hastened on to heavenly justice. Treated as chattel, Virginia had given birth to a son by the colonel's uncle, Senator Musgrave, and the son was lynched. Colonel Musgrave is disinclined to discuss the matter with his wife, the not-so-patrician Patricia, who replies, "But don't you see? That colored boy was your own first cousin, and he was killed for doing exactly what his father had done." Cabell's casual treatment of this painful subject is analogous to Ellen Glasgow's more intense treatment in *Virginia*, published two years earlier although *Rivet* antedates it in composition. Further, in his work Cabell castigates the whole "Marse Chan" school of southern writers. In chapter 12 of part 4, through his fictional author Charteris, Cabell satirizes Thomas Nelson Page, then at the apogee of veneration by Virginians: "I love to serve that legend. I love to prattle of 'ole Marster' and 'ole Miss,' and throw in a sprinkling of 'mockin'-buds' and 'hants' and 'horg-killing time,' and of sweeping animadversions as to all 'free niggers'; and to narrate how 'de quality use ter cum'—you spell it c-u-m because it looks so convincingly like dialect—'ter de gret hous.'"

Charteris goes on to defend the self-esteem and civic virtues of the romanticists; he will never write a true story about Lichfield-Richmond, for it could only be a tragedy. "Yes, it is only in Lichfield I can detect the raw stuff of a genuine tragedy." Charteris-Page cannot write that tragedy, nor does James Branch Cabell although he moved tentatively toward it in *Rivet*. Ellen Glasgow produced it in 1932 with *The Sheltered Life*. The anomalies of the situation may have been too difficult for Cabell to convey at this stage of his development. Page was enjoying his success as a sentimentalist in the flamboyance of the Gilded Age, and Colonel Musgrave, an exponent of the traditional, marries a Gilded Age wife. At the end of *Rivet*, a dying Rudolph Musgrave is rejoined by the spirit of his dead wife: "He understood, for an instant, that of necessity it was decreed time must turn back and everything, even Rudolph Musgrave, be just as it had been when he first saw Patricia. For they had made nothing of their lives; and so they must begin all over again (368)."

The ending is pure Thomas Nelson Page, but James Branch Cabell was attempting to cut an umbilical cord. Though *Rivet* was a painful book for southerners to read, it indicated that its writer was headed in a new direction. What had remained unspoken, what had indeed been treated as sacred in literature as well as in society, would be treated as comedy. And the comedy continued in other ways. Ever concerned for redemption in his home town, Cabell was dismayed that local book shops had stocked so few copies. He wrote the distributor for McBride on 15 December: "The *News-Leader*, with its strong insistence that the *Rivet* deals viciously with local celebrities, has actually created an honest and urgent demand for the book here. But the bookdealers have sold out their meager first orders, and today not a copy is to be had in Richmond. . . . Without exaggeration, any dealer who had the book in Richmond could have sold a whole edition last Tuesday. But by next Tuesday, as we know, it may be quite another story."

Two months after *Rivet* appeared, *The Majors and their Marriages* came off the press on 13 December 1915. Though not termed a comedy on its title page, the book grew out of Cabell's apprehensions about the social role Priscilla would play in Richmond society. Amusingly *Majors* proved that Gabriella Moncure, Priscilla Cabell, and James Cabell were all related, however distantly. Percie Cabell accepted her inheritance of distinguished ancestors with aplomb, and proceeded to join a number of lineage societies. Before the work's appearance, Cabell sent out handsome circulars soliciting orders: "I am getting out this book at the cost of considerable time and labor, and with no chance of monetary profit, simply because I am resolved to see perpetuated the history of that distinguished family." Complimentary copies far exceeded the number sold, going "gratis to the public libraries and to the leading genealogical experts and to the historical societies of the United States in general, but of Virginia in particular." The work was handsomely reviewed in the few publications that treated family histories. It was dedicated "TO/BALLARD HARTWELL CABELL/ IN COMMEMORATION OF HIS CHRISTENING." The christening associated with this sixth child of Priscilla Cabell carried over indirectly to her previous offspring, as the Shepherds were given middle names in the society columns of Richmond papers: Miss Grace *Guerrant* Shepherd, Miss Priscilla *Macon* Shepherd, Miss Virginia *Waddill* Shepherd, and Mr. Emmett *Albin* Shepherd, Jr.

Compared with the Cabell-Shepherd family's peaceful seclusion at Dumbarton Grange, the outside world seemed a turbulent place. In Europe, France and England were locked with Germany in the most fratricidal war in history. American newspaper accounts were full of atrocities along with stories of war profiteers in this country. Sometime during 1915, Cabell wrote a sonnet about King Midas. "Let all I touch be gold!" he cries. The sestet of the poem poses some problem of interpretation. Is it simply an anti-profiteer poem? With its reference to France and England, are we to read "Cabell" and "Branch?" Have marriage and publishing contracts made its author into a Midas?

> Today who follows Midas?—Nay, let be
> To whisper of lost friends I knew of old
> When England gave me life which France made free!
> I trade unbiased; and my guns are sold—
> Whoever buys—now all need buy of me,
> And all I touch or handle turns to gold!

The poem was published in the Richmond *News-Leader* on 20 January 1916 and, like most of his poetry to date, was included in *From the Hidden Way*, under the title of "Sed Risit Midas." Another somewhat bitter sonnet entitled "Paschalia" appeared in the Easter issue of the Emmanuel Episcopal Church *Parish Light* on 23 April and reappeared in *From the Hidden Way* as "Easter Eve." The poem is a conversational exchange between Caiaphas and Pilate. Their hearts have been wrung by Mother and Son, but their consciences are free; they have fulfilled their duty. The anniversary of his mother's death gave rise to Cabell's bitterest poem, "IV—Lex Scripta Est (February 14th, 1916)," a sonnet which he also included in the 1925 edition of *From the Hidden Way*:

> Time rounds a twelvemonth since you died,—most dear
> And brave of women!—and he thrives as yet
> Whose craven heart found courage to beget
> The lie that slew you;—who, with fame made clear
> And past his poison, rest till High God hear
> Our prayer, and smite with godlike plenitude
> This lean gray snake, and spill the venom spewed
> In vain to guard his lewd blood-brother's bier.
>
> Not yet—most dear and brave!—may faith foretell
> Fate's fixed inevitable hour, nor be
> Rewarded by its advent, to compel
> This liar's exile from all less vile than he,
> And startle in the loneliest nook of hell
> Iscariot and Cain with company.

During the spring of 1916 Cabell continued to send out the manuscript of "In the Flesh," the novel that juxtaposed a writer's dual life—comfortable domesticity and troubling dreams. The first draft had been written in 1914; it had gone out to various publishers in 1915 and had suffered universal rejection. Its very first rejection had come in January from a young reader at the George H. Doran Company. Sinclair Lewis, yet to make his own name in literary annals, in a long critique judged the characters of the novel deficient in attractiveness and unable to awaken a reader's sympathies. Not even Guy Holt, when Cabell met him in April and sold him three manuscripts, had been impressed with "In the Flesh." Having now received more rejections, Cabell began to give thought to rewriting the work in an attempt to imbue it with life.

After missing the 1915 season at the Rockbridge Alum Springs, the Cabell-Shepherd family returned the following year "early in the summer, having closed their home, 'Dumbarton Grange,' for the season." Again, the Shepherd daughters entertained the VMI cadets. Their activities appeared in headlines, always giving their new middle names, and the news "Concerning Mr. Cabell" was inserted as well. One suspects that Cabell was again the resort's society reporter. "It is of much interest in literary and social circles here and throughout the state," one report read, "that James Branch Cabell is correcting the final proofs of his two books, 'The Certain Hour' and 'From the Hidden Way,' which will be brought out in the fall by the Robert M. McBride Co. 'From the Hidden Way' is in verse form and Mr. Cabell's friends here are looking forward with the keenest interest to both publications."

Ballard Hartwell Cabell's first birthday party took place on the lawn in front of Kentucky Row, 25 August, with both parents entertaining a small group of resort children. Pictures in the baby's "Biography" show a middle-aged father in shirtsleeves, thinning hair ruffled by a breeze, serving as nurse to a round-faced, chubby infant. The infant's eyes seem unfocused.

On the same day that Ballard's birthday was celebrated on the lawn of the Rockbridge Alum, Cabell penned a letter to H. L. Mencken, the revolutionist of American letters, then editor of *Smart Set*. Mencken's immediate response was to send Cabell a petition to sign on behalf of Theodore Dreiser whose "genius" was being suppressed; he also wanted something from Cabell for *Smart Set*. In his reply of 20 September, the Richmonder recalled fondly his debut years in the publication. Thus began an extended literary friendship that helped place Cabell in the mainstream of the revolution brewing in American letters.

The Certain Hour appeared on 4 November. It was dedicated to the author's father, as Richmond newspapers noted approvingly. The stories won the cachet of those who preferred Mr. Cabell in his older, more whimsical, romantic vein. The Richmond *News-Leader*, under the headline "James Branch Cabell Appearing Twice in Literary Limelight This Fall," reminded Richmonders that his "latest preceding work, '*The Rivet in Grand-father's Neck*,' created a sensation among Virginia gossips." Perhaps realizing that *The Certain Hour* was not destined to be a strong seller, its author sent out an extraordinary number of complimentary copies to other writers. His scrapbook for this work contains fulsome acknowledgments pasted between its pages of clippings. One finds hand-penned notes of thanks from Margaret Deland, James Lane Allen, Agnes Repplier, Amélie Rives Troubetskoy, Ellen Glasgow, Mary Johnston, Owen Wister, and Alphonso Smith, Poe Professor at the University of Virginia.

From the *Hidden Way* appeared two weeks later, on 18 November. Its dedication to Beverley Bland Munford was followed by the sonnet Cabell had written on his uncle's death. The middle-aged author of these mostly youthful verses delivered a copy to Mary Branch Munford at 503 East Grace Street. She responded with a letter of appreciation. "I was so glad, as it happened, I opened the door myself Saturday evening, when you came in person to bring me this, the first copy of your book of poems." Cabell had spent considerable time polishing and arranging his poems for publication. Confessional in nature, they were a record of his emotional life. Indeed, the collection in book form constituted an intellectual biography. Many of the poems speak directly of a love unconsummated and forever lost:

> They have ordained for us a time to sing,
> A time to love, a time wherein to tire
> Of all spent songs and kisses; carolling
> Such elegies as buried dreams require,
> Love now departs, and leaves us shivering
> Beside the embers of a burned-out fire. (204)

Reviews of the work, though modest in number, were favorable. Again the author sent out complimentary autographed copies in large numbers to fellow versifiers and critics. One went to Professor Lewis Worthington Smith of Drake University, who had written in the April *Atlantic Monthly* that fifty contemporary American poets—including Cabell—were doing better work than Longfellow. Cabell cited the perceptive professor in the preface to *From the Hidden Way* and sent him an inscribed copy. In his joyful reply Professor Smith confessed he had Virginia ancestry.

Cabell's new editor-friend Guy Holt had influenced the final form of this publication. Holt objected to the excessive attribution of poems to other poets, to the author's Latinity and his archaisms. Cabell was eager to please, having already agreed to exempt 750 copies from royalty in exchange for 25 free copies. For his part, Holt accepted an unmarketable product in order to oblige a writer who promised better things to come. By December, Cabell had finished his revision of *The Cream of the Jest*. Holt came down to Richmond that month to discuss this new work among other business matters. The manuscript was sent off on 20 December with a cover letter to Holt: "Write me candidly as to 'Cabell on the Cosmos' now in your hands. I think it far and away my best work, but that is because I really 'let myself loose' in many parts of it: for which sufficient reason you have no earthly call to agree with me. At worst, you will see that your remonstrance against too-clever dialogue, as being unnatural, had been considered by me before our talk. . . . And, as I have told you, you make intelligent suggestions, so that I would appreciate and heed any and all admonition short of advice to burn the manuscript."

From previous versions Holt was not predisposed to like *The Cream of the Jest* and put off a new analytical reading. Even though it was not a pastiche of previously published stories, a quick scanning indicated it was still a work with the looseness of structure endemic to this author. As Holt indicated in several critiques, he felt fine writing should be not an end in itself but an adornment to a plot that went somewhere. His Christmas gift to Cabell was an inscribed copy of James Stephens's *The Crock of Gold*, a work in the style of Cabell that delighted from beginning to end. Writing on 30 December, Cabell defended his new offspring: "I shall continue to assure myself that it is beautifully written, from the technical side, and so truthful that when it is published, if it ever is, I shall have for the rest of my life the feeling of going about unclothed."

Holt's analysis of *The Cream of the Jest* was dated 3 January 1917. He agreed with its author that "it is the best thing you have ever done—at least, in part." It is "vital," a new quality in the Richmond writer's work, but Holt was annoyed by digressions and distractions, in particular the evasions of attributing the work to other authors, the childish parodies of publisher's names with paraphrased letters of rejection, the satirical treatment of Cabell's visit to the White House of Theodore Roosevelt. The critique, however, was joyfully received at Dumbarton Grange. If the main character, Kennaston, had life, then the peripheral objections could be accepted and the offending passages altered. Indeed, in his reply of 7 January, the compliant author suggested that Holt might be in a better position than he to remedy the chapter on publishing: "Suppose you alter that chapter yourself, and let me see specifically what you do mean. I am agreeable to any arrangement which preserves the essential points of the chapter."

As Cabell revised the manuscript, he allowed the character of Kennaston to become even more autobiographical; Kennaston is the author of "Men Who Loved Alison" (in *The Soul of Melicent*) and "The Audit at Storisende" (in *Gallantry*). Cabell interpolates his essay "Why People Should Own and Read Books," which had appeared the year before in the Boston *Herald*, and attributes it to Kennaston. Characters from *The Eagle's Shadow*, *The Cords of Vanity*, and *The Rivet in Grandfather's Neck* enter *The Cream of the Jest*. When Cabell sent the final version off to Holt on 16 April, he wrote: "I have now 'linked' the book with *The Soul of Melicent*, as well as *Gallantry* and the three modern books, with Balzacian Thoroughness." Thus we see Cabell moving toward the concept that all his work was a *comédie humaine*, later to appear in a perfected version, the Storisende Edition. The relationship of Kennaston and his wife is treated as part of a universal comedy, although it is peculiarly that of James and Priscilla Cabell. In his memoirs, this period is touched on in detail:

> So I was permitted to have all to myself the library upstairs, which was lighted by the same three windows that eventually got into Don Manuel's castle at Storisende. And nobody upon any pretext was allowed to disturb me while I was writing books.
>
> Immediately after breakfast, when the Shepherd children were packed off to their schools and kindergartens, just so was I packed off to the library to write books until lunch time. After lunch I returned to the library, and there, for an hour or two hours, I typed out yet a little more of *The Cream of the Jest*, or as I then called it, *In the Flesh*. Meanwhile, and all day long, that intrepid woman who had married me would be about her own activities, which were numerous and varied and incessant and, to me, for the most part incomprehensible.
>
> She saw to the housekeeping; she supervised the farming; she drove the car into Richmond and back again some three or four times a day so as to attend to the family's requirements in general. We maintained a chauffeur, so far as I could judge, simply in the event of an emergency; for Priscilla Bradley Cabell preferred to do her own driving, thank you. . . .
>
> She in brief did I know not what: but she managed everything while I wrote books undisturbed in the library upstairs. . . .

Yet in the evening she was not tired. She, to the contrary, would have liked, I believe, either to go to a party somewhere every evening, or better still, to be giving a party every evening. And I, who did not in the least desire to do these things, I obeyed her complaisantly. At her behest I endured all sorts of social gaieties, evening after evening, in those days. (*As I Remember It,* 38–40)

Formulating a Creed

1917–1919

During the spring of 1917, with *The Cream of the Jest* essentially behind him except for minor revisions, Cabell diverted himself with writing two genealogical articles and composing essays on literature, a carry-over from college days. "A Discourse for Friends [Quakers] of Virginia and Carolina, by Joseph Glaister" appeared in the *William and Mary College Quarterly* for April, and "Thomas & William Branch of Henrico and Some of Their Descendants" appeared in the same publication for October. Lyon Gardner Tyler of Cabell's college days was still editing the *Quarterly*. Referring to the literary essays, Cabell wrote Holt on 26 May: "I have quit fiction and am writing a book to elucidate my 'aesthetic creed'—being persuaded by you and Mr. Follett *et al* that I have one—and have found that, subconsciously, it was just what I wanted to write. Some day you will see it, and some day, too, I hope to have your rebuttal. Meanwhile I have invented a new essay-form, and am having a delightful time playing with it." College professor Wilson Follett was then the reviewer for the *Dial* and had accorded *The Certain Hour* praise for its artistry.

The United States had entered the war against Germany on 6 April, but Cabell, who turned thirty-eight on the 14th, saw that drama as the work of an inferior playwright and devoted his efforts to more artistic thaumaturgy. On the other hand, his cousin Henry Sydnor Harrison had volunteered as an ambulance driver for the Red Cross before the United States's entry into the war. Harrison had gone overseas in January 1915, shortly before the publication of *Angela's Business,* and had served in the Dunkirk sector. Upon the entry of the American forces, Harrison had enlisted in the navy; because of his age he was assigned to naval communications. He was only a year younger than James Cabell, and his younger brother, to whom he had dedicated *Angela's Business,* was killed in France. Cabell, already jealous of his cousin's literary and social success, was galled by the contrast that patriotic fervor shone on his sheltered existence at Dumbarton. His ancestors had figured gallantly in the Revolution and in the Civil War; every eye of the past would judge him critically—save one. Every transgression had been forgiven in the sight of Louisa Nelson. He dedicated the new work about to be published to his black nurse. "At me ab amore tuo diducet nella senectus." Later in the year Cabell confessed to Holt: "This war annoys me so that I cannot really get to writing. I am still dabbling off and on at *Something About Eve,* which, if I ever finish it, will be a Comedy of Fig-Leaves—but it all pivots about a woman, and I seem nowadays obsessed by the desire to write exclusively about myself, under an alias." It was at this time that Cabell wrote a biographical sketch for publicity purposes and sent it to Holt. It found its way into Wilson Follett's "discovery" of Cabell in the *Dial* the following year.

In late June the final revision of *The Cream of the Jest* was sent to Holt, the author anxious for a September publishing date. With the country mobilized for war, austerity was the order of the day; but staying quietly at Dumbarton instead of going to his summer retreat was no sacrifice for the basically sedentary, reluctantly social Cabell. While the essays that were to become *Beyond Life* took form, Cabell found congenial reading in H. L. Mencken's fulminations on publishing and on American culture in general. Essentially a newspaperman at that time, Mencken had recently ended his association with the Sunpapers and shifted to the New York *Evening Journal.* Though this paper was not widely esteemed, its pages saw the first drafts of Mencken's most controversial essays. Some, such as "The Sahara of the Bozart," were dressed up for *Smart Set.* "The Sahara," still delightful reading today, outraged the defenders of the Old South. In his diatribe against the intellectually impoverished ex-Confederacy, Mencken spared only one contemporary—Cabell. The essay was really a critique in progress, a series of joyful attacks on the Bible Belt. Cabell wrote Mencken on 22 August 1917: "It was exhilarating to read your fine, truthful and damnable article in the September *Smart Set*, so that I am duly rendering thanks therefor. Your tribute to Virginian culture and statesmanship is, I regret to say, no more than the repayment of a debt which common-sense everywhere owes our general befuddlement. About your dirge over Georgia I am not so certain, being less intimately acquainted with the corpse, but it is delectable reading. Please go on with the articles as indicated a year ago, and use the writers of the month as texts rather than targets." "The Sahara of the Bozart" was expanded for *Prejudices: Second Series* in 1920, when it drew the collective wrath of the South.

On 20 September Cabell expressed his essays on literature to Guy Holt, congratulating himself on a "remarkable production" that was "beautifully written" and deeming his "Greek sentences" a type of noble "architecture." He had been playfully condescending about such popular writers as Henry Sydnor Harrison. But Holt did not have time to critique the essays then, being preoccupied with the production of *The Cream of the Jest*. Holt had, however, bought a secondhand or remaindered copy of *The Soul of Melicent* and had not cared for it. Cabell received his copies of *The Cream* on 27 September, the publication date. He was pleased with its appearance and set about seeing that it was reviewed in the local press. He had received a handsome review of his total career in a new Richmond paper, the *Evening Journal*, the year before; the owner-editor, Samuel T. Clover, was himself a literary man, who gave extensive coverage to books. Two of his young reviewers, Emily Clark and Hunter Stagg, later became associated with Cabell in producing the *Reviewer*. Clover gave *The Cream of the Jest* a laudatory review on 6 October and followed it up on the 13th with a deciphering of the sigil that Cabell had devised as a key to his work. Cabell expressed one of his copies to Mencken and was rewarded by an admiring review in the November *Smart Set*. A letter of profuse thanks is dated 19 October: "Generosity could not have said more, and I fear that veracity would have said less." He appealed to the Baltimore critic for a boost for Arthur Machen, the Welsh writer, one whom Cabell had long appreciated. The Welshman was soon to enjoy a revival of interest in America and to develop a literary friendship with Cabell. Machen's *The Hill of Dreams* had been in Cabell's mind while writing his dream work, and he sent the older man a copy of *The Cream of the Jest*.

The New York and Boston critics were entertained but generally saw the new opus as appealing only to the literati. In Chicago, however, several champions spoke up. Burton Rascoe writing in the *Daily Tribune* and Lewis Galantiere in the *Examiner* were the critical voices Cabell had long sought. Galantiere had detected the Machen influence as had Vincent Starrett, then associated with the Herald-Examiner. Starrett had earlier written Cabell a long, friendly letter praising the stories in The Certain Hour and commenting on his own infatuation with the work of Machen. In his reply of 8 November Cabell confessed that The Hill of Dreams and "A Fragment of Life" had been influences, and he invested a copy of The Cream of the Jest, suitably inscribed, in his new admirer. Rascoe and Galantiere were close friends, and when the former came across The Cream of the Jest in the Tribune office and liked it, Galantiere reminded him that Guy Holt of McBride's had asked them both to read it. So unknown was Cabell to Rascoe that he took the listing of Cabell's previous works on the flyleaf as a hoax. His review was entitled "Here Is Your Chance to Own a First Edition" (29 December). Cabell also received "a ream of private encomiums" from Hans Hertzberg, an editorial writer, then editor of the Chicago Inter-Ocean Fashion Art Magazine. Chicago was home to a host of writers soon to emerge as America's titans—Edgar Lee Masters, Carl Sandburg, Ben Hecht, Ring Lardner, Sherwood Anderson—and was also home to the venerable Dial (transferred from Boston), Poetry: A Magazine of Verse, Art, the Lantern, the Little Review, all contributing to the literary fermentation of the city. In his memoirs, Vincent Starrett called what became known as the Chicago Literary Renaissance a "gaudy and stimulating moment in time." The Chicago critics had championed outsiders such as H. L. Mencken and T. S. Eliot as well as European authors, and now the Richmond writer was to become a cause. Writing of Rascoe's influence on the Tribune, Starrett observed: "He it was who blew the first great trumpet blast for James Branch Cabell which made that obscure Virginian a classic almost overnight."

The appearance of The Cream of the Jest prompted a letter from Sinclair Lewis, who as a publisher's reader had been the first of many rejecters of "In the Flesh," the work's first title. Cabell's reply of 26 November was a cordial confession that he had profited from Lewis's criticism of the original; he looked upon the published version as a "collaboration." He also confessed to knowing the work of few contemporaries, in part because Richmond bookstores stocked only the most popular writers' novels, such as "the latest offense by . . . Mr. Harrison." In Richmond, Kate Langley Bosher, whose Mary Cary had been a best-seller in 1910, spoke glowingly of Lewis and his wife whom she had met in St. Paul. Cabell asked whether St. Paul was a permanent residence. Lewis replied that he, his wife, and young son were indulging in an "experiment of living as much like Respectable Persons as possible, for one winter." Come spring, they would head east, perhaps to Dumbarton. Lewis's decorous behavior in St. Paul flowered into *Main Street* three years later.

That October also saw the appearance of cousin Nellie Tompkins's second book, published by Dutton. *The Enlightenment of Paulina* was an advance over her earlier *The Egotistical I*. A northern woman who marries for money comes south to a counterpart of Richmond, and there her better character unfolds. But true to the romantic tradition she finds meaning in the arms of a good man. Ellen Wilkins Tompkins herself never married. Cousins Nellie and James had grown closer over the past four years, thanks to Percie Cabell's friendly hospitality to her husband's kinfolks, especially the talky ones. Nellie's autographed inscription in Cabell's copy of her new book read, "Dear James:/I hope you will like/this book/I owe you a/ great deal of thanks for/your kindly encouragement:/and I want to think/ *The Enlightenment of Paulina* is worth while./Nellie/Oct. 19, 1917."

Over a four-month period Cabell asked for Holt's opinion of *Beyond Life*, but on that manuscript his young editor remained disturbingly silent. Praise from Vincent Starrett and others for *The Cream of the Jest* salved Cabell's ego. On Starrett's suggestion, Cabell sent Arthur Machen in London a copy of the novel, and a mutually gratifying correspondence ensued. On 5 January 1918, Cabell wrote Holt once again concerning the essays: "But when—ah, when indeed—do you expect to write me as to *Beyond Life*? We stand just where we did four months ago, as touches that, so that really your verdict ought to be mature. For my part, I have not read a line of the thing since I expressed you the fair copy in September, so that my notions about it are hazy. In consequence, I may be more or less fairminded."

On the same date, Holt was at his typewriter putting in final form his assessment of the essays. "My first essay with pencil and paper this year was an attempt finally to set forth the celebrated rebuttal of your artistic creed—and performances," he wrote. The letter is typed on four oversized sheets of paper. It was the most remarkable letter James Cabell had ever received. Never in his seventeen years of publishing had his work been assessed so truthfully or so mercilessly, the glossy surface stripped away to reveal the ambivalent heart of its creator.* "So much by way of

---

*Truncated, relatively polite, versions of this letter appear in both collections of Cabell letters. The complete letter is reproduced in Dorothy Scura's doctoral dissertation, "Ellen Glasgow and James Branch Cabell: The Record of a Friendship."

apology. As for you, sir, I shall say at the outset that not in a long time have I read so fascinating, so ingenious and withal so insincere a book as 'Beyond Life.' It is an apology for romance by a man who believes that romance is dead beyond resurrection, and who knows therefore that it is perfectly safe to lament it. It is a tissue of delightful misconceptions—the more delightful because intentional—and has so blandly honest an air that I protest, upon my first reading I was entirely taken in by it and really fancied its author sitting in honest grief over the lost youth of the world. And the style of it!"

Holt compliments the simplicity of style and then goes on to comment on the speciousness of Cabell's treatment of romance versus realism. He then turns his attention to Cabell's list of the seven qualities that made for a good book. He adds another and castigates the work of the Richmond writer for ignoring it:

> But let me defer this matter for a moment and point out in entire serious-
> ness one quality you have overlooked in your catalogue of desirable ingredi-
> ents of literature: You have said that these are the auctorial virtues *par excel-
> lence*: distinction and clarity, beauty and symmetry, tenderness and truth and
> urbanity. These are good, I grant, and it may be upon a mere matter of words
> that we differ. Yet it seems to me that all books have been made re-readable
> through the possession not of these qualities alone, but of one other, which
> is salt to them all—namely, gusto. To me it appears that all enduring books,
> of however delicate a texture, have possessed a heartiness akin to the smack-
> ing of lips over a good dish. It is not joy, for many joyless writers have dis-
> played it, and it is inherent in the blackest of tragedies. It is not ecstacy, al-
> though this it may approach. I think it is almost a physical thing, an
> unconscious recognition of life, and an abandonment of self in the very act
> of being. It is a drunkenness of the soul, perhaps, and blood sister to the
> fierce pain and joy which we call ecstatic living and which the creative artist
> must always seek to reproduce in his work, just as the fully living man does
> in his life—and whether through sin or holy fervor is immaterial. Gusto, I
> should say, is the very life-blood of art; and in the measure of its possession
> does the artist overtop life, for he is by so much enabled to produce the
> image, constant and enduring, of that which is in reality only of the moment.
> It is in this, both in its larger and smaller aspects, that your own dream has
> so often faltered. Nowhere in your writings do I find either that earthiness
> which makes all men Falstaffs for the moment, or that madness which makes
> them monsters or saints. They are weak, they are melancholy, they are mildly
> regretful; but always, even though you say otherwise, are they restrained and
> calm voiced—always, because their author is seeking beauty in the phrase

and not in the thing which the phrase clothes. And so people admire your books in restraint. They know a mild wonder at the beauty of phrasing, at the keenness of insight, at all the delicate tinsel and lace in which you have costumed your thought but the thought itself escapes them, and they may contemplate a soul's tragedy and say, "Pretty" over it. It is not their fault, entirely, either. They come to you for a story, and you give lovely sentences and a graceful gesture. But never do you—despite your theories—give them even that romance that you seem to promise. For underneath you are all realist, as you well know.

It comes to me that you have always deceived your readers, either by preying upon their ignorance with invented celebrities, or by imposing upon their tendency to take you at your face value, by pretending to be what you are not—what seemed expected. And with whatever pleasing glamour you have tinted the surfaces of the people of whom you wrote you looked with the realist's eye in viewing their inadequate souls.

And in doing so you have missed not only popularity but truth.

His pretty little stories were sugar-coated pills. As for style, what did it matter how a writer captured a splendid truth? The letter went on and on. The lecture ended as any great exhortation should; he could do better. "James Branch Cabell is a realist who, if he would, could tell a story more simply, more humanly, and more appealingly than he has yet done, without sacrifice of beauty or of truth."

Here was a letter for many readings. First he had to suppress the outrage and dismay. Then he had to put aside the sorrowful wonder and, yes, accept the possibility that there were some therapeutic truths seeded in the attack. Was it just possible that some of his bright dreams had been tinged with Confederate gray? Young Holt had concocted a bitter brew and in effect had said "Drink!" Rabelais emerging from the Middle Ages had given that advice to the new age dawning. Cabell drained the cup and smacked his lips. Urbanity restored, he wrote Holt that the patient was annexing the diatribe as the penultimate chapter of *Beyond Life*, "and in return will immortalize you with the volume's dedication when the thing is published."

"Your rebuttal, my dear fellow," Cabell wrote, "is so precisely what I wanted, if only to lend an air of fairmindedness! You see, here I shall break in indignantly and say what you say, with brief retorts by Charteris. Your scurrilous onslaught upon my books I shall put in the mouth of Charteris, as a *tu quoque* after my advocacy of gusto: the question of my books' permanency being of course with him a vital matter since his existence hinges on it. And then I shall go on to the end." Holt's letter ended up in the final chapter of the manuscript, becoming a part of the dialogue between Charteris (Charles Coleman) and the now anonymous Author. The work as published contains Holt's charges of insincerity; it appropriates Holt's paean to gusto, his jibes at Cabell's effete pessimism, his questioning of methods, and his comparison of art and religion. It understandably does not include his attack on Cabell's narcissism and consequent failure to attract a large reading public.

Cabell's urbane acceptance of Holt's stinging criticism resulted in another letter from the twenty-six-year-old critic, who was rapidly becoming the Richmond writer's alter ego. Holt suggested further revisions to the essays: Cabell should remove references to his own works in the manuscript, should strive for a universal approach to literature in general, and in fact should "eliminate James Branch Cabell from the text entirely." As a lure to an obedient author, Holt further suggested that as editor he might possibly impose his will on a reluctant McBride to get an unsaleable product published; his position with the firm was secure, because the draft had removed possible replacements. "McBride will, I am sure, bear with me in my unaccountably obstinate attempt to foist your wares upon an unawakened public." In another long epistle written 17 January 1918, Cabell fell joyfully into the task of joint creation, "since you are evidently determined to have the book precisely what you want it." The revisions went rapidly, with both correspondents sparring over details. The manuscript again in Holt's hands, Cabell worked fitfully at the embryonic *Something About Eve*.

In Chicago, Burton Rascoe was again at his *Tribune* lectern admonishing mid-westerners. He declared, in "On a Certain Condescension in Our Natives" (16 February 1918), that "there is an American conspiracy to keep hidden the disturbing idea that literature has been, is being and will be produced in this country." Taken to task was *Some Modern Novelists*, the recent book by Helen Thomas and Wilson Follett that included British contemporaries. "But the Folletts omit to mention an American who is as great as the greatest of them—James Branch Cabell." Rascoe went on to compare the Richmond writer with Anatole France, "probably the greatest literary figure on the European continent." On 2 March Cabell wrote Rascoe, "It grieves me that you did not send me a copy of 'On a Certain Condescension in Our Natives,' as the clipping bureau might have missed it. . . . your generosity overwhelmed me." Rascoe, however, was then on a sojourn east. He had seen Holt in New York and had liked the glimpse he had had of *Beyond Life* ("the tastes I had of it were most relishable"), and he proposed serializing it in the *Sunday Tribune*, with payment. Rascoe had also called on Mencken. While the latter agreed to write an article on the Richmond author for Rascoe, he observed, "I am afraid your man, Cabell, is not *vital* enough." Rascoe, as he informed Cabell, had risen to the defense and upon returning home had dispatched a three-page letter to Mencken that summed up "some of the more salient features" in Cabell's work. Cabell, deeply indebted to Rascoe, acknowledged his gratitude on 13 March. In return for receiving a copy of Rascoe's letter to Mencken, Cabell agreed to review a new biography of Booth Tarkington for the *Tribune*, and he acknowledged Rascoe's request for a first draft of one of his books:

> If I possessed the manuscript of any of my books it would be at your service. But I must tell you that as each book was published, and indeed each magazine tale, I have regularly burned the manuscript, just back of the stable. It has become a sort of recognized ceremony. A manuscript, to its writer at any rate, betrays too nakedly the author's poverty of thought and his makeshifts: it constitutes a quite positively indecent exhibit. I am still almost sure all manuscripts ought to be burned— "Almost," I say, because Holt came to talk with me about this very matter, and with some eloquence presented the other side. He wrung from me a promise to—well, to consider preserval of my manuscripts for the future. I don't think I went further than that. In that event, I promised him the rough copy of *Beyond Life*—typewritten, but with some million alterations and additions—and that will leave me scriptless save for the two books I have in hand. . . . I can only say that if I finally give him *Beyond Life*—and I feel that I ought to—I hereby promise you the manuscript of the next book by me as ever is.

Caught between praise from Rascoe and others in Chicago and criticism from Holt and Mencken in New York, Cabell determined he would show the latter he was a monstrous clever fellow. Mencken wanted a short story for *Smart Set*. He should get one. The very first of Cabell's stories, "Love-Letters of Falstaff," written in 1901, was still, to his chagrin, his most popular story. Also rankling was Holt's statement that "nowhere in your writings do I find either that earthiness which makes all men Falstaffs for the moment, or that madness which makes them monsters or saints." Mencken felt that he lacked vitality. Very well, he would write another Falstaff story, one about Jurgen, a merchant of discarded dreams. It would have the gusto decreed by Holt, and the model embodiment was not far to seek—Uncle Jim Branch, who in his mid-fifties still roamed the byways in search of forbidden pleasures. "Some Ladies and Jurgen" was written rapidly and was dispatched to Mencken in Baltimore. The allegory of a middle-aged pawnbroker rejecting three queens of romance, Guenevere, Cleopatra, and Helen, enchanted the Baltimore scribe. As embodiments of chivalrous, gallant, and artistic ideals, the women were rich foils for a male of remarkable vitality. Mencken dashed off a letter to Rascoe:

> I wish you could see a story that Cabell sent in to the Smart Set a week or so ago—a superb piece of writing. I only hope we can come to terms with him: he deserves five times as much as our cash-drawer can afford. The thing is really almost perfect. He has done nothing better, and very little so good.
>
> In the midst of your encomiums I begin to detect a central fact, to wit, that Cabell mirrors the disdain of a defeated aristocracy for the rising mob. He is the only articulate Southerner who is a gentleman by Southern standards: all the rest are cads. Thus one may account for his "decadence" in the midst of a crude and Methodist society. I shall pursue the point in a book I am doing for the autumn. (*Letters*, 118–19)

Cabell's review "The Tragedy of Mr. Tarkington," in which he maintained that Tarkington never wrote a book as good as he was capable of writing, appeared in the Chicago *Tribune* on 6 April; for the next seventeen weeks, through 11 August, installments of *Beyond Life* also ran weekly in the *Tribune*. "Some Ladies and Jurgen" came out in the July *Smart Set*. The 18 July *Dial* featured a selection from *Beyond Life*, and Cabell had genealogical contributions in the April, July, and October issues of the *William and Mary Quarterly*. Cabell was elated with his serial appearances in the Chicago *Tribune* and wrote asking Rascoe to send copies although he had arranged for a Richmond news-dealer to procure Sunday editions of that journal. Rascoe was only too happy to oblige, and their correspondence grew apace. Despite the midwesterner's self-interest, his letters reveal a depth of reading, and they stimulated a flow of ideas from Cabell's pen treating influences, literary assessments, and social perceptions. Cabell wrote Holt that "Rascoe and myself are now corresponding at the rate of some three or four letters a week." The result was that their letters became the most extensive in the Cabell correspondence, lasting until Rascoe's death in 1955. Cabell's correspondence with Holt bears more directly on his bookmaking, but that with Rascoe touches more on the creative process. Others who knew Rascoe did not feel the warmth toward him that Cabell felt. The yokel from Oklahoma, the Babbitt of newspaperdom, a useful but "drooling piece," as he was called, Rascoe nevertheless managed to insinuate himself into the center of the literary scene of his day and to survive several changes of the literary guard.

The essays appearing in the *Tribune* irritated some readers, drawing attacks that made for publicity. Ben Hecht writing in the Chicago *News* belittled Cabell as a clone of Arthur Machen, and Rupert Hughes sent the *Tribune* a twelve-page letter listing Cabell's "historical inaccuracies." Hughes, a versatile author of stories, novels, plays, poetry, and biographies, had also had a distinguished career in World War I as an army officer. Cabell's lengthy rebuttal on 6 May took a lofty, sportive tone toward Hughes, to whom he referred throughout as *Captain* Hughes. A modern reader may feel that the Virginian exceeded the bounds of good taste, and even the latter admitted to Rascoe, after seeing his reply in print, that it was a little "underbred." His irritation had made him display "very little of the auctorial virtue called urbanity." Hughes, stung by the personal references to his education and his army career, submitted another twelve-page, single-spaced, typewritten rejoinder to Cabell's attack. Again Rascoe ran it gleefully in the *Tribune*. Captain Hughes defended his upbringing and career and amusingly disparaged Cabell's literary postures and arch style. In the same issue, 18 May, appeared a one-paragraph riposte that Cabell had wired to Rascoe the day before, having been privy to Hughes's defense before it was published. While Cabell's distaste for the works of both Henry Sydnor Harrison and Rupert Hughes may have been objective, some of his attitudes toward both men may be attributed to their military careers in an era when patriotism was the current national religion. Even young Ben Hecht had been a war correspondent in Germany and Russia and later proved his literary capability with one of the most successful plays of all time, *The Front Page*. But the literary debate that took place in Chicago served to make Cabell's name known nationally in literary circles. Mencken had added gusto to the colloquy with an attack in *Smart Set* on the "intellectual slums" endemic to New York, Boston, Philadelphia, and other culturally pretentious capitals. As a result, a book that had few chances of paying publication costs sold over three thousand copies, "mainly in Chicago and environs."

The stimulation of Holt, Mencken, and Rascoe was augmented by that of another literary personage, Joseph Hergesheimer, who came to see Cabell the first week in May. Their names had been linked by Mencken in the *Smart Set*, and Wilson Follett was making amends for leaving Hergesheimer out of *Some Modern Novelists*, just as he had done for Cabell in the *Dial*. Hergesheimer had the good fortune to be popular, having appeared frequently in the *Saturday Evening Post*, and also to be gaining literary approval. *Three Black Pennys* (1917) had established his reputation at the same time that *The Cream of the Jest* had enhanced Cabell's. Writing of

Hergesheimer at this period, Carl Van Vechten commented on his flamboyant personality, an adjunct to his style: "Joe was fantastic in dress, extravagant in conversation: more he was brilliant." The introduction of Hergesheimer and Cabell was brought about by Nellie Tompkins, Cabell's Richmond cousin. Nellie had met the Pennsylvanian on the beach at Cape May, New Jersey, and with her sister had visited Joe and Dorothy Hergesheimer at Dower House, their historic mansion in West Chester. When Joe was invited to Richmond, he accepted, for it would give him the chance to meet the writer with whom he had been linked.

Cabell had read none of Hergesheimer's writings when they met and was reduced to "feeble equivocation." Fortunately, Hergesheimer's extravagant personality compensated for Cabell's inhibiting shyness, so that the two "got on." Cabell wrote the ever-curious Rascoe:

> I shall certainly read *The Three Black Pennys*, at least— Between ourselves, Hergesheimer as a person rather disconcerted me. He informed me, for instance, that he and I were the only real artists in America, were kindred souls, and so on—and as yet, I don't know whether or no this was a compliment. Then, all the while, I did not dare confess that I had read none of his books, if merely because he assumed, as an affair of course, I had read every one of them. Still, we got on, I believe, fairly well— His article in the *Sun* was about Ellen Wilkins Tompkins, who wrote *The Egotistical I* and, more recently, *The Enlightenment of Paulina*: and was but flagrant log-rolling, inasmuch as Nellie has written but two chapters of the novel he puffed— I say "Nellie" because she is my second cousin and told me of all this, though I did not see the article. I wonder if you came across *The Enlightenment of Paulina*, as published by Dutton last autumn? It did not "sell," but I found it surprisingly good—largely, no doubt, because I knew the author and thought well of her as a person—not merely, I assure you, on account of the cousinship. (17 May 1917)

Cabell read *The Three Black Pennys* and was relieved to find he liked it, though he objected mildly to its Jamesean appositional style. He wrote Hergesheimer on 27 May declaring his joy—"I had read none of your books"—and avowed that he looked "forward to the other three Hergesheimer volumes."

At this time Cabell met another flamboyant personage, John Macy, with whom he formed a friendship. Macy had published *The Spirit of American Literature* in 1913 and had served briefly on the faculty of Miss Jennie Ellett's school in Richmond; he was unhappily married to Anne Sullivan Macy, the teacher of Helen Keller. Miss Jennie introduced Macy to Cabell, whom she regarded as her most literary pupil. Though Macy's bohemianism was a small barrier for Cabell's prudery, it served to liberate the Richmonder further from provincialism of place. Cabell found Macy's literary discussions congenial. There were echoes of Coleman-Charteris.

June at Dumbarton was given to the birth pangs of a new book and to long letters to the new friends that Cabell began to regard as champions. A 4 June letter to Rascoe commented on his own interest in the creative process, "the author's mental processes." His thoughts turned to the emerging book and to his promise that the manuscript copy would be Rascoe's: "And for the rest, I am trying, in the intervals between being a person, to write you a book manuscript. It gets on very, very slowly, and has an excellent chance of being suppressed, though whether on the score of salaciousness or blasphemy is not yet determinable. My agreement with Holt was to write the thing as it came to me, and that done, for us to cut out the really impossible portions—" On the same day he wrote Vincent Starrett and sent him a copy of The Hidden Way, "my favorite book. . . . I still consider that it was an interesting boy who lived and wrote these verses." A letter to Hergesheimer on 8 June rendered thanks for the loan of Wilson Follett's treatise on Conrad, "but your own book I am reading with leisure and careful consideration." Of his work in progress, in "that terrible stage of making a first draft," he finds "the labor of writing unendurable until one has a whole of sorts, to be revised and made better indefinitely. I am thus candid without solicitation because some day I mean to wring from you a confession as to your 'methods.'"

Another letter to Hergesheimer on 12 June brought forth a long confessional letter from the Pennsylvanian. He compared their writing experiences, which had forged a bond between the two writers and served to make them both more analytical. Neither writer wished to look directly at contemporary life, their vision fixed on "an age slightly removed from our own." "If your inability to get North stretches out too long," wrote Hergesheimer, "perhaps I shall be South within a reasonable time. You might send me a word of the mountains of which you spoke." Cabell's reply of 29 June was again a passionate defense of why they wrote—"for the same reason that the coral zoophyte builds his atoll"—with further justification for avoiding the contemporary: "You should, I think, stick to the age sightly removed from your own. I wonder if you have done this in Java Head, of which I hear proud rumors?"

The heyday of Virginia's smaller mountain resorts was waning, and the young Shepherds found the old-fashioned social rituals of the Rockbridge Alum Springs devoid of pleasure. Virginia Beach now lured young Richmonders. Though pale, sedentary James Cabell was not a sun-worshiper, with the help of a writing table set up on a screened porch he gradually adapted to his surroundings. Like all environments in which he wrote, the beach entered into the work at hand, in this case *Jurgen*. Cabell wrote Holt in a letter dated 11–12 July:

> *Jurgen* gets on as well as could be looked for, in these surroundings. We have taken a little house within a hundred feet of the Atlantic Ocean, and, being a large family, dwell therein in appalling promiscuity. But I have retained a porch, rather bigger than a postage stamp, for writing purposes, and so between thunderstorms manage to spoil my share of paper. Meanwhile I must certainly manage likewise to use this idiotic ocean in *Jurgen*: it is a sleek and fat ocean that for ten days has been solemnly spanking the sand, and really the longer you look at it the more futile appears the whole performance— How does the short story title, "Some Ladies and Jurgen," impress you as a name for the otherwise unchristened book—a brown book, I too hope, in course of time.

Cabell liked the brown covers of the two McBride imprints, which evolved into the format of the Kalki Edition of his works. In mid-August he fretfully put aside "The Pawnbroker's Shirt," his preferred title for *Jurgen*. Without a typewriter and therefore the means of making a fair copy, his manuscript was becoming indecipherable with interlinear insertions. He was ready to return to the comfort of his study at Dumbarton and extracted an agreement from his wife for a 1 September departure. In the meantime he read the works of others and penned long, confessional letters. Under Rascoe's tutelage he read Bennett's *The Pretty Lady*, confessed he was "unable to appreciate" Nietzsche, admitted Ezra Pound was only "the shadow of a name," observed that the Folletts' formula was to "take the author as [their] starting point," felt ambivalent about Anatole France ("*Bonnard* I liked: one has no choice"), fretted over Booth Tarkington ("But you, I believe, do not take Tarkington as seriously as I").

Back in Richmond, Cabell had his ego further expanded by a visit from Alfred Knopf whose publishing firm was rising in esteem. The handsome young publisher and his wife aspired to feature the best contemporary work of American and European authors in handsome formats. Cabell wrote Rascoe, "We parted amicably but without promises." Then came a report on the work to be dedicated to the Chicago scribe: "The *Pawnbroker* I have been re-copying at odd intervals, until a little more than a third is done. But this time I will not be foiled, and will make of the thing a book of noble and majestic propositions, though it involve the squandering of every idea I possess. Besides, there are all sorts of ways to pad it, once the paper shortage is relieved."

Cabell letters were so engaging and confiding that Rascoe could no longer resist the impulse to meet the artist in his atelier. Surprised by Rascoe's visit, Cabell journeyed into Richmond via a long walk and street-car ride. Rascoe recorded his impressions in his biography, *Before I Forget* (1937):

> I went down to Richmond to visit Cabell in his large colonial-Virginia house with mullioned windows, in Dumbarton Grange, where he wrote most of the biography of Dom Manuel. Mrs. Cabell was away visiting one of her daughters at Randolph-Macon College. Cabell cannot drive an automobile; Mrs. Cabell was family chauffeur. He met me at the station, and we boarded a streetcar. I did not notice the Jim Crow signs and started to sit down in the section reserved for colored people. Cabell said, "You'll get arrested if you do that," and smiled. We found a seat and rode to the end of the car line. Then we had to walk about half a mile to the house.
>
> It was wartime, and servants had left their service and were drawing high wages in the munitions plants. The Cabells were without hired help in that big house. Mrs. Cabell's daughter Virginia cooked a marvelous dinner of fried chicken, cream gravy and hot biscuits. We went into the living room for coffee. Cabell had warned me that he had had little experience in conversation. That night it would seem that neither he nor I had had any. There had seemed so many things I wanted to talk about when I should meet him, but there we were sitting together and I could think of nothing. (361)

Cabell had written earlier, "I am very clever at repartee if you give me a week or two." In the company of Holt, Hergesheimer, and Macy, the reclusive Richmonder had been relieved of taking the conversational initiative, but Rascoe was another whose ideas flowed more readily on paper. Rascoe continues:

> Occasionally he would break the silence with a grieved neighborly statement about the sorrow already inflicted thereabouts by the deaths of Richmond boys at the front and of influenza in the training camps; or he would say something about the difficulties of writing when the young folk were having parties at the house; or he would drum into me vocally the demand he had already made . . . to get out a book or books made up of my journalistic writings, as Mencken, Nathan, Van Vechten and others had done.
>
> His manner is quiet and rather humble; his accent is that of Tidewater Virginia; he seemed then to me to be a man who outwardly fitted himself perfectly and unobtrusively into the whole social scheme of things domestically

and communally in Richmond and yet lived an inner life that was realized in the dreams of his novels.

In the room in which I slept that night there was a photograph of Cabell when he was at the College of William and Mary: he was then a fat boy with eager and challenging eyes; now he was thinnish and wore glasses and was losing some of his hair at the sides of the top of his forehead; and his face had taken on angles and lines of quiet dignity and inner serenity. I arose so late that I scarcely had time to snatch a bite of breakfast and drink a cup of coffee and make the train I had planned to catch back to New York. When Cabell waved to me from the platform while I stood on the steps of the train there was an expression on his face which told me that I had found a personal friend in Cabell as well as an author whose work I admired greatly and meant much to me. (362)

On 28 September Cabell wrote Holt: "Well!—The most important event of the month has been my meeting 'in the flesh' with Rascoe, whom you must have encountered since. I shall always regret that his first visit took place in such horribly upset circumstances, but with him I was delighted. Then too, of course, I have since recollected some 709 things I had intended to ask him about and did not: indeed, now I think of it, neither of us talked enough for what ought to be a Historical Occasion."

The projected trip north in October was postponed. Spanish influenza had descended on America like a medieval plague, and casualties were epidemic along the Eastern Seaboard. Even in the safer Midwest, when Sinclair Lewis and his family "had to take a trolley, they sat at an open window and if any one coughed they left the car at once." A 26 October letter informed Rascoe that the Dumbarton household was "still cowering in the bushes while the influenza ravages Richmond: but now 'they say' it is abating, however gradually, so that we hope to get back by and by to normal living—But will that ever really come again?" A winter sojourn in Richmond was planned. Priscilla Cabell justified the move on the grounds that her girls needed some social life and that it was impossible to acquire enough coal to keep the large frame house at Dumbarton habitable in severe weather. In Richmond they rented the house of Dr. Arthur Cabell, the writer's bachelor uncle, and on 12 November the Cabell-Shepherd ménage moved to 3 East Franklin, a short block from James Cabell's birthplace. The thirty-nine-year span of time had seen few changes in that section of Franklin. Today both houses are gone. Cabell was annoyed that the house contained no table suitable for typing, but it did contain an extensive library on strange sexual practices. His readings therein found their way into the Cocaigne chapters of the manuscript he was unable to type.

With the children and their nurse established in Richmond, James and Priscilla Cabell fared north on the first of December. Cabell recounted this episode to Rascoe in a 28 December letter:

> On—let me see—the first of December my wife and I paid an extempore visit to New York, she to do Christmas shopping, and I for no especial reason except just "to go along." So I bundled up the Jurgen manuscript as it stood, and dropped in on Holt without any preparation. Of him I saw a great deal, and we threshed out the matter of the next book pretty thoroughly. Mencken was not in the city, nor was Hergesheimer: Knopf also was out of town. Cook [Howard Cook of Moffat, Yard, & Co.] I met at a Small Fry luncheon, and was by just the glimpse I had of him delightfully impressed.
>
> Well, we had planned to stay on for some two weeks, during which I was to call at Cook's office, and Knopf was to be back the end of the week, and on my way home I meant to stop off at Baltimore. But we had reckoned without the influenza: for on the fifth day of our visit we were summoned home posthaste by the news that four of the children—including the three you saw—and the nurse were all down with it. . . . Ballard had the closest call of any. . . . Ultimately, though, he did not have pneumonia, and the others too recovered. So all ended well.

This letter became the basis of an imaginary interview by Rascoe of Cabell and Hergesheimer. It took the form of "Jim and Joe, Authors," a playlet which he published in the Chicago *Tribune* on 1 February 1919 and later as an appendix to his biography, *Before I Forget*. Therein he mistakenly recalled the event, a meeting of the two authors in New York, as really taking place. The portraits, however, are telling:

> Hergesheimer is, say, 5 feet 9, possibly less, rather heavily built; in the thirties (or looks it), with a rotund mouth, full-lipped, somewhat protruding, which helps to give him a look of puzzled and anxious inquiry when he directs his gaze toward you from those small, blue, keen (yes, keen) eyes with which he regards you altogether absorbedly through the thick-lensed, horn-rimmed glasses. His nose is ample. You are rather startled by his voice at first: it has a tenor pitch and becomes the more nasalized the more interested he gets in the conversation. His hair is dark and his color is good, though he is not what you would call a handsome man.
>
> Nor would the discriminating observer apply the word "handsome" to Cabell; his nose is long, but it has a squatty aspect at the tip; it looks snubbed, but isn't, as a profile view would instantly reveal. And his hair is thinning on

the sides of his forehead, where it might be parted if he didn't roach it back. This impoverishment of the hirsute heritage of his youth gives him an appearance of a more than normal expanse of brow. If he loses much more hair his cupola will suggest the droll wig worn by the Irish comedian of the old burlesque school. His mouth is distinctly Southern—if you know what I mean—the sort of mouth that cannot pronounce "rs" without difficulty, a mouth with few motions. But if there is a lassitude in his mouth, there is not in his eyes—grayish blue, quizzical eyes which observe you from the angle of a depressed chin, and then from the angle of a thrust-out chin, and then from the corners. When he talks you don't at first know whether he is jesting or is speaking in sober earnest. You learn later that he is doing both. He speaks with his head thrown back, and he listens with it bowed. He and Hergesheimer are of a height and almost of a build: Hergesheimer says they are of a mind, but that remains to be seen.

Hergesheimer is easily the better talker—one of the best, in fact, I have ever heard. . . .

Cabell says little, but he is vastly interested, and there is an agreeable touch of humor to all he says. Throughout the scene Cabell smokes cheap, domestic cigarettes, and Hergesheimer smokes excellent cigars. The latter offers the contents of his case to the others, and there are encomiums for the flavor of the weed. (409–10)

The publication of *Beyond Life* in book form was set for 18 January of the new year, 1919, but its author received his free copies earlier. Inscribed, they were dispatched to Holt, Hergesheimer, Mencken, Follett, Machen, Starrett, Rascoe, and Samuel Travers Clover, owner-editor of the Richmond *Evening Journal*. The previous November, Clover had been one of the founders of the Virginia Writers' Club, bringing together a miscellaneous group of newsmen, editors, historians, amateur poets, and published writers of some repute. At the club's second meeting on 14 December, which Cabell did not attend, he was elected president and Clover was named program chairman. The *Evening Journal* was the most book-conscious of the Richmond papers; Clover himself reviewed books, and he had a strong staff of reviewers including Vera Palmer, Emily Clark, and Hunter Stagg. The copy of *Beyond Life* autographed for Clover resulted in an extended review on 11 January. A poor performer in public, the reticent Cabell attended meetings of the Writers' Club sporadically, although members felt that he was "genuinely anxious to be helpful and accommodating." He encouraged all to persevere, referring to his own long years of rejections. If the programs were frequently frivolous and the talk mainly social, the club facilitated Cabell's press relations and gave the curious access to the mythmaker who had long been the subject of their own mythmaking gossip.

On 10 January Cabell sent Rascoe "half of Jurgen's story, upon which I would value your advice. First, as to whether you will accept the dedication, judging this far. Then, as to whether you find the book 'improper.'" Rascoe was pleased with all and urged no changes. Revisions to Jurgen brought Guy Holt to Richmond in February to spend three days. Cabell agreed to six modest expurgations in the manuscript, yielding to what he termed Holt's "pruriency." Even though the allusions to sex were veiled in allegory and artful language, the young editor feared, with reason, that they would not pass the moral censors. Cabell prevailed upon his loquacious guest to address the Writers' Club, where Holt's charming talk on book publishing from an editor's viewpoint was well received. The next day Cabell took Holt out to Emmanuel Church. "The more I think of it the gladder I am I took you to Emmanuel," he wrote afterward; "you now perceive the milieu in which I was reared. Season with your glimpse of the Writers' Club, and you will have a very fair notion of our highest cultural standards."

Alerted by the "Chicago Debate" over the publication of Beyond Life in serial form, critics nationwide were prepared to give it their close attention when it emerged as a book on 18 January. Its ivory-tower thesis that human beings live by deception was alternately admired and damned. Cabell was a scholar-artist; he was a "poseur." The work was intellectually stimulating; it was insincere "sophomoric erudition." Cabell liked the assessment it received from Dorothy Scarborough in the 2 February New York Sun Books and Book World, widely quoted in provincial papers. He later chose her to review Jurgen for the Bookman. In return for Scarborough's encomiums, he agreed to review her From a Southern Porch which came out later in the year. As she recalled in her autographed copy to the Cabells, she had often sat on their porch at Dumbarton.

After Holt left, Cabell longed to tinker with Jurgen, to make it conform to Holt's notions of what public prudery demanded and yet have it remain an uninhibited expression of the male libido. He repeated fretfully to his wife that he could only work "at home," meaning his library at Dumbarton. He was free to take the streetcar out there anytime he chose, but then he was a totally incompetent furnaceman. He wrote Holt on 15 March from Dumbarton: "Just now I can write no more. I am alone in the house—for we do not sleep here until Monday—and the furnace is refractory and I am chilled through. So I shall go into the yard to get warm. To-day, you comprehend, I am marooned here, to get the library in shape." Finally he was back, after "ten days of unmitigated misery" of moving via automobile. As he typed the final draft of *Jurgen*, he wondered what his next creation would be. He wrote Rascoe on 25 March: "Give me some notion as to what sort of book I should write now that *Jurgen* is practically off my hands. The request has a droll ring, but I have the feeling that you have created a sort of legend (I omit any allusion to Frankenstein, as pro-German) to which I am in a manner bound to live up. Come tell me, now, about this Cabell of whom you write so delectably: what sort of book would he in your opinion write next? For my mind is just at present To Let Unfurnished— I mean this."

Cabell expressed "The Pawnbroker's Shirt" (as he was still calling *Jurgen*) to Holt on 7 April, having worked on it for some fourteen months. He recognized clearly that the work was now two things: "I find it, after all, autobiographical" and probably his claim for remembrance by posterity as well. *Jurgen*'s spiritual journey through the notions of humankind was a record of Cabell's own intellectual awakening. Also it was infused with the presence of Louisa Nelson, Gabriella Moncure, and nearly every family member who had shaped his development. While future readers interpreted every episode as fantasy, each had its genesis in a moment of past time. Personalities of the present nudged the mage's pen. The idea of Jurgen as a nature myth, the procreative sun, is attributable to Wilson Follett, the college professor-critic who had opined that Cabell was a myth. Holt and Cabell had argued in circles in hammering out *Beyond Life*; all came back to an unresolved question: Is there meaning in experience? Every man's story was a circular journey home. As his fortieth birthday approached, Cabell began to feel that his work might live and that he should clean up the imperfections of his earlier writings. He wrote Holt on 8 April: "I have really begun on the Intended Edition of my complete works, that is, setting aside one copy of each for marginal corrections and improvements, to be made in spare moments."

Cabell's feeling of exhilaration at being on the threshold of redemption, of having overcome all obstacles to reigning in a world of his own creation, was augmented by a visit from Hergesheimer. Returning from Florida where he had gone to recuperate from a breakdown after finishing what he deemed his best work, Cabell gave newsman Rascoe details: "Hergesheimer came down, after the completion of his masterpiece, with violent and inexplicable bleedings at the nose: I, immediately after finishing *The Pawnbroker's Shirt* was smitten with almost complete blindness which lasted all one cheery morning. The doctor tells me it was 'probably eye-strain.'" After commiserating, the two writers congratulated each other over their expanding literary fortunes. Cabell wrote Holt of the pleasurable four days spent together.

> We have sworn, upon the whole, eternal amity, and, upon the whole, I like him immensely. We talked of all things: and have decided to be twin emperors reigning upon equal thrones. His next book, from what he tells me of it, will be curious and by far his best. It is not to appear in bookform until next January, though, running first in *Everybody's*. Of *The Pawnbroker's Shirt* I have promised him an early proof, so that he can review it for the *Sun*, and, he believes, one or two other papers. That we will take up later. Meanwhile I arranged, through our friend Clover, to have him interviewed here, in full length, and he declared me the finest prose artist &c. therein. So it goes—And again Hergesheimer pleaded the cause of Knopf: but I got out of it gracefully by explaining that I could not well publish through a man who declared Hergesheimer to be the only honest-to-God literary artist in America. (16 April)

Along with the shop talk, the two writers discussed revisions of earlier works, a practice that Cabell had always indulged in; he termed it his "Economist Theory," because the writer got the most return out of every effort. Hergesheimer gave him some excellent advice which the Economist unwisely ignored. "It was one of the many topics over which I wrangled with Hergesheimer," Cabell wrote. "'Never revise,' he insisted. 'Your best work will live and the rest will be forgotten anyway'—and then went home and set about a revised edition of *The Lay Anthony*. So I must have won the debate." While Cabell may have won the skirmish, he lost the battle in time, expending his creative powers in fruitless attempts to reanimate the lifeless puppets of past years. Anticipating a rise in his stock with the appearance of *Jurgen*, he labored to dress up and sell its forgotten siblings. "My notion is to get twelve books in which the 'style,' anyhow, will stand up under criticism." Significantly, he started with the two earliest autobiographical novels. He confided to Rascoe, "I have revised *The Cords of Vanity* all through, and made it, I really think, infernally good. *The Eagle's Shadow* I am submitting to similar treatment, and the result promises to be—well, pretty fair. I do not claim more." Townsend, the cad-hero of *Cords*, had characteristics in common with Jurgen, and, more important, Cabell saw that both were projections of his fantasy persona. His introspection and analysis of his past work took the form of a Yeatsian gyre, a viewing of the past from a high and expanding circle of comprehension, aided in large measure by discussions with Holt, Rascoe, Hergesheimer, and other critics. The hero of *The Eagle's Shadow*, however, remained nebulous even for Cabell. Inspired by Rascoe's mistaken surmise that his list of books were all made-up titles, he began to attribute this early nebula to a fictitious author.

13

The Redeemed

1919–1920

On his fortieth birthday in 1919, James Cabell seemed at the point of realizing a dream with the writing of "The Pawnbroker's Shirt." The dream
encompassed fulfillment, justification, apotheosis. It was more real than
marriage, than any comfortable humdrum domesticity, and something
deep in his psyche revealed this truth to him graphically.

> At Dumbarton Grange the library in which I wrote for some twelve years,
> between 1913 and 1926, was lighted by three windows set side by side and
> opening outward. It was in the instant of unclosing the most westerly of these
> windows, on a sunlit afternoon in the April of 1919, to speak with a woman
> and a child who were then returning to the house (with the day's batch of
> mail from the post office) that, for no reason at all, I reflected it would be
> regrettable if, as the moving window unclosed, that special woman and that
> particular child should prove to be figures in the glass, and the window
> should open upon nothingness. For that, I believed, was about to happen.
> There would be revealed, I knew, beyond that now moving window, when
> it had opened all the way, not absolute darkness, but a gray nothingness,
> rather sweetly scented. . . . (Preface to the Past, 41–42)

This moment of revelation, termed "panic surmise," a "second-long
nightmare," by the hallucinator, soon passed, but its significance was not

lost on the visited: "that evening I made a brief memorandum of this historical circumstance."

Other emerging writers began to enter Cabell's orbit. William Rose Benét, Carl Van Doren, Sinclair Lewis. After having written some sixty short stories, Cabell got around to reading a treatise on how to write them. He was amazed that he had never heard of the limited viewpoint. He wrote Hergesheimer in wonder: "Have you ever tried composing, in the third person, a tale all told from the viewpoint of one of the characters, and conscientiously included nothing except what that character actually would notice at the time it, actually, would be noted or thought of? It is rather fun; it shuts out local color and scenery and so much else that you can hardly get the story told at all." The results of his reading were two short stories, "The Wedding Jest," which appeared in the September issue of the *Century*, and "Porcelain Cups," which appeared in the November issue. The former was included in *The Best Short Stories of 1919* and the latter in the *O. Henry Memorial Award Prize Stories, 1919*. Both were incorporated into a revised *Line of Love*.

As summer advanced, Cabell's eyes continued to bother him. His oculist attributed his discomfort to "getting accustomed to new lenses," a theory the victim doubted. "I have taken to copious weeping without any provocation, and in company this is embarrassing and suggestive of some secret sorrow." As Priscilla Cabell and her children made plans to spend July at Virginia Beach, Cabell decided he would remain at Dumbarton with Ballard, Isabelle (the invalid), and their nurse. He wrote Hergesheimer that July and August were usually his mentally gray months. In these barren periods, he tinkered with a completed manuscript. "This year there is nothing. But I am cloudily groping, I think, toward another dizain." Magic-seeking would be their mutual goal until death. Hergesheimer would find the "local color" of heaven irresistible; Cabell had already "done" his impression of "both places" in *Jurgen*. When the vacationers returned, the family journeyed for the month of August to the Rockbridge Alum where Cabell was used to working on the cool back porch of their favorite cottage, its decline into seediness no deterrent to his sensibilities. There he penned a long letter to the ever-importuning Rascoe, in which he recounted in detail the genesis and evolution of *Jurgen*. Earlier he had heard from Sinclair Lewis, who was heading east by automobile via Tennessee and Virginia in search of a civilized place to live. In the middle of August Lewis and his charming first wife, Grace Hegger, arrived at the Rockbridge Alum.

Seated under the maples on the lawn, the two writers read each other's latest literary efforts, Lewis the proofs of *Jurgen* and Cabell the first draft of *Main Street*. While they argued contentedly, Gracie Lewis amused herself by playing with Ballard and accepting good-naturedly the disapproval of the Richmond ladies for leaving her baby behind: "We like our babies under foot at all time," she was told. The clear-eyed outsider wrote her impressions of the scene in a memoir, *With Love From Gracie* (1955). The mountains were the Alleghenies, not the Blue Ridge, and the cottages were nineteenth century, but she knew she was in Poictesme.

> James Branch Cabell was at Rockbridge Alum Springs, Virginia, with his wife, step-daughters, and small son. The Alum was a one-time fashionable resort, a spa, where Thomas Jefferson himself had come to drink the mineral waters. The eighteenth-century red brick hotel and cottages were set about a parade ground with circular beds of tired cannas and a hazardous croquet ground, and the Blue Ridge Mountains rose on all sides. In 1909 thirteen hundred people had strolled about the place. In 1919 there were only eighty paying guests, including thirty boys from the Virginia Military Institute who were making up their winter work. Yet the manager was obviously bored by the advent of these two new guests, who when they registered were warned that all they need expect in the way of service were the air and the waters.
>
> We were given one of the little red brick cottages with a fireplace in each room, and when I asked for some firewood against the chilly evening I could have sworn I saw a colored man removing pieces of the porch to make kindling for the fire. During the night it rained on Hal's bed and next morning he complained at the desk.
>
> "Move from Cottage Three to Cottage Five," he was told sharply. "Don't leak so much."
>
> There was an air of fantasy about mealtimes in the decrepit dining room, sitting at table with the creator of Poictesme and surrounded by VMI students and pretty Richmond debutantes, whose mothers wore the smartest of sports clothes and with be-diamonded fingers drank from handleless cups and never resented the lack of cream in their coffee because the manager preferred to give the whole milk to his calves and chickens. (128–29)

From the Alum, the Lewises continued their house-hunting journey north to West Chester where they visited Hergesheimer. Gracie wrote that they outstayed their welcome at the Dower House, but even so Lewis dedicated *Main Street* jointly to Cabell and Hergesheimer.

Back at Dumbarton, Cabell turned his attention to doing chores, writing book reviews, and beginning his encomium of Hergesheimer for the *Bookman*. Cousin Nellie Tompkins was visiting in West Chester, and the

Hergesheimers found her lively chatter more congenial than the literary talk of realist Lewis. September saw the publication of "The Wedding Jest" in the *Century*, a story that found its way into a later edition of *The Line of Love*. *Jurgen* made its appearance on 27 September. Hergesheimer was among the first to write, terming it "a very strange and very beautiful book." Further, he saw it as a projection of its author, "truer than truth, and made to a marvelous extent from your innate being." An anonymous review of *Jurgen* appeared in the New York *Times Book Review* on 28 September, the day following its publication; its author had "become the willing slave of quaint fancy, fecund inventiveness, and unleashed imagination." W.H.C. in the New York *Tribune*, 18 October, commented on his "dramatic use of sex." H. W. Boynton in the *Review*, 25 October, stated that Cabell used too much "erotic symbolism." Heywood Broun in the New York *Tribune*, 17 and 29 November, found Cabell immoral in *Jurgen*. The reviewer for the New York *Globe* compared the work with James Stephens's *The Crock of Gold*, and Samuel Clover in the Richmond *Evening Journal*, 11 October, compared Cabell favorably to George Bernard Shaw.

The sexual implications in *Jurgen* were a calculated risk. Though they were made to appear an inherent part of the work, what is accepted today as natural and integral to life was in 1919 still taboo, considered unnatural and abhorrent. As an author, Cabell was determined to be thought "vital" by Mencken, virile by Holt. Even more, he wanted to jolt what he perceived as popular indifference to his works. Both he and his publisher were aware that the line between the admissible and the inadmissible would be tested. During this anxious period of waiting for the reaction to his calculated gamble, he read Hergesheimer's latest book, *Linda Condon*, and worked on his Hergesheimer paper. He also read Mencken's new book, *Prejudices: First Series*. He and his wife planned a trip to New York for the first week in November, as he wrote Rascoe, "to discover what is being done about marketing *Jurgen*." In this postpartum period he was as yet unaware that *Jurgen* would reel into a life beyond his control, and he confided to his Chicago confessor: "I am appalled by the yawning void which is my mind when I probe thereinto tentatively after the makings of a new book. The last three volumes have been so very cosmical in theme: I cannot go on writing with the universe in general as my topic: so you must prepare for a letting down in scale at least. . . . What to write! I have no notion, and no idea of any sort." "The Feathers of Olrun," published in the December *Century*, flowered into *Figures of Earth*, but as Cabell made clear in his later preface to that work its psychic inception took place the previous April when he opened his study window on a sweet-scented void.

In New York the first week in November, Cabell found that Holt had issued a small first edition of *Jurgen* and that orders far exceeded supply. His indebtedness to Holt, however, made him resist Knopf's continued courtship, although Cabell agreed with others that Knopf's publications as artifacts were the envy of the publishing world. Another publisher's representative, Howard Cook of Moffat, Yard & Company, also continued his campaign of flattery to lure Cabell from McBride. Back home, Cabell heard from two he had long admired and whose approbation he sought: Kipling wrote that he had read *Jurgen* with interest; Maurice Hewlett disliked it at length, saying that he had always "been concerned with love as a passion, and not as an appetite." As *Jurgen* became increasingly attacked and defended by the press, Cabell as a person became increasingly an object of public curiosity. Exposing himself to the scrutiny of the curious was distasteful to his temperament. Shy, misjudged in earlier life, he affected a pose of imperturbability. The curious turned to those who knew him best. Asked about the man behind the writer, Hergesheimer responded to an inquirer: "I am rather overcome at the thought of giving you a picture of Cabell. . . . he is a solidly built man of middle height, with a smooth immobile face, deep-set impressive eyes and a mouth touched with humor. A very aristocratic individual. His essence is an extraordinary combination of irony and romance—commonly supposed to be destructive one of the other—the former increasing with his years." No one, including himself, Hergesheimer perceived, was spared an irony that bordered on the corrosive. As Jurgen learned in the forest, when the brown man with queer feet, Pan, stamped his foot, the earth moved and to the sound of swelling laughter.

Just when Ballard Hartwell Cabell's parents admitted to themselves that he was an "exceptional" child is difficult to determine. In the early years of this century little was published concerning childhood illnesses, and the term "Down's syndrome" did not come into the language until later. The earliest pictures of Ballard show a round face and slanting eyes, but in other ways he appeared a normal child in babyhood. Rather round faces were a family characteristic. Dr. Cabell is said to have realized immediately that his grandchild was born with mongolism but that he did not have the heart to tell the doting parents. Ballard's baby book, a record kept in intimate detail by his father, gives no direct clue to the parents' realization that all was not right with their child. His life is copiously illustrated with photographs through his second year. Ballard did not speak his first word until he was two, an ominous sign today but perhaps not then. A drawing of his hand made on 18 February 1919, when he was three-and-a-half, shows the broad palm and short fingers associated with Down's syndrome. The last entry, still in his father's hand, records Ballard's first attendance at church, 13 June 1920, when he was not quite five. Cabell must have known by then that Ballard was "exceptional," the term he always applied to his son. He may have even been aware that Richmond knew all along.

Ballard's christening in the Victorian Gothic Emmanuel Church at Brook Hill on 11 December 1915 was considered by those assembled to be a symbolic occasion that healed all past grievances. Both sides of the family were witnessing the beginning of a new life that would add an illustrious chapter to their saga. As the rumors about the Cabell baby out at Dumbarton made their way through Richmond, various interpretations were given to Ballard's condition: "Mrs. Shepherd" was too old to be having children; the baby was the victim of uterine exhaustion; the mother had defective genes; her oldest child was an imbecile, (in truth, the victim of spinal meningitis); the father, a profligate in earlier days, had been given to strange sexual preferences; Cabells married late and produced few offspring. The psychically wounded saw the child as divine retribution: a blasphemer, a seeker after strange gods, had fathered an aberration of nature. While the child for Richmonders became a part of the myths surrounding his creative father, at Dumbarton an endearing, strangely wonderful child was bonding two dissimilar parents into a union no normal offspring could have effected. In time, they confessed that they would have rejected "any miracle which might have made him utterly and how far less lovably normal."

As Christmas drew on, James Cabell was attempting to breathe new life into *The Cords of Vanity*. Jurgen the middle-aged poet looked back nostalgically on Townsend the youthful poet. Cabell confided to Rascoe on December 20: "I shall do three more short stories when I have finished the revised version of the *Cords* which is to come out this spring. I am having a fine time with Townsend: definitely dating him first of all from 1898 to 1903 . . . and accounting for and realizing him to the point of convincing myself. With the women I am doing what I can, but some of them stay hazy." Townsend's dates correspond to those of his creator's from the time he left college, through the newspaper years, until the writing of *The Eagle's Shadow*. Alice Serpell, Gabriella Moncure, Norvell Harrison, and Annie Cabell were fading into the past.

As 1919 ended, Cabell was happy with Wilson Follett's review of his work in the *Atlantic*, and the January *Smart Set* also gratified him, with Mencken, George Jean Nathan, and Carl Van Vechten paying their compliments to *Jurgen*. Van Vechten, a newspaperman aspiring to become a serious writer, was soon counted as a Cabell champion. On the other hand, writers on the staff of the New York *Tribune* continued to carp about the work's salaciousness. Walter Kingsley, writing on 3 January, said it was heavily laden with sex and claimed it was being read by chorus girls on Broadway titillated by its innuendos. Troubled by those recent news items, Holt wrote Cabell on the 7th. Even though the better periodicals were praising *Jurgen*, he hesitated to quote them; "shall we dare advertise at all in the newspapers with that damned fool on the N.Y. *Tribune* doing his best to have the book suppressed? For that must be his purpose?" Cabell may have been amused at the conceit of chorus girls reading his work. He replied: "The *Tribune* free advertising, I note, continues, and if it adheres to last Saturday's vein should do no harm. Only I would much prefer to have it shut off altogether."

The *Tribune* notices came to the attention of John S. Sumner, secretary of the New York Society for the Suppression of Vice, whereupon he secured a grand jury indictment in the Court of General Sessions in the county of New York on 14 January charging *Jurgen* with being a "lewd, lascivious, indecent, obscene and disgusting book." Holt's call to Cabell threw the book's author into a state of turmoil, as visions of having to defend his work from the public dock haunted the recluse. At last a letter from Holt saying that his presence was not needed for the book's initial defense relieved that anxiety. Almost immediately Cabell heard from his closest literary friends, Mencken, Hergesheimer, Rascoe, Lewis, Follett. Other sympathetic letters followed, and letters of protest appeared in the newspapers. Englishman Hugh Walpole, at the height of his literary success and lecturing in America, wrote in Cabell's defense, and Ernest Boyd, an Irish critic, wrote from Dublin. With the trial set for 8 March, Holt came down to Dumbarton in mid-February to consult with Cabell. Earlier they had written literary figures for testimonials of support; Mencken, however, had warned that the courts seldom allowed such evidence to be admitted. The scrapbooks were gleaned for evidence of Cabell as an artist, and it appeared to the two that they had a strong case, as Cabell wrote on the 16th. Dreiser, an earlier victim of censorship by moral zealots, wrote suggesting that a defense fund should be established by publishers to hire competent lawyers for the protection of all writers.

Robert M. McBride, the publisher of *Jurgen*, wrote on 1 March that he had "found the biggest lawyer in the United States on questions such as are involved in the *Jurgen* case." McBride went on to list, rather curiously, the political alliances of his expert, John Quinn. Then Mr. Quinn rendered the strange opinion that Cabell would be convicted by the court in ten minutes. The lawyer suggested, "therefore, the plan of having the case put off on the ground that he has just come into it and has not had time to prepare the case, and then later on will have the case set over until the Fall, then the case will very likely be dropped when the Court hears that the book has been stopped and will not be continued to be published." McBride saw no other way out and asked for the author's concurrence. Heartsick, Cabell agreed to Quinn's plan, but he was soon in New York, "drawn thither by the *Jurgen* imbroglio." His publisher attempted to mollify him with publishing plans for new editions of his older works. While there the dispirited Richmonder met Hugh Walpole, who was fascinated by fellow creative spirits, especially males at the center of public attention.

Walpole, in America on his first extended tour as a lecturer, had visited Hergesheimer in West Chester the previous October. Hergesheimer had written Cabell: "Hugh Walpole has just left me after one of the happiest times of my life; and this was added to by the fact that his discrimination applauded you very liberally. I hope you will make an effort to see Hugh while he is in America, he'll be here some five months more, for I can assure you that it would be pure pleasure." When Holt had requested a publicity endorsement for Cabell, Walpole had replied handsomely. In Baltimore, Walpole had challenged Mencken's opinion that the last part of *Jurgen* was inferior to other parts: it "was by far the best." Thus when Cabell received a letter from Walpole on 15 March asking if he could be the Cabells' guest at Dumbarton on 7 and 8 April before going on to visit Ellen Glasgow for the weekend, Cabell readily agreed. The Englishman's popularity was in the ascendancy, and he could help moribund *Jurgen* find a British publisher. Cabell read as many of Walpole's books as he could put hand to and ordered the four latest from Holt. To help entertain Walpole, the Cabells invited the members of the Virginia Writers' Club to tea on the 8th, giving instructions how to reach Dumbarton Grange by train. Nan Lightfoot, the club's secretary, commented in the minutes: "Inside, the uncaged literary lion was prowling to and fro. Mr. Walpole is an affable lion without any whiskers, but with a handsome, young-looking face, although his mane is slightly grey. A number of ladies surrounded him; however, as many, if not more, clustered about Mr. Cabell, for we were determined not to allow our President to be eclipsed by anybody."

Hugh Seymour Walpole was the son of an Anglican clergyman, one who was then bishop of Edinburgh. A product of English public schools and Cambridge, he was as gregarious as Cabell was reclusive. Walpole had a wide acquaintance in the international world of art, music, and theater. Though his extravagant overtures frequently frightened new acquaintances, he most often left people feeling good about themselves. Anglophile Ellen Glasgow was enchanted with the luminary who had burst upon the scene, and his visit was the occasion for the two Richmond writers to draw closer together. Six years older than Cabell, Glasgow shared the same social milieu; her brother Arthur had married Margaret Branch, Annie Cabell's first cousin. Ellen Glasgow, however, did not share James Cabell's neurotic fear of Richmond society, which she regarded with an attitude of amused if critical acceptance. Walpole doubtless sensed a lingering Victorianism in Richmond that amused him. He enjoyed his stays at Dumbarton and One West Main, declaring that Richmond was his American home. Glasgow hoped to establish closer ties to Walpole, whose talk of literary friendships with a menagerie of lions bedazzled her. Walpole, however, was more interested in shy, ironic Cabell, "a friend after my own heart, whom intellectually I can look up to and admire." His biographer, Rupert Hart-Davis, observed that Walpole made a lifelong quest for the "ideal friend," usually among the older men of his acquaintance, especially writers and artists.

Whatever else Walpole may have seen in Cabell, he saw a writer whose major work was the subject of a court case and who thus needed a champion. Himself a facile writer who rarely revised, the Englishman marveled at the studied craftsmanship of the American. Socially he saw an introverted male whose marriage appeared totally devoid of passion. Priscilla Cabell, the antithesis of the dream women, was a prototype of the earth woman, dedicated to the care of her family. The illnesses of her first husband, Isabelle, and Ballard were not burdens for her but rather the focus and justification of her protective instincts. If her seventh child, James, was fretful about his real or imagined woes, she treated him with the same tolerant but therapeutic firmness she accorded all her charges. Walpole easily recognized Cabell's assumed urbanity as a protective shield.

In her efforts to impress the Englishman with Virginia's ties to England, Glasgow arranged an excursion to Williamsburg and Jamestown. Cabell had not returned to the scene of love and sorrow since leaving twenty-one years before. Williamsburg had not yet been restored to colonial splendor, and its homely seediness held associations for him that touched anguished memories. Glasgow knew and doubtless savored the irony, and Walpole too may have sensed Cabell's inner emotional state. Many aspects of Walpole's personality reminded Cabell of Charles Coleman, and the ghost of Gabriella Moncure was everywhere. In Jamestown the three writers gazed at the brown river. William Cabell had settled on the upper reaches of the James, and James Read Branch for whom he was named had drowned beneath its surging waters. It was a river of memories.

For his part James Cabell, wounded socially and artistically, basked in Walpole's healing presence. Convinced that *Jurgen* was a masterpiece second to none, Walpole knew whereof he spoke. He was the protégé of Henry James, the friend of Kipling and Hardy, an intimate of Conrad and Bennett, and indeed was acquainted with a constellation of literary stars. Affectionate inscriptions were written into the Walpole books that Cabell had hurriedly acquired. It was immediately "James" and "Hugh," while others were addressed as "My dear Holt," "Rascoe," "Mr. Hergesheimer" and their letters signed "James B. Cabell." Last-minute complications prevented Cabell from seeing Walpole off when he left Richmond, but he stood beside the tracks at Dumbarton as the Englishman's train sped north. The latter was to spend part of the following week in West Chester with Hergesheimer. In the meantime, however, Hergesheimer stopped off in Richmond on his way home from a four-week sojourn in Cuba. He urged Cabell to join Walpole in West Chester, but Cabell refused. On 18 April Cabell penned a letter to his new friend there:

> . . . Well! Joe will tell you that he and I had at least one good talk, wherein I curiously avoided talking of you—though probably he did not notice that feature. He asked me, be it also known, to come on to West Chester with him, but I could not comfortably imagine the three of us together. "It certainly is" a disconcerting, droll, fine personage, whom I trust you will duly lecture upon the unimportance of externals, before leaving West Chester. For example: he was all excitement as to his recent discovery that a girl with blue eyes and red hair appears to have violet-colored eyes, and that seemed to me an excellent instance of his pre-occupation with such superficial "truths." The love for truth is his tiger, to quote another distinguished author.
>
> I am still wondering about that same distinguished author. Meanwhile I have retired into the not at all lonely solitude that he temporarily invaded or dispersed. . . .
>
> I think obscurely of so much, and set down so little in this letter, which visibly attests little more than my dependency upon the typewriter. And you leave us this week, after, I rather think, an unequaled conquest of affection from coast to coast. For my part, I must leisurely return to a re-reading of your books, finding in them this time your voice and accent and an astounding change— I hope—I repeat, dear Hugh, that you are not going to be a

Shirley or a Massinger among the Limited. I hope you will coldbloodedly comprehend that your endowments will be more profitably invested in writing than in friendship. To love and to be loved is at best your avocation, or in somewhat lower terms grist for your mill. Joe understands this—this much anyhow—far better than you. All is grist. Even you, I hazily foresee in the next story but one by a brown glittering river in the wind.

The letter is signed "Affectionately, JAMES."

A week later, on board the *Mauretania* bound for home, Walpole wrote "My dearest James: I have made four great friends in America, you and Joe are two, and you are outside and beyond all the others. Throw yourself out then to meet it; launch out and come along. You can give yourself up to me and be perfectly safe; look on it as a kind of Jack-in-the-box spree to be indulged in once a year—and then back into your box you may go. . . . Joe is different. I care for him deeply, he is a fine creature, but you I want to protect and help and care for to the end of my days."

Cabell, too, expressed more than common friendship in his 5 June reply. "I am jealous for you, Hugh. I want you to do more than you, or anybody, can achieve. . . . As for our protecting each other! art certainly, and living too, I suspect, must always be a lonely adventure. But one can love, and hope."

Years later when Rupert Hart-Davis asked Cabell about Walpole's letters to him, Cabell lied, saying he had destroyed them. "Hugh's epistolary manner I considered too compromising." To whom? Many of the Englishman's letters to fellow authors read like love letters. The Virginian's letters are far more remarkable, uncharacteristic of his guarded reticence to others. When Walpole's letters to A. C. Benson were returned to him after Benson's death, Walpole himself was shocked by their intimate expression, acknowledging that if he had received such letters from a younger man their tone would have alarmed him. Cabell attributed the cooling of his friendship with Walpole to the 1929 publication of *Frances Newman's Letters*, wherein Cabell is quoted as telling Newman of a remark made by Walpole. Five years earlier when the latter made a list, in his diary, of his closest friends, he named Carl Van Vechten and Joseph Hergesheimer but not Cabell. In *As I Remember It* (1955), which contains his unflattering last words on many of his contemporaries, Cabell touched on Walpole's homosexual aggressions, terming them a "nuisance." In our later-day assessment of the Cabell-Walpole friendship, perhaps we should note a letter that Walpole wrote to Hergesheimer in 1920: "Your saying that you think of making a man's friendship your theme interests me enormously. I could tell you many things about that. They have been the finest things in my life simply because I've never yet found the right woman, but it's a dangerous and difficult subject simply because so many people will see it only as homosexual, which is the last thing it generally is."

In his own first affectionate letter to Walpole, Cabell had written, "All is grist. Even you." His next work, *Figures of Earth*, metamorphosed Walpole into the wayward, adorable Sesphra of the Dreams, Sesphra an anagram for "phrases" and symbol of the suppressed *Jurgen*. Cabell-Manuel is bewitched by the love song of Sesphra and is ready to kill wife and child to follow after his creation. Early in June Cabell received proofs of the Walpole article scheduled to appear in the July *Yale Review*. Cabell wrote: "I love it and I love you." Plans were immediately made to have McBride publish it as a publicity pamphlet, one that would include favorable reviews of Cabell's earlier works.

As one of the first major writers to assess Cabell's total output, Walpole's assessment remains remarkably valid after seventy years:

> Let it be said at once that Cabell's art will always be a sign for hostilities. Not only will he remain, in all probability, forever alien to the general public, but he will also, I suspect, be to the end of time a cause for division among cultivated and experienced readers.
>
> His style is also at once a battleground. It is the easiest thing in the world to denounce it as affected, perverse, unnatural, and forced. It would be at once an artificial style were it not entirely natural to the man. Anyone who reads the books in their chronological sequence will perceive the first diffident testing of it in such early works as "Chivalry" and "Gallantry"; then the acquiescence in it, as though the writer said to himself—"Well, this is what I am—I will rebel against it no longer"; and the final triumphant perfection of it in "Beyond Life" and "Jurgen." (Walpole, 6)

Further, Walpole's assessment of Cabell's position in literary history remains accurate. He saw Cabell as a transitional writer who began in the style of the late nineteenth-century romantics with their stock characters and plots and who emerged after World War I as a leader of the individualists reflecting "independence of thought, courage, and above all what George Moore has called 'the great realism of the idea.'" Cabell is less interested in his characters than in the stream of life that flows beneath them. "In the accepted, conventional sense of the word he is scarcely a novelist at all." His characters are puppets; thus "he is not a modern realist," being basically unaware "of the motives that move ordinary minds." As a writer, Walpole cautioned other critics, Cabell should not be judged by the criteria applied to others. He was strongest speaking in his own voice, "but it is a legitimate criticism, I think, that, being what he is, he would be wiser to leave alone themes that demand realism and psychological analysis for true revelation."

Walpole's analysis strengthened Cabell's own growing conviction that he was essentially a biographer and that all his work was indeed only chapters in an extended biography. If Walpole did not sow the seed of the Storisende Edition of the Works of James Branch Cabell, he was certainly the first attentive gardener to the sprouting acorn. *The Art of James Branch Cabell* appeared in its booklet form later in 1920, and the "books by Mr. Cabell" appendix lists them in "Genealogical Sequence" rather than in their chronological order. The Storisende Edition grew out of the new sequence.

Cheered by Walpole and the resulting publicity of his *Yale Review* defense, Cabell gave himself to writing the episodes that would become his next "novel," *Figures of Earth*. Holt had written earlier that John Quinn, the political lawyer employed to defend *Jurgen*, had been unsuccessful in his ploys to deflect the attacks on its alleged obscenity. Quinn assured Holt that the case would be lost in court with heavy fines imposed; having "earned" his $1,000 fee, he was ready to drop the affair. Because another lawyer would have to be retained, Holt asked if the *Jurgen* royalties could go toward legal fees that had eaten up all of McBride's profits. Cabell agreed, writing Holt on 11 May: "I refuse to defend *Jurgen* on any count: the book must speak for itself: and those who don't like it can go to hell. So I am out with my platform before any of the political parties." With no profits coming in from *Jurgen* despite its inflated sales on the black market, he made plans for reissuing some of his moribund works. The public was curious about the author, and his older titles could be rejuvenated with new prefaces written by his defenders. He asked Hergesheimer to preface *The Soul of Melicent*, to be retitled *Domnei* (Woman Worship). Follett agreed to perform a similar service for a rewritten *Cords of Vanity*, and Mencken took on *The Line of Love*, noting that he was "tempted to write the preface before reading it." Meanwhile episodes of *Figures of Earth* were making their periodical appearances: "The Hour of Freydis" in the May *McClure's Magazine*, "The Head of Misery" in the July issue, "The Hair of Melicent" in the September issue, "The Designs of Miramon" in the August *Century*, and "The Image of Sesphra" in the October *Romance*. Cabell had written all these episodes by 1 July, on which date he wrote Hergesheimer thanking him for the *Domnei* introduction: "Well, my excursus into short story writing is happily concluded, and it is rather good to be back at a book. But my methods of composition invariably appall me at the beginning, with a dispiriting conviction that nothing endurable can possibly come out of such disconnected drivel, so that I view life gloomily these hot adhesive days."

Back up at cool if seedy Rockbridge Alum Springs, Cabell heard from Sinclair Lewis, who was at cool Kennebago Lake, Maine. The latter's magnum opus, *Main Street*, dedicated to "James Branch Cabell and Joseph Hergesheimer," would be out in September.

In his letter to Lewis on 7 August, Cabell described his summer work: "I am 'writing' here, in a sort of somnolent fashion, to the extent of patching together, more or less coherently, the various Manuel stories—I don't know if you have encountered any of them—into a book, for appearance some time after Christmas. Then we are reprinting the earlier ones, in a revised and uniform edition, the first in which, *The Cords of Vanity*, should be out before long with a preface . . . , and later I may be calling on you for an unblushing puff of one of the others. So be prepared. I am using my friends, you see, à la Meredith."

On 22 August, Cabell wrote Walpole: "You are to imagine me, then, exalted by some 2,000 feet of Virginia mountains, and more or less contentedly laboring at (I think) *Figures of Earth* on the same porch whereupon I concocted *The Cream of the Jest* four years ago. We have a little four-room brick cottage here, all save the bathroom rather over a century old, and are content in a queer place to which I have been coming since I was two, and which I mean some day to get into a book."

On 28 September the revised *Cords* was issued by McBride, and Cabell duly dispatched autographed copies to his friends. Certainly Townsend, Cabell's youthful persona, was no more popular in his second appearance than in his first, and the press gave the book scant notice. Cabell later wrote that this was not only his least popular work but also the most actively disliked. Its author, however, could never admit to disliking his creation though he saw clearly enough the structural deficiencies. In it a youthful Gabriella Moncure moved unseen by casual readers. In his preface Follett made a valiant attempt to link it with *Jurgen*, furthering Cabell's efforts to sell his multiple and diverse output as a "biography." This viewpoint was repeated in *Jurgen and the Censor*, privately printed by the Emergency Committee Organized to Protest Against the Suppression of James Branch Cabell's *Jurgen*, a committee composed of Edward Hale Bierstadt,

Barrett H. Clark, and Sidney Howard. Handsomely produced in a limited edition as a collector's item, *Jurgen and the Censor* contained reports, editorial opinions, and numerous testimonials from leading writers who had been solicited for comments. In his report, Barrett Clark observed: "It must be borne in mind that *Jurgen* is no isolated phenomenon; it is an integral part of the world of Mr. Cabell's imagination. It is the crowning episode of the artist's comedy of life. It seems to be his ultimate word upon the subject that underlies all his books, from *The Eagle's Shadow* to *Beyond Life*."

In October, Hergesheimer was rewriting *Steel*, which Cabell had read in periodical form and urged its author to revise. Hergesheimer proposed a trip to Richmond later in the month, but conditions at Dumbarton were not favorable. "I wish I could put you up," Cabell responded. "But we have not had a servant in the house since last spring . . . and you would not be comfortable." He closed with the observation, "I am two-thirds through *Main Street*. I incline to believe that Lewis has really and deeply honored us." A letter to Lewis two days later confirmed the Richmonder's admiration. Mencken wrote that he too was amazed: "I always had a notion that Lewis was a talker—that he planned good books but always wrote bad ones. But *Main Street* is full of genuinely distinguished stuff." Cabell was reading and enjoying Mencken's new *Prejudices*; he wrote to Holt that it was "a really great book in its first 150 pages. Perhaps my interest flagged after he had ceased mentioning me." Mencken credited Cabell with having a large impact on *Main Street*'s better qualities: "I suspect that you preached it into Lewis." *Domnei*, the revised version of *The Soul of Melicent*, prefaced by Hergesheimer, was published on 22 October. A few reviewers suggested that the reissued titles gave their author a chance to trace his growth, but despite the interest in the author of *Jurgen* others questioned "if books such as these . . . should be published again."

Back in Richmond, the local literary scene was undergoing a metempsychosis. The Richmond *Evening Journal* under the guidance of Samuel Clover had done more to champion literary news locally than either of the two other local journals, its Sunday magazine section publishing extended reviews by young feature writers. Emily Clark had developed a column entitled "Browsings in an Old Book Shop," and Hunter Stagg had begun producing extended critiques such as "The Art of James Branch Cabell" (27 June 1920) based on Walpole's *Yale Review* article. Cabell had come to look on the *Evening Journal* as his voice in the community and had alerted its staff to visiting luminaries. Unexpectedly, the publication announced its demise on 25 September 1920, ownership of its assets passing to the Richmond *Times-Dispatch*. The last issue appeared on a Saturday. "Hunter Stagg and I had assisted at its death-bed," Emily Clark wrote of the *Evening Journal* in *Innocence Abroad* (1931), her account of the birth and death of the *Reviewer*, a literary magazine about to be born and intimately associated with Cabell. A few weeks after the demise of the *Evening Journal*, the two reviewers conceived the idea of continuing their literary careers in a publication of their own, and Margaret Freeman, a close friend, agreed to find credit and a printer. Another acquaintance, Mary Dallas Street, contributed seed money to get the project started. A prospectus was sent to possible subscribers in the South and to editors, publishers, and critics in New York. Armed with their prospectus, Clark and Stagg sought endorsements and literary contributions from local writers; the first on their list was James Branch Cabell, president of the Writers' Club. Cabell agreed to meet the neophyte editors at the Virginia State Capitol, where he was attending a meeting of the Virginia War History Commission. Awed by their surroundings and by their quarry's reputation, the editors learned later "that Mr. Cabell arranged to receive them, like honored guests of the State, in the Capitol of the State and of the Confederacy, instead of in his study at home, because it would be a simple matter to get rid of them politely there." Cabell's politeness continued. He recognized that the friendly voice of the defunct *Evening Journal* might be continued in the new publication and indeed might be heard outside Richmond. "His name headed a list, later photographed and broadcast, of every living writer and artist born in the state." Mencken took the list to be the board of directors of the magazine; the New York *Times* saw it as a list of contributors.

Fortunately for Richmond's literary history, the four "editors" of the *Reviewer* suffered from varying social liabilities. Emily Clark, daughter of a deceased Episcopal clergyman, was long on family, short on money, and devoid of beauty. Margaret Freeman was the outspoken, overly positive daughter of a Methodist bigot and a mother sensitive to a restrictive social position. Mary Dallas Street was from a monied family but was a large, masculine, red-faced woman termed by younger contemporaries "Mr." Street. Hunter Taylor Stagg, darkly handsome, subject to seizures from a near-fatal head wound at the age of seven, was a younger son of a father sinking into financial straits. All four knew and associated with the "best people" in Richmond but were excluded from the inner circle based on family, money, and personal beauty, and consequently turned to cultural interests. Thus four social misfits joined forces to bring the *Reviewer* into being. This literary magazine gave Cabell a new voice and introduced him to the woman who became his second wife.

Another stimulus to literary activity in Richmond occurred earlier in November when Miller and Rhoads, a leading department store, instituted an annual book fair. Cabell, Nellie Tompkins, and Nan Maury Lightfoot were the first day's luminaries, each with a booth in which to autograph works. Cabell wrote Holt the following Monday that the fair "passed off splendidly. Miss Duzan, and incidentally Mrs. Cabell, is profoundly enraged with you for having none of my books in. Luckily I had some *Domneis*, a few *Cords*, and a stray volume or two of my other works, which I let Miss Duzan have for my afternoon. I must proudly record that I autographed and sold out every Cabell book in the house, so that dozens were turned away lamenting . . . we could easily, I think, have sold 50 more books if only we had had them. What happened?"

The Miller and Rhoads book fair was the occasion of Cabell's establishing a literary friendship with Frances Newman, an Atlanta librarian, who had come to the notice of authors and publishers for her trenchant reviews in the Atlanta *Constitution*. Miss Newman's sister, Margaret Patterson, was married to a Richmonder, and she took her visiting mother to the book fair. Mrs. Newman wrote Frances on 4 November:

> Armed with Jurgen, we went. A lady M. knew introduced us to Mr. Cabell—he looked at your name on the fly-leaf and said, "Is this Frances Newman of the Atlanta Constitution? I have been thinking of writing to ask her who she is—several things of hers have been sent me by the clipping bureau. One thing she says of me—and he laughed—is that I am 'a man of one idea, but that is more than most people have.'" Also he would like you to send him something you have written of other people. Margaret told Mr. C. she hoped you were coming soon to R. and he asked her please to let him know when you came. Your Jurgen is the most valuable—being of the "suppressed" edition. "With cordial friendly regard. James Branch Cabell" is what he wrote. So you see what has come back to you from casting this Jurgen on the water. A Mrs. Bosher, author, was near him when introduced to Margaret, and Mr. C. said, "You had better be very polite to Mrs. Patterson. She has a sister who is a critic"—and he spoke as if you were quite out of the ordinary.

Frances Newman, herself an aspiring writer and a formidable lion-hunter, wrote thanking Cabell for the autograph and enclosing clippings of her reviews. Ever one to cultivate a friendly critic, Cabell wrote her on 16 November; on the 21st he became the fourth in her series of Literary Introductions to leading authors. Miss Newman's own literary career blossomed, and she and Cabell became admiring advocates until her death in 1928.

14

The High Place

1920–1922

On 15 November 1920, Cabell wrote a long, wooing letter to Rascoe. Pleased with the progress of *Figures of Earth*, which was appearing in periodical fragments and was scheduled as a book for February, he forewarned his least critical critic: "It is, I really think, a good book—not at all cosmic, as I remember foretelling to you a long while back, but vital, and with very lovely bits of gymnastic writing, which upon Untermeyer's suggestion, I shall henceforward describe as contrapuntal prose— However, you can best judge the book when it appears. To Holt it was a hideous and pathetic disappointment, because nothing I could say to him in advance could prevent his looking to find in this book an attempt to rewrite *Jurgen*, and when he found no shadow of such attempt he grieved, as will, I know, a many others."

The reference to "contrapuntal prose" was a hint to future reviewers that the Author of *Jurgen* was resurrecting in prose form more of his college poetry. Louis Untermeyer had admired similar passages in *Jurgen* and had credited Cabell with inventing a new form of prose-poetry. Cabell went on to propose that Rascoe do a preface for one of the earlier works planned for reissue. "I do not offer you *The Eagle's Shadow*, which evidently I must reserve for my own prefacing, under the title probably of *Vingt Ans*

Apres. Any of my literary friends, even you, would handle the book too ferociously." Other writers could relinquish their earlier works, but Cabell saw them all as mirrors. Rascoe, between jobs and temporarily living in his native Oklahoma, was happy to comply with a preface.

A second and slightly revised printing of the collection of stories entitled *The Certain Hour* appeared in December. It bore the brown binding of the Kalki Edition, and the publisher had hopes for the Christmas trade, the suppressed *Jurgen* still stimulating interest in its author. On 11 December Cabell contributed "The Taboo in Literature" to the New York *Evening Post,* utilizing a satirical play on the verb "to eat" as a reference to copulation. Revised as *Taboo,* it was privately printed and distributed by McBride the following March as another attack on the suppressors of *Jurgen.*

At this time, Hollywood as a market for story material came to Cabell's notice via Hergesheimer whose works were attracting filmmakers. *Tol'able David,* based on Hergesheimer's story of the same name, was to prove one of early filmdom's major hits. Barrett Clark, one of the Emergency Committee organizers to defend *Jurgen,* had made a dramatization of *The Rivet* which inspired hope in Cabell that he too would be discovered by Hollywood. The composer Deems Taylor wrote admiringly, Cabell replied charmingly, and a *Jurgen* suite resulted in time. Cabell also received a charming letter from Zelda Fitzgerald, cajoling him to send a copy of *Jurgen* as a Christmas present for her husband. Along with an autographed copy, Cabell sent praise of the twenty-four-year-old Fitzgerald's *This Side of Paradise.* Fitzgerald, according to Rascoe, had written the novel with a copy of *Jurgen* propped before him, being "deeply impressed with the chapter entitled 'The Brown Man with Queer Feet'" and using "the description in several of his stories and in *This Side of Paradise,* without understanding Cabell's use of the symbol." A Christmas Day note of thanks from the rising star revealed he had just finished his second novel, *The Beautiful Lady Without Mercy,* later retitled *The Beautiful and Damned;* Cabell professed looking forward to reading it. Fitzgerald, too, was hearing the siren call of Hollywood, and again Cabell turned his thoughts to dramatizing one of his own works.

Frances Newman arrived in Richmond to spend Christmas with her sister, and on 31 December she was out at Dumbarton. Cabell met her with the greeting, "Well, you don't look so formidable." He showed her the study on the second floor where he created his magic, a ritual he accorded visitors he wished to impress. The ebullient critic and the reticent author got along well. Her acerbic wit and "proper sense of literary values," plus her desire to become a novelist, he found congenial. Rebutting her low estimate of Fitzgerald, he maintained that *This Side of Paradise* had a future in literature; "I began with 'The Eagle's Shadow,'" he remarked, "so I can't afford to be hypocritical." Cabell proposed that Holt should look over Newman's manuscript "Parthenos," an early title for *The Hard-Boiled Virgin*. They discussed Hergesheimer, the next author to be treated in her column. Cabell confided that he himself was trying his hand at drama but feared the strictures of Richmond's Little Theatre League, especially their demanding ladies. Though only nine years Cabell's junior, Frances Newman played the ingenue-soubrette to Cabell's worldly savoir faire. Less than a week later, she wrote from Atlanta, "There are quite five hundred things I grieve that I forgot to speak to you about, so I hope that you will find yourself bold enough to confront the ladies of the Drama League." Their friendship remained firm for the remaining eight years of her life.

In the days that followed, Cabell attended rehearsals of his play and worked on the publicity for *Figures of Earth*. Concerning the latter, he forwarded his ideas to Holt on 26 January: "Herewith a suggestion for the catalogue. It is tentatively rendered, to do with as you like. Of course there are at least two other available "lines": to play up the continuous reliance of mankind upon appearances, as the book's theme: or to assert that the main question raised is, What is success? Grandfather Death ultimately suggests that success consists of being yourself, but there is no reason to suppose that Death is the best possible judge of life— It is distressing to be the author of books so multiplicative in significance that you cannot swear they mean anything in particular."

Listed as a founder and "Honorary Vice-President" of the Little Theatre League of Richmond, Cabell had been cajoled into dramatizing the short story called "Balthazar's Daughter" (1913). The play, retitled "The Jewel Merchants," underwent considerable revision during rehearsal. Louise Burleigh, the director, and the three actors all helped to revise it. On 11 February 1921, Cabell, with an eye on a larger audience than Richmond, wrote his champion Mencken:

> Recently I have ventured into dramatic composition, to the extent of a one-act play, and I am wondering if you would be favorably disposed to consider it for *The Smart Set*. This paragon, I should explain, is based upon my short story, "Balthazar's Daughter," in *The Certain Hour*, and is to be produced by the Richmond Little Theatre League the end of this month. We are now rehearsing it, and as I am learning by experiment what "goes" and what doesn't "go,"

and alter accordingly, the manuscript stays yet in a fluid state. The "literary" graces thus are being steadily eliminated, but, though I say it, the thing acts very nicely. And by about the twenty-fifth *The Jewel Merchants* will have taken its final form.

Performances of the play took place on 22 and 23 February in Binford Junior High School Auditorium, and the local press was enthusiastic. Nan Lightfoot, in the *Bookman* (April 1921), recorded how it was received by the local audience:

> As the curtain fell there was a lone cry of 'Au-thor!,' which, not being taken up, sounded like the voice of one crying in the wilderness. Then we—the audience—'caught on' that we were actually urban enough to be having a first night in our midst, and 'Au-thor!' 'Au-thor!'—'Cabell!' 'Cab-bell!!' resounded.
>
> The dramatist, however, would not take his cue. Mr. Cabell, who under criticism is about as sensitive as the Rock of Gibraltar, is quite the contrary when enduring admiration, and so he sat for some time trying to ignore the outcriers. At last, however, less in response to them than to his wife's urgent whisperings, he rose and bowed twice.

While the putative author pushed for the publication of "The Jewel Merchants" and hoped for other productions, he saw that his melodramatic short stories were not truly dramatic, just as he had seen that his books were not novels in the classic sense. The philosophical conte was his forte, as those who compared him with Voltaire pointed out. The theater Cabell reluctantly ceded to others. He felt some satisfaction when Hergesheimer wrote a little later that "the moving picture people . . . think that they own me" and when he witnessed younger contemporaries squander their talents in Hollywood.

Meanwhile the neophyte editors of the *Reviewer* were putting their first issue together at Margaret Freeman's house on North Harrison Street. Cabell wrote a welcoming letter to another emerging little magazine in New Orleans, *The Double-Dealer*; "A Word from James Branch Cabell: a Letter" appeared in the first issue in January. "Cabell on Degeneracy," another letter, was published in the New York *Globe* on 21 February. The first issue of the biweekly *Reviewer* made its appearance on the 15th, its lead article by Mary Johnston envisioning Richmond as a literary center. Ellen Glasgow graced the third issue, and James Branch Cabell contributed a bit of verse to the fifth. On 26 February the eagerly awaited *Figures of Earth* came from the press. The work made its anticipated impact, rallying the Cabell-oriented coterie and baffling a large segment of the reading public.

Figures of Earth emerged as another allegorical biography. If *Jurgen* was the far-ranging youthful persona of James Branch Cabell, Manuel was the older, more reflective author, although Cabell went to pains to point out in the Foreword that this new hero was not a man of reasoned action but one who acted on chance and impulse. This plot more closely parallels Cabell's career as a writer than does the *Jurgen* journey. Both are circular. Jurgen returns to uncertainty, Manuel to his unrealized dream. "What is that thing?" asks Miramon (Mirror-man) at the beginning and of Grandfather Death at the end. "It is the figure of a man, which I have modeled and remodeled, sir, but cannot seem to get exactly to my liking." Cabell's psychology is impeccably modern seventy years later. Self-identity was the goal. If the mirror of art could truly reveal James Branch Cabell to himself, he would know completion as a man. Manuel stares into the dark pool. "Mistily," he says, "I seem to see drowned there all the loves and desires and the adventures I had when I wore another body than this." Priscilla Bradley Cabell enters as Niafer, first disguised as a boy, mirroring shifting visions of her. Gabriella Moncure enters in several guises, as Suskind (Unkissd), who has shorn a lock of Manuel's hair as Gabriella had of a boy in Williamsburg; also as Freydis, who has the power to animate lifeless figures. The "geas," the bond that was placed on Manuel "to make a figure in this world," had been placed on a boy by the elder Dr. Cabell (who had known Poe), by Martha Patteson Branch (who had known the heroes of the Confederacy), by happy-natured, head-strong Annie Cabell (who had expended beauty, wealth, passion in frivolous pursuits). Somewhere in the mirroring pool was the real James Branch Cabell, who stared back with haunting eyes. Glaum of the Haunting Eyes, another incarnation of the writer, became a character in *Something About Eve*, a work put aside which emerged a few years later.

The appearance of the new novel was anticipated by reviewers nationwide, owing to its predecessor's continued suppression. The extent and depth of its critical notice in the press was exceptional. Cabell's portrait gazed from numerous book pages; headlines heralded reviews. The responses varied greatly, but obviously the work puzzled many. The author as a person was relatively unknown, even in his native Richmond. His publicity over the years, for much of which he was responsible, overemphasized an aristocratic heritage, an aloof refinement, a distaste for popular pleasures. The fact that *Figures of Earth* was a confessional work, an artistic biography, was lost on most reviewers. As Cabell had foreseen, it could not be dissociated from *Jurgen*. "Sad," wrote the critic for the New York *Times*, of the new work; "cheerful," remarked the *Nation*. "Uneven . . . overwritten . . . underwritten," said the *Dial*; "a classic," Ben Hecht declared in the Chicago *Daily News*. Cabell added the names of Fanny Butcher, Vernon Lewis Parrington, and Carl Van Doren to his lexicon of champions. An old idol, Maurice Hewlett, provoked wrath with "The Essentials of Nonsense" in the New York *Evening Post Literary Review*, wherein *Figures* was termed "excessively tiresome." Two assessments appear justifiable today: the judgment of *Booklist*, which prophesied that *Figures* would be "understood and enjoyed only by a few," and that of J. A. Thomas in the *Yale Literary Magazine*, who categorized Cabell as "a writer for the elect—but for the elect of all time."

The following month, McBride launched another attack against the suppressors of *Jurgen* with a distribution of 920 copies of *Taboo*. Dedicated to John S. Sumner, it credited him with waving his fecundating wand over the writer's moribund works, and investing them with life. Satirical innuendo could hardly go further. From Chicago, Margaret Saunders wrote asking permission to make a play of *The Cords of Vanity*, a proposed vehicle for Henry Hull. McBride decided to publish *The Jewel Merchants* in the fall for Little Theatre use.

Responding to autographed copies of *Figures of Earth*, Fitzgerald and Lewis wrote letters of praise for the new work. Mencken, while laudatory, ranked it below *Jurgen*. Walpole found some things in it "too hard" but promised to read it again; his review in the *Nation* pleased Cabell for not comparing *Figures* with *Jurgen*. Letters of appreciation for every kind word flowed from Richmond, Cabell usually devoting Saturday to his correspondence. Frances Newman found the new work greater than *Jurgen*, and of her paeans in the Atlanta *Constitution* Cabell wrote that "all else pales before the delight I got from your review." Carl Van Doren had, to the author's pleasure, "recognized in Manuel the deflected artist." Frances Newman wrote, "Someday . . . you must do an edition after the manner of Henry James' New York edition, with an auctorial introduction for every one of your opera" (March 13). While Cabell professed not to like Henry James, this was advice sweet to the ear, and encouragement for his Storisende Edition.

In April Hergesheimer, on his way from Aiken to West Chester, stopped in Richmond, and on Cabell's forty-second birthday he lunched at Dumbarton. Another guest was Margaret Newman Patterson, sister of

Frances Newman, about whom the talk centered. As a strong voice in the Sahara of the Bozart, Newman's reviews were widely reprinted in other southern papers. Cabell and Hergesheimer had become critics and were a mutual promotion team. Cabell's *Joseph Hergesheimer*, scrapped together from laudatory reviews appearing earlier, was about to be published by the Bookfellows in Chicago and would be included in *Straws and Prayer-Books*. Hergesheimer's April visit to Richmond was the usual occasion for festivities where he was lionized. Lodged in the prestigious Westmoreland Club, he was a guest-of-honor at a reception given by the Cabells to which members of the Writers' Club and the fledgling editors of the *Reviewer* were invited. At Margaret Freeman's he debated "the artist" with voluble, opinionated pianist John Powell, then at the height of his fame.

Hergesheimer was also the center of attention at a meeting of the Writers' Club, where he graciously autographed copies of his works. There, at the home of Nan Lightfoot, he again met Emily Clark. An editor of the newly established *Reviewer*, she was aggressively determined to make it the vehicle for personal recognition. Approaching thirty, impecunious, thin before it became modish, with a nose termed a "snout," she fixed on bewildered, fascinated Hergesheimer as the wizard who could make her dreams come true. Her letters to him over the next four years, until she captured a wealthy overage knight, are the counterpart of her verbal histrionics, a breathless monologue in southern intonations rendered unintelligible by a lisp that left her Yankee victims, her favorite prey, gasping in befuddlement. Carl Van Vechten said upon meeting her, "Your voice and accent are enchanting, but I can understand scarcely a word you say." Later Hergesheimer observed that a man was lucky to escape Emily with the shirt still on his back, but in April 1921, beguiled by his Richmond acceptance, he agreed to call on her with suggestions for the *Reviewer*. In *Innocence Abroad*, Clark speaks of the success of that meeting: "There burst upon our incredulous but enraptured ears the statement from Joe that he not only would contribute a series of articles to the magazine, but would collect for us six other articles by eminent writers of America and England. We had not then dreamed of such magnificence. Mr. Galsworthy and Sinclair Lewis were among the names he mentioned. Mr. Cabell maintained an almost Chinese calm. 'What will *you* do, James?' Joe pointedly inquired. Mr. Cabell, who later did many things, refused to commit himself." (89)

While the Hergesheimer-Cabell alliance grew stronger, older allegiances fell away. When Maurice Hewlett, Cabell's youthful idol, attacked

Figures of Earth in the New York *Evening Post Literary Review* on 23 April, the Richmonder uncharacteristically counterattacked the following day, saying that Hewlett, fortunately, had confused the real authorities cited in *Figures* with the fictitious. "Mr. Cabell Replies" appeared in the 30 April *Literary Review*. His explanation to Holt was "that nobody is interested in a defense, whereas everyone delights in an attack." On 29 April Cabell had written Sinclair Lewis congratulating him on the sales of *Main Street*, adding, "And you appear, too, to be winning almost equal laurels at the lecturing—wherein, by the way, you are proving the best advertising agent I ever had."

On his return to West Chester, Hergesheimer pressed the Cabells to visit him at the Dower House. His promise to "shoot Mrs. Cabell around in my little Fiat" was probably the persuasive lure for her whose love affair with driving lasted a lifetime. At the end of May the Richmonders made their long-delayed visit to West Chester, an event widely reported, the occasion for visits by other notables with pictures made for rotogravure sections of newspapers. In his *We Were Interrupted*, Rascoe left us a picture of the Dower House and of Hergesheimer's style of living:

> I visited Hergesheimer for a week end at Dower House, West Chester, Pennsylvania. Dower House was an ancient Pennsylvania Dutch house built of local boulder stones, with all the original timber still intact. He had made almost enough money to pay for the house and modernize it by writing about it in the *Saturday Evening Post*; he was especially proud of the Dutch-oven fireplaces, five feet tall, six feet wide, and about four feet deep, which had been walled up when he bought the place and behind the sealing walls of which he had found ancient hand-wrought iron hooks, cranes, cooking utensils, fire prongs, and lighters.
>
> Joe was an epicure and an exponent of charming living; he delighted in glassware, fabrics, and fine wines; he had become a collector of book rarities and first editions and he pored over the new collectors' catalogues that had been delivered in the morning's mail while we ate a fine breakfast of fruit, scrapple, sausages, eggs, toast, and coffee served on antique Dutch china. He was an entertaining monologuist and his lovely wife, Dorothy, was a pretty and gracious hostess. (93)

While gregarious Joe Hergesheimer thrived in the bustle of worldly excitement, after his visit to the Dower House Cabell confided to Holt, "What I need is a desert island with a good mail service."

Back in Richmond, Cabell was induced into joining local socialites at Reveille, a pre-Revolutionary War estate in the western environs of Richmond. There Pernet Patterson had built a log cabin on his sister's property where amateur theatricals were given. Richmond had become drama crazy, and the Cabineers, as they called themselves, brought covered-dish suppers and invited visiting celebrities such as Hergesheimer to join them in their rustic revels. There in early June, Cabell was cornered by Emily Clark and Mrs. Stuart Rennolds, a sophisticated beauty. The latter reproached Cabell for allowing himself to be "vamped" by Emily. He demurred, but he was assured it was the "most insidious kind, being disguised by an ingénue manner." Nervously Cabell admitted that it must be an entirely new and unrecognizable variety. Later in June, Cabell refused to journey north on his wife's urging; she could visit her sister on Long Island, but he had no business to attend to in New York. Emily wrote Hergesheimer on the 18th: "Mrs. Cabell has just come back, and she's sort of edgy, like Dame Lisa in Jurgen. She was so put out with him. He looks very stubborn."

In July the Dumbarton ménage made its annual hegira to the Rockbridge Alum Springs. Long in decline, to the dismay of the sociable Percie, the Alum with its associations continued to be an irresistible lure for Cabell. For one with no hobbies, no interest in sports or in being entertained, the Alum's decline was no deterrent. Let the social-minded continue their revels at the White or the Hot; Percie could motor over to those meccas of pleasure. It turned out to be the last season for the venerable spa, and on arrival Cabell caught "a peculiarly vicious cold in the head" that affected his eyesight. Admittedly, the Alum was not a good place to enjoy bad health. Joe and Dorothy came for a visit in August. Dorothy and Percie had their domestic interests, and the two writers had their craft. Hergesheimer's Tol'able David was being filmed in nearby Highland County. There Joe and Dorothy had lived in a tent during a rainy spell so that, unlike the Sinclair Lewises the previous summer, they were not appalled by the Alum's primitive comforts. Joseph Hergesheimer's career was still in the ascendant, his heroes seen as embodying American virtues although their single-minded actions echoed the older success-or-failure formula. In his critiques of his friend's work, Cabell commented on this "mimic" hero, "hagridden by one or another sole desire." Concerning his essay the "Feminine Nuisance," appearing in the July Vanity Fair, Cabell chided Hergesheimer, "You have, I see, been at it again—I allude to the pernicious practice of reading Henry James." Hergesheimer, in turn, was distrustful of Cabell's intrusive irony. While the two writers had their critical differences, they shared artistic concerns over the effects of time and change, particularly the way in which the tyranny of the past inhibited a person's present. Hergesheimer may not have seen that Cabell's irony sprang from the autobiographical nature of the latter's hero, which precluded elegiac apostrophes to the perfection of the past. The Pennsylvanian's unquestioning allegiance to the presumed perfection of the past made some of his fiction read like that of Thomas Nelson Page.

Inspired by Hergesheimer's interest in the *Reviewer*, Cabell made its editors a handsome offer: he would edit three issues of the monthly magazine beginning in October. The prestige of his name and the contributors it would attract brought ready acceptance. Cabell had attended Emily Clark's tea with Joe Hergesheimer in April, and he continued to meet with the editors in her Park Avenue residence, a typical "Lower-Fan," late-Victorian structure. At these meetings, the admiring, charming Hunter Stagg impressed Cabell; Hunter's childhood illness had allowed a wide reading in the English classics that gave his reviews a rich texture. Cabell considered them the best feature of the new magazine, somewhat to Emily's chagrin. This offer to edit stemmed from Cabell's warm memories of his sophomore year at college and his editorship of the college literary magazine. Further, he saw that with the interest of Mencken and other established writers, the fledgling publication could focus the attention of the literati on Richmond, bemusing the locals. It was another distraction for those who remembered the old gossip of deviance and murder. Ironically, however, it stimulated their memories. Emily wrote Hergesheimer, "I've heard such an interesting and authentic story about him, but I can't write it—it happened a long time ago."

Cabell found editing the *Reviewer* both irksome and amusing; it preempted his creative writing time, but he enjoyed soliciting material from the titans and playing editor to the aspiring. Mencken promised to contribute, "once I get the sand out of my eyes," a reference to "The Sahara of the Bozart." Guy Holt, Frances Newman, and Carl Van Vechten were appealed to, the latter on the eve of his literary celebrity as a novelist of twenties sophistication. Cabell was miffed that the usually toadying Rascoe did not respond in time for the October issue, the first issue of the *Reviewer* as a monthly publication. The four novice editors had produced twelve fortnightly issues. With an expanded format to play with, Cabell led off with Mencken's "Morning Song in C Major," another treatise on the arts in the South. Soon-to-be-well-known Julia Peterkin made her bow, and Frances Newman proved to an enlarged readership that she was a stylish literary critic. Disliking wasted space on a page, the editor penned amusing fillers, attributed to Burwell Washington, Henry Lee Jefferson, and A. C. Fairfax. The October issue also saw the debut of another Cabell amusement, "The Lineage of Lichfield," wherein he began to link all his protagonists in an elaborate fictive genealogy. "A bore," Emily wrote Joe, but it resulted in another "chapter" of the biography-to-be.

Emily Clark's pleasure in being associated with Richmond's local literary lion was tempered by his editing edicts. She wrote her confessor in West Chester on 26 October: "Mr. Cabell is being arbitrary about The Reviewer, but his regime only lasts through the December issue. He edits things and changes our proof, and he has made me say 'sonorous balderdash' in my November article—a phrase I would never have used in a thousand years. Don't tell *anybody* I said this." In the same letter she waxed hilarious about Margaret Freeman's flattering attentions to Cabell, attentions remembered by the author at seventy when he was again looking for a wife. Emily also included news of Percie Cabell: "Mrs. Cabell left for New York last night without Mr. Cabell. She thought until the very last minute that he was going, just as she did last spring when you came down, but he got in the same stubborn fit and stayed behind. She's furious. He's implicated in a vortex of parties, as Grace Shepherd is a debutante. They are giving a big dance for her in a few weeks, and I wait with interest to see if he really will stand in a line and receive with his wife and family. I know he'll crawl out of it, don't you?"

Although thirty, Emily Clark's social ambitions rivaled those of Percie Cabell for her attractive daughters. Though Emily adorned her person, she had decided that she would attract by being a "personality." She studied other "personalities." Using Amélie Rives's interest in the *Reviewer*, Emily cultivated the older celebrity and her husband, Prince Pierre Troubetzkoy. The latter had painted a stunning portrait of Ellen Glasgow a few years earlier and had been commissioned to paint Miss Jennie Ellett, Cabell's early teacher. In July Emily visited Castle Hill, the ancestral acres of William Cabell Rives, Amélie's father and home to the Troubetzkoys. There she made much of her association with Cabell and Hergesheimer and was urged to bring them to Castle Hill. Emily relayed a wealth of gushing detail to Hergesheimer, later recapitulated in *Innocence Abroad*. Further, her visit allowed her to invite the princess to Park Avenue when the latter consulted a Richmond dentist in October. At Emily's house, James Cabell met his celebrated older cousin. Although born in Richmond, Amélie Rives rarely visited the city. Cabell assured his cousin that he had read *The Quick or the Dead?*, her literary *cause célèbre*, in the year of its appearance, when he was nine. A shocker for its time (1888), it may have elicited the curiosity of non-literary Annie Cabell, and a curious boy may have picked it up. Cabell, knowing of Amélie Rives's interest in Hergesheimer, presented her a copy of his panegyric on the Pennsylvania writer which had just arrived from the press.

In a letter to Frances Newman on 24 October, Cabell observed that his correspondence had suffered owing to his "trying simultaneously to write, conduct a magazine, sit for a portrait, and bring out a debutante step-daughter." Later in the month, while visiting her sister, Newman entertained the Cabells, with Emily Clark and Hunter Stagg calling later. "Hunter," Frances wrote a young friend, "is far the cleverest and most attractive of the Reviewers." Newman was invited to attend a meeting of the *Reviewer* staff at Emily's house, but there the visitor devoted her attention exclusively to Cabell so that Emily and Hunter "retired unobtrusively to another room, where we gave way to uncontrolled mirth at our insignificance in her cosmos of that moment." Frances Newman journeyed on to New York and learned from Guy Holt that a new lawyer had been engaged by McBride to take over the defense of *Jurgen*, deemed a hopeless case by the pessimistic Quinn. Frances wrote Emily, "It's the oddest thing that *Jurgen's* lawyer is an old and intimate friend of ours—Garrard Glenn, who grew up half a block from us. We are going to a play with them Friday." Garrard Glenn was a brother to Isa Glenn, soon to make a literary name for herself. Isa later became a friend of Hunter Stagg. Frances Newman wrote Cabell in November concerning the new lawyer: "Margaret is very anxious for Garrard and his wife to come down to visit her so that he may see you—his wife was a girl from Albemarle County, a really charming woman." Alerted by the gossip, Cabell wrote Holt, "What is the status of the *Jurgen* case? and what imports the nomination of this Garrard Glenn for the defense?" Glenn, he was informed, was with the firm of Goodbody, Danforth & Glenn and had been engaged by McBride. A native of Atlanta, Glenn held a law degree from Columbia. He later became a distinguished professor at the University of Virginia.

Cabell's emergence as a personage in the national media was noted in Williamsburg. The June issue of the *William and Mary Literary Magazine* contained "Cabell: Short Story Writer." That fall the Kappa Alpha fraternity, assuring Cabell that they ranked him among their distinguished alumni, invited him to a rush party along with a congressman and a senator; they asked him to send an autographed picture. The November *Vanity Fair* featured "The Comedian," wherein the Richmond author postulated that life is essentially the same comedy played over and over, enacted on various stages and in diverse costumes. It became the preface to *The Lineage of Lichfield*, which appeared serially in the *Reviewer*. A revised version of *The Line of Love*, with a preface by Mencken, and a revised *Chivalry*, prefaced by Rascoe, appeared on 15 November. The critics frankly accepted these reprints as apprentice works by the Author of *Jurgen* trading on his notoriety. What else could he do with the masterpiece suppressed? A theater impresario in New York wrote asking the Richmond author to translate Brieux's comedy *Les Hannetons*, Cabell's "a name glamorous to link with Brieux's."

For some time Hergesheimer had been planning to bring Mencken to Richmond to meet Cabell; he proposed coming about 25 November, a Friday. Cabell replied on 2 November: "It will be fine should you both come. I shall be turning out a debutante step-daughter at just that period, and you might help me to stand it." Two days later he elaborated:

> Your telegram has just been telephoned out to me. But of course do you and Mencken come just as you had planned. We are giving on the evening of the twenty fifth a dance, for the younger set, at the Woman's Club, and this I shall have, I suppose, to attend. But it would be to me a joy, and a real comfort in tribulation, if both of you would come too. Invitations are duly going forward to both, and to all the Reviewers, and I shall reserve the library for the literary guests, so that we can withdraw utterly from the dancers when we so elect. It would be an addition to the party, I candidly confess, should you bring something on the hip, as by force of circumstances the affair will be Saharan.
>
> So come. I really want you to. And all the remainder of that weekend is free.

Although Mencken had reservations about wearing dress clothes to the party, Hergesheimer was enthusiastic about the occasion—"it ought to be chaste, refined and elevating, noble in thought and deed." The metaphorical hip would be remembered, although Emily Clark remarked later that the two visitors remained impeccably sober. Emily entertained them at a dinner before the party to which she invited her stepmother, Cabell, Pierre Troubetzkoy, and one other patrician lady who, according to Emily, was descended from "practically everyone on the Washington monument [in Capitol Square]." At the Woman's Club, while the debutantes danced, the Reviewers retired to the library with the literary luminaries and were promised increased help for their magazine. The party was considered a great success. On the following evening in Hergesheimer's room at the Jefferson, Cabell amused himself by defending the immortality of the soul against the excited scientific rationality of Mencken. The visitors were taken to see Tuckahoe, where the Sales lived in the ancestral home of the Randolphs. They were entertained at Reveille by the Crutch-fields, and by the well-to-do Triggs. Handsome, charming Emma Gray Trigg with her sultry voice captivated the dandy Pennsylvanian. Rascoe observed of him, "He winks at women with an air of self-confidence and smiles at them as if there were something between him and them." Other handsome matrons in Richmond flowered under his gaze. It was a game that Cabell had played only in his writing; in real life it made him uncomfortable. Indefatigable Emily Clark hustled Hergesheimer up to Castle Hill for a visit to the Troubetzkoys. On the train, usually affable Joe maintained a glum silence. In a long letter of mingled praise and reproach, Emily wrote to him upon his return home:

> Mr. Mencken says you are insane. Why? The Troubetzkoys were charmed with you, even though I was not. You were very kind and sensible in many ways and I'm ever so grateful for it and the wonderful manuscripts for The Reviewer, but I can't see why you were so cross with me unless you didn't want to go to Castle Hill and I let you in for it. But it didn't last long and you did like the other people I arranged for you to meet here. . . . Amélie says Mr. Cabell lives in an ivory tower, and Alice says he's the only person she's ever seen who has achieved complete detachment like the people in India. . . . Mrs. Cabell says you told her you didn't like anybody in Richmond any more, and that you were never coming back again. I think it was very unkind of you—and to her, of all people—and several persons' feelings are hurt. . . . Did you say those dreadful things to Mrs. Cabell? (*Ingénue,* 38)

Doubtless Priscilla Cabell, like other Richmond women, had spoken to Emily Clark about her harassing pushiness, especially in regard to Herge-sheimer whom Emily monopolized. When Hergesheimer assured her that he had not disparaged his Richmond friends, Emily's neurotic response was, "I'm glad you didn't say those things to Mrs. Cabell—she's a very common woman and it's better not to forget it." Emily's uncharitable view of a wife protective of her husband's writing time, especially when she had to listen to his grumblings about the Emily Clarks of this world, was shared by Margaret Freeman and others who wished to claim him as their playfellow. Of the Reviewers, Priscilla Cabell was fond only of Hunter Stagg. His undemanding manner, his politeness, and her husband's admiration for his perceptive reviews made him a congenial guest. Emily Clark, who felt herself better born than Priscilla Cabell, avidly read *Town Topics: The Magazine of High Society.* In its columns the activities of Richmond's elite followed those of Baltimore, where Emily had relatives, and came before those of Washington. Its tone was knowing, amused, and Fitzgeraldian in its awe of the privileged. Emily Clark never saw her name in its pages, but Priscilla Cabell and her daughters were featured almost as frequently as Lady Astor, soon to visit Virginia with her titled husband.

In a series of review-critiques appearing in the *Nation*, Carl Van Doren was according Cabell high praise as a growing artist, and Cabell wrote grateful responses. "Van Doren," he wrote Holt, "has the best sense of form, I mean in what he himself writes, of anybody now criticizing . . . a joy and wonder." Hergesheimer's new work, *Cytherea*, was scheduled for publication on 3 January, but Cabell received an advance copy and read it over the Christmas holiday. A novel again treating a man's obsession with an idealized female, it was the Pennsylvanian's greatest success to date. On the day of its publication, Cabell wrote glowingly, "I am very proud to know you." Their friendship allowing a relatively frank exchange of critical opinions, Hergesheimer had awaited Cabell's verdict with anxiety. He answered two days later with relief. He had reached a stage in his career where he was safe to write as independently as he was able. Further, he was setting out on a journey that would "include literally everything in the United States, north and east and south and west. . . . Lorimer is sending me, and I am to write in a pattern entirely to my own liking and of my own choice." It sounded very much like Manuel in *Figures of Earth*, setting off to redeem Poictesme. Cabell too had attained the high place, but he could not be totally free as long as *Jurgen* was suppressed in the United States. It was, however, being published in England with illustrations by Frank Papé. Louis Untermeyer wrote Cabell on 10 January: "The English edition of *Jurgen* has finally come from The Bodley Head. It is, in many ways, a beautifully made volume. But it is an unevenly illustrated one." In *Figures of Earth* Cabell foreshadowed the course of *Jurgen* through the world; it would become an alter-ego, with a life of its own. Sesphra, anagram for *phrases*, is amoral, pagan, and walks with a limp, but at this time it had not overshadowed its creator's persona. Cabell still held his identity as a growing artist, yet to be defined by the critical establishment.

The pedagogue-critics of the day saw Cabell as the leading exponent of a revival of romanticism in literature that ran counter to the entrenched realism of Howells and Dreiser. Even so, while he did not treat the contemporary scene, except allegorically, he was not distanced from Sinclair Lewis and Scott Fitzgerald, perhaps because of the close and cordial interest that these three entertained in one another's work. Fitzgerald's romanticism was that of the adolescent, and Lewis was a romantic cynic who viewed modern society satirically. At this time Lewis was writing *Babbitt* (whose hero was the quintessential American go-getter) from the vantage point of Europe, while savoring its culture for a year. On 22 February 1922 he wrote Cabell a long letter from London, saying how frequently he had thought of the Virginia writer. Despite Lewis's admitted appreciation for European refinement, the intellectual stimulation, the seductive luxury, he thought of it as more properly Cabell's milieu: "I remain, I suppose (perhaps to my advantage) incurably a brash and provincial American." But "you, who are of essence European," would be properly at home. Even though he had found Cabell's favored retreat deplorably primitive, "last summer I thought of the Alum. Even in Kent, with shadows forever crossing the North Downs just above the Pilgrims' Road, I longed for that little porch, and the cornfield, and the hills."

On 24 February Cabell wrote Scott Fitzgerald, thanking him for a copy of *The Beautiful and Damned*; he had read all but the closing episode in the *Metropolitan*. As an ardent reviser himself, he was especially attentive to the changes Fitzgerald had made. Writing from St. Paul, "this swollen Main Street," Fitzgerald observed that he had met Hergesheimer and asked, "When do we meet?" He consciously borrowed Cabell's complimentary close, "Yours faithfully." A few days later he wired Cabell asking permission to cite part of Cabell's letter for publicity promotion. In a follow-up letter he explained: "Maxwell Perkins of Scribners had heard from some editor in Richmond that you liked the book. He had tried to get in touch with that editor [Emily Clark] to see if it was quotable— realizing how invaluable a word from you might be." On 21 March, Mencken wrote Cabell: "Fitzgerald blew into New York last week. He has written a play, and Nathan says it has very good chances. But it seems to me that his wife talks too much about money. His danger lies in trying to get it too rapidly. A very amiable pair, innocent and charming." Writing from New York on 27 March, Fitzgerald thanked Cabell again for his endorsement and exulted over the sales of the new book. Then he made a suggestion: "Why do not you publish a geography of the lands of your own creating on the inside, front and back covers of your next book, much as Conrad has in the last edition of *Victory*. I think it would be very amusing both for you and for your public." Cabell began to amuse himself with such a map, which appeared in Carl Van Doren's 1925 monograph on Cabell and still later in *Townsend of Lichfield*.

On 25 March Cabell wrote Van Doren asking when his new treatise on the American novel would be out, and the following month he received an inscribed copy of *Contemporary American Novelists*. Cabell was grateful for the book and his place therein, but he had reservations about Van Doren's suggestion that he should write a modern comedy of Virginia. In light of Cabell's closeness in spirit to Lewis and Fitzgerald, the suggestion would appear valid, but he wrote, "I distrust the contemporaneous." Further, his parenthetical "In passing, I have never laid the scene of a book in Virginia" is pure evasion. Lichfield and Fairhaven have no fixed locale, but they are all too obviously Richmond and Williamsburg and therefore "in Virginia." His distrust of the contemporary scene grew out of the pain of his formative years, which led him to mask his social satire in allegory; it was set in mythical Poictesme whose map he began to draw. Faulkner too, consciously emulating Cabell, drew a map for the setting of his great epic. Cabell's slight epic, *The Lineage of Lichfield*, was published in an elegant format in April. He was again indebted to Van Doren for its most perceptive review. "I am the more grateful for that I still insist, in the teeth of my publisher's skepticism, that the opus is an illuminating, if not an actually requisite, approach to the shape and sum of my writing." It was another step to the Storisende Edition—not truly an end but a summing up, a statement for posterity, a reassurance to his daemon. The artist was in a reflective mood, for his father (from whom he had inherited a certain reserve) was uppermost in his mind.

Dr. Cabell, now in his seventy-fifth year, lay dying. He had retired as superintendent of the City Home and was living with his oldest brother, Caskie Cabell, and Caskie's wife, Nannie Enders Cabell. Also living at 903 Floyd Avenue was Dr. Cabell's widowed sister, Agnes Bell Cabell Lottier. Their three-story late Victorian house faced for a while the present James Branch Cabell Library, but in 1922 none of its occupants could have foreseen that a library would honor James Cabell. True, he was attracting a certain notoriety, just everywhere, but that book *Jurgen* was suppressed for being obscene. You were kind of embarrassed when friends asked if you had read it. It was all just a lot of fairy-tale nonsense. Poor Annie's son had always seemed to get himself talked about. But that fine woman he married, despite her pushiness, had just established the Virginia chapter of the National Society of Daughters of the American Colonists; as regent, her photograph appeared with a headlined article in the social section of the Richmond *Times-Dispatch* for 16 April.

Recently turned forty-four, Cabell was desperate to reanimate his youthful works while *Jurgen* cast a lurid but commercial light on its author. He refurbished *Gallantry*, scheduled for publication in June with an introduction by Louis Untermeyer. One of his short stories from this collection had been dramatized and was being produced at the Woman's Club. Emily reported to Joe: "It was Mr. Cabell's story, 'Simon's Hour,' from Gallantry, dramatized as the Little Theatre League did the first one last year. Douglas Freeman was the most important person in it and was remarkably good—a debauched English vicar and loathsome beyond words. John Powell was asked to be in it and refused. It was a better play than the one the Little Theatre gave. I don't know whether Mr. Cabell liked it or not. He sat in the first row and looked perfectly phlegmatic" (58). Douglas Freeman, editor of the Richmond *News-Leader*, had not yet adopted his spartan regimen nor stunned Richmond with his monumental four-volume *R. E. Lee*. John Powell was the celebrity of the hour; his concerts in New York the year before had drawn rave reviews, the *Evening Post* declaring that the mantle of Paderewski had descended on his shoulders. At the time "Simon's Hour" was being produced, Powell was informing friends that he had only a few months to live, an announcement received with disbelief; he was obviously enjoying his celebrity status too much. The old stone house on Main Street was being turned into a Poe Memorial by the Archer Joneses. For its opening, Emily reported to Joe, "a weird collection of Virginia 'artists' will be guests of honor, from Mr. Cabell and John [Powell] to Miss [Margaret] Montague and Mrs. Bosher." James Cabell, withdrawn, reticent, attended the obligatory social functions with his loquacious wife, but these scenes were to him unreal, a theater of puppets. He longed to return to the "reality" awaiting him in his study. Vibracious (Ballard's word) Frances Newman had again descended on Richmond, visiting her sister, but she was in deep mourning for her mother who had just died.

On 7 May 1922, Dr. Robert Gamble Cabell, Jr., died. His passing was front-page news in the Richmond papers. One of the last gray heroes had entered Valhalla. The boy-soldier who at seventeen had caught his mortally wounded brother as he fell at the Battle of New Market, the selfless physician who had dedicated his later years to the care of the indigent in the City Home, was interred with appropriate honors in Hollywood Cemetery. His grave was near those of his Presbyterian parents, just as Annie Cabell had been buried in the same cemetery alongside her Episcopalian mother and father.

James had never enjoyed intimacy with his courtly, reticent father. After his fifteenth birthday the son had rarely seen the man who had given him life, but now that the elder Cabell was dead his son felt a compelling need to understand him. James Cabell now stood on another plateau from which to view the past. His father, he began to perceive, had very early raised his eyes to the high place where beauty and holiness are enshrined. For a while, like many another chivalrous youth, the young Robert Cabell, Jr., thought he beheld the ideal in the face of a woman. Annie Cabell, longing to remove the garments of an elegiac South, to give herself to the joy of life, had no desire to be idealized. Now, at midpoint in life and career, the writer began to understand his parents' relationship, the conflicting ideals, the disparity of temperaments, the financial stresses. James Cabell's teen-age suppressions had resulted in fictional matricide and patricide, but with the real deaths of his parents a more compassionate "reality" of understanding could give them rebirth. Dr. Cabell's virtuous reticence and Anne Branch Cabell's gallant attempt to embody abstract concepts were seen in a tenderly ironic mood. Cabell longed to translate their pain into healing art. Another chapter in the biography had to be written. Cabell's tenderest, most understanding evocation of lost love, lost dreams was burgeoning into life.

"The writing of 'The High Place' was begun in 1922," its author later recorded, and he remembered "the book was planned, at Dumbarton, in the early spring of 1922." Dr. Cabell's death on 7 May removed the last restraint from telling his story. Cabell was now a master of the philosophical quest. He understood fully its function, artistically and philosophically. His father's death liberated him psychologically as well. The painful details of his parents' unhappy marriage underwent a metamorphosis, emerging as a comedy of disenchantment. Indeed, theirs was a universal drama, inherent with the ironies that underlay all great literature. Moved by his theme, and at the height of his creative powers, James Branch Cabell began to write his best work.

The Journey to Antan

The Magic Circle

1 9 2 2 – 1 9 2 4

In May 1922, Cabell's friendliest critic, Carl Van Doren, asked him to review Arthur Machen's republished *House of Souls*. "No, you must not tempt me to write now about Machen." Cabell replied. "I am already tied up with family affairs and disordered vision . . . and these arranged, there is still a story to be done before I can get down to the writing of that long-overdue book." "The Candid Footprint" was appearing in the May *Century*, and "the story to be done" was "The Bright Bees of Toupan," scheduled for publication in early August by the United Feature Syndicate in newspapers across the country. Both stories became episodes in *The Silver Stallion*. "The Appeal to Posterity," *Literary Review* (25 March); "A Note on Alcoves," *New Republic* (12 April); "The Thin Queen of Elfhame," *Century* (December) all were incorporated into *Straws and Prayer Books* (1924). "Alcoves" also appeared in *The Novel of Tomorrow* (Bobbs-Merrill) in December.

Cabell was consciously working against the clock to mine his creative lode. As he had confessed to Burton Rascoe, he had put nearly all his art and philosophy into *Jurgen*; although his energies were not depleted, his younger persona was becoming more and more a mocking alter ego. A sense of loss was emerging more strongly in his work. In *Figures of Earth*, the work that followed *Jurgen*, the creative spirit Freydis tells Manuel that "she loves Sesphra [*Jurgen*] because he is all that Manuel once was, possessing comeliness, wit, youth, and courage." Cabell-Manuel's successive failures lead to an ultimate loss—his sense of self. The conceptual notions that created a unified reality for the Richmond of Cabell's youth—for the Cabells, the Branches, and Virginians of an older day—had been replaced by uncertainty, and Cabell himself had led in the dismemberment of the older structures and ontology. He had played the Richmonder rather than the Virginian in this respect, the opportunist out to get ahead in an exchange of goods and services. Aristocratic mansions fell to the wreckers and democratic apartment houses rose on their sites. Cabell felt strongly he had not completed his fictional house. With no sales from a suppressed *Jurgen*, its author refurbished older works and hawked every least scrap from his pen. An aging Manuel-Cabell confessed to an ever-young Freydis-Gabriella, "We must meet each other as best we can, not hoping to succeed, just aiming not to fall short too far."

Even with a sense of loss weighing heavily upon him, Cabell had hopes for "that long-overdue book." Unlike most of the longer works he had written, it would not grow out of a previously published story. It would have sustained vision, an organic wholeness. While biographical, this book would not be another reworking of his loss but the story of his parents' marriage. He approached it in a nearly reverent spirit, its satire muted with tenderness, with compassion. He longed to escape to the mountains of Virginia where he had always done his best writing. The old Rockbridge Alum, so intimately associated with parents and youth, was closed. Industrious Percy Cabell leaned to Mountain Lake in Giles County. There her fretful husband could find cool repose, and she and her family could enjoy pleasant society. At Dumbarton, Cabell had taken to writing in a nearby log cabin, returning to the house to eat and sleep. His vision continued to bother him, and a long consultation with an oculist left him less than assured that he would recover.

In late April, Priscilla journeyed to Washington as Virginia regent of the Daughters of the American Colonists. While Cabell disliked having her away, he abetted her interests in historical societies, filling out her genealogical forms, writing her reports. He had refined her colloquialisms so that she presided at meetings with a calm and gracious competence. "Not that I was ever admitted to these gatherings," he wrote. "But . . . I used to sit upon the hall stairway outside, whence I could listen with approval to the earnest voice of Priscilla Bradley Cabell speaking, speaking never so tranquilly and with a quiet friendliness, to the assembled gentlewomen in her quaint drawing room" (53). Cabell made this statement in his final book, *As I Remember It*, dedicated to his dead wife. Here he expanded on the myriad ways that man and wife had altered each other: "Our marriage improved both of us, in short; and in chief, because we did not have any traits whatever in common. Here was a deficiency which enabled each to supply for the other very nearly all that which the other lacked. She attended to every practical matter, unquestioned, because she understood about such matters. But to me she relinquished—completely, and shruggingly, and with a flavor of compassion—any affairs which displayed a cultural or aesthetic aspect, because of my being, as concerned these minor features of our shared living, just a perpetual old fuss-budget" (55).

In May the engagement of Priscilla Shepherd to Hopkins Davis was announced in the local papers. *Town Topics* (8 June) picked it up, adding a gratuitous comment: "Miss Shepherd is the stepdaughter of James Branch Cabell, whose marriage to her mother, the former Priscilla Bradley, a few years ago created quite a stir, as Mrs. Shepherd had been a widow several years and was considered an excellent *parti* for the brilliant young novelist, who was not overburdened with the goods of the world." He was still not overburdened, but he had hopes that his current publicity would rectify that embarrassment. Creative energies were diverted to refurbishing *Jurgen*'s predecessors. *Gallantry* (1907) with a preface by Louis Untermeyer made a reappearance on 14 June.

Also in early June, Priscilla Cabell persuaded her reluctant husband to accompany her on a visit to Long Island where her sister lived. It was his plain duty, and his Aunt Mary Munford concurred. If Emily Clark could claim his attention for the *Reviewer*, then his family should have equal rights. The trip was not without interest for the reluctant writer. He was invited by his editors to dine in Greenwich Village and to attend a party in his honor later. Ernest Boyd recorded his impression of the Virginian in his *Portraits: Real and Imaginary* (1924):

> A serious and clearly very shy man advances, smiles wanly and is soon absorbed in the problem of ordering from a menu long since conned and rejected by the earlier arrivals. The author of "Jurgen" is with us. A sober figure, in truth, with the formal manners of a country gentleman, but without the hearty, downright manner which might be expected from so *farouche* a devotee of open air and rural life. He wears glasses which gives him the air of a lawyer; austere, old-fashioned glasses, which eschew the modernity, the intellectual connotations of tortoise-shell and its convincing substitutes. He

says little. His demeanor is that of a layman, high in the favor of the reverend clergy, who is privileged to attend a meeting of the General Synod of the Episcopalian Church. (172)

. . . After dinner we journey up town to a party—not too large, at Mr. Cabell's urgent request—convened to do honor to the rare occasion of one of these always deferred visits to New York. . . . Well, the champagne has been put on ice, and we are moving in the right direction. Suddenly some commotion is perceptible, Mr. Cabell is gazing anxiously about him. He must not stay out late. He has a train to catch. He is expected somewhere down on Long Island. He must leave here. He is gone.

The party for Mr. Cabell continues. (173)

On 17 June Cabell wrote Sinclair Lewis, who had recently returned from a year in Europe: "On the afternoon of the thirteenth, that proverbially unlucky day, you were seeing someone off on the train at Forest Hills, so that I, already on the train, passed helplessly within a foot or two of you, on my way to New York and home. The maddening part is that I was for a week at Nassau Boulevard, while you were, to appearances, at Forest Hills and were supposed by me to be in New Hampshire. . . . At all events, I know you are now in thrall to *Babbitt*, and this is just to wish luck to the book, and, however belatedly, to bid you welcome to these States." Cabell's acquiescence to the New York trip was owing to his desire to consult with Guy Holt over the upcoming court hearing for suppressed *Jurgen*. Holt wrote Cabell that the official date was 26 June, "but we are mentioning that to no one as there is a strong possibility that matters will be quietly dropped. We may not learn of this latter development until the day before the trial." Owing to a crowded court docket, the hearing was postponed until the fall.

Cabell was concerned about the arrangements for his writing this first summer at Mountain Lake. A creature of habit, he missed the familiar surroundings of the Rockbridge Alum. While the settings of his creative fantasies were technically in Poictesme, their geographical details usually corresponded to the Virginia surroundings of their author. The setting of his new work was altered to conform to the elevated vistas of Mountain Lake. That, he admitted grudgingly, proved no great deterrent to creativity, but a wobbly writing table vexed him unbearably. Despite his fretful mood, by 27 July he had completed seven thousand words of "The Place that Ought Not to Be." Twelve days later he wrote Holt that the framework of the new book was complete, "the skeleton ready for decoration and festoons." In addition, five stories had been completed for the *Silver*

Stallion, projected for 1924 but not to see print until 1926. Further, French and German translations of *Jurgen* were scheduled for publication, news to Holt who was offended that Cabell had conducted the negotiations himself rather than through McBride, his American publisher. Cabell "would have done much more but for unfavorable conditions here which have interfered with work." While Mountain Lake was undeniably a cool retreat in a generally hot Virginia, Cabell looked forward to September and a return to Dumbarton. Despite his mood of discontent, he was giving birth to a work that would rival *Jurgen* in critical esteem, and other forces were conjoining to bring about the release of the suppressed work.

Back home, Cabell read *Babbitt*, in which he was mentioned, and found it even better than *Main Street*. Holt came for a visit to discuss legal matters complicated by not knowing just when and in what fashion the trial was to be conducted. Still plagued by a bad eye, Cabell was cheered by letters from two women, one wanting to dramatize *Domnei* and the other *The Cords of Vanity*. Emily Clark was full of chat about her pilgrimage to West Chester where Van Vechten had amused himself by making her rather than their host the subject of talk. In her letter of apology to Hergesheimer she interjected, "Another thing—don't lose patience with Mr. Cabell, ever. You and Hugh Walpole are the only men he cares a straw about, and he needs you. I know he doesn't amuse you. He doesn't me, either, but he is so tragic." She was convinced that his marriage was unhappy, although she considered Dorothy Hergesheimer "perfectly splendid." Dorothy never attempted to protect her husband from demanding females, but then the ebullient Pennsylvanian was the antithesis of the inhibited Virginian. Hergesheimer had long urged Cabell to change his publisher from Robert McBride to Alfred Knopf, and Emily revealed that Alfred and Blanche Knopf were coming to Richmond. Knopf had wooed Cabell before, and Emily planned to woo the Knopfs; they would later publish her two books. The *Reviewer*, having sold stock, now had a business manager, Russell B. DeVine, a great-grandson of one of the men who had founded the *Southern Literary Messenger* of Poe fame. Emily advised Joe Hergesheimer that "Mr. DeVine is doing splendidly."

On 5 October Isabelle Shepherd, the oldest of Priscilla Cabell's children, died at the age of twenty-six. A bright and beautiful child, she had been afflicted with spinal meningitis at an early age and had been a chronic invalid since. In New York, Robert McBride, just returned from Europe, and Garrard Glenn conferred on the upcoming trial and felt the need for more enlightenment on Cabell's scholarly references in *Jurgen*.

Holt wired that publisher and lawyer wanted the author in New York. After the funeral of his stepdaughter, Cabell fired off an angry letter on Sunday the 8th:

> What in the name of all the fiends is going on at your office? You spend the working day within some fifteen feet of Mr. McBride, with whom you presumably stay on speaking terms. You have all written out in your Law's Serious Call &c., absolutely all the information which he and Mr. Glenn are at this late date demanding. The whole thing seems absolutely the last word and straw in the way of incompetence.
>
> It would perhaps not so utterly madden me but for our present family circumstances. . . . It causes me furiously to think, I can assure you, of the talk I had with Knopf last week— But that can wait. What I want to say is that, if you insane people consider it absolutely necessary, I can manage to be in New York Wednesday from morning until midnight, with every inclination to get you all in jail . . . you are all insanity-provoking people to have dealings with.

Cabell had lunch at Emily Clark's where he met Frederick B. Eddy, a Cabell fan and bibliophile who had purchased *Reviewer* stock and contributed an appreciation of Walter de la Mare to the October issue. He succeeded in getting his extensive collection of Cabell works autographed. Dr. Beverley Randolph Tucker, who had also bought *Reviewer* stock, was inflicting his appalling plays on the Writers' Club. Having shareholders for the magazine was rapidly losing its appeal for Emily.

On Monday, 16 October, the long-delayed hearing of *Jurgen* took place in New York. Garrard Glenn in a scholarly brief asked Judge Charles C. Nott for acquittal, and the judge took the motion under advisement. On the morning of the 19th he rendered his opinion, finding the suppressed work "one of unusual literary merit" and containing "nothing 'obscene, lewd, lascivious, filthy, indecent or disgusting' within the meaning of the statute." He concluded: "The motion, therefore, is granted and the jury is advised to acquit the defendants." Holt immediately wired Cabell the news, and Cabell replied that afternoon:

> Your telegram when received this morning was—need I observe?—good reading matter, the best that your firm has put out for a long while. I must, while I think of it, ask for a copy of that thaumaturgic brief, which, in its final form, I never saw.
>
> Well, what is to be done next? I mean, for one thing, is it possible to put the book again upon the market at once? and will the firm bring suit against

the society? . . . I await your plans, and tender in turn my warmest congratulations.

That same day Louis Untermeyer wrote Cabell:

> I was almost expelled this morning for rising to my feet when his honor charged the jury (you should have seen those twelve hundred percenters!) to bring in a verdict for Holt, McBride et al. I was about to congratulate the justice upon his excellent decision as well as his discovery that Jurgen (which he pronounced Yourgen) was founded on a well-known mediaeval legend.
>
> As it was, both Redman and I felt cheated. Had the case gone to the jury, Redman, as you know, was going to read—God and the Smith Brothers willing—the entire work to the twelve (technically) good men and (legally speaking) true. The recitation would have taken six and one-half hours. At the very conclusion, just as Redman was tottering from the stand and the jury was being waked by the clerk of the court, I was to tower to my five feet seven and cry "Encore! Encore!"
>
> As I say, I feel that Justice Nott has cheated me of a brilliant and dramatic jesture. In spite of which I congratulate you, as I have already congratulated Holt, not only on the delayed evidence that Truth, Beauty and Allied Generalities will prevail but on the adroit and altogether admirable brief prepared by Garrard Glenn. My renewed felicitations.

Holt made plans to publish Glenn's brief along with Judge Nott's decision as *Jurgen and the Law*, a bit of scholia for literary historians. Heywood Broun apologized in his columns for his role in publishing Walter Kingsley's spoofing letter three years earlier, the letter that brought *Jurgen* to the attention of its suppressors. Thomas Caldecott Chubb, a young man with literary interests, wrote Cabell expressing the hope that the liberated work would now appeal on valid grounds rather than on the basis of prurient rumors, but Broun saw more clearly that "irreparable damage has been done to the book." More difficult to assess, even today, is the subtle alteration it made in Cabell's creative psyche. A matter of self-debate for his remaining years, the episode was seen as positive in the vindication of the work as an artistic endeavor with its resulting publicity but negative in its insidious coloration of all his subsequent work. Author and publisher made plans for getting *Jurgen* again on the market. McBride had lost Cabell's list of misprints in the American edition, and the author had to reread for flaws once again. A month later he had the pleasure of seeing his wayward offspring on the sales tables at Miller and Rhoads, in time for a brisk Christmas trade.

Also in October, Priscilla Cabell made one of her frequent trips to New

York. There she saw Holt and again met Burton Rascoe. The latter's account of this visit was commented on by Cabell after his wife's death:

> Her first newspaper interview was granted, unconsciously, in the October of 1922, to Burton Rascoe, whom at the time she had known for some two or three years; and Burton, somewhat to my confusion, printed it in the New York Tribune, of which he was then the literary editor.
>
> Mrs. James Branch Cabell (he recorded in his "Bookman's Day Book") is up from Richmond to see her children who are at school here. . . . Like most Southern women, she refers always to her husband as Mr. Cabell, never calling him James, Jim or Jimmy. . . .
>
> Mrs. Cabell told me that Cabell was "still fussing" about her choice of a place to take a vacation this year. . . .
>
> After we came back he said he hadn't been able to do a lick of work all summer; his whole summer had gone to waste; and for me to tell Mr. Holt that his book wasn't even started yet. But I am not going to tell Mr. Holt any lie about it; Mr. Cabell's book is most finished." (*As I Remember It*, 58–59)

Cabell interpolated here that "the book referred to was *The High Place*, which at the time of this interview was some eight long months from being finished."

> "He really is the most helpless human being that you ever saw in your life. And he wrote all right, but grumbling all the time. Now that he is back home, he pretends he hasn't written anything and that I am to blame for it, for taking him to the mountains when he wanted to go to the beach. But I know better. He just likes to be stubborn.
>
> "So I do not pay one bit of attention to him. I just ignore him, and see that he has everything he wants, and I keep people away from him. He doesn't like it now because I am up here in New York; and he keeps writing that he can't do any work because he has to answer the telephone all the time. Of course, when I am home, I answer the phone for him; and I tell people he is not there when he doesn't want to see them. So he really wants me to hurry back because he likes to have me to wait on him." (*As I Remember It*, 58–60)

Back at Dumbarton, Cabell received copies of Hergesheimer's *The Bright Shawl* and Mencken's third *Prejudices*. He worked on galley proofs of the revised *Cream of the Jest*. This "fifth printing" appeared in December with a preface by Harold Ward. Edwin Bjorkman's appreciation "concerning James Branch Cabell's Human Comedy" in the *International Book Review* for December pleased the author, and Cabell determined that it would be the preface to a revised *Eagle's Shadow*. Since so little could be said for that early effort, it was best to intimate that better things followed. A film version of Mary Johnston's *To Have and to Hold* was attracting large audiences in Richmond, and Cabell longed to have one of his works attract a producer. Even as a "successful" author, he had yet to know economic freedom. Mary Johnston was able to travel and to build her palatial house at Warm Springs. Ellen Glasgow, besides having a wealthy and generous brother, had always enjoyed good sales. By contrast, James Cabell, of distinguished ancestry and a world-renowned writer, was still living on the charity of Mr. Emmett A. Shepherd, "nobody in particular from Fluvanna County . . . an ornament to the lumber trade."

Other writers had become wealthy from their labors. Dorothy Hergesheimer did not have to support Joe. Sinclair Lewis was able to maintain his wife and wander at will over Europe and America. Even young Fitzgerald could support his frivolous southern belle in style. And there was the Englishman Hugh Walpole, soon to visit Richmond again. The man published his novels faster than one could read them, and the public clamored for more. His latest was *The Cathedral*, a clone of Trollope's Barchester novels. Emily Clark found reading Walpole a bore and vowed not to read this latest, but her idol Hergesheimer praised it, weakening her resolve. Frances Newman, writing in the 19 November New York *Tribune*, roasted it. Walpole, who was visiting the Cabells over the Christmas holiday, moaned, "My God! and what have I done to the woman! It was the only really vicious review the book got! And I liked her so much, too!" Again the ebullient Englishman overcame Cabell's reserve, the talk centering on writers and books. Tonsillitis, however, drove Walpole back to New York on the 27th. On the same day, replying to a letter from Frances Newman, Cabell unfortunately repeated Walpole's remark. Published seven years later, after her death, the indiscretion ended the friendship of the two men. Frances Newman was again in Richmond in January 1923 and wrote a young protégé that Cabell was amusing and "very grand seigneur." He assured her of her importance as a lady of letters, and she left for Europe in a happy glow.

About this time, Cabell was disturbed to hear that Guy Holt had thoughts of leaving McBride. On 3 February he wrote Holt, "I would hardly have any alternative to publishing elsewhere; and as a creature of habit, I would much prefer to go on being published by you."

Later in the month Hergesheimer was again in Richmond, playing Sir John Falstaff to a coterie of young Richmond matrons and submitting to Emily Clark's importunings, ostensibly on the part of the *Reviewer*. After he left, Emily resumed her Cabell assault. Perhaps responding to momentary pique, he entertained himself by telling her that Joe never read her magazine but encouraged her in her childish amusements. Furthermore, he said, Joe was not impressed with her character sketches appearing in Mencken's *Smart Set* as well as the *Reviewer*. Cabell's stunning revelation prompted a flurry of letters from Emily to Joe. "He said you had never told him you took me seriously in a literary way at all, or thought there was any future for The Reviewer," she wrote. "Was that just Mr. Cabell's perversity, or do you think I can write at all?" At a party given by the Richard Carringtons in honor of Marguerita Silva, a famous Carmen at the Opéra-Comique who was booked for a recital in Richmond on 5 February, Emily reported to Joe:

> Delia's party was the best I've been to for a long time. . . . The man [Mme Silva's companion] talked about Mr. Cabell and said terrible things. Usually it makes me mad, but I was too cross with him from the day before to care, or to defend him. They wondered if his child was imbecile, but I explained that he wasn't—he's really worse than that, something queer. He remembers things better than most children do, and whenever I see him he kisses my hand in a dreadful sticky way and catches the hem of my skirt and holds it. I think he is a stray figment of Mr. Cabell's brain—a nature myth . . . . Lots of people have read the Bookman piece [featuring Cabell, in the February issue] and are twittering about it. . . . Please hurry and tell me you think I can write, because Mr. Cabell said you considered The Reviewer a plaything. He *always* says that.

Still smarting, Emily returned to Cabell in her following letter to Hergesheimer. "He seemed so amused when he said you didn't read The Reviewer and didn't mention my writing. He laughed and laughed more than I have ever known him to."

Then Montgomery Evans, another lion-hunting young man, arrived in Richmond. A Yale graduate from Philadelphia, Evans first met the editors of the *Reviewer* and other local literati and on 14 February was a guest at the Writers' Club. Cabell was unable to see Evans on the 15th because Percie was entertaining the national head of the Daughters of the American Colonists, but the next day Hunter Stagg and Montgomery Evans caught the afternoon train out to Dumbarton. Evans leaves us a contemporary's impression of Ballard Cabell, then eight-and-a-half. It is a painful portrait for those who knew Ballard and grew fond of him; in their eyes his singular appearance and speech impediments were replaced by his acute perceptions of others' feelings and his generous and affectionate nature:

Someone who saw him at Dumbarton has since referred to him as "The nature myth," and the term is not ill chosen. He is about 9 years old, yet his speech is as incoherent as that of a child of 5. He looks like a caricature of a hod-carrier and his over-large face seems poised at a precarious angle on his shoulders, as if someone had lifted his [head?] off and carelessly replaced it with another.

In his eyes lies all the craftiness of an eerie madman of the woods, and his movements are not quite human in some intangible feature.

He had been romping about the study when Mr. Cabell asked him to post some letters. At once he assumed an air of absolute exhaustion while his eyes laughing belied his words. "I too tired, I very tired" as he fumbled with his cap in which he occasionally hides his face.

Later Mr. Cabell called attention to his shirt which was coming out of his trousers: "Might I suggest that you effect some closer connection between the two." Ballard squirmed delightedly in the chair and shaking his head vigorously called out "You crazy zing, you, crazy zing!" pointing with his cap, and chortling as if at some prodigious merriment within himself.

In March Emily Clark reported to Joseph Hergesheimer: "Mr. Cabell's little boy is very ill with pneumonia. I talked to him over the telephone today and he said he was critically ill, and seemed very depressed. Of course it will be much better if the child dies before Mr. Cabell discovers that he is really abnormal, but all the same it will break Mr. Cabell's heart because Ballard is the only thing he really cares about except his books." She wrote later that "Mr. Cabell is shut up with his little boy" and then in April that "his little boy is getting better now, and I think it is a great pity, but he is almost bubbling, for him."

In his study, Cabell polished his latest work, *The High Place*, and attempted to revise *The Eagle's Shadow*, his first. Acutely aware of its dated style and total lack of content, he debated whether it should be republished. Hunter Stagg relayed to Montgomery Evans news from Dumbarton:

Moreover, he tells me, in the midst of the disturbance [Ballard's illness] he is trying to re-write The Eagle's Shadow for the intended edition, which task he describes as hellish: considering that the book was written twenty years ago I can well believe it. He said a year ago he was not going to do it over, but Guy Holt has immense persuasive powers. I asked Mr. Cabell what on earth he was able to do with it after twenty years, and was he adding anything to it, or cutting anything out. He said, "Mostly cutting out." "But," I protested, "it was already such a little book—" "I know it," said he somewhat glumly: "That's the trouble. I expect it'll be republished finally as a blank book."

On May 1, Cabell wrote Holt that "*The Eagle's Shadow* is now virtually done in its second form. It is not even now a masterwork. But after some dejected days, wherein it seemed that nothing could be done with this stuff, I got my teeth into it and wrought really astounding improvements. But you shall see. Meanwhile a contract."

Working simultaneously on his earliest book, written twenty years before, and his latest gave Cabell a strange sense of déjà vu, a double perspective of looking forward and backward. He saw that he had attained the national attention the Author of *The Eagle's Shadow* had longed for, but he also saw that he was not the writer his younger persona had aspired to be. While writing *The High Place*, the mature writer became convinced that all his work was really one extended biography, the story of his will to be a major romancer. The revisions of his earlier works, first dictated by economic concerns, now pointed the way to an artistic realization. By imposing the framework of the Manuelian saga of *Figures of Earth* on his earlier output, he could advertise these works as components in an epic project of many volumes planned as early as 1901. The imposition of this arbitrary unity on every last story posed problems of falsification. The eyes of the novice looked on in consternation as his later incarnation ruthlessly and cynically altered the younger man's work. Who was the disembodied, and who was the possessed? That would have to be debated in another "chapter" of what Cabell was now calling the Biography. The cost of "success" in terms of human intimacy, of the irrational passion of the heart, was not lost on the forty-four-year-old writer. As Marie Clair (Gabriella Moncure) observed: "You and I are not enamored of flesh and blood." Dr. Tucker's ridiculous play about Poe came to mind. The lost poet whispered in his heart, "It was many and many a year ago."

On 28 April Stagg reported to his new confidant, Evans: "The large and expansive Joseph [Hergesheimer] is, at this writing, in Richmond, having arrived here unheralded no longer ago than Tuesday night [24th]. He is leaving again Monday. On Wednesday evening Miss Clark had a small party for him, at which was present the elusive Mr. Cabell, who— conditions at Dumbarton Grange not being favorable—did not after all leave Richmond. As he hates to go away I really think he was glad that his son did not get better soon enough for him to take the trip he had expected to take. He was in a genial humor the other night, however." At this time Hunter Stagg, learning that Montgomery Evans was planning a trip to London and Paris for a summer of literary lion-hunting, decided to borrow money to accompany him; he would put up his library of signed first-editions as collateral. On 15 June he reported to Evans, referring to Cabell by the sobriquet Koschei, the character in *Jurgen*:

> I passed an afternoon and evening last week with Koschei the Deathless. Do you know, I am one of the only two friends of Mr. Cabell who are ever asked "to stay to supper" by Mrs. Cabell? And I am the only one who lives in Richmond. Even Joseph Hergesheimer has never been asked to take but two meals out there, and they were "parties," not just informal family meals. Do not mention this last piece of information, though, for I understand that it is a source of irritation to Joseph that he is never asked out there. It hurts his vanity, for one thing, but more than that it hurts his feelings, for he is honestly fond of Mr. Cabell, and admires him, both as a man and a writer. Well, after this pardonable bit of boasting, I proceed to say that Koschei was very delightful and sweet, and contributed a sum to my fund, thereby astonishing several people, who declare that he is fearfully "stingy." I don't think myself that it is stinginess. It is just that the old dear has never had any money in his life till lately, and his habit of making what he has go as far as possible naturally clings to him. One can't break such a habit after all that while. And besides he hasn't much now, in spite of the boom, though some appear to hold the impression that he has.

Emily Clark had written Hergesheimer early in June, "Mr. Cabell is *crazy* about my writing now." She had not dared publish her sketch based on Henry Anderson, friend of Ellen Glasgow and glamorous Queen Marie of Romania, in the *Reviewer*. "Lustre Ware," published under the pseudonym Patricia Hale, appeared in Mencken's *Smart Set*. "Mr. Cabell thinks it the best thing of mine he has seen yet." She also reported that Cabell had defended Frances Newman against the term "wicked"—"truly evil people were never openly malicious": "He said he had known wicked women, and that they were sweet and charming to everyone, but meant nothing by it. And that no one ever suspected them of a thing, and often felt extremely drawn to them. And he said *they* were the people who worked havoc and were really evil. It was interesting, because he so seldom expresses an opinion. . . . I tried to find out who some of these deadly females are, but, as usual, he wouldn't tell. So now I shall be suspicious of all amiable women I know, and comparatively at ease with Frances. Mr. Cabell is *so* aggravating" (*Ingénue*, 145).

Hergesheimer, planning to write a novel set in nineteenth-century Virginia, was soliciting background reading from Emily. "I'm very excited about your writing it," she responded. "It is shrieking to be done, and no one down here can do it. It isn't Mr. Cabell's sort of thing, and none of the women can do it at all. I never can, even if I write better than I think I shall. Mr. Cabell can't write about early Virginia. He is always writing about modern Virginia, but the things he wants to say about it are so dreadful they terrify him, and so he calls it Poictesme. But no one seems to know that but me" (Ingénue, 153).

In July the film of Hergesheimer's The Bright Shawl was shown in Richmond. Dorothy Gish and Richard Barthelmess were popular stars, but Emily felt they were unsuited to their roles. The Cabells had left for Mountain Lake, Hunter Stagg and Margaret Freeman were abroad, and pianist John Powell was boring everyone with his much-publicized friendship with Joseph Conrad. "John Powell has left for Mountain Lake," Emily wrote, "which seems to have become a Home of the Arts. I'm quite sure he is annoying Mr. Cabell. He went down to Oyster Bay twice to spend the day with Mr. Conrad at the Doubledays'" (Ingénue, 165).

Cabell wrote Holt from Mountain Lake, "I have returned . . . to the high place, and I find it vastly inferior to my description of it. Still—since this year—we know what necessaries to bring with us—we are not now uncomfortably established for, I estimate, July and August." He reviewed with Holt his fall publication schedule, juggling the appearances of The High Place and new editions of Jurgen, Jest, and The Eagle's Shadow. This summer, finding Mountain Lake more to their liking, the Cabells decided that it should become the site of their own cottage. The lodge was all very well for meals and the social activities required by Priscilla Cabell and her family, but the querulous writer needed the privacy of his own work space. They determined to build higher upon the mountain slope overlooking lodge and lake.

Back in Richmond in September, Emily Clark wanted to embroil Cabell in the Reviewer's financial problems, but he held aloof, limiting his advice to literary contributions. Mr. and Mrs. Archer Jones, establishers of the Poe Memorial in the "Old Stone House" on Main Street, were conniving to move the Reviewer there and call it the Southern Literary Messenger. Cabell suggested that it should be called The Reviewer, Formerly The Southern Literary Messenger. The Joneses offered to underwrite publication costs if Emily would drop Mary Street and Hunter Stagg as editors. She refused and, as she confessed to Hergesheimer, cried for the first time in five years. A visit to West Chester and a restored Dower House refueled her spirits. Back home, she wrote: "Mr. Cabell has been here to bring me The Eagle's Shadow, and I have told him about Dower House and your lovely, lovely workrooms. Poor darling, he has a terrible time and will have to spend this winter in an apartment at the Chesterfield. But he will at least be accessible, and when you come you and I must go to see him frequently, and amuse him, and annoy Priscilla. She is such a blight. . . . I've told her how wonderful Dorothy was, quite innocently" (*Ingénue*, 190).

Hunter Stagg was home from Europe and in charge of the Sunday Book Page in the *Times-Dispatch*. He asked Cabell's opinion of Carl Van Vechten's *The Blind Bow-Boy*, just off the press. Like Queen Victoria, Cabell was not amused although his own new novel touched on homosexuality. Hunter was asked out to Dumbarton the afternoon of 12 September to tell Cabell of his literary conquests. Van Vechten had opened doors for the young, good-looking Richmonder and had procured contributions for the *Reviewer* from Ronald Firbank and Gertrude Stein. Van Vechten, as Emily observed, had become Stagg's patron saint. Cabell and Hunter Stagg laughed about John Powell's zealotry for the Anglo-Saxon League and racial purity. Stagg had admitted to Powell that he felt "a strange indifference," an admission James Cabell was loath to make. He would stick to allegory to convey dangerous opinions. Even Hunter, having met Sylvia Pankhurst by accident in a London bookstore, was questioned by the Secret Service when he returned to Richmond. Guy Holt came down to Richmond later in the month to show Cabell the Papé illustrations for *The High Place*; Hunter reported to Montgomery Evans: "Much better than the Jurgen pictures, and done by the same man. Mr. Cabell says Guy doesn't like the book at all, and complains of it constantly, but his complaints do not seem to upset the author, who confided to me that it was better written than anything else he had done."

Hunter was in despair over the appearance of his Book Page. Sensational "screamers" headlined reviews. "Mr. Cabell says it is not nearly as bad as I consider it, though he admits there is room for improvement." Cabell had always cherished publicity, even the bad publicity which he had taken delight in appending to the new edition of *The Eagle's Shadow*. Stagg's review of *The Blind Bow-Boy* prompted Van Vechten to ask for ten copies and permission to reprint it elsewhere. Van Vechten made plans to visit Richmond, and the Cabells made plans to visit West Chester. Richmond as a literary center was being frequently commented on in the New York *Times* and other journals.

Joseph Hergesheimer, Carl Van Vechten, and James Branch Cabell were guests of honor in late October at a luncheon given by the Architectural League in Philadelphia. According to Bruce Kellner in his book on Van Vechten, "The three were introduced, and each spoke briefly but apparently without much individuality. At the conclusion, one of the members approached Carl with a copy of Jurgen under his arm, addressed him as Mr. Cabell, and invited him to sign. Carl was agreeable, and so was James, who signed Carl's name to the architect's copy of Peter Whiffle" (164). Van Vechten wrote Hugh Walpole from the Jefferson Hotel in Richmond on 7 November: "Starting out a week ago with a luncheon given in Philadelphia for Cabell, Joe [Hergesheimer] et moi, my life has been a succession of entertainments. Spent five days at Dower House—not only the Cabells were there but several others. Joe has almost ruined Dower House by making it so perfect. . . . Joe and I came down to Richmond yesterday, Joe to start work on Bale Hundred, his new Virginia novel, and me in search of adventures! We are going out to the Cabells this afternoon.—I shall write you more about Cabell later. He is very difficult but on the whole we got on better than I expected" (Letters, 59).

Hunter Stagg, writing Montgomery Evans on 5 November, reported that Cabell was "furious" to discover upon his return from West Chester that he had not yet received a copy of The High Place. Nor had Stagg received a review copy. The book was on sale in Richmond book stores, "disappearing like hot cakes," and by the time the reviewer decided he had better buy a copy, they were sold out. Finally Holt rectified the oversight. Cabell promised to write in Stagg's copy before he read the latter's review. Hunter reported their exchange of banter to Evans: " 'I hope you didn't see anything ambiguous in the book?' 'NOT A THING!' said I heartily. 'I never read a less ambiguous book.' 'Why, I don't know what you are talking about, Mr. Stagg,' he said severely." Hunter Stagg's review was centered at the top of the Sunday Book Page on 2 December, with a large photograph of the author at the Rockbridge Alum Springs. It was headlined, "Latest Novel of Cabell is Vivid and Beautiful." He was "one of the greatest writers of his time and one of the greater writers of all time." Stagg had won a friend for life. Mencken too liked The High Place, but other critics found it, oddly, a rewrite of Jurgen. Its sales, however, were gratifying.

While in West Chester, Cabell had been accorded the central position in a galaxy of literary stars. At the country club he was photographed, sitting glumly in blue serge, surrounded by jovial colleagues in Halloween dress. In the photograph, vivacious Dorothy Hergesheimer addresses him on his right, and glamorous Phoebe Gilkyson snuggles on his left. In the left of the photograph, a placid Priscilla Cabell gazes into the camera, and a placid Hergesheimer gazes at Priscilla Cabell. On the far right, Blanche and Alfred Knopf sit quietly. Three rows back, an animated Van Vechten appears to be dressed as a sailor, perhaps an allusion to the notorious Duke of Middlebottom in *The Blind Bow-Boy,* hot off the press. The Duke's motto was "A thing of beauty is a boy forever," and he affected sailor garb. Van Vechten saw to it that things stayed lively in Richmond. Later in the month, Hunter Stagg wrote Montgomery Evans details of the revels:

> I think I have not written since the visitation of Hergesheimer and Carl, yet on the other hand it seems to me I must have. It was a lively week, at any rate, and so well equipped were those gentlemen in the way of liquids, that I hardly drew a sober breath the whole week they were here. There were lunches, at the Jefferson — just me and them — following an hour of drinking, and preceding several hours of drinking. There were dinners, both at the Jefferson and at the houses of friends, after the same program. And Mr. Cabell had a tea at which he served cocktails and plenty of highballs— the first time I have ever known him to do it. He and Carl liked each other immensely —I had not been able to make up my mind whether they would or not, and had strongly suspected that Cabell at least would not like him. But he did very much — though I think he was prejudiced against him before hand. Cabell came back from Westchester a wreck, and took to his bed, rising only to give the aforementioned tea, and then going back again. Yes, he did bob for apples. He also played forfeits, and was made, by Carl, to kiss all the women in the room. Everybody else here was crazy about Carl— he made more friends in that one week than I have, I believe, in my long residence here, and left with the firm intention of coming back as soon as possible, so he said. Fancy him liking Richmond —he said it is adorable, and thereby floored Emily, who thought he would be bored to death by the proper and unsophisticated souls who here abide. (27 November 1923)

Van Vechten wrote Alfred Knopf from the Jefferson on 12 November, "I've had a marvelous time here & almost cried when I said good-bye last night to a lot of them. Cabell, who has not yet received The High Place, told me to tell Guy Holt he was barking like a Borzoi." Knopf's books featured a Russian wolfhound, a borzoi. When Van Vechten wrote Walpole that he had at first found Cabell "*very* difficult," he touched on an essential facet of the Richmonder's personality. Though Van Vechten was only a year younger than Cabell, he was at least a generation younger in his social attitudes. In his mannered prose Cabell could touch on any subject, but in social intercourse he was struck dumb by the levities of contemporary sophisticates. A few years later, he confessed:

> Oncoming antiquaries, I suspect, will not ever give us sophisticated writers of the 'twenties our due credit for the pains with which we learned to converse in drawing-rooms about brothels and privies and homosexuality and syphilis and all other affairs which in our first youth were taboo,—and even as yet we who have reached fifty or thereabouts cannot thus discourse, I am afraid, without some visible effort. I have noted a certain paralytic stiffening of the features (such as a wholly willing martyr might, being human, evince at the first sight of his stake) which gave timely warning that the speaker was now about to approach the obscene with genial levity. (*Restless Heads*, 39)

Despite Van Vechten's flamboyance, Cabell recognized in the transplanted mid-westerner a fellow esthete, one who was generous in his praise of his contemporaries. Van Vechten's mission later in November was to save from oblivion a new novel that had received a bad review in the New York *Times*. Elinor Wylie, known as a poet, had just published her first novel, *Jennifer Lorn*. Van Vechten found it "the most enchanting book of all time" and recruited Cabell, Hergesheimer, Lewis, and others to rally to its defense with encomiums for publicity purposes. Cabell genuinely liked the work, as did Emily Clark and Hunter Stagg. With its eighteenth-century-style binding and title page, it was a picaresque extravaganza that deliciously satirized many of the notions well-born Virginians cherished concerning their English and Scottish heritage. It sold out in Richmond, being in truth more to the tastes of the locals than Cabell's allegorical retributions in *The High Place*. The rally saved *Jennifer* from obscurity.

The elderly Edwin Swift Balch, explorer and writer of Philadelphia, had been smitten by Emily Clark's charms in Baltimore the previous summer, and he journeyed to Richmond to visit her. She wrote Hergesheimer on 7 December, omitting the name of her suitor: "Something quite miraculous has happened to me, so I must tell you. You have borne with, and doubtless been bored by, the sorrows of The Reviewer during the last few months to such an extent that I owe it to you to tell you that they are over. An amazingly philanthropic person in the North has bought the remaining three thousand dollars worth of stock, half of the whole magazine, and put it in my name. Nothing like this has ever happened to us before, and it seems incredible." When Emily telephoned Cabell the news of the *Reviewer*'s escape from the Archer Joneses and their Poe Shrine, the romancer marveled in a hushed voice: "Why, it's just like a fairy-tale." Without naming her suitor, Emily began to question her Richmond friends about the married state and about the expectations of husbands regarding conjugal duties. On 16 December she observed to Hergesheimer, "Mr. Cabell thinks it doesn't matter who you marry and I'm wondering if that may not be true, and if it isn't sensible to do it for Continental reasons just as he did."

Frances Newman, just returned from Europe, was again visiting her sister in Richmond. She gave a tea for the literati, and Emma Gray Trigg drove Hunter Stagg out to Westhampton. Emily, reporting to West Chester, boasted: "I took Frances Newman to Ellen Glasgow's party yesterday because she wanted very much to see her, and she was ecstatic over the house and Miss Glasgow—although I now say Ellen!—together. She said she wished some of the New York writers with wild apartments and wilder clothes could see it. . . . Hunter called Mrs. [Archer] Jones 'Mrs. Poe' the other day by mistake. Poor, put-upon Poe!" (*Ingénue*, 204).

In February, Montgomery Evans was again in Richmond petitioning Cabell for autographs for his extensive collection. Priscilla Cabell was in New York where she was lunched by the Van Vechtens. Cabell found Hunter congenial company during her absence, but he drew the line when petitioned to autograph magazine stories for Evans. Cabell urged Stagg, soon to turn twenty-nine, to propose to the capable, efficient Margaret Freeman, already thirty. Margaret had served as an army nurse and was admirably suited to take charge of Stagg, who was subject to epileptic-like seizures from a childhood accident. Stagg proposed, but Margaret was planning a career in interior decorating, having studied in Paris. She also had reservations about Hunter's sexual orientation, just as she had the eye of suspicion on Carl Van Vechten's. Paris had made her much more alert to these matters than had her Methodist family background in Richmond. Hunter for the previous year had been pursued by a woman of Russian descent from New York. Stagg confided to Van Vechten, "It is one of my pet vanities that I have never had to solicit a lady's favors in my life. They have always done the work. This does not mean that a great many have done so, but isn't it, anyway, a record for a fellow nearly twenty-nine?" Many years later Cabell wrote that he had admired Margaret Freeman as "talented and handsome . . . whom any man would be proud to have as his wife." Without naming Hunter Stagg, he added, "I had actively hoped for her marriage, I had encouraged him, for his well-being's sake, to attempt to marry her." But Hunter drifted into sexual ambivalence, and Margaret Freeman married James Branch Cabell some twenty-six years later.

Having enjoyed his visit to Richmond the previous fall, Van Vechten recruited Hergesheimer for another descent on Richmond. He had entertained the Triggs and Carringtons in New York, and they had urged him to return. Priscilla Cabell asked him also. Unlike her reluctant husband, she enjoyed the social aspect of his notoriety. While Emily Clark deplored her total lack of interest in writing, it bothered the visitors not a whit. In his memoirs Cabell marveled over his wife's enjoyment of their company and theirs of her engaging simplicity:

> But she got on swimmingly with every one of these large literary figures, even with those among them who seemed right sort of funny; because it remained, when all was said, my wife's unshakable if politely unvoiced opinion that anybody who wrote books, or who talked about books quite seriously, ought not to be regarded as a rational person. And in consequence, with a flavor of maternal pity, she was always especially pleasant in dealing with the sophisticated and flamboyant, world-famous Titans of literature who made glorious the 1920's.
>
> She had not read any of their books, nor did she pretend to have done so. She did not hearten these great writers with any least fraudulence as to intending by-and-by to read their books. And yet they every one of them regarded Priscilla, as they termed her—excepting only Ellen Glasgow, to whom she was Percie—with an unaffected affection. It was a miracle that I could never understand in the light of my knowledge as to the sustaining vanity and the egoism but for which no one of these writers—including myself, I daresay—would ever, quite so visibly, have thought either his or her most recent book to be wholly worth the labor invested in writing it. (*As I Remember It*, 57–58)

Van Vechten and Hergesheimer prevailed upon Elinor Wylie to join them while they were in Richmond. Her *Jennifer Lorn* was now attaining the public notice accorded to *The High Place* and *The Blind Bow-Boy*, but Cabell dreaded the disruption of out-of-town revelers. He confided to Hunter Stagg, "I shall be glad to see them all, but I don't mind telling you they aren't welcome." Others in Richmond, however, felt differently. Two letters of Hunter Stagg record the festive moment with élan. The first is addressed to Montgomery Evans, who had visited Richmond earlier in the spring.

Wednesday. [9 April]

Dear Monty,

It is a distrait, demoralized, and almost prostrate young man who writes: he is not, either, the only person in Richmond in that condition. Emily Clark and Mr. Cabell are quite as bad off.

For a week ago last Sunday [30 March] Carl and Joe arrived. I had dinner with them that night, getting somewhat full of gin. Next afternoon Mr. Cabell and I called on them, afterwards leaving to go to a performance at the Woman's Club. When that performance was over, Mr. Cabell, greatly desiring to escape the crush of women, the tea and talk, was led by me out of a side entrance, and to the back gate. Alas, that was padlocked: no escape. Someone pursued us, telling Cabell he must come in and meet the star of the afternoon, who was Percy Haswell, or Mrs. George Fawcett — the aging actress you've heard Margaret speak of. Cabell told this person we'd be in in a moment, were just smoking a cigarette. Left alone again, we scouted wildly about till finding no other way, I observed a heap of wood piled against the brick wall. "We can climb that," I suggested. And so we did, mounting to the top of the barrier and — Ah, Monty, think of climbing over the back wall of the Woman's Club with James Branch Cabell! We then sat in the car till Mrs. Cabell came, when I left them and went back into the club to meet and talk with Mrs. Fawcett, who is very sweet.

Next day, or evening, rather, Ellen Glasgow had a delightful dinner, at which the dear lady served champagne — only one glass though. Next day, Wednesday, I visited the Jefferson in the day, got nicely stewed, and that afternoon Elinor Wylie arrived, and that night Emily Clark had a grand dinner party. Mrs. Wylie was liked, but not enthusiastically. Next day more drinking at the Jefferson, and at night a perfectly riotous dinner party at the Cabells. Scotch flowing like water. Mine enemies the Joneses arrived drunk as lords, both of them, and Mrs. Jones was the scandal of the evening. Mr. Jones embraced me, and apologized almost in tears for his behavior to me during the winter, and I was furious, preferring that matters should remain as they were—and doubtless still are, since he probably doesnt remember a thing about it. Mrs. Wylie was observed to grow on you, with closer acquaintance. By the way, that day Mr. and Mrs. Knopf had also arrived. There were then, at Cabells, five of the most prominent American novelists, and two of the most prominent publishers. Next day I lunched alone with Mrs. Wylie, liking her still more. That night there was a gathering at the Jefferson, though no formal party was given. Saturday Virginia Reynolds had a luncheon at the Commonwealth Club, and Hergesheimer was observed to become suddenly very friendly with me. That afternoon there was a tea at Ellen Glasgow's. That night Mrs. White had a small dinner, just Joe, Carl, Elinor (it became Elinor and Hunter then) Emily, Mr. and Mrs. Trigg and me. Champagne flowed like water at this affair, in the old style, your glass being filled as soon as it was emptied. Next morning Carl and Elinor departed. At midday Margaret called me up to say that a telegram had come offering her a job in New York, and she was going the following evening. This was a stunning blow. So I broke several engagements and spent the afternoon weeping at her house. That night Joe had a dinner, the first to which he has invited me for three years. It was a wonderful affair, at which I was reproached for not having called him Joe a year ago, and bidden to start at once. It also became Alfred and Blanche, and Hunter on that occasion. Intoxicated by all this I almost called Cabell James, and dont doubt that I would have by the end of this week if they had all stayed on, with all that sort of celebration. I left this party at ten, however, and went up to Margaret's where I stayed weeping till after twelve. And she departed Monday night. What I shall do without her I do not know. Richmond is hard enough to endure anyway, but when she is not here it is completely rotten. Monday night I spent half with the Knopfs, and half at the Conquests, who I forgot to mention, have had a beautiful lady named Mrs. Gilkyson staying with them, an old friend of Joe's and Carl's, to whom Cabell has been attentive to a degree heretofore unprecedented, for him, in Richmond. She is charming. Tuesday morning the Knopfs left, also Mrs. Gilkyson, and I sunk into a state of weary relaxation which makes the writing of this letter a terrible effort. Joe remains a week longer, but there are no more parties, so I should worry. Well, it was marvelous, but thank god it is over. I could not have lived through another week of it, what with the constant drinking, the late hours, and all the rest of the excitement. Mr. Cabell looked quite wan Sunday night, and Emily has taken to her bed.

Despite her suspicions concerning Van Vechten's sexual orientation, Margaret Freeman and he "got on like a house afire," she deciding that he was capable of anything but that his interests were "almost entirely intellectual and very little physical." Just as Hergesheimer had become an epistolary confessor for Emily's intimate thoughts, so too did Stagg's letters to Van Vechten become confessional. On 7 April, the day Margaret left for New York and her new job, Hunter wrote Van Vechten: "Margaret, by the way, thinks you are marvelous (her own word), clever to a degree described as appalling, also interesting, amusing and doubtless a perfect fiend." Later in this letter he records Elinor Wylie's comments about Cabell: "I remembered her telling me two days before that he did not really like her (which is true, I discover), and that it didnt matter. 'Now if Cabell did not like me, I would feel it was through a lack in me, something wrong about me,' she said. But, though I'd like Joe to like me, it doesnt upset me that he does not."

Emily Clark left her vignette of the meeting of Elinor Wylie and Cabell. They met at her house "for supper, not dinner." At thirty-nine, Wylie was still a beautiful woman and had recently married for a third time, to William Rose Benét. Emily wrote in *Innocence Abroad*: "She appeared in a dark dress with a string of black pearls around her throat, slightly remote, almost non-commital. . . . Several young men who came in later, and had heard of her oftener as a beauty and a femme fatale than as a writer, found her to their surprise, detached and unresponsive to masculine interest. But Mr. Cabell, who approached her with a respect seldom offered by him to any woman, with one or two almost shy questions about *Jennifer*, soon established for her an atmosphere of confidence and security" (167–68).

16

Tea and Intrigue

1924–1926

With the revelers departed, Cabell retired contentedly to his study. His forty-fifth birthday came and went, and April reawakened those first awakenings in Williamsburg. The young woman who was the prototype of Marie-Clair in *The High Place* was much in his mind again. It puzzled Richmonders at this time that he was urging the Theatre League to put on a play about Poe, but Cabell was feeling like a bereft poet. Gabriella Moncure was his Annabelle Lee. If all the mature work of James Branch Cabell was truly an extended biography, then her chapter, his college verse, was its beginning. He was giving the verses *From the Hidden Way* their second refinement, having first published them in 1916, and was now planning their second exposure for September. In reality he was further removing them from the exuberant freshness of their first forms; the author of *Jurgen* was editing a boy's poetic effusions very much as Henry Alden of *Harper's* had edited Mr. Townsend's stories. Earlier in the year a group of Cabell admirers had published *A Round-Table in Poictesme*, a symposium of laudatory essays, and Cabell had contributed "The Author of The Eagle's Shadow." That youthful author confessed to his famous counterpart whom he was interviewing that he did not entirely like the older man's books. Why had the irony crept into the romances? "What did you want . . . that you never got?" The increasing dichotomies in Cabell's work, especially between pre- and post-*Jurgen*, were becoming the subject of critical analyses.

The revised "Apologia Auctoris" that prefaces the 1924 edition of *From the Hidden Way* is signed by "Robert Etheridge Townsend, Lichfield, April, 1924." Townsend is the errant hero of *Cords*, the quondam lover of Bettie Hamlyn, alias Gabriella Moncure, to whom that episodic extravaganza is dedicated. This new "Apologia is a collaboration" with Mr. Cabell. Subtitling this edition a "Dizain des Echos" is "a bit affected," the apologist observes, but Mr. Cabell believes it will please reviewers, "enabling them to start off with a smart witticism about its applicability to other books." He had determined, in constructing his mythology of a biography, "that all went by tens," obliquely referring to his first ten titles, now attributed to others, before *Beyond Life* and *Jurgen* catapulted James Cabell into the constellations. The first ten "chapters" of the Biography would be followed by ten more. The epic romancer was planning to reveal this master design in a work already underway, *Straws and Prayer-Books*, termed an "Epilogue," just as *Beyond Life* was the "Prologue." While their epics fell into multiples of six, Homer and Vergil could claim no greater design. Thus Horvendile, Koschei, Miramon wavered between egoistic euphoria and keening despair over the imperfections of the results.

Straws and Prayer-Books, like *Beyond Life*, was a synthesis of ideas scattered in articles and book reviews. By late April Cabell had sent Holt an outline. In follow-up letters he saw *Straws* "like Villon's Grand Testament." He prided himself on his skill in melding its disparate elements: "And I have utilized everything rather nicely, too, as a pretext for talking about, under whatever veiling, myself and my own books." He invited Holt to pick all possible faults and admitted he had low expectations for the work's sales. On 3 May Holt requested a "formal elaboration" for publicity and, since the book was already essentially written, said that he hoped to receive the typescript soon. *Straws* gave Cabell another chance to pose as the seer, one who had foreplanned all his works as a cycle from the very beginning of his career.

In his domestic life, Cabell's stepdaughter Priscilla Shepherd Davis gave birth to a son, allowing the seer to pretend to be indignant that he was so soon a stepgrandfather. Ballard was delighted to be made an uncle at nine. On 22 May Hunter wrote Montgomery Evans, then in England:

Yesterday afternoon I went out to the retreat of Koschei and spent the afternoon, and even stayed to supper, and had part of the evening there . . . Take your Garnetts and your Crowleys! I don't think I ever had a better time there, and Koschei was excellently in vein, talking more liberally, and more wittily, and ever and anon more sincerely than usual. He autographed your "Round Table", and your "Rivet", and, rebelliously, your "Chivalry." Twice he started to do it, and then said he didn't see any reason why he should, but I persisted, and repeated what you had said about preserving it in its uncut state, and finally he relented and did it. He also autographed Miss Fullerton's "Jurgen"—and my Bibliography, and my "Reine Pédauque", and gave me a Modern Library "Beyond Life," and kept a commercial edition of "The High Place" I carried out to write more invocations to the devil in at his leisure. He also promised to do something for me which if he really ever does do will cause you and all other Cabell collectors such anguish of spirit as will near end your lives. As I do not for a moment believe he ever will do it, however, I shall not reveal what it is. If he does, you will know all right.

Cabell was pleased to hear from Holt that he had no major criticisms to make of *Straws and Prayer-Books* and that Carl Van Doren, after thinking it over, had agreed to write the booklet on Cabell that McBride wished to issue for publicity purposes. All during June, Cabell was concerned with the new cottage being built at Mountain Lake. Plumbing, gas fixtures, screen doors all were subjects of letters. In July the Cabells repaired to Mountain Lake where, to their dismay, roof and walls leaked. In Richmond, the film of Hergesheimer's "Wild Oranges" was playing, and Frances Newman was again visiting her sister. Only Emily Clark was in town, agonizing privately over marriage to the fat and elderly Edwin Swift Balch and giving up the *Reviewer*. Hunter Stagg was off on an extended series of visits, through West Chester and western Pennsylvania and on up to Maine. Good-looking Hunter, "the black lily," was a congenial guest. He met museum directors, artists, horsemen, and after excessive partying in Pennsylvania and New York, he found the cool, lofty boredom of Kennebunkport relaxing. Carl Parsons, a wealthy literary dilettante, had invited him there for a visit. Hunter called on Booth Tarkington while in Kennebunkport. He next accepted invitations to Atlantic City and Provincetown where his host, a young doctor, introduced him to a more sophisticated life than Richmond had provided. Back home, there were new novels to review. He found the writing of Van Vechten's *The Tattooed Countess* "superb." On the other hand, Hergesheimer's Virginia novel, *Balisand*, was "rather a frost."

In mid-September, Hunter wrote Van Vechten: "I have seen James once and conversed with him on the phone several times since his return. He is emphatic about the excellence of the Countess. He said also that he must go and condole with Emily about her approaching nuptials. Condole? said I. Yes said he. Losing one's innocence is a very disappointing experience." A week later Hunter wrote Evans: "I went out to Cabells, with Emily, the other day, but had no talk with him, Emily being there. I have seen him, too, at several more or less literary teas, but only had a real talk with him at one of them." Cabell professed to be glad that Emily and Hunter were giving up the *Reviewer* after the October issue. It had served as his plaything too for a while, but now that there was contention over who would direct its policies, he was relieved to bow out. In his study he autographed copies of *From the Hidden Way*, just republished, for friends and' friendly critics. He also autographed signature leaves for a limited first edition of *Straws and Prayer-Books*, one that was happily oversubscribed. Ellen Glasgow had agreed to review his book, and he was to reciprocate soon with a preface to one of her books. It was the beginning of their mutually supportive publicity, destined to last almost twenty years.

Carl Van Doren had become Cabell's most prolific champion. In August his "Irony in Velvet," in the *Century*, postulated that Cabell's short stories were ironic, thereby distressing "readers who prefer to have their romances entirely romantic." In the 19 October *Nation*, Van Doren determined that *Straws and Prayer-Books* and *From the Hidden Way* ranked Cabell with Hawthorne and Melville. In the *Century* for November, the critic expounded on the mutual dependence of *Jurgen* and *Figures*. And in the December *Literary Digest International Book Review*, he treated Cabell's "world-vision" in the essay "Getting the Ground Plan of Mr. Cabell's Work." Cabell had drawn a map of Poictesme, and he and Holt debated where it should first appear. Holt had wanted it to be published with Van Doren's article in the *International Book Review*, but Cabell held out for its debut in Van Doren's monograph, *James Branch Cabell*, published the following year.

Emily Clark made her last request of Hergesheimer for a contribution to "a little magazine which was the pet charity of the literati." She added, "As *Vanity Fair* would say—I am retiring from The Reviewer. After this month I shall fall into a well of silence and you will not be troubled again." Her long-suffering sustainer failed her in this last request, but Cabell contributed a cryptic, abstruse sonnet entitled "The Second Way." Her last issue was one of her best, leading off with three episodes of Frances Newman's *Hard-Boiled Virgin* and ending with a poem by Allen Tate. Emily was denying to everyone in Richmond that she was engaged. A sympathetic Hunter Stagg explained to Carl Van Vechten: "Though they know she is lying it is easier for her if she doesn't have to act as if it were so. Also she is not in good health. Her nerves are troubling her and she looks a wreck—really pitifully. My heart aches to see her. The poor thing is frightened to death. And her heart is having palpitations, or something, caused by nerves, so that she has to go to the doctor. The same thing happened during the summer before she got herself up to the point of actually accepting the poor man." Emily Clark's anguish was not too dissimilar from Cabell's at an earlier period, an agony that he relived from time to time.

On the whole Cabell had to be gratified with the critical reception of *Straws and Prayer-Books*. While few reviewers went so far as Van Doren, neither did they wish to appear outside the mainstream. Louis Bromfield found "delicious humor" in the footnotes. Ernest Boyd termed it a "Literary Diversion," and Ellen Glasgow wrote that "Mr. Cabell . . . reveals himself again as a moralist and a merrymaker." Not all was unrestrained praise, however. John Farrar's *The Literary Spotlight*, a collection of anonymous essays caricaturing the current establishment, contained some telling truths about the Richmond writer. "When Cabell tries to be topical he is usually lumbering." His polished prose, according to Farrar, was really a cover for a lack of any kind of conviction. "The truth is that Cabell's work is almost entirely subjective. He is constantly in the throes of explaining and justifying himself to himself." At this point in Cabell's career, these words were prophetic, foreshadowing much of his later writing. Farrar touched on the writer's essentially dowdy home life, his "astonishingly meager" library, all indicative of an indifference to reality, of a realization that he could never attain a perfection once envisaged. The critic castigated Cabell's habit of forming coteries of mutual admirers (Hergesheimer, Mencken) to further his works. "Cabell cannot stand criticism, a weakness that serves his work poorly. The success that has come to him in such a strange and ironic way after years of neglect and even contempt has embittered rather than mellowed him." As to the epic Biography of Man, in his intention "to embrace all life, he has succeeded in embracing Cabell." The image in the pool of thought, Farrar maintained, had all along been the ambivalent self. He also touched on another truth: Richmond's dislike of Cabell, which stemmed not really from the old gossip but from the city's desire to patronize him. His celebrity prevented that, however, and "Richmond realizes that while Cabell knows it inside and out, it can really never know Cabell."

Hunter Stagg's reviews of Cabell's verses and essays appeared in the Richmond *Times-Dispatch* on Sunday, 20 October, the same day that Miller and Rhoads announced its coming book fair. Hunter saw Cabell's penchant for attributing his poems to others as a ruse to avoid writing modern verse. He observed that much of *Straws and Prayer-Books* was on the subject of how and why books were written. He added perceptively: "And incidental to this is much inevitable discussion of himself, which we must take, with thanks, in place of the autobiography which he, alone among modern writers, seems determined not to write."

Carl Van Vechen had been announced as one of the celebrities attending the book fair, but he wrote Hunter privately that he preferred coming to Richmond solo. Hergesheimer was in attendance, and the *Times-Dispatch* ran his *Linda Condon* serially during that week. Henry Seidel Canby, editor of the *Saturday Review*, was a guest as was a young Louis Bromfield, author of *Green Bay Tree*. Beale Davis, the Petersburg author of *One Way Street*, was an object of interest, especially for his social behavior. The Virginia Writers' Club provided hosts and hostesses for each of the six days. On Monday, the opening day, those announced were Cabell, John Powell, Kate Langley Bosher, and Robert Lancaster, author of a book on old houses. On Friday, the Writers' Club gave a dinner at the Commonwealth Club, with Guy Holt as featured speaker; Dr. Tucker made an impassioned plea for keeping the *Reviewer* in Richmond. Emily and Hunter saw the club as antipathetic to the publication, however. Doubtless they regarded themselves as professionals and the members of the club as provincial amateurs.

Hunter went on to Baltimore for a visit with the Kinsolvings. Did Cabell remember "Kinny" Kinsolving, his rival for the attentions of Alice Serpell at the Rockbridge a quarter century before? In Baltimore Hunter saw Walter de la Mare, whom he had met in England in 1922, and was taken under the wing of charming David Bruce, his distinguished diplomatic career a future legend. In Richmond, Cabell made notes on the galley proofs of Carl Van Doren's *James Branch Cabell*. Van Doren defended anew Cabell's circular plots, "returning . . . to the same 'situation,' seen differently, with which all started." He admitted, however, that the formula might appear overworked. Cabell wrote Ellen Glasgow on 15 November, thanking her for her masterly review in the *Herald Tribune*. His business correspondence with Holt shows him concerned about illustrated editions of his works, motion picture rights (especially for Jurgen), translations into French and German, and inclusion in anthologies of American literature. He resolved to review no more books save Ellen Glasgow's forthcoming Barren Ground.

Again winter at Dumbarton was attended with problems, the furnace breaking down and Percie's health impaired. Again they resorted to rented quarters in Richmond. For Cabell these were "hellish weeks"; for Hunter Stagg, they presented golden opportunities to drop in on the master. Frances Newman's penchant for colds drove her to the protection of her sister in Richmond. Cabell thought her novel The Hard-Boiled Virgin should come out in the spring, but as a longtime librarian Newman had a prejudice against spring books. Her Mutations of the Short Story was actually selling and making money.

Just as John Farrar's The Literary Spotlight had been irreverent to the leading writers of the day, so too did Charles Baldwin's 1924 edition of The Men Who Make Our Novels provide titillation for the Richmonders who knew Cabell, Hergesheimer, and Van Vechten. Baldwin's opening remarks on Cabell were personal indeed.

> In Richmond the most unpopular (and probably the loneliest) boy at school—dubbed "Sister" by the young rowdies who, with their uncouth manners and half-formed thoughts, already, so early, had permanently alienated him from our common (oh, so common) humanity—teacher's pet then, and now the pet of such critics as, in his entourage, have taken teacher's place, the pedants, professors of an interest in connotation and commentary—that is Mr. Cabell, the (I should say) most distinguished writer in America, a precious and precise reveler strayed from the narrow confines of the Eighteen-Nineties, an ironic Pound with no memories of Idaho to lend pathos to his present disillusion. (86)

Of Cabell's celebrated style, Baldwin observed that he wrote English "as though it were a dead language." As to the man, he quotes Cabell as saying, "My books must stand for my biography. My personality is, even to me, entirely devoid of interest."

While Cabell was pleased with the concept of all his work as an extended biography and was happy that the idea had been sold to most of the literary critics, he was aware of evidence to the contrary. He was pleased with Van Doren's encomiums which appeared in February of the new year. Even so, he realized that the so-called Biography was an imperfectly patched together opus and that it lacked a conclusion. *The Silver Stallion* would remedy the latter omission. Writing it was demanding his best effort, and he resented the intrusions that robbed him of concentration. This book was to be a capstone, a farewell to an important phase of his career. Yet he was tired of the restrictions of Poictesme. The province he had invented to liberate him from the restrictions of time and place had become as exigent in its way as any real place had been for a Dreiser or a Sinclair Lewis. Only one place held any semblance of reality—his study at Dumbarton. Unfortunately, just when he most longed for that three-windowed room where the creative spirits seemed most friendly, he was exiled. Hunter Stagg wrote Montgomery Evans of Cabell's acute unhappiness:

That gentleman, by the way has been dragged by the seat of his pants and the scruff of his neck in town, and forced to live for at least a month (dating from two weeks ago) in a small apartment. Mrs. Cabell, unable to cope with the difficulties of keeping house in winter out there in the country, effected this move, which she has been threatening since last winter. They may stay two months, though Mr. Cabell swears that HE will not, whatever she does. Following, as it did, close upon the heels of a term of service on the jury, the move precipitated Cabell into a horrible mood, combined of despair and fiendish temper. I went to see him the second night he was in the place. Indeed, he called me up and asked me to come down, which fact will show you to what depths of woe he had sunk. For the second time in my life I saw him, that night, so unhappy that he couldnt hide it—and indeed, he made no effort to. I had an odd feeling of being actually in the presence of the forces which had been called together from out of the spaces to make certain works of genius signed James Branch Cabell, which is a feeling one doesnt often have in his company. . . . Mrs. Cabell said he was behaving like a devil. He wouldnt read, and he wouldnt go out, though urged to, and he swore (and still swears) that he wont write a line there. He works cross-word puzzles! Now however, he has started to read, and is in a more cheerful humor. He comes up here every two or three days to borrow books, and, sometimes finding me out, talks to mother, whom he likes a lot, and says it is a pity I didnt take after her.

Speaking of Cabell, I have just received a check from Brentano's for fifty three dollars!—the same arriving as I ended that last paragraph. It is, of course, for the Cabell article. A week ago I had a letter from Stuart Rose, and not to conceal anything from you, he wrote: "Your article is the best thing of its kind that I have ever seen. It compares more than favorably with Cabell's monograph on Hergesheimer. Whether you know it or not, you have done a first-rate job; one of which you will live to be proud." Mr. Cabell endured my teasing, about the more than favorable comparison with him, with equanimity — indeed, he was almost as pleased as I, having been a bit anxious when Stuart waited so long to give his verdict. (12 February)

By mid-March Cabell was back in the Dumbarton study, and Holt was requesting a new title for autumn publication. Unfortunately, it would not be *The Silver Stallion*, which could not be dashed off on demand. He was carefully crafting, he hoped, another masterpiece that just might be his last. Life was full of traps, and innocent-looking adversaries were constantly turning up. On 17 March, Hunter Stagg alerted Carl Van Vechten that another caravan of visitors was to descend on Richmond for the visit of Carl and Irita Van Doren, guests of Ellen Glasgow. Van Doren was to lecture at the Woman's Club on the 30th, and Cabell was too heavily in his debt to ignore his visit.

A lengthy opus from Hunter to Van Vechten gives us another intimate account of the farcical events that took place. After describing Emily Clark's efforts to upstage every other entertainment held in honor of the Van Dorens, Hunter recounts her behavior at the lecture and afterwards:

> After the lecture there is always a reception, with tea and coffee drinking, and much introducing of people to the lecturer. But not this time. Emily planted herself under Mr. V. D.'s chin, turned up her snout and talked. Nobody could get near him. Time and again people took people up to be introduced to him, and in the middle of the introductory sentence threw up their hands and turned away, for Emily never stopped talking, with her eyes fastened on his. Everyone was furious, except those who were laughing at her. Mrs. Cabell was nearly strangling, with rage. She came up to me and chattered with fury, and grabbed my arm and said, "Come here! Come here! You've got to meet him, you've got to break this up." I was led up to the pair, stuck my elbow in Emily's ribs, she turned to see who struck her, and Mrs. Cabell seized the instant and introduced me. The minute the formal words were over, though, Emily went on talking. I laughed at Mrs. Cabell's fury, and walked away, with her. "I was wondering," I said, "if you could get Mr. Van Doren, and bring him with Mr. Cabell up to my place after this is over, and finish up those Martini cocktails Monty brought down. I want him to autograph the book he wrote about Mr. Cabell." She said she would, if she could ever get near V. D. to arrange it. "But if you ask Emily Clark I shant do it. I shant come." . . .
>
> On good authority, I hear that after we left, Emily went completely crazy

and ran from person to person saying, "Oh do you think they are going to Ellen Glasgow's to dinner? Oh, Do you think they are? Or, do you THINK they CAN be going there and not me? Oh, how CAN they be going to Ellen Glasgow's and not ME! I dont BELIEVE Hunter lost his hat. It was a LIE, a LIE' Oh do you think its POSSIBLE that they've . . . etc." So that someone remarked that they had heard that a social climber was the most wretched creature in the world, but if there was any more pitiable wretch than a literary climber they didnt want to see it, after that exhibition. She was utterly distraught, and completely mad, for the moment.

Well, when Monty and I got to Miss Glasgow's, there was Emily. Miss Bennett told me she had called her up and asked her ten minutes before supper time, and that she had got there almost before she finished talking over the phone. She paused long enough, however, to call up several people and tell them that she "had found her invitation to Miss Glasgow's waiting for her when she got home from the club. At the dinner she made an ass of herself talking continually about how lovely Mencken was to her, so that Miss Glasgow had many occasions to roll her eyes with humorous patience over to meet mine. Emily also told Mr. V. D. that she had had a book she'd have liked him to autograph, only she had been too considerate to ask him. That before me. It didnt make any hit with him, though, I think. (20 April)

In April, Hunter lost his job as a paid staff member of the Richmond *Times-Dispatch*, an austerity cut. Both Cabell and Van Vechten suggested that it relieved him from the burden of reviewing so that he could to do more serious writing, and Hunter considered job opportunities in Baltimore and New York. His article on Cabell, commissioned by Stuart Rose, appeared in *Brentano's Book Chat* for March/April and was entitled "The Absence of Mr. Cabell." Asked to write a Richmonder's intimate portrait of a fellow Richmonder, Hunter had resorted to the ruse of writing about Cabell's personal elusiveness in his home town.

"Above Paradise," an episode from Cabell's work in progress, *The Silver Stallion*, had appeared in the February *American Mercury*. In May, Cabell dispatched another episode, "The Mathematics of Gonfal," to the *Century*. Also in May ever-stimulating Joseph Hergesheimer was back in Richmond, and the following month ever-vivacious Frances Newman was again in town. She and Hunter journeyed out to Dumbarton. As usual Hunter was burdened with books to be autographed for friends, in particular Montgomery Evans and Margaret Freeman. Cabell bibliophile Carl Parsons, whom Hunter had visited in Maine the previous summer, had just lost his young wife and had decided to allay his grief by taking Hunter to Europe along with another young man. Parsons knew that Hunter had established literary friendships in England and France on his 1923 visit. As Hunter crossed the Atlantic again, the Cabells headed for Mountain Lake.

Cayford Cottage again needed repairs. Among its other drawbacks, its flat-roofed porch conducted water into the living quarters rather than outside. Some sixty-five years later, however, Cayford is still in use as a summer lodging at Mountain Lake. Among matters literary, Cabell reported to Holt that *The Silver Stallion* was progressing, the cool heights of the Alleghenies making his pen flow smoothly. The tone of the work is elevated, elegiac, its style Cabell's best blend of wit and irony. The author's wisdom is biblical, and he steps easily into each character, each being a manifestation of his multifaceted persona. In a sense, he burlesques each of his former selves, recording the evolution of a collective society. The passing of the Fellowship of the Silver Stallion reads very much like the passing of the Confederate veterans from the Richmond scene. Another episode, "The Mathematics of Gonfal," appeared in the August issue of the *Century*. An untitled preface was added to the seventh printing of *The Rivet*, issued in September. In October, Cabell had hopes that the motion picture rights to *Jurgen* would bring fifteen thousand dollars.

Now that all her children except Ballard were past childhood, Percie decided that the large frame house at Dumbarton was too empty and too isolated for the needs of her declining family. Her husband was loath to leave. His career had moved into its major phase when he moved into Dumbarton Grange; leaving it would parallel his departure from Poictesme. Would he be leaving the place where the magic spirits had congregated to give his work life? Still, he had been only a guest; it was his wife's house and her money. Cabell resigned himself to her inevitable decision, and she promised him another upstairs room in which to write his books. Percie settled on a thin, pie-shaped sliver of a house, 3201 Monument Avenue, its façade on the avenue making it appear larger than it is. The house had been built in 1910 and was considered somewhat old-fashioned, compared with the new neocolonial and neo-Georgian mansions rising along Monument. When Cabell received a copy of Hergesheimer's *From an Old Stone House*, an account of the metamorphosis of the Dower House with handsome pictures, he wrote on 28 November: "All my thanks come to you for that most superb looking volume. It perforce stays for the while unread, now that we are finally, actually, and agonizingly, 'moving.' We have taken over a rather suitable, much smaller house several hundred miles up Monument Avenue; and trust, if we survive the transit, to be settled in it, for all time, by the end of the week."

Deems Taylor's symphonic composition *Jurgen* was at last scheduled to be performed in New York on 19 November. Cabell hoped that McBride would publish the illustrated *Figures of Earth* on the same day. Hunter Stagg wrote Carl Van Vechten on the 3d: "James, to whom I talked today, says he is not coming to New York to hear Deems Taylor's *Jurgen*. He is dying to hear it, but is appalled by the thought that he'd have to say something to the composer afterwards. Of the novelists' dinner he seemed to think it would be endurable if you and Joe and he could get speechless together before dinner, but none the less he isn't coming. It is the same old story. Mrs. Cabell says he is, and he says he isn't. She is coming north, however, whether he comes or not."

Later in November, Cabell invited Hunter to the Woman's Club to hear a lecture by John Cooper Powys. Hunter, through the influence of Van Vechten, had become interested in Negro writers, artists, and musicians. He wrote his mentor on 18 November:

> I saw James the other day. He took me to a lecture by that Powys man. He asked if the Anglo Saxon league had been after me, and said that John Powell has threatened to have it after me, on account of my meeting Negroes last June. How'd he know? I asked, but Mr. Cabell didn't know that; he said somebody had written it down here, and that John was furious. I suspect that somebody was me, and that Cabell told him himself. I said I was sorry John knew, because I had been looking forward to the pleasure of telling him myself. I told Ellen Glasgow the other day. When she got well she asked me down to tea, alone. She wasn't, apparently, shocked.

November saw the publication of another episode from *The Silver Stallion*, "What Saraide Wanted" in the *Red Book*. In December Cabell's works were generally selling well. "A Brown Woman" was included in *Great Short Stories of the New World*. Cabell hoped for the sale of twenty thousand copies of *The Silver Stallion* when it appeared in the spring. Papé, the illustrator of choice for nearly all his current reprints, was also requested to draw a map of Poictesme based on Cabell's map with emendations. Louise Burleigh, lured to Richmond to direct the Little Theatre League, was trying her hand at a dramatization of *Jurgen*, and a Ruth Ehrich asked his approval of her dramatization of "Simon's Hour." Cabell approved of a Yiddish *Jurgen*. In February 1926 he wrote Holt that Norman Bel-Geddes was enthusiastic over Burleigh's scenario of *Jurgen*; everyone agreed that Jurgen was a dramatic character, but he seemed resistant to translation. Papé's map, with place-names misspelled, disappointed Cabell. Indeed, a number of small annoyances began to fret an aging poet, nearing forty-seven.

Moving from Dumbarton marked a prophetic transition in his life, and now it was definite that Guy Holt was leaving McBride. Cabell had frequently considered leaving that publisher for Alfred Knopf's firm, but his close association with Holt had deterred him. Now that his collaborator-editor was leaving, would this not be an appropriate time for him to make his move? The John Day Company that Holt was joining was not large enough to buy the Cabell copyrights from McBride. He would do as Holt suggested—send the John Day Company a small, symbolic work as a gesture of good will. The sales reports from McBride were currently satisfactory, and that firm had suffered through the long drought of Jurgen's suppression. Then, too, there was the revised, uniform edition that Cabell longed for; few publishers would be willing to assume the economic risk of such a project. Even so, Cabell sorely missed Holt's carping criticisms and advice: "I merely repeat that, after eleven years, I feel so utterly at sea as to be almost seasick."

The reception of The Silver Stallion in April was mixed, but on the whole its author could be pleased, for most reviewers appeared to accept the work as an integral part of an ongoing saga, albeit one winding down. Frances Newman in the Bookman observed that no one need try to understand the work "unless he has read and understood Jurgen and Figures of Earth." The underlying tone of most reviews was that the writer was now a known product and that one either savored his writing or did not care for it. Cabell himself decided he had been wasteful of his creative talents in The Silver Stallion. When he had forwarded the typescript to Holt on 30 September 1925, he had observed that four of the characters were each worth a whole book. He went on to explain his difficulty in letting go of this work:

> The book manuscript was bundled up and sent to you in some haste, in part because I knew I would never get on with anything else so long as it was in the house and subject to revision, and in part because I was rather afraid that if I continued to brood over the fiasco of the Figures of Earth tailpieces I would in some sudden fit of rage mail the manuscript to Knopf. I really think that if he had not selected this especial juncture to announce his taking over of Fanny Hurst his chances would have been excellent. Even then, fate tried to intervene, for as the mail train snatched the mail bag from the hook the bag was ripped open and that one package spilt out in the ditch, where it

spent the night. The mail carrier retrieved it the following morning, and the postmaster remailed it, without letting me know about the accident: I can, thus, but hope it reached you in good order, and try to disregard the omen. . . .

This book completes the history of medieval Poictesme. I shall deal with that province no more; and the temptation to quote Prospero is considerable. I still plan, when time serves, to enlarge greatly the Afterword of *Domnei*: otherwise, the Biography now runs without a break to the end of *Gallantry*.

In April 1926, Cabell was again writing Gilbert Porterfield at Mountain Lake about repairs to Cayford Cottage. He had not settled comfortably into the new study at 3201 Monument and began to look upon the retreat in the mountains as his inspirational home. Richmond was really a distracting place. That spring Carl Van Vechten came down to Richmond, urged on by Emily Clark Balch and lured by his passing interest in handsome, amusing Hunter Stagg. Hunter wrote Montgomery Evans, referring to Emily's visit: "She had her motor car and, with Carl and her mother and me, motored about to various points of interest in Virginia. There were also dinner parties, one or two of them a bit hectic." They saw the University of Virginia on a perfect spring day. April seemed to awaken old desires in Cabell. *The Music from Behind the Moon*, which he was writing for Holt's new publishing firm, allegorized once again the troubling music Gabriella Moncure had produced in his schoolboy's heart. This nostalgia may have been inspired by the publication of *Retractions*, a collector's edition of fifteen sonnets; all twelve copies had been sent to Cabell for his autograph. While copyrighted in 1924, this bit of scholia did not emerge from the press of the Cat's Head Club until 24 April 1926. These are the love poems of a middle-aged man addressing a woman loved in youth. To Cabell they were like distant music from another time and place, from behind the moon.

Responding to an invitation to visit the Hergesheimers, Cabell wrote Joe on 12 June:

> At this writing we are packing and parcel posting the houseful of stuff which annually we must convey to Mountain Lake, and all is turmoil. It would be soothing in this time of agitation to think that Dower House were anything like a near possibility. But, naturally, it is not a possibility before the fall. . . . Anyhow, do you and Dorothy ask us again toward autumn, and I can promise an acceptance. You should well know that I enjoy and envy Dower House.
>
> The *Stallion* has done quite nicely, and I have completed an astoundingly

short novel which appears in September as a limited and, I hope, rather strikingly illustrated volume. The title, anyhow, is beautiful,—*The Music from Behind the Moon*. This too I am hoping you may like when I exchange it for a copy of *Tampico*.

Back at Mountain Lake, Cabell began to look through his files for a project. He no longer felt chivalrous or gallant; he was an aging poet like Madoc in the small work he was writing for Guy Holt at the John Day Company. He had excelled as the comic poet, beginning as Sir John Falstaff and culminating in Jurgen, but he felt himself a failure as the poet-lover. And why had he failed? The enemy was within, he decided, and the enemy may have been a benefactor. He had earlier put aside *Something About Eve* to work on *The Silver Stallion*; now he took out the unfinished manuscript. It would serve admirably as the vehicle illustrating whether domesticity or fear of failure itself had robbed the poet of his powers. In its later preface he wrote that it was "already an aging and much interlined manuscript when, in 1923, Guy Holt compiled his Bibliography." The discontented author had burned the first version in the fireplace at Dumbarton in the spring of 1925, along with other manuscripts he felt to be stillborn. When he had complained to Holt the previous fall of his wastefulness in *The Silver Stallion*, he exempted one of the characters—Ninzian, "for he, I gather, plans to visit Lichfield" (Richmond, the theoretical setting for *Something About Eve*). The symbolic setting for the work, however, is Mispec Moor, an anagram for *compromise*. Gerald Musgrave, the writer, is another comic treatment of the author himself. "I came back to Gerald Musgrave in the July of 1926. I found in Cayford Cottage, just such a cottage as Gerald inhabited." The work took a year to complete. Gerald's journey to Antan, the place of immortality, is interrupted when he meets the domestic woman, Maya of the Fair Breasts. This wholly maternal woman's magic is of a different order from the seductions of the other temptresses Gerald has encountered. While Gerald-Cabell made his compromises at Cayford Cottage, Percie Cabell found her own contentments. Some thirty years later, the story was retold:

And then, in those untroubled days, then every summer she enjoyed our two or three months' stay at Mountain Lake, where we had builded Cayford Cottage—with a glass-enclosed small porch-room, for me to write books in—and where, because virtually the same persons returned to Mountain Lake every summer, she had scores of intimate acquaintances with whom to go fishing (in which, precisely as Mr. Shepherd had done, she delighted), or with whom to play bridge (in which likewise she delighted, all-scientifically, in accord with Mr. Culbertson's very latest rulings), or with whom to tramp the wide sprawling hills in a search for mushrooms.

She had come, somehow, to know all about mushrooms. Without hesitating could she distinguish between the edible and the poisonous varieties. It was to her an unfailing joy to wander abroad gathering in a wicker basket all such mushrooms as would not, according to Charles City, kill you dead as a door nail, and then, with the aid of a small electric heater, to cook these mushrooms upon the back porch of Cayford Cottage. After that, she would carry down the hill toward the hotel a sizzling, huge kettleful of them for our supper, in the hotel dining room, sending over by our waiter a liberal portion to the table of this or the other of her special friends, and glowing visibly, with an artist's fond pride, over their enjoyment of her unparalleled cooking.

Yes, very certainly Priscilla Bradley Cabell had a talent for living; and out of every one of these homely, everyday avocations at Mountain Lake she got a constant and companionable contentment. (*As I Remember It*, 69–70)

17

Mispec Moor

1926–1931

For a child growing up in late-Victorian Richmond, being a writer meant having your name on the spines of a long shelf of uniformly bound books. In his inner heart James Cabell knew that all his diverse writings were not an organic whole; but as a believer in outward appearances, he might have felt that if all his works were so bound, perhaps they were truly of a piece. Guy Holt had helped create that shelf of books, and Cabell sorely missed the exchange of letters with his editor. Now that editorial discussions were underway about the Storisende Edition of the Works of James Branch Cabell, he needed familiar counsel he could trust, and he also needed Holt's criticisms during the writing of *Something About Eve*, which seemed to be getting more digressive than some of his previously wandering tales.

And now, in September, Ellen Glasgow, six years his senior, had followed up the success of *Barren Ground* the year before with a sparkling comedy that was winning huzzas in the critical world. Asked to review *The Romantic Comedians*, Cabell declined on the grounds that he was over exposed. His own contribution to the September book world, *The Music from Behind the Moon*, was being accepted for what it was, a collector's item, noteworthy primarily for its eight woodcuts and the art of bookmaking.

Carl Van Doren termed it "the essence of Cabell," and Benjamin De-Casseres, an ardent new apologist for the Richmond author, found "poetry, humor, and laughter" in the slight volume. The following month Cabell was offered the O. Henry Prize for 1926 for "Between Worlds," which had appeared in the September issue of the *American Mercury*. Cabell was also reading the proofs of Frances Newman's *The Hard-Boiled Virgin*. Responding to her appeal as a protégé, he had agreed to supply a publicity statement for her publisher, and along with a flattering letter he dispatched the following on 5 October: "This appears to me the most brilliant, the most candid, the most civilized, and—always within the limits of its chosen field—the most profound book yet written by any American woman. You have here—for, to be sure, the discerning and the tolerably tolerant reader alone—a small masterpiece." Mencken, who read a carbon copy, agreed with Cabell's assessment and was also quoted on the book jacket.

Mencken, on a trip through the South, was entertained by the Cabells on Thursday, 14 October. Hunter reported details to Van Vechten, always curious about the Richmond scene:

> Cabell's dinner for Mencken was not an unqualified success. Mencken had written asking to see only a selected few of the newspaper men. So Mrs. Cabell got four of five from the News Leader, through Virginius Dabney, and not knowing any on the Times Dispatch, got me to bring any I wanted to from there. But for some reason Cabell had nothing to speak of in the way of drink, only two rounds of cocktails—so it wasnt that kind of party. Then Mrs. Cabell, who hates to do anything purely for Mr. Cabell, with nothing in it for herself or her daughters, up and asked Dr. and Mrs. Tucker (I've no objection to the doctor—like him fine), and Miss Julia Sully, and Miss Glasgow, and her brother from England, and Robert Cabell and his wife, and Emily. No young and pretty girls either for Mencken or for the young newspaper men. So it wasnt that kind of party. It was neither one thing nor the other. And I have an impression of phalanxes of black coated young men standing around talking to each other, and they see each other every day at the offices or drinking coca colas on Seventh and Broad. Whereas they had come in considerable excitement at the prospect of hobnobbing with both Mencken and Cabell at once. True they saw and met both these personages, but in such a gathering nobody got much more than that out of it. Mencken got nothing out of it either, unless he was amused at the spectacle of Miss Glasgow perfectly consciously immolating herself—with a fretful, pained look on her face upon the altar of log-rolling, by eagerly and rather pathetically agreeing with everything he said, even when it was perfectly plain that she had not caught what

he said. She made a mistake. Not being used to doing that sort of thing, she doesnt know how. She didnt get away with it, and couldnt conceal that she knew very well she was in a false position, doing something that she resented having to do and despised herself for doing. In spite of the fact that she is displeased with me for some reason or another, I hated to see the poor lady put herself in that position—which is certainly not a position for Miss Glasgow. Mr. Cabell, fiendish as usual, sat with his hand over his mouth—but his eyes gave him away. As one of the few people in the crowd who he had seen before, Mencken was unexpectedly cordial to me. (28 October)

The *Hard-Boiled Virgin* appeared on 20 November, and Carl Van Vechten wrote Hunter Stagg on the 30th: "The hard-boiled virgin reads like an exposé of a soft-boiled nymphomaniac. I was delighted with your review. I saw Ellen last week. She is furious, naturally, with Cabell's blurb. So is Miss Wylie. What did he mean by it? Emily, by the way, is not a bit perturbed. She considers it extremely flattering that Frances took so much trouble to include her. I cannot imagine any one who did not know Frances reading the book."

Stagg's reply (6 December) is probably near the truth.

As to what James means by writing all that on the jacket of the book, it is very simple. He really does think the book extraordinary, but that's merely by the way. The real thing is his well-known natural perversity and contrariety which made him delight in setting everybody by the ears with his encomiums, his "most brilliant," and most everything else, while he reserves an avenue of retreat, if challenged, through the simple phrase "always within the limits of its chosen field." This phrase he, of course, makes the least conspicuous. He masses the sentences so that the phrase is the one that no one notices or remembers—*precisely* so that if anyone says anything to him he can, if he wishes, point to it and make them feel foolish because they overlooked it. That's his old trick. Of course, if you invest that one phrase with much meaning, it makes all the rest mean—precisely *nothing at all*. Trust James to see to it that he has a way out of anything that may look like a jam. Of course this way out won't do him much good with Miss Glasgow and Elinor Wylie. If they are inclined to say anything to him about it (and Miss Glasgow might, though I doubt if Elinor will), by merely pointing to it he can stop their arguments, but it wont stop their feeling the way they feel. But what does he care about that, or anything else, except his liberty to chuckle and snicker all by himself in his library over the neat and tricky little piece of mischief that he has pulled? All this is merely my own interpretation of the matter, quite unauthorized. . . . Nothing could be more characteristic of James than this small boyish prank, and I expect he is enjoying it thoroughly. And the chances are that he is enjoying even more the simple absence of dignity in Mr. Mencken's support of his remarks, both on the jacket of the book and in that ridiculous interview in the Atlanta paper.

Cabell mailed Stagg a copy of a limerick, he had written, with a note: "This review of the Hard-Boiled Virgin has just reached me, and seems apt":

> An erudite spinster named Frances,
> Who delighted in ribald romances,
>> Resolved to find out
>> Beyond physical doubt
> What the point of the joke in men's pants is.

Late in life Cabell amused himself by penning similar bawdy limericks.

Hunter Stagg was again employed, the esteemed historian and editor Douglas Southall Freeman offering him the Book Page of the Richmond *News-Leader*. In December, Cabell was visited by an artist, Bernhardt Wall, who did sketches of the writer, his study, and his house that resulted in another collector's item entitled *A Visit to James Branch Cabell*. Cabell is presented as uncharacteristically jovial and chubby. He also received a letter, dated 8 December, from his cousin Henry Sydnor Harrison, asking him to consider rejoining the Author's League which needed the support "of our most distinguished writers." Evidently Harrison was willing to overlook Cabell's condescending remarks relative to Harrison's earlier popularity. He hoped to renew their acquaintance begun in the ancient days of Mrs. Tyler and the *Times-Dispatch*.

Weighted down with the Storisende Edition and struggling to complete *Something About Eve*, Cabell wrote his former editor in January of his sense of loss. Other writers seemed as vibrant as ever. Hergesheimer and Frances Newman were again in Richmond. The former's *Tampico* was favorably received, and Newman was the literary sensation of the moment, being interviewed by the local press everywhere with *The Hard-Boiled Virgin* in its fifth printing. Hergesheimer, who liked staying at the Westmoreland Club when in Richmond, entertained her and the Cabells at dinner on 12 January. The Cabells entertained at lunch on Saturday the 15th, and they were all included in a party given by Ellen Glasgow on Sunday. Cabell outlined to Newman the next book he wanted her to write. At the time Newman was working on a novel tentatively titled "The Golden Lover," which she later changed to *Dead Lovers Are Faithful Lovers*. Percie Cabell liked Frances Newman as another talkative female, and when Percie was in New York in May, Frances wrote Cabell: "It was awfully nice of Mrs. Cabell to call me up and we had a grand gossip." Frances Newman entertained Virginia Shepherd, Cabell's stepdaughter, in New York. In May Newman wrote Cabell: "I had Lamar [Trotti] down to meet Virginia and he is already very anxious to marry her—both because of her own charms and because he fancies receiving a bride from the hand which wrote The Cream of the Jest."

In May Cabell was having eye problems. On 9 June he wrote Hergesheimer: "The blindness, thank you, is at least temporarily removed, though the doctor yet harbors discomfortable and truculent designs against my tonsils. Meanwhile new glasses serve me nicely, the last part of *Eve* went yesterday to the publishers, and I live waist deep in proofs for the Storisende Edition." He gave Holt a more extended report on 17 June.

> For myself, the spring has been rather hellish. On the last lap of [*Something About*] *Eve*, just at the opening of May, I was smitten with inexplicable and very painful eye-trouble which led the doctors generally to favor pulling my teeth and cutting out my tonsils and operating for sinus, on the principle, I gathered, that I might thus quite possibly be helped and, anyhow, nobody else would be hurt. Ultimately, it turned out that one eye had changed its shape, so that my glasses were wholly wrong, and we compromised on a new pair. That settled on, a day or two ago, the oculist managed to make a mistake in following the prescription, so that my new pair was much more wrong in another way, and in the while that I tried to get adjusted to them, made matters worse. Literature in such circumstances cannot thrive, but I in some not yet comprehended way did get the manuscript finished and delivered. It has gone to the printer, without, I gather, having been read by anybody, although Jones writes me that he read the first half. Anyhow, it is quite nice, with a wholly proper hero who conducts himself chastely throughout the book in howsoever trying circumstances: it is a book with which no moralist can quarrel, with any pretence of justice. Still, we know what they are.
>
> The Plimpton people seem to be making quite a good job of the Storisende Edition, and thus far orders have been coming in with gratifying frequency. The *Stallion* needed very little revision, the other two a great deal, just in phrasing. The three prefaces are so-so and quite handsome in length. I incline at present to hold the set down to eighteen volumes, since it is now, to my partial eyes, a complete whole—I mean, with *Eve* finished.

Holt in turn expressed his regret in not working with Cabell on *Something About Eve*. The absence of his therapeutic editorial criticisms left Cabell feeling less secure in the days ahead.

As usual, Cayford Cottage needed its annual repairs before the Cabells settled in. While all of them enjoyed the cool heights of Mountain Lake,

Cabell sat figuratively on his literary mountaintop. His time was spent writing prefaces, revising the previously revised, and autographing sheets to be included in the Storisende Edition. In September the *Bookman* published "Confusions of the Golden Travel," the twelfth chapter of *Something About Eve* in which the hero enters the great Mirror of Caer Omn, anagram for "Romance," and the "novel" itself was published the same month. The New York *Times* review was entitled "Something, but Not a Great Deal, About Eve." Critics friendly to Cabell cautiously continued to find great beauty in the writing. Hunter Stagg in a letter to Van Vechten on 12 October summed up the attitude of many Cabell admirers:

> I would like to know what you think of "Something About Eve." I like it much, much better than the Silver Stallion, but I find (between you and me) that Mr. Cabell's isolation from human affairs has brought him at last to the logical point — an inability to inject life and personality into his hero. However, Mrs. Cabell tells me James thinks it is the best book he has written. I wonder if he does. To me he said nothing except that he would see that I got a tall paper copy if the book stores disappoint me, which, though mighty white of him, is hardly an expression of opinion. All of which sounds more disparaging than I mean it to sound. I really found the book vastly entertaining, and full of beauty, though Gerald himself was flat, and made me sigh for the irrepressible vigour of Jurgen and the suave, cynical vitality of Florian.

Something About Eve was dedicated to Ellen Glasgow, whose national prominence ranked with Cabell's. Her social standing in Richmond, however, ranked higher than his in local judgment, and he stood in awe of her commanding presence. If her deafness was a tribulation to her in society, it was not so inhibiting an affliction as his shyness. On 14 October Cabell wrote her expressing the hope that she liked the work dedicated to her. His reputation as a collectible author saw the book through multiple editions. Although *The White Robe* and *The Way of Ecben* were yet to appear as codas to the Biography, *Eve* was to be its author's farewell to the writer he set out to be twenty-six years earlier. It was not, however, an adieu to the writer he had become, the essential biographer. In his review of *Eve* in the *Nation*, 12 October, Carl Van Doren called for more interpretive criticism of Cabell's works, a congenial summons to the author, for Cabell himself had evolved into a student of that work, discovering therein a fascination that would hold his attention for his remaining years. He had already attracted the attention of a young scholar who was the first to study his oeuvre in depth in an academic context.

Warren A. McNeill of Lynchburg first wrote Cabell in 1924, when he sent an editorial he had written for the Lynchburg *News*. Returning to the University of Richmond to complete work on a baccalaureate degree, McNeill inquired into Cabell's sources and proceeded to write a thesis of ten thousand words. A pleased Cabell wrote that he would indeed like to see the thesis in print. When McNeill reviewed *The Silver Stallion* in 1926 for the Richmond *Times-Dispatch*, he was invited to 3201 Monument, and the writing of *Cabellian Harmonics* began with Cabell's active collaboration. Discussing the poetic passages in his later works, Cabell confessed in a letter dated 27 November: "Your letter and analyses I found, naturally, of no little interest. In some places—I admit—you seem to have found more than I consciously put there. I shall profit by it, of course, and protest that it was all quite intentional." In the same letter, he added: "I have just typed my full permission for the Lynchburg Little Theatre to produce at some near date your adaptation of 'In Ursula's Garden.' All luck to the performance!" Over the next year Cabell worked closely with McNeill, writing long letters outlining and analyzing the Biography. Cabell was pleased that McNeill had lined up a major publisher for his study and was happy to provide a preface in April 1928. Random House published an edition of fifteen hundred copies of *Cabellian Harmonics* later in the year.

In December Cabell wrote Holt that he had resolved to inscribe no more books, a vow he broke the following June when he autographed 840 copies of *Ballades from the Hidden Way*, an "art book" that would bring an inflated price. His signature on a book was worth the inflation, and the experience of actually making money was a novel one for Cabell. He began to consult Robert Cabell about investments, just like any other bourgeois householder in Philistia. Frances Newman, again in Richmond for Christmas, conferred with Cabell about her second novel, *Dead Lovers*. She had put Cabell in her first as Charles Carrington, and he had agreed to accept the dedication of her next work. Newman wanted a picture of them together. She wrote her young protégé Hansell Baugh on 6 January 1928: "Mr. Cabell was still intact, though he also had a cold, and he has the hundred and five pages you read of DLAFL—I am surviving this cold merely to find out what he thinks, and though I don't want him to like it as well as the HBV, I don't want him not to. He is considering whether to have it laid at his feet, or whether to wait for the sophistication." The latter reference was to her intention of writing a history of sophistication, "for which," she wrote Cabell, "you'll be the only possible dedicatee." She later decided that *Dead Lovers* was unworthy of Cabell's name as dedicatee. She hoped to sell it to Hollywood, which was attracting the fond gaze of the most respectable writers. In late March, on her way to France in search of sophistication, she stopped by Richmond to bid farewell to the Cabells. She wanted to leave before the new novel appeared in early April. She was fleeing on a new liner, the *Ile de France*, which had "a red grand salon upheld by round red columns that make me think of the palace Mr. Cabell gave Suskind."

The first of the eighteen volumes of the Storisende Edition had begun to make their appearances, and on 25 May Cabell wrote Mencken a letter of appreciation for a publicity puff. "As for the appearance of the books, I incline, sometimes, to share your feeling. The set then reminds me of some minor Victorian author like William Black or Charles Reade." At Mountain Lake Cabell continued to labor over the remaining volumes of his collected works. He agreed to have six of his sonnets published the following January as *Sonnets from Antan*, another collector's item. The market could absorb about one of these minor limited, signed editions a year. He wrote Carl Van Vechten from Cayford Cottage thanking him for an autographed copy of *Spider Boy: A Scenario for a Moving Picture*. He added: "With me the year is unfertile. But we are bringing out in October a 10,000 word story [*The White Robe*] which I rather hope you may like, as the trend of it is wholly moral and edifying. Meanwhile I slave on my collected works, than which Frankenstein never dreamed of a more relentless monster."

Back in Richmond, Cabell's friendship with Ellen Glasgow began to establish itself on firmer ground. Oddly, her growing abilities seemed to contradict his oft-repeated theory that all of a writer's best work came before the age of fifty. Glasgow at fifty-five was writing better than ever. Both Richmond writers had reached the stage in their careers that called for prefaces to their earlier works, prefaces written not by outside critics but by the authors themselves. Cabell acknowledged that he admired Glasgow's prose style; it had weight as well as wit. He felt that *The Romantic Comedians* highlighted her gifts for irony; moreover, Glasgow was at work on another social satire, *They Stooped to Folly*. She began to interest him as a personality.

Then Cabell had shocking news about the other female writer who interested him. Frances Newman died in New York on 22 October. As her most ardent sponsor, Cabell wrote her fellow-sponsor Mencken on 27 October: "I was horrified by Frances' death. I had not seen her since last April. *The White Robe* is dedicated to her, in words that have become rather grimly apt. Despite the error of her last book, the planned History of Sophistication would have made her future assured and enviable. As it is, the one author that I really thought I had raised, among so many failures, has failed me too. I shall essay the making of no more writers."

Hunter Stagg had become increasingly dissipated, drinking bouts alternating with brief periods of reform. Almost totally dependent on his mother for his personal care, he yet retained the friendship of many Richmonders for his honesty, charm, and contacts with a larger literary world. He wrote Van Vechten in December that "the Cabells reopened diplomatic relations this fall and I've seen them a few times, and attended luncheon there." Hunter, "along with the greater part of the population of Richmond," was recovering from the flu and his usual charitable attitude toward Cabell was not in evidence: "Between you and me I am in a state of high irritation with James Branch Cabell over 'The White Robe.' Why don't you bring out a similar $10 edition of one of the installments of Pistaches and Pastiches which you used to toss off for the Reviewer? Such a move would be equally justifiable if not more so—at least it wouldn't be repetition."

Now in his fiftieth year, Cabell had already acknowledged to himself what Hunter Stagg was shocked to see taking place. In *Townsend of Lichfield*, the coda of the Storisende Edition, Cabell was explicit:

> For, after forty-five or thereabouts, it is inevitable that a writer should cease to develop as a writer, just as he ceases to develop as a mammal. No one of his faculties, whatsoever else may happen to them, can improve after that all-arresting date. Some few—although not many authors, it more or less inexplicably appears—begin to fail earlier. But the average writer has reached his peak at, to my finding, forty; and with favoring luck, with all that he has learned of technique to counterbalance a perhaps lessened exuberance in creative power, he may retain that peak for some years. Yet this retention profits him little. He has nothing new to give: and you may look henceforward to get from him no surprises. (25)

As 14 April approached and the fateful birthday drew near, the Cabells felt neglected at 3201. Here one of the greatest literary achievements of all time was being brought to a successful conclusion, and no one in Richmond seemed aware of this extraordinary event. Percie Cabell went to the telephone and called Hunter Stagg. The latter wrote Van Vechten on 5 April: "You will be amused to hear that I have written a paper about Mr. Cabell for a magazine published here by the Chamber of Commerce. . . . Cabell is to be fifty years old sometime soon, so Mrs. C. tells me. She also tells me she thinks we ought to do something about it in a public way, arrange a sort of demonstration in honor of the 'anniversary,' she called it. I agree that it would be fitting and interesting to do something, but I am unable to suggest any ideas." Fortunately for Cabell's ego, the occasion did not slip by unnoticed in the press. Stagg wrote Van Vechten again on 22 April: "Mr. Cabell asked me Saturday, over the phone, if I had heard from you recently, and what did I hear, etc. I said only an occasional postcard. He spoke appreciatively of a birthday telegram received by him. He called me to thank me for my 'very nice' article about him. It isn't good, so I don't send it to you. . . . the Times Dispatch took occasion to write a fairly long editorial very complimentary to both of us, and to the Chamber of Commerce for turning its patronage to Belles-Lettres."

Cabell heard from his faithful friend Hergesheimer, as industrious as ever, and Cabell wrote him on 4 May: "I labor at that endless Storisende edition, and have a small book of verses somewhere in the printer's hands. It was due a month ago, but was held up by one of those habitual blunders for which I have now ceased to ask even an explaining. Anyhow, the set is now all in type save for three volumes, so that I am virtually prepared to meet posterity in the best garb I could manage."

Cabell saw two additional books growing out of the Storisende Edition. First, an anthology of selections should be culled from the eighteen volumes, a sort of Poor Man's Portable Cabell. Then the eighteen prefaces were too good to stand alone at the head of each volume; they should form another book, one that illustrated, once and for all, the superb unity of his collective output. Both author and publisher wanted a "name" as editor of the anthology. A letter to Mencken on 28 July is revealing:

> You are to accept all my apologies for McBride's having bothered you—I believe, twice—about the anthology scheme. It was a matter in which I had flatly declined to approach you, inasmuch as, I explained to him, you had nothing to gain by it, and you had already done for him and me a great deal more than we could fairly expect. But publishers are queer. To be sure, if they were over distinguished by retiringness we might starve. Meanwhile I can but apologize for a molesting about which I knew nothing.
>
> I begin nowadays almost to be perturbed by the nearness with which my Collected Works approach to completion. I begin to suspect that Sindbad must have felt rather lonely once he was rid of the Old Man of the Sea. In any case, there is to be a brief new book this fall for which the prayers of your chaplain are requested. And all the volumes of my set save one only are now in the hands of the printer.

The brief new book was *The Way of Ecben*, a transparent allegory of a poet's fall from popular favor. Holt saw it as "the tragic end of a chapter—mine in a sense, though it is entirely your own. I know enough that you cannot stop writing. . . . But you've closed a door on yourself."

In July, up at Mountain Lake, Cabell was reading an advance copy of Glasgow's *They Stooped to Folly*, Which he considered her best book to date. The New York *Herald-Tribune* wanted an article on her, but Cabell coyly suggested Virginius Dabney. A week later Cabell had finished reading the Glasgow novel, a satire on three generations of "fallen women" in Richmond with a central introspective male. He enumerated his favorite passages, much to Glasgow's pleasure, and she dedicated the novel to him.

Nearing the end of the Storisende Edition, Cabell must have anticipated financial security at long last. The edition sold for $10 a volume, or $180 for the set. With every volume autographed, it would become a collector's item and would increase in value, better than money in the bank. Rising stock prices, based mainly on speculation, had created unprecedented wealth in the country. Yet about 550 banks had failed from 1 July 1928 to 30 June 1929, the period of greatest prosperity. Then Black Thursday, 24 October 1929, saw the first catastrophic drop in the stock market. The economic implications had probably not dawned on the reclusive Richmond writer when he journeyed to New York in November to confer about the final three volumes of his cherished Complete Works. He and Holt were disappointed not to see each other, but Cabell wrote on 8 December that he had finished the Biography. To Holt's admission that he was unhappy with the John Day Company, Cabell responded on the 13th: "Meanwhile the indefiniteness of your plans is a trouble to me. I need not state what I would prefer that future to be. Meanwhile I do most earnestly want to hear at the first moment possible what you decide upon." In January, Cabell was still laboring over seventeen hundred remaining signature sheets for the Storisende Edition. Holt found a new job at McGraw-Hill, and Cabell hoped that his old editor would take on the "guide book" to the Biography of the Life of Manuel, eventually titled *Preface to the Past*.

Ellen Glasgow too was appearing in a multivolume set, the Old Dominion Edition published by Doubleday. Cabell wrote her on 18 January 1930 that "your publishers have done more than nicely by you as goes the general appearance of the volumes." He then offered a word of advice about prefaces: "It is of real importance, I think, that the future prefaces be longer, so that your customers may see, and cannot miss seeing, the plain and ponderable addition. When I next see you I shall submit a simple formula by which you can do a 2,000 word preface without the least mental strain." Cabell had agreed to take on the rather large order of reviewing the eight volumes of her Old Dominion Edition for the New York *Herald-Tribune* (20 April 1930), and Glasgow had taken on the even more arduous task of reviewing The Biography of the Life of Manuel for the *Saturday Review of Literature* (7 June 1930). Having submitted her essay to him for his approval before she sent it off, Cabell replied on 27 April:

> Please do not change one word of this. I find no fault anywhere in this tropic jungle of wit and common sense—both highly poisonous.
>
> I protest only that Jurgen's virtue was considerably fortified by the discovery that he was embracing, not a girl of eighteen, but a woman of forty. Yet in the main you are quite right. My birth condemns me to remain one half Scotch Presbyterian, for all that I have wandered after the gauds of the Protestant Episcopal Church.

The beginning of the Great Depression took Cabell back in memory to the economic hard times of 1893, which had wiped out his father's thriving drugstore and had contributed to his parents' separation. Now another economic cataclysm heralded social changes, and new values would supplant old. Just as the societal values of his parents' day had been derided by his generation, so too would his by a new set of social and literary critics. It was remarkable how the crash came just as he was bidding his fictional province adieu. Before the new critics could write him off, he determined to lead the way with a series of "epitaphs" for writers who had shared the literary spotlight of the 1920s. Thus *Some of Us* began to take shape. He intended that his assessments should make a book, but as usual he first wanted to place its chapters in periodicals. Cabell wrote Mencken on 3 May: "I have become a humanist critic. I am now completing three papers on Elinor Wylie, Lewis, and Hergesheimer severally. The first is virtually disposed of to the *Virginia Quarterly*. I am wondering if you would be interested in seeing the one on Lewis when it is completed. Of the Hergesheimer paper I do not speak, because my notions are yet vague as to just how it will shape itself."

The essays went well, but Cabell continued to miss Holt's criticisms while a work was in progress, observing aptly that criticism after a book was published was of little use to him. Fortunately his old friend Burton Rascoe was not associated with McBride, and Cabell wrote him on 27 May: "To-day I mailed McBride's the copy for *Some of Us*. I hope you will look it over before I reach New York, D.V. next Wednesday. Advice in general would be appreciated. My main difficulty is about Miss Cather.

She ought not to be left out: to the other side, I simply cannot write an article about her. But, if I put in something, howsoever brief, the book would then have, as it manifestly ought to have, ten chapters. So it goes. I am tempted to ask you to write in something complimentary about her. At all events, do look the thing over." The chapter on Willa Cather emerged as a one-page intrusion rather than as a logical inclusion. Cabell was less and less interested in contemporary authors, with the exception of those he knew personally. Van Vechten, included in *Some of Us*, was pleased "that a formal farewell was rather to a series than to the art of literature." The book was "charming and incisive." Sinclair Lewis, also included, was "enchanted," and his new wife, Dorothy Thompson, "devoured it with incessant low chuckles."

For one who professed to write solely for his own amusement, Cabell went to extraordinary lengths to cultivate anyone who could promote his writings. As Ellen Glasgow's "famousness" grew, he became ever more attentive to her blandishments. He was also well aware of his debt to the professorial ranks in academe; most local reviewers of books took their leads from the pundits at the top. Thus he reluctantly took part in the Southern Writers' Conference in Charlottesville on 23 and 24 October 1931. Glasgow, who originated the idea, had prevailed upon her friend James Southall Wilson to organize and host a meeting at the University of Virginia. Guests could stay at either the Monticello Hotel in town or at the Farmington Country Club. A remarkable assemblage of thirty novelists, poets, critics, historians, biographers, and playwrights gathered. On Friday, in the unlikely company of Mary Johnston, William Faulkner, Donald Davidson, and Allen Tate, Cabell heard Ellen Glasgow's charming welcome address, attended luncheon at Wilson's home, rode out to Castle Hill where the Troubetzkoys entertained, and attended dinner at Farmington. There the guests unwound and, gathered around Glasgow and Sherwood Anderson, enjoyed "good-natured raillery and good talk." Cabell, ill at ease, remained sardonic and mistrusted; he had declined giving the welcome speech. On Saturday, after a trip to Monticello and another round-table discussion at the university, Garrard Glenn (defender of *Jurgen* in the court) and his wife entertained at lunch. His sister Isa Glenn, novelist, was there. After a third discussion period, the final scheduled event was a tea at the Colonnade Club on the West Lawn. Most of the guests found the conference graciously informal and enjoyable, if lacking in substance. Emily Clark loved it, and Ellen Glasgow made new friends. Cabell satirized it in *Special Delivery* (1933). Twenty-five years later

Robert Cabell III endowed a chair at the university in memory of his brother, and Faulkner returned as Virginia's most distinguished Writer-in-Residence.

In October 1930, Cabell wrote Rascoe, "As for my next book, my plans stay vague. An essay affair is partly taking shape in my mind, but the temptation is small to publish anything in the immediate future." A year later he was still toying with his essays; on 14 November 1931 he thanked Hergesheimer for a copy of *Sheridan* and added: "For myself, I continue to work holes in the typewriter ribbon contentedly. There is to be next spring a slight book which has in a sober fashion diverted me with the most handsome paragraphs of fine prose about nothing in especial. You will be seeing it by-and-by." *These Restless Heads* appeared in February 1932 in an art deco format, marking visually a sharp break with the romantic past. Its author was Branch Cabell.

18

The Possessed

1932–1943

In dropping James from his name, Cabell declared that his youthful persona was dead. That writer had been the voice of Gabriella Moncure, Charles Coleman, Martha Patteson Branch, Annie Cabell, and others who spoke through James Branch Cabell. True, Branch Cabell had inherited the aged body of James Cabell, but that boy no longer existed psychologically and could no longer serve as a medium for ghosts. The work that might follow would be from the pen of an author who had learned the craft of writing from James Cabell, but it would be a record solely of the remarkable intelligence and creations of the boy. The Biography now existed outside either persona. In the prologue of *These Restless Heads*, Branch Cabell compared himself to Prospero in Shakespeare's *The Tempest*, saying farewell to his magic. The central section is a long confessional structured on the four seasons. Rambling Branch is still mighty interested in predecessor James, but still he records the routine of the writer's current existence. Richmond and Mountain Lake have replaced Poictesme, with only mild regret. Discursive, self-congratulatory, the stream of consciousness that flows through the writer's mind is sufficient to move the pen. It is biography in a purer form than the artfully constructed allegories of ghostly James. The epilogue is a brief excursus back into the being of the author of the Biography, but Gabriella Moncure loses out to Percie Cabell in this farewell allegory.

The Literary Guild had chosen *These Restless Heads* as one of its selections for its members. The edition was boxed with Carl Van Doren's *James Branch Cabell*, and the Guild gave a reception in New York for the "new" author. Carl Van Vechten, writing on 5 February 1932, gave Hunter Stagg a report on the affair:

> I liked These Restless Heads a lot, more than you do, I fancy, and more than I have liked any other book of Cabell's since, perhaps, Jurgen. It is, of course, an apologia pro sua vita, a little naive in its studied sophistication, and certainly a description of what must be a very narrow and somewhat chilling existence, but none the less charming. His frank preference for the approval of posterity is perhaps a bit of necessary perversity. He and Priscilla lunched with us yesterday. They had never been here before and never met Fania before (he hadn't; Priscilla has) but it went off very well. Marinoff burst a bomb just towards the end when she said she thought we looked alike. Am I as handsome as that? was Cabell's gallant retort. I was utterly unequal to words. This morning she has amplified her original statement to include everything. She thinks we *are* alike. She *feels* that we are. The reception given by the Literary Guild at the Chatham was unhinging to the reason. As I said to the guest of honor: Branch Cabell seems to be doing all sorts of things that James Branch Cabell never would have done. Corey Ford, Woodward, Burton Rascoe, Krutch, Carl Van Doren, Hendrik Van Loon spoke over the radio in praise of Cabell and themselves. I spoke briefly to Boyd, to Rascoe, to George Jean Nathan, to Horace Liveright. It all seemed very 1920 and I wondered if I were still alive.

It was probably on this trip to New York that Percie Cabell was again queried as to her remote and mysterious husband, an interview that Cabell mentioned in *As I Remember It*, finding in it sound portraiture colored with flights of imagination. This interview, by Ruth Seinfel, appeared in the New York *Evening Post* (4 February, p. 8). What Cabell did not comment on was another article in the same paper (p. 6) that pointed out how poorly Cabell handled himself during interviews:

> Behind the musical slurrings and elisions of her Virginia speech there emerged a picture of an author's wife who is what you think an author's wife should be. When her husband retires into his study to work she stands like a wall between him and disturbance, firmly turning away ladies who come from California bearing a book to be autographed and gentlemen who put their foot inside the door and protest that Mr. Cabell has agreed to look at

their manuscript this morning. She turns down invitations for him, takes him home from parties when he shows the first signs of fatigue, and graciously pours the cocktails at his literary afternoons.

And there is a slight suspicion that, although she would never dream of saying so, she looks upon the world of fancy in which her husband spends his days as a little—oh, ever so little—touched with madness. Perhaps the interviewer was mistaken, but there seemed to be something derisive about the look in Mrs. Cabell's eyes—which are of an almost tawny brown—and in the curve of her lips as she said:—

"James is a perfectly normal man until after he has had his breakfast coffee and opened his mail. Then he goes upstairs, into his library, to write his books." . . .

Nor is she jealous of that witch woman who, as Mr. Cabell has pointed out in *Beyond Life*, is never a man's wife, and who in the guise of Helen, or some other lovely wraith, haunts the dreams of all men, including Mr. Cabell.

"That woman is only a woman in a book," Mrs. Cabell pointed out, "and it never occurred to me to be jealous of anybody on paper. I have never known a jealous moment since I married James."

Mrs. Cabell approves of her husband's books, which she reads, not in manuscript, but as soon as they have been published. "I read them right through and get it over with," she said. . . .

Mrs. Cabell herself is quite the antithesis of a woman in a book. Her life is concerned with such realities as telling persistent telephone callers that Mr. Cabell does not autograph books, and mending Mr. Cabell's clothes, and finding time meanwhile to bring up her five children by her first marriage and her young son, who is also Mr. Cabell's son, as well as giving advice and counsel on the upbringing of her grandchildren, of whom there are now five.

"For James married me when I was a widow with five children—wasn't he brave?" she demanded. (*As I Remember It*, 65–66)

In early May, Cabell received a letter from Bennett Cerf of Random House; that firm had acquired the American rights to James Joyce's *Ulysses* and proposed publishing it in the near future. It was still banned in some states, and Cerf hoped for Cabell's help in freeing it. His frank opinion of the book was sought, not so much a strict literary appraisal as a social statement. His opinion, along with that of others, would be offered as indicative of the ban's preposterousness. The suppression of *Jurgen* was probably uppermost in Cerf's mind in soliciting Cabell's endorsement, but Cerf may have also felt that the Irishman's extended interior monologue had much in common with the Virginian's discursive confessionals. A copy of the 1924 Shakespeare & Company's edition of *Ulysses* accompanied Cerf's request. Cabell was doubtless curious to read the work. The stream-of-consciousness technique was a *cause célèbre* in avant garde literary talk, and earlier *Vanity Fair* had "nominated" Joyce and Cabell for "immortality." Oddly, Cabell did not respond as anticipated; he answered Cerf's questions but not in a way that helped to lift the ban on a work that remains a twentieth-century classic. His reading, however, stimulated his thinking about the craft of conveying experience in literary forms outside the conventional modes. Lewis Carroll had pointed the way, but Freud and Jung had added to our knowledge of free-flowing reverie. The seed of Cabell's dream trilogy, *Smith, Smirt, Smire*, was sown. But the dream could not be utterly formless. The psychology of the dream state imposed its restrictions on the dreamer as inexorably as chemistry and economics placed theirs on the realist. In matters of technique, Branch Cabell was no freer than James Cabell, nor, for that matter, was Branch much freer in choice of subject than James. The fantasies of the boy had been inspired by Gabriella, and those of Branch were inspired by James's accomplishment. Inside and outside, the psyches of James Branch Cabell and Theodore Dreiser were not so far apart. Cabell had already written the great American Realist that, relative to matters of faith, "I have always felt that you and I regarded . . . the universe from very much the same point of view."

Then there was that other "realist," Richmond's own Ellen Glasgow, who at fifty-nine was growing as a writer. Her appraisal of Cabell in the *Saturday Review* was really splendid, and he wrote her on 10 June, praising her expository style. His letter closed: "In any case, all luck and pleasure to you this summer. Then do you buckle down to *The Sheltered Life* as becomes America's foremost (woman) novelist." Ellen, he knew, would stiffen at the modifier. Her novel came out in August, and it was accorded accolades, J. Donald Adams leading off in the New York *Times* on 28 August. Even the younger Southern Agrarians, Allen Tate and Caroline Gordon, were impressed by its strength. Cabell wrote on the 30th: "Your reviews have been splendid and I begin to regard you with low envy. The *Times* notice was, I submit, a superb example of unintentional comedy—but superb publicity also. I would rather like to see Mr. Adams, just out of morbid curiosity. I would even like to talk with him as to that mellow wisdom with which you have come to terms with life. Acquiescence hereabouts had not, I confess, struck me as your leading trait."

Early in the summer Cabell was invited by Earnest Boyd and George Jean Nathan to be one of the founding editors of a new literary newspaper, *The American Spectator*. He agreed, as did Dreiser and Eugene O'Neill. Cabell sent his contributions and wrote that he would be in New York for editorial consultations. Nathan responded: "It is grand news that you will be in New York the latter part of October. Dreiser has urged Boyd and myself to try to persuade you to spend an evening with us. He is most interested to meet you. Let us know in advance of your coming and we will arrange a quiet editorial party with appropriate tipples." Surprisingly, in the midst of the Great Depression, *The American Spectator* was a resounding success, its first issue selling out several times over. Its demise two-and-a-half years later was owing to its editors' boredom with the physical production of the paper rather than any drop in circulation. For its time, it kept Cabell in the center of the literary establishment and disguised his own declining fortunes. The socialist critics coming to the fore found him irrelevant. Joseph Warren Beach in *The Twentieth Century Novel* titled his chapter on Cabell "Hors d'Oeuvres." Ludwig Lewishon in his *Expression in America* found that Cabell never progressed with the literary history of the country. Granville Hicks, in some circles called Granville "Hacks," in *The Great Tradition* dismissively called him "a fraud . . . a sleek smug egotist." Cabell utilized this invective in a later work.

On the surface Cabell remained impervious to criticism, but in reality his reaction was to attack his critics in his subsequent works, weaving his scorn into the fabric of the matter. In the fall and winter of 1932, he amused himself by writing and revising materials published in various journals. The ten letters that comprise *Special Delivery: A Packet of Replies* were forthcoming in March 1933. Based on his correspondence, each request from a typical correspondent—the school girl, the book-reviewer, the aspiring writer, the autograph collector—is answered in a brief typed form usually sent by Cabell, followed by a diatribe on the real thoughts that passed through the author's mind. While highly diverting reading, the range of the attacks further narrowed Branch's readership. Nevertheless, Cabell wrote Holt that he was pleased with the response. He found the genre so congenial that he continued to pen letters, addressing them to historical personages, real and literary. These letters emerged the following year as *Ladies and Gentlemen: A Parcel of Reconsiderations*. Beginning with an apostrophe to Odysseus' wife, Penelope, a portrait modeled on Priscilla Bradley Cabell, its final letter is addressed to Jurgen, who came home to his domestic Dame Lisa. Warren McNeill observed that Branch Cabell was beginning an autobiographical phase in his writing career. The verb "continuing" would be more accurate. Cabell's "Prologue: Which Treats Writing without Tears" embodies an attack on literary editors in general, from Henry Mills Alden of *Harper's*, through Henry L. Mencken of *Smart Set*, to Henry S. Canby of the *Saturday Review of Literature*. He attacked literary symposia then becoming a vogue on college campuses in the socially conscious days of the New Deal. Cabell made no attempt to disguise his dislike of FDR and the new proletarian advocates. The *Saturday Review* responded anonymously (24 November 1934) that "it is an astonishing and a melancholy thing that any man should wish to present himself to the world in such a character" as he does in these letters.

In May 1933 Cabell met one of the leading pundits of academe, William Lyon Phelps of Yale, who had openly expressed his dislike of Cabell's writing. The embattled author wrote his editor at McBride that he had "been cheered by the meeting." "We got on together to admiration, both before and after the lecture in which he denounced my evil doings." Phelps wrote Cabell the following month with kind words for his latest contribution to letters. The response from Richmond was warm: "The one thing which of late years has pleased me more than did our historic meeting was the receipt of your letter. It was delightful of you to write it, the crowning touch of your amiability."

In October, Cabell told Holt that he was writing *Smirt*, the first volume of a planned trilogy. It was to be a departure from anything he had attempted before. A new editor at McBride, Richard Butler Glaenzer, was coming to serve somewhat as a replacement for Guy Holt, a debater of a work in progress; he would share in this new work's genesis. Not since 1927 had Cabell attempted a full-length work of fiction. The trilogy was also, he claimed, his first attempt to interpret contemporary life since *The Eagle's Shadow*. It would shatter the myths that Cabell was a romantic dilettante, an escapist, a one-theme writer, a master of only the shorter forms such as the conte. It would incorporate all the themes of western civilization, becoming a compendium of comparative literature, and its tripartite structure would be based on nothing less than the Holy Trinity. It would fall into Northrop Frye's fourth category of literature—the anatomy. In this mode, as Joe Lee Davis observed in his study of Cabell, the writer transcends the experience of "feelings and their tendency to blur clear outlines" (58) in order to impose the reductive simplicity of the intellect through deliberate oversimplification and distortion. If his critics accused Cabell of ego, very well, he would give them ego. As Smirt reasons, "What theme other than Smirt could be esteemed quite worthy of Smirt's employment?"

   Smirt was published in March 1934. In its "Author's Note" Cabell paid his respects to Lewis Carroll and made the claim to be the first to treat the dream in a realistic manner, with no perception of time and with the awareness that one neither eats nor smells odors in dreams. Lest one miss his intent to satirize the Joycean vogue, early on he injects into a Faulknerian sentence the statement that "nobody gives Dickens credit for inventing the stream of consciousness method . . . in *Little Dorrit*, but it is a poor art that never re-Joyces nowadays"; the sentence closes with an admonition by his black nurse, Louisa Nelson, to go to sleep. In the penultimate chapter, Cabell-Smirt says farewell to Louisa Nelson: "Then there was only the first of all his memories, in the coffee-colored, thin and gray-haired face of his nurse. But this Negro woman's face he could not well see, because of the tears in his eyes." In the chapter entitled "Heir Presumptive," Cabell-Smirt is castigated by a proletarian writer in language of the gutter; some of the invective is borrowed from Granville Hicks's *The Great Tradition*. The reviews of *Smirt* were few; few cared to be quoted in his sequel. The reviewer for *Herald-Tribune Books* admitted she did not know what Cabell was doing in *Smirt*.

   In the same month that *Smirt* assaulted Cabell detractors, its author received a call from Henry Seidel Canby, a pillar of the critical establishment. Cabell wrote Glaenzer, his editor, on 31 March concerning a fourth edition of *Smirt* and added that Canby had admired his "work in conversation—'ah, but why not,' you remark, of course, 'in an article?' Why not, indeed! Anyhow, it was a case of William Lyon Phelps all over again, in that we got along beautifully." The following year Canby invited Cabell to contribute some verse to the *Saturday Review*. Cabell refrained: "You see, I have figured in the *Review* for so long and so uninterruptedly as a doddering imbecile that for you to be printing a contribution by me really would give you an air of not taking your reviewers quite seriously. That would never do. And moreover, now I think of it, not for long years have I written any verse except for the lowly utilitarian purpose of dedicating this or the other book with an acrostic (12 October)."

   Yet Cabell longed to be vindicated in the pages of the *Saturday Review*. Ellen Glasgow had survived the changing of the critical guard. She had been accepted by the critics of high moral seriousness in the early part of her career, she had fit right in with the sophisticates in the 1920s, and now she was the darling of the socialist establishment. No one would turn down a review by Miss Glasgow, not even H. S. Canby. Cabell set about to woo her. He determined to realign her on the side of the aristocrats even though her forthcoming novel, *Vein of Iron*, was about the "good" people rather than the "best." From Mountain Lake he wrote her on 19 July 1935, concerning a highly flattering squib about her aristocratic virtues: "In preparing this for the *Book of the Month Club News*, I made you a special carbon copy. Now if there is anything whatever about this 1000 word eulogy which you do not like, then do you say so, loudly and clearly, in time to have it changed. I am tolerably sure the angle is right and can do no harm. Now that the riffraff is out in full force armed with corncobs, we have to wear the label of aristocracy whether we like it or not; so let's carry it off defiantly." Neurotically receptive to flattery, ever ready to be a woman for all seasons, Glasgow swallowed the bait. Cabell responded immediately: "I will be around for my pound of flesh later, because—through an astounding coincidence—I too have a book coming out this fall. It would be nice if you could review it, preferably for the *Saturday Review*, which otherwise will manhandle it sight unseen; but there is no great hurry about the manifestation of your natural gratitude, inasmuch as the first lot of proofs are just being mailed me. Do you but go ahead and enjoy the assured success of *Vein of Iron*."

Glasgow was not averse to playing the game. She would review *Smith*, the second installment of the trilogy, due out in October. McBride and Cabell were so anxious for a favorable review that the latter labored over a set of galley proofs in order that Glasgow could read the work before publication. McBride thought the review should be tendered to the New York *Times* but sent it instead to *Herald-Tribune Books*, because the *Times* would not publish unsolicited reviews. Along with the galley proofs, Cabell gave his reviewer some instructions: "A word for the intending reader: *Smith* starts as virtually pure romance and shifts toward irony in the third book, the fourth book being all irony, the fifth book turning into something rather like burlesque, whence we work back as well as may be to the tone of the book's beginning. At least, that is what I tried to do."

Smith, A Sylvan Interlude, was the least abrasive of the Nightmare Triplets, and Glasgow's review reflected no positive pain. Oddly, Cabell retained a fair and rather faithful reviewer in Fred T. Marsh of the *Times*. His summary concluded with the observation that Cabell "is a rare and gifted ironist in whom we miss a certain balance." Even Joe Lee Davis, a friendly scholar, felt that the four tales of Smirt's four sons "are 'leftovers' from the 'Biography'—and none too impressive ones at that."

Gertrude Stein, under Carl Van Vechten's guidance, began a lecture tour of America in late 1934. She spent Christmas Eve with Scott and Zelda

Fitzgerald in Baltimore, had tea with Eleanor Roosevelt at the White House, and in early February descended on Richmond where Ellen Glasgow entertained at dinner and invited other guests afterward for eggnog. The Cabells were invited for dinner, and it went well. Alice Toklas was appreciative of the hot breads; Stein and Glasgow shared a fondness for dogs and woolens. Glasgow, owing to her deafness, usually dominated the conversation, but on this occasion she deferred to the voluble Stein, whose talk perplexed Cabell:

> "Is Gertrude Stein serious?" he asked.
> "Desperately," Alice Toklas replied.
> "That puts a different light on it," Cabell admitted.
> "For you," said Alice, "not for me."
>
> (Kellner, *Carl Van Vechten*, 267)

After dinner, Hunter made his appearance. He had resolutely dried himself out for the occasion. Upon his arrival, Stein moved across the room and planted herself beside him for the rest of the evening. Alice Toklas flew to him crying, "The Myth—the Myth!" Cabell had left before Hunter arrived.

As Cabell's literary fortunes began to spiral downward gently, so too did his domestic life undergo changes. As he tells us in his memoirs, he developed his first case of pneumonia in Richmond on 14 January 1935 and was taken to St. Augustine, Florida, for recovery. "But upon the fourteenth of January in 1936 I again had pneumonia; and again I was returned to St. Augustine for recuperation." The pattern was repeated for a third year. The following year, anticipating the worst, the Cabell ménage established itself in St. Augustine well before the fateful date, with auspicious results, and each winter thereafter sojourned in Florida. In the midsummer of 1936, Percie Cabell was stricken with crippling rheumatism. Cayford Cottage, on its steep hill above the lodge at Mountain Lake, became inaccessible, just as the fifteen-year lease on the ground rights expired. To replace it, strong-willed Percie had another summer cottage built at the mouth of the Potomac near Ophelia, Virginia. This modest structure was christened Poynton Lodge, after one of the baronial estates associated with her distinguished ancestry. It became the summer refuge for Percie, James, and Ballard for the rest of their lives.

Guy Holt's sudden and premature death in April 1934 robbed Cabell of his closest literary advisor. Even after Holt left McBride in 1926, Cabell had continued to confide in his former editor. His subsequent relationship with Richard Glaenzer, also of McBride, never blossomed into the close, uninhibited exchange of criticism that stimulated Cabell's best efforts. Over the years, he had grown increasingly disenchanted with McBride as a publisher, and *Preface to the Past* (1936) was the last title published by that firm until a reconciliation almost twenty years later. Cabell turned to his most faithful champion, Burton Rascoe, now literary advisor at Doubleday-Doran. Rascoe, essentially a newspaperman, usually interjected himself into his reportage, a tendency that trivialized his subjects. Cabell was blind to Rascoe's faults and for the rest of his life remained grateful to him for his championship in Chicago. Cabell's letters to Rascoe during this period are less concerned with the evolution of his work-in-progress than with his outrage over his declining critical acceptance. The publication of *Preface to the Past* could have been interpreted as an act of charity by McBride. This reissue of the eighteen prefaces contained in the Storisende Edition had little appeal to a nation struggling with economic and sociological problems in an unprecedented depression, especially in view of the fact that they were prefaces to works dating back to 1904, many of which had never enjoyed popular or critical success.

Cabell wrote Rascoe on 12 July 1936: "Relative to *Smire*, I think we may call it a deal—"think," I say, since the matter is, after all, subject to the approval of Doubleday-Doran. As goes McBride, I had notified him, before I talked with you, that *Preface to the Past* was the last book by me—barring some miracle—that he would manhandle. . . . I have since had two other approaches from publishers. I needn't, I hope, say I would much prefer to work with you." He went on to outline his demand for royalties and format; then amazingly, after stipulating a spring publication date for *Smire*, he discussed a fall publication for *Smirt*, *Smith*, and *Smire* under one cover entitled *The Nightmare Has Triplets*. Sales of the first two had been poor, and the reprinting of *Smire* so soon after its initial appearance could hardly be justified. Rascoe, however, encouraged Cabell's buying the plates for the first two from McBride for the planned omnibus. Rascoe was also an editor for *Esquire*, and Cabell confided on 6 August, "Only yesterday did I see the current *Esquire*, and I protest that I did not find *Gone with the Wind* to be even readable." *Smire* was finished by late August, and Cabell begged, "You would . . . do me a great and actual favor by criticizing it with the utmost severity à la Holt, so that I may profit by as much of the fault-finding as seems to me rational. I am not thin-skinned prior to publication, but only afterward." Cabell planned a trip to New York for late September, to dicker with McBride over plates and to discuss with Rascoe the planned trilogy publication.

In the following March 1937, the large frame house at Dumbarton burned. The scene of Cabell's most creative years, a potential museum, it had become a sleazy nightclub, and arson was suspected. The fire coincided with the publication of Smire, leading Cabell to write Rascoe, "I rejoiced, wistfully, over this somewhat gaudy commemoration of Smire's debut." He had seen only the reviews in the Richmond Times-Dispatch and the New York Times, and they depressed him. He protested that he had not burlesqued the Holy Trinity or prattled about himself, a protest that still rings somewhat hollow. By May he knew the book was not selling. "This outcome disgusts me, because (a) Smire contains much of my handsomest writing, and (b) because it imperils my main object, which was to see the trilogy complete in one volume." Cabell was objective enough to see that Doubleday-Doran had produced "a good-looking volume" and that they "advertised to a fair extent and in a suitable fashion." Somehow, the dedication of the work to poor, wasted Hunter Stagg seems apt.

In his dream trilogy, Cabell may have created a more significant work than the patched-up Biography, more cohesive, more encompassing, both contemporary and universal, but one has to know the Cabell of the Biography to appreciate the Cabell of the trilogy. The latter could be considered The Divine Comedy of the twentieth century, as representative of its day as "The Waste Land" or, for that matter, Ulysses, the work that provoked it. In Cabell's library one finds Henry Hazlett's The Anatomy of Criticism: A Trialogue, wherein Cabell figures in the discussion of literature and literary criticism. Hazlett's book was published in 1933, the year Cabell was writing Smirt, and is unrelated to Northrop Frye's Anatomy of Criticism: Four Essays, published in 1957. It and other evidence indicates that Cabell kept abreast of contemporary criticism while defaulting on contemporary literature. He confessed to Rascoe near the end of his life that he had never read any of Faulkner's books. "I felt in duty bound to dispose of Gone with the Wind and Anthony Adverse, and perhaps some of Pearl Buck, before beginning on Faulkner." Mickey Spillane "strengthened" him.

In the summer of 1937, down in bucolic Northumberland County, Cabell observed that his agricultural future was provided for, "however gloomy be the auctorial present." He had begun a new book, The King Was in His Counting House. Based on Italian Renaissance history and Jacobean drama, it took at first the form of a play. Later, with some fault-finding of a new editor, its form was altered. When the book was sent to Random House in March 1938, Cabell was stung by "his majesty" Bennett Cerf's rejection. Rascoe suggested sending it to Harcourt, but he sensed a sinking cause and declined to act as agent. On 19 April Cabell wrote his former champion, "I am sorry that I ever bothered you with the notion." On the same date he wrote John Farrar of Farrar & Rinehart: "My recent publishers and I have agreed to part, on the general ground of incompatibility, so that I now look about for their possible successors. I am finishing a story, and I wonder with how much or how little enthusiasm your firm would consider the chance of bringing it out." Cabell had found his publisher for the next ten years. Farrar became his new confessor, Cabell pleading for a Guy Holt relationship, for "any editorial suggestions, however acerb, toward a book's betterment." Hoping for a permanent alliance he warned, "I expect no large sales for this book; yet my main desire is that you should not expect them, and be disappointed when they do not materialize." Writing in the *Times Book Review* of *The King Was in His Counting House*, Thomas Caldecott Chubb, a former admirer, admitted that he had grown tired of Cabell. The reviewer in the *Saturday Review* lamented that "the old flavor is gone." A consolation for the work's author was a British edition by the Bodley Head.

Ellen Glasgow too had a new publisher, Harcourt. Although *Vein of Iron* was a bleak picture of the Great Depression in Richmond as witnessed from One West Main, it had been critically acclaimed and had sold well, being a Book-of-the-Month Club selection. Now Scribner planned a subscription edition of her works, requiring twelve prefaces by the author. She remembered Cabell's 1930 offer of a simple formula for preface-writing, and she addressed a note to him. "There are many things I should like to talk over with you," she wrote, "especially the art of prefaces, in which you are vastly proficient." With her fortunes still in the ascendant while his declined, Cabell was eager to strengthen their alliance. Neither writer liked to talk on the telephone. Her deafness and Percie Cabell's illness were further deterrents. He responded with a note dated 16 September 1937:

> I, none the less, am much interested in the notion of your Scribners' set, and I share gladly with you my own formula for a preface.
> There are just four points, I think, to be covered always: the place and the significance of the book in your complete work, that social history of Virginia; your own personal view of the book nowadays, as well as, if you like, of the dead person who wrote it; the book's origin and the circumstances in which

it was written; and how, and when, and what happened after the book was published—which of course gives you a free hand with its reviews and the acquaintances you may have made through it.

With this formula once firmly fixed in mind, and with a little juggling about of its four parts, the writing of a 2,000 word preface is really no intellectual effort at all, as you will soon find. But only through trying. So please do try!

Glasgow was happy to accept her Richmond colleague's help; what she found a chore he rather enjoyed. A series of notes from Glasgow that accompanied drafts of her prefaces sent over to Cabell attest to his considerable help. If he enjoyed the labor, she detested it.

A review of the correspondence also shows that Cabell had a large hand in helping her to select novels for the Virginia Edition that would fit into the concept of her work as a social history of Virginia. Cabell proposed that idea in his 1925 review of *Barren Ground*, but he tells us that she came to accept it as her very own, becoming convinced, "in all honesty," that she had conceived of a social history in 1899. He had an ironic chuckle in *As I Remember It* that by ill luck her first two novels would not fit into the plan. But then his own two first novels are very ill at ease in the more illustrious companionship of the Biography. Glasgow appeared the wiser of the two in omitting several of her early works from a more ambitious, if later, plan. When Glasgow sent the first six volumes of the Virginia Edition to Cabell, he wrote on 19 July 1938: "Of the books with which you so prodigally provided me, I read first of all your prefaces; and the more I consider these, the more steadily my admiration grows. You owe the age to make a book of these prefaces by-and-by, and you must do that."

In November Cabell journeyed to New York and was handsomely received by the staff of Farrar & Rinehart, balm for his wounded self-esteem. He wrote Farrar on the 14th: "I returned home pleased cordially by the thought that intelligence and sympathy yet thrive among publishers, for I liked all of you, howsoever uncommunicatively. I have not the gift of tongues." Later in the month he informed Farrar that his next work would be the Hamlet story with Hamlet's uncle as the protagonist. It was again a matter of self-identification, having married a widow himself. Hamlet would be afflicted, somewhat like Ballard. Ballard had recently acquired a rat terrier named Hamlet.

This year, to avoid the inevitable pneumonia on 14 January Cabell was to be driven to St. Augustine before Christmas. Percie would have to give up her annual Christmas party in Richmond, a ritual that Cabell described in Victorian detail in his memoirs. She had surrendered once again to "her not ever failing common sense." Cabell wrote Glasgow on the day after Christmas that "I had hoped we would see you again before we left Richmond, but everything stayed in what my Mammy used to describe as a perpetual swivet up to the last minute. . . . It follows we are now settled in our old, quite comfortable quarters, and I begin vaguely to think of writing something once more, under the bland influence of sunshine and springlike weather. I do not think I can ever stand the dark winter of Richmond. Besides, it was so pleasing to spend Christmas among complete strangers, as compared with one's dearest and bothersome relatives."

In the new year Cabell "toiled through" the first draft of his Hamlet story. He considered "The Hobby-Horse is Forgot" as a title. While the Florida sojourns warded off pneumonia, he was still subject to frequent colds that affected his eyesight. Cabell had been a heavy smoker since college days. Those days were again in mind, for his research into background materials for Hamlet took him back to Professor John Leslie Hall's lectures. While the critics entreated him to be contemporary, he retreated farther into the historical past. Agreeing with Glasgow, he found the news of the day increasingly depressive. He wrote her from Ophelia on 4 September 1939: "Even here it looks rather like war. A tornado passed just a half mile of us on 18 August and blew down all our trees from the south. We got them set up again just in time for a tremendous north-easter which, a week later, blew them all down again from the north. All is propped up once more, but I doubt if many of my pet trees will survive, whereas all my vines of course were ruined utterly. We were more lucky than our neighbors, though, many of whom lost their houses. In brief, everything seems to be smashing up everywhere."

Cabell's imagery doubtless extended to his career, in his mind. Writing Farrar later in the month about his work in hand, he suggested to his publisher: "Consider . . . this possibility: what if the tale were issued under a pseudonym? My books are no longer reviewed. It has been my misfortune to impress myself upon the mind of the reviewer too strongly. So he or she writes out an opinion of me, to almost the full extent of the allotted space, and then fills in with a brief mention of my last published book. Weigh well this point." Later in the year, with the typescript at the printers, Cabell inquired of Farrar: "When do we publish? I still hope to get a most unwilling Ellen Glasgow to review it in the right way, and have started her to reading the source story as a preparative. If you could manage it, by long odds the best thing would be to have the *Saturday Review* ask her to do this romance, because otherwise any notice of it there is quite certain to be vituperative, while *Books* will be at any rate tepidly fair-minded. How handsome an art is criticism!" (22 November)

Glasgow, in deteriorating health, was urged by Percie Cabell to join them in Florida. She entertained the idea but Christmas found her confined to her bed in Richmond. *Hamlet Had an Uncle* was published in January 1940, its appearance coinciding with a convention of Pen Women in St. Augustine. Cabell attended the convention to promote his book but he found the experience exhausting. "Deeply as I regretted your absence," he wrote Glasgow, "I grant that upon the whole you were wise to keep away from the Pen Women." On the whole, Cabell received rather good reviews of his new work. Even the *Saturday Review* found it in a class with *Jurgen*, and the *Times* critic recommended it as an antidote to thinking about the war. In Richmond, no less a personage than Douglas Southall Freeman received it with paeans. Another bit of cheering news was that *The Jewel Merchants* had been set to music and was performed at the Peabody Institute in Baltimore on 26 February. Ever-faithful Mencken gave a report, and Cabell responded on the 29th:

> As always, you are good. It is a comfort to know that, in your competent opinion, the opera passed off with good effect. Had I been present I would have been horribly embarrassed by my complete ignorance of music, so it may be all was for the best. As the affair stands, I regret only the absence of a leitmotif, because, without knowing what that be, I infer from the *Sun's* tone that the lack of one is culpable if not out and out indecent. Anyhow, I am grateful to everybody concerned; and I hope for an encore, with me to attend it.
>
> I deplore, but yet sympathize with, your reports of the intangible effects of senescence. As for this Hergesheimer, who (like Sylvia) is he? I recall cloudily somebody of the name who for no given reason dropped me as an acquaintance long years ago.—In all earnest, though, it is sickening, how these things just happen through nobody's special will or action. And in my own romantic fashion I still cherish Joe, if but tacitly.

The convention of Pen Women in St. Augustine was the occasion of Cabell's meeting Marjorie Rawlings of Cross Creek fame. *The Yearling* had been a best seller two years before and was being made into a film. On meeting Rawlings, Cabell's first remark was, "How does it feel to be a great writer?" Sensing the trap, she avoided this pitfall whereby he "at once established the ego, the vanity, and the hopeless condition of whomever" he assailed. With her earthy sense of humor and a dedication to the drudgery of writing equal to his, they became fast friends, a friendship that stimulated Cabell in the gathering twilight of his career. Glasgow's friendship continued to sustain his self-esteem. In May Glasgow attempted to rally support for his election to the American Academy of Arts, a proposal he cautiously agreed to. In May he sent Marjorie Rawlings a copy of the pamphlet *Of Ellen Glasgow: An Inscribed Portrait* by Ellen Glasgow and Branch Cabell, signed by both authors, one of a hand-printed edition of 109 copies. Mrs. Rawlings replied that she felt she had received a visitation from God and the Virgin Mary. During the summer both Percie Cabell's and Ellen Glasgow's health continued to deteriorate, and Cabell wrote consoling letters to Glasgow urging her to complete her autobiography and a novel tentatively entitled "Give Us Our Lives."

With this last work, to emerge as *In This Our Life*, Cabell had ample opportunity to repay some of the debt he owed Glasgow for her labors in his behalf. Both writers later commented on the help he gave her in the fall of 1940 after she had suffered a second heart attack. Their accounts agree that Cabell rendered aid in preparing a final draft of her novel for the publisher. He reveals that her determination to see it in print was motivated by the promise of the Pulitzer Prize; it is doubtful that her pride would have allowed her to accept his help otherwise. He refers to the "not unlaborious task work" over a period of three or four months; after each visit to her bedside, "I would kiss her cheek and depart with a fresh batch of typescript for me to revise and to make tidy during the next three or four days." In contrast, she writes that "James Cabell would come to spend hours by my bedside, reading chapters, and assuring me that this book did not require the usual third writing." He wrote of his "revising for her, in chief out of love and friendship and my honest sympathy, but in some part out of the derisive pleasure which I got from knowing that at long last I was completing a Pulitzer prize winner." She would have the final product her very own: "In the end, when my publisher left, and James went to Florida for the winter, I gathered my strength and wrote over the whole novel, chiefly for style and manner, in proofsheets." In her letter to Cabell dated 15 January 1941, she makes no mention of rewriting "the whole novel." She writes that she "pruned," that she cut out a number of paragraphs; "I think the novel has been shortened by several pages." *In This Our Life* appeared in 1941 and duly received the Pulitzer Prize the following year, although, as Cabell lamented, no one could assess it as her very best novel. Critics made it plain that they were recognizing her total work rather than the merit of the work under review. No public acknowledgement to Cabell for his considerable aid was made at the time. Thirteen years elapsed before an acknowledgment appeared in her posthumous autobiography. In *Let Me Lie*, published two years after her death, Cabell himself did not reveal this detail in his generous assessment of her.

From 1940, Ellen Glasgow's letters became more and more elegiac, owing to her sickness and her depression about World War II. Cabell's letters were invariably efforts to cheer her. When she complained of her letdown after seeing *In This Our Life* off to the printer, he wrote from Florida: "But you can now shift easily, and without undue effort, to getting together the prefaces. Looking them over, it seemed to me, that, after a brief Foreword, you should begin with the Battle Ground preface; using after that the Voice of the People one, and then go on in the order the books were written, and ending with a sort of Epilogue for In This Our Life. After all, though, I tend to forget it is your book." She took to the idea and sent off for page proofs of the prefaces to the Virginia Edition.

While Cabell aided Glasgow in seeing her final works to fruition, he was at work on two projects of his own. In May 1940 he had volunteered to write, with a collaborator, the projected volume on the St. Johns River in Florida for Farrar & Rinehart's Rivers of America series. Also, he had already started on the tale of his Indian youth who would journey from Northumberland County, Virginia, to Florida, be received as a prince by King Philip in Spain, return to Florida where he would be present at the founding of St. Augustine, and finally return to Virginia to protect his people from the white man's civilization. After the usual shiftings of title, *The First Gentleman of America* was settled on. Cabell observed to his publisher, "This title also would show that at long last my theme is American." He claimed to stick close to historical fact and appended a five-page bibliography. By late September he sent off the typescript and hoped for a mid-January publication, "so that if there be any Florida tourist trade this winter, we may hope to benefit by it." Though the deadline was met, bookstores were loath to stock up on Cabell titles.

In January 1941, Cabell established a close literary friendship in St. Augustine with Stephen Vincent Benét. St. Augustine was the ancestral home of the Benéts, and a family convocation was the occasion for Cabell's meeting the poet. Benét was an editor for Farrar & Rinehart and had critiqued *The King Was in His Counting House*, *Hamlet Had an Uncle*, and *The First Gentleman*. When Cabell inquired who was to author the St. Johns volume in the Rivers of America series, Benét, knowing of Cabell's interest, asked, "Why don't you do it?" When the Virginian professed ignorance of Florida history, Benét suggested that Professor A. J. Hanna of Rollins College to whom Cabell had dedicated *The First Gentleman* be asked to help with research. Thus began a two-year collaboration with Hanna as co-author and Benét as supervisory editor, a relationship that Cabell found exasperating, stimulating, and rewarding. At a time when world events were sweeping him into irrelevance, this was his umbilical with the world of publishing.

Cabell was settling into his background reading suggested by Hanna when Percie received shocking news on 18 March. Grace Shepherd, now Mrs. Wirt P. Marks and the mother of two children, had committed suicide. She was thirty-nine. Percie, in a nearly crippled physical state and emotionally devastated, hurried back to Richmond with her dependent husband. Marjorie Rawlings, passing through Richmond from a trip to Washington and not knowing of the Cabells' bereavement, called. Cabell wrote on 9 April, the same day that Marjorie wrote Percie:

> We have had, as you now know, a great many sorrows since you and I fell to brawling in our cups, most enjoyably, but I want to assure you that the impossibility of our meeting during your passage through Richmond was an additional grief. It simply could not be managed in the horrid confusion of all our family affairs.
>
> I can but hope for better luck, all around, in the future. Meanwhile I learn that with Ellen Glasgow you scored a tremendous hit. She informs me that you both, figuratively, let down your hair and babbled out your pasts to each other without any auctorial embellishments. If only I could have been privileged to sit by and blush in silence!

Glasgow and Rawlings' friendship remained firm for the rest of Ellen's remaining years.

In this summer of 1941, Cabell was again serving as Glasgow's collaborator in letters. She wrote him on 3 July:

> It was so good of you to spend your day in Richmond with my Virginia Edition. I cannot tell you how much I appreciated your letter. All your ideas are excellent, and I am arranging the flyleaves between the different groups. The proofs came ten days ago, and I have given all my strength to them, . . .
>
> The title still bothers me. *A Certain Measure*, as you suggest, would be good, except that it might be the name of a novel; and the only chance for this book is with people, the small minority, who read critical essays.

What do you think of *Life and the Novel* or *Life in the Novel*? I want a title that is alive, and yet one that indicates the nature of the book.

Cabell replied from Ophelia, Virginia, on the 28th of the same month: "I still think a title which might be the title of a novel is better than one which might be the title of a text book; yet I do not believe that, upon the whole, any title is apt to prove misleading." Cabell's suggestion that the prefaces should be entitled *A Certain Measure* was not readily accepted by Glasgow; it was too close to the title of his collection of stories *The Certain Hour*. She finally accepted his suggestion, however, with obvious reluctance; on 1 August 1941, she wrote: "Well, you have a crafty wisdom, and after changing the title a dozen times, I have actually decided that 'A Certain Measure' is the best name we can find, even if it does not seem to hit the nail on the head. Anyway, I have ceased to feel that hitting nails really makes any difference. I am so grateful to you for your interest. May you never know the horror of coming to the end of your work before life is finished."

Cabell answered this letter almost immediately, on the 6th. He reproved her for her depression, reminding her that she had "a superb book, already complete, in A Certain Measure." He assured her that her fame was secure, that she had received more recognition than Shakespeare or Homer in their lifetimes. On 31 August he wrote to thank her for the gift of a sign for Poynton Lodge; "the gift troubled my conscience with the thought that I might have been of use to you with the preface proofs this summer, and I wonder if you have now completed them?" He had virtually finished his *First Gentleman of America* and was at her service. His services were accepted, for on 18 December 1941 he wrote from Florida: "I had hoped to see you before leaving Richmond, and get straight the bibliography. It needs only the insertion of the magazine appearance of your short stories; after which, the three lists, of magazine contributions, of criticism in books, and of criticism in periodicals, ought to be straightened out into the chronological order of their publication. You will then have a complete job; and should hie to Lavinia's bedside." More than a year was to go by before the subject of *A Certain Measure* came up again. Glasgow's reluctance to publish it may have been due to the war, as she suggested, but there is also the large possibility that she took stock of how much Cabell was in the book. The metrical arrangement of a passage from *Vein of Iron* was all too obviously Cabell's work.

Glasgow reciprocated Cabell's labors in her behalf by writing his publisher expressing her admiration for *The First Gentleman of America*, compliments to be used in advertising the book. On 31 January 1942, Cabell wrote Glasgow from St. Augustine that "the last week has been wholly insane with parties in honor of *The Gentleman*, of which Florida approves, with naivete, because it is about Florida and has been mentioned by Kate Smith over the radio." In response to Glasgow's curiosity about the man Marjorie Rawlings had married at the age of forty-five, he commented: "Marjorie is married to a most agreeable person, considerably her junior, called Norton Baskin, who is the manager of a new hotel they have lately opened in St. Augustine. You too would like him; yet I cannot but regard through tear-blurred eyes anyone who is pledged to share life intimately with an author."

Cabell also had his publisher send a copy of the new book to Carl Van Vechten and requested the latter to write Farrar "as to your delight in this solid historical opus." By April the author was lamenting to Farrar: "I am heart-sick—if that needs saying—over the fate of *The First Gentleman*. Even in Florida, where people clamored at least mildly for the book, I faced always the difficulty that the book dealers 'had sold out all they had, but could order you a copy.' You know what that means. At the Florida Historical Society's annual meeting there were fifty or more persons who tried to buy the book—with but three copies on sale." Again, while not copious, the reviews had been generally favorable. Responding to a query by Burton Rascoe, Cabell replied on 10 February: "*The First Gentleman* has had but indifferent luck,—in the main, I think, because his reviewers do not know anything about early American history. They do not know whether my tale really happened or happened only in part or is made up out of the whole cloth. So they hedge dubiously and with an odd flavor of resentment. Let me add here, for your private information, that every bit of it did happen, nor is there in the book even one invented character. So does it come about that a solid historical work is judged as a more or less plausible romance." Rascoe's review appeared in the Chicago *Sun* four days later under the gratifying title "The First Writing Gentleman of America," wherein he reappraised Cabell's writing career from the vantage point of a confidant.

Over the summer of 1942, Cabell labored over the St. Johns history, exchanging manuscripts and letters with Hanna in Florida. In July, Cabell commiserated with Glasgow over their addiction to "the drug called writing." She was at work on a sequel to *In This Our Life* entitled *Beyond Defeat* as he assembled the "Parade of Diversities" associated with the Florida river. The World War II gasoline shortage drove the Cabell ménage back to

Richmond in mid-September. From there Cabell wrote his co-author, "It is my private opinion that our book is becoming about as dull stuff as I ever read. I do not doubt the material is of value . . . but the slump . . . leaves me appalled and drowsy."

From St. Augustine, Cabell wrote Glasgow four days before Christmas:

> You have been much in my mind during the last month, howsoever little evidence my Corona has given as to this fact. But I have been living in slavery to the St. Johns river. Every morning, directly after breakfast, I have begun work on the accursed stream, and have continued at work until four P.M., when I go out for an hour's walk, and then get back to the hotel in time to make ready for dinner. Then after dinner, I take yet another walk before going to bed. It is an existence which can hardly be defined as living, but it has got the book virtually finished. I now hope to turn in the typescript the first of the year—for publication I do not know when. . . .
>
> We have made out fairly well. Percie, as was to be expected, lost her gasoline card, and since it has not yet been replaced, we can get nowhere except afoot. That does not very much matter in St. Augustine, which is small, but then Percie is not always able to walk even a little way. We at all events have not had to bother about keeping warm.
>
> Even so, we have a plenty of acquaintances among the townspeople to provide Percie and Ballard with society. Even I expect to expand when my slavery is over, but thus far, I have not mingled. I have not so much as seen Marjorie Rawlings, to talk with, as yet.

In the new year, the St. Johns continued to occupy Cabell's attention at a time admittedly unpropitious for the arts. In March, the death of Benét "horrified" Cabell, and he proposed to Hanna that they dedicate their work to the poet who had guided their labors to completion. Oddly, Cabell made sport of compiling an index, which he saw as an "ornament" for librarians. The drawings by Doris Lee delighted him. Hanna solicited his aid in writing blurbs for War Bonds; Cabell complied, hoping "that in the event of any official notice of our plea for War Bonds as an investment, we can obtain at Atlanta adjoining cells."

Late in January Cabell had inquired of Glasgow, "So what, please, are you doing to help literature?" Glasgow decided to release *A Certain Measure* for publication. Cabell's response was positive: "No new news has pleased me more than that you now plan to let the book of prefaces appear this autumn. The times are—need I mention it?—unfavorable to anything except journalism or nostalgia in the way of writing, but even so, there must be a sound, sane, very much frightened minority of intelligent persons busied in keeping quiet, whom the book will both delight and reassure. . . . A separate publishing of the prefaces will aid to help interest in the novels they treat of." Their next several letters touch on the book's appearance, and Cabell's enthusiasm can only be accepted as genuine. In contrast to his optimism, Glasgow continued glum even after the book was off the press. On 7 September 1943, she wrote from Maine:

> The first advance copy of "A Certain Measure" has just come, and it goes straight off to you. It will be published October 14th. Of course, the inevitable disappointment has set in. I am not satisfied with the appearance of the book. The print is very good. I selected that, and the best paper we could find for the first edition, which will take all of this particular kind of paper.
>
> But I dislike the smooth edges, and I think the book looks too much like a text-book. Then, of course, as soon as I open the pages, I see things I should like to do over, and so differently.

Two statements stand out in this letter: "The print is very good. I selected that," and "I see things I should like to do over, and so differently." Her presentation to Cabell is also dated the 7th, and its inscription runs: "For James Branch Cabell, With affection and admiration unbounded, from Ellen Glasgow." The book records no acknowledgments of any kind, printed or written. Cabell still had not received this copy in Ophelia, Virginia, on 14 September writing that "postal service in these parts has been virtually suspended" owing to his mail carrier's appendicitis. However, on 18 September, he wrote that he had received it the day before and read it; he proceeded to praise it handsomely: "It establishes the wide variety of your talents, or rather, it attests them with a more definite tangibility. I believe that is even more important than the fact that the book affords grand reading."

In October both authors were back in Richmond, where face to face she made a request. She asked him to review *A Certain Measure* for the New York *Post*. This request was followed by a remarkable letter the next day, 28 October 1943:

MY DEAR JAMES:

> You are most unselfish, I think, to write this article. I know writing about other people is not the pleasantest work in the world.
>
> I tried to tell you this yesterday, but, somehow, we never seemed able to finish what we began; and now I have become rather shy about writing to you since you tell me you carefully preserve all your letters. For I do not write

letters. I merely dash off impressions and impulses in the most inadequate typing. . . .

But what I tried to explain yesterday was only this: You asked the meaning of a social history, and my answer was, or would have been but for an interruption, that I meant by a social history the customs, habits, manners, and general outer envelope human nature had assumed in a special place and period. My place happened to be Virginia, and my period covered the years from 1850 to the present time. But the inner substance of my work has been universal human nature—or so I have always believed—and if the great Balzac had not been ahead of me, I should have called [my] books the Human Comedy. As I remark in one of these prefaces: "My major theme is the conflict of human beings with human nature, of civilization with biology."

This was what I started to say.

Blessings on you, dear James. I haven't had so merry an hour for a long time.

Yours ever,
ELLEN

This letter presents three ironies. First, she asks him to review what both knew to be his work to a large degree. Either she was consciously asking Cabell to review Cabell, or unconsciously she was already denying his role as collaborator. Second, she instructs Cabell in the meaning of the phrase "a social history." Evidently, she had taken seriously a beautifully ironic question posed by him the day before. He who conceived of her work as such and helped her to sell the idea to posterity is now patiently instructed. Third, she was obviously writing the review she wanted to see in print. Cabell had only to sign his name and send it in. (Was this an acknowledgment that the ideas were his?) Another friendly critic, Howard Mumford Jones, had already agreed to review the book for the Herald-Tribune.

Considering the ironies of her request and his large role in the genesis, development, and final form of A Certain Measure, it is not very difficult to imagine Cabell's emotions. An objective review was impossible; a pretense at a serious, straight-faced review would likely be suspect, at best dull. What resulted was a long, ebullient, seriocomic spoof of a scholarly critique. He termed it "the very best of her books . . . by far the most interesting." Picking up the "Social History of Virginia" theme, he compared her work with The Decline and Fall of the Roman Empire and declared she had surpassed Gibbon, even going so far as to sport with the fact that the initials of both historians were E. G. Her prose was "luminous and accurate." And surely she recognized the double-edged irony of "It is, in brief, all Ellen Glasgow." Perhaps his most serious bit of buffoonery was in exalting her as a historian rather than a creative artist: "And it follows that I do not applaud the result as being fiction of the first quality. My point instead is that, when viewed properly, as a whole, the work of Ellen Glasgow is history of the first quality." Howard Mumford Jones was much more in line in comparing her with Henry James.

Perhaps Cabell thought that Ellen Glasgow would realize he was burlesquing his part in *A Certain Measure* and would consider the review a private joke between them. Perhaps he felt that his previous comparison of her fame to Shakespeare's and Homer's and his expansiveness about *A Certain Measure* in letters just prior to publication had prepared her for a lighthearted review. Perhaps he even thought she would be mildly piqued but still pleased by its excessive flattery. On the other hand, it is quite possible that Cabell was piqued that no word of public recognition appeared in any acknowledgment or even privately in Glasgow's presentation copy to him. (That, too, would have been acknowledgment for posterity.) Whatever his motive, he could hardly have been prepared for her outrage and bitterness.

The review appeared in the *New York Post* on 2 December and in the *Chicago Sun* on the 5th. After over a week of ominous silence on her part, Cabell wrote cautiously from Florida on 11 December: "If you have yet seen the complete article concerning you and Gibbon as it appeared in the N.Y. Post then you have the advantage of me. They promised to send me copies here, but none has reached me. The extract printed in the Times-Dispatch appeared carefully to omit the more complimentary parts; and Romeike, whose once fine service has collapsed, has forwarded no clippings dated later than the middle of November." Silence ensued.

19

The Past Reclaimed

1943–1949

The St. Johns made its appearance in September 1943. Contrary to Cabell's expectations, the *Saturday Review* treated it kindly, its reviewer finding the work "scintillating, cynical, and singularly candid." The New York *Times* considered it a better book than either author could have produced alone, making it the best of the Rivers series. Marjorie Rawlings, having read a pre-release copy in August, wrote Cabell in flattering terms, objecting only to including Stephen Crane's common-law wife Cora in the history. Rawlings did not tell Cabell that she was reviewing *The St. Johns*, and her review came as a complete surprise when Cabell read it in the New York *Herald-Tribune Books* on 5 September. He wrote her two days later:

> You are a treacherous woman with many redeeming traits—which means that having had no hint you were to review *The St. Johns*, I yesterday was both astounded and delighted when *Books* arrived. Still, though, you harp upon Cora. Cora teaches an inspiring lesson, and besides, she gave me a chance to invent her physician friend through a patois which I had not ever attempted before.
>
> Although I liked every word of your review, I got an especial pleasure out of "the course of the book flows as steadily as the river."

Mencken too remained faithful in his praise, and Cabell wrote him grate-fully. Van Vechten also responded, doubting the existence of a co-author. Cabell assured him that Hanna was "a most professorial professor whom I have learned to regard with impatient affection."

Back in Florida for the winter, the Cabells were invited to visit Marjorie Rawlings at Cross Creek. Cabell wrote her on 19 January: "Heaven is not kindly enough disposed toward us, it seems, to let us visit Cross Creek. My Wife's poor hands have so stiffened that for her to attempt to drive now would be, if not an absolute impossibility, an unblushing flirtation with suicide. I record this fact with my eyes full of tears which are but partly caused by the influenza germ that infests all three of us at present, because I did want to see, as it were, Macgregor upon her native heath." The invitation was renewed for early March. Rawlings' new husband, Norton Baskin, had volunteered as an ambulance driver in the American Field Service and was with British troops in the India-Burma sector. The Cabells again had to decline, not only because of their infirmities but also because of "the difficulties of getting enough gasoline ever to return to Virginia."

With *The St. Johns* out of the way, Cabell began to feel at loose ends, having no absorbing project at hand. Benét's replacement on the staff of Farrar & Rinehart was himself a novelist and critic—Philip Wylie, whose *Generation of Vipers* castigating American motherhood had created a literary sensation the year before. Cabell sent off his incomplete manuscript of "Virginian essays" for a critique. Instead, he received a mannered, care-fully worded rejection such as Cabell himself might have written. He re-plied testily at length and closed with the resolve to finish the work, "and I shall then go on playing with my text for, in all probability, the rest of the summer." Rinehart had turned down Hanna's life of Achille Murat who had migrated from France to Florida, and Cabell offered to read the typescript to see if he could "make it more sprightly": "To be candid already, I am not over eager to write any more Floridian history after Florida's reception of the St. Johns. Outside the state, the book had, as you know, a mild triumph; inside, there seemed to be an obscure resent-ment that the history of Florida had not been presented, as is customary, in a form which nobody could read."

In this summer of discontent, Cabell heard again from Ellen Glasgow after a half-year silence resulting from his sporting review of *A Certain Mea-sure*. She wrote from Castine, Maine, on 16 June, touching first on impersonal matters in a genteel way. Having established her exalted remoteness from the petty cruelties of the world, she brought up the matter of his perfidy:

> In this life-giving air, lifted high above a blue rippling bay and a chain of hills, I find that only a war on the other side of the world, with mankind destroying itself and other more innocent animals, appears really important enough to bother about. Even the sharpened edge of what Berta Wellford felicitously called your "all-time low" has become harmlessly blunted.
>
> You alone, I suppose, my dear James, know the reason for this abrupt change of front after thirty—or is it nearly forty—years? I am willing to grant you any number of reasons, though I cannot quite understand all the long endeavor to build up a charming appearance of sympathy and comprehension, if this were simply for the need of releasing, in the end, a sudden gust of inhibited malice. Literary smartness must depend, of course, for its best effects upon caricature and misrepresentation, and, as we both have learned, from the wise or the witty, caricature demands the spicy flavour of malice or flippancy. And yet, even so—the only literary right I deny is the right of misrepresentation. But all this is beginning to sound over-serious. Perhaps, without suspecting it, I am still incurably romantic at heart, and I dislike seeing destroyed a perfection that cannot be restored. I find, as I grow older, that I cling more firmly to certain ancient beliefs or illusions: to steadfast loyalties, and to truths of the written or spoken word, and to the abiding sincerity of a long friendship.

His response, dated nine days later on the 25th, ignored her homily on friendship; it opened pointedly with no separate salutation but an observation: "It is uncommonly good to be hearing from you at long last, my very dear . . ." The letter continued in an impersonal vein; castigating the moral fervor attendant to the war, he remarked in passing that his current project was lacking in "sturdy patriotism" so that its publication would be delayed, and he quipped that "I pray to God every night, as befits an Episcopalian, to make people stop being so high-minded." That remark could just possibly apply to Ellen, and now it was his silence as to their relationship that was a sting to her sensibilities. Her silence this time lasted only three months. She wrote from Maine on 25 September 1944:

> Well, James, your letter was most agreeable, but its rightful place was in another summer. It told me everything, except the one thing I was rather curious about, and that is:—Does the pleasure of releasing an inhibited gust of malice make the effort, or the satisfaction, worth more than it costs? In this past year, I have learned how easy it is to destroy anything, whether it is a

bird or belief; and I have learned, too, that there is no literary magic, white or black, that can restore either a bird or a belief. Not that I wish to appear over serious. What you might care to say in a newspaper would certainly be no solemn matter, if only it had not denied everything you had said or written, and I had believed, for the past thirty or forty years. And this is true, even when, by minds less subtle or less literary than yours, what you say is misconstrued as cheap smartness.

This year there was no fall meeting in Richmond as in years past. In a letter from Florida, dated 23 November 1944, Cabell again placed his salutation in the opening remark. "It had been our hope to see you before we left Richmond, my hitherto dear Ellen, but after our furnace broke down of a sudden, there was nothing left for us except a few days of misery." Almost a year would elapse this time before Glasgow wrote again. In that time, she had become seriously ill and had decided to forego publishing her last short novel.

Norton Baskin returned home in November 1944 debilitated from tropical illnesses, and Marjorie Rawlings spent more time in St. Augustine that winter helping her husband to restore his health and his hotel business. The friendship of the Florida writer was a cordial for Cabell, who was increasingly nostalgic for past glories. Rawlings migrated on a circuit of Cross Creek, St. Augustine, and a cottage at Crescent Beach below St. Augustine. In the spring of that year, a disastrous fire had swept through a wing of Castle Warden, the Baskin hotel, killing two women; one was a friend of the Baskins who had been using their penthouse apartment. In addition to other trials, Marjorie was embroiled in a legal one. She was being sued by Zelma Cason, a cracker neighbor who alleged she had been libeled in *Cross Creek*. As winter residents of St. Augustine, the Cabells had settled into a restricted routine of movie-going, cards, tea-parties, and the local cultural events associated with a small city, but Rawlings was still a star in the publishing firmament and was courted by book and periodical editors.

The Cabells suffered through a damp and servantless summer at Ophelia. They determined that a bedroom had to be installed on the first floor of 3201 Monument so that Percie could avoid stair-climbing. They consulted with Carrie Duke, a friend of Glasgow and an antique dealer. The remodeling plans made a small reception room opposite the front entrance into a dining room, the latter became a sitting room, and the former parlor became a spacious bedroom. By 30 September, Cabell wrote Rawlings that they were living in a pig sty where nothing ever seemed to get finished. They planned to return to St. Augustine in late November.

After many months Cabell heard again from Ellen Glasgow, and this time she did not allude directly to their estrangement, although it was in her thoughts. Almost as a reward to a child who has at least disciplined itself not to cry, Cabell replied almost immediately on 30 August and referred cryptically to the cause of her discontent. "I must certainly see you in October. There are so many things which may not be written about with profit, because a face to face quarrel, but not a letter, can end with a kiss."

Glasgow returned to Richmond in late October, and Cabell went to see her. He wrote Rawlings on 3 November:

> Two days ago I saw Ellen Glasgow, and her condition horrified me. She is a mere wisp and has reached really an advanced stage of melancholia. She has been able to do virtually no work for some two years, and she now faces with horror the notion of living inactively in her dark house throughout the winter with not even any literary contacts. I myself do not see why anybody should want to talk with writers (present company excepted, of course), but she does; and she talks morbidly about being starved mentally as well as physically.
>
> Now then do you please write her a letter. Tell her how wonderful she is in comparison with all other writers, living and dead; that is treatment to which she responds purringly. And urge her to try spending the winter in St. Augustine. I believe this to be a possibility, now that I have discussed the matter with her companion, Miss Bennett, who believes that some such course is imperative. She could then get out and about; she loves to walk; and there would be enough people to make a to-do over her to induce complacence. You and I could acquire merit by discussing literature with her on, say, alternating Thursdays. It is a scheme on which I am working hard, and in which I hope you may aid. Please do.

Marjorie Rawlings wrote Ellen Glasgow on the 9th, a long, cordial letter discussing work, and begging Glasgow to join her and Cabell for the winter. The idea was entertained by Ellen and her companion, Anne Virginia Bennett, but Glasgow died quietly in her sleep on 21 November. Ellen's companion and sister arranged a high-church Episcopal service with the Apostle's Creed recited twice over the remains of the agnostic writer, but Cabell did not attend. He wrote Hunter Stagg from Florida in late January:

> As yet, I have not wholly recovered from Ellen Glasgow's death, which, as you may know, was of a bewildering suddenness. The last time I saw her was two days before, when she stopped by 3201 in the afternoon and we talked

uninterruptedly for two hours as to her future plans, now that her strength was being recovered. She was frail looking, but in high spirits, and even drank two entire old fashioned cocktails. The next news I had was when Miss Bennett telephoned at eight o'clock in the morning the news of her death. I admit that I went all to pieces and displayed a depth of emotion which I could not but admire.

Well, and immediately afterward we came to St. Augustine, where nothing in particular has happened. John Farrar, though, has at last established his own firm, and it will be bringing out a brief story by me about pirates . . . as early as may be in the summer, and the non-fiction book about the State of Virginia as soon afterward as may seem advisable. You may find extracts from the latter in the March and April *Atlantic Monthly*, which I take to be a strange harbor for an erstwhile indecent and obscene author to be reaching.

Although Cabell had written Professor Hanna that he intended to avoid Florida history in the future, the historical character Jose Gasparilla began to seize his imagination, and in August 1946 he wrote his former collaborator asking about source materials on Gasparilla. The writing of the tale provided a type of occupational therapy, and the account of the pirate's childhood allowed Cabell to escape into his own. By early December he had finished *There Were Two Pirates*. His publisher had evolved into Farrar, Straus & Company, and Cabell was again in communication with John Farrar, whom he could generally count on for prepublication criticism. Increasingly, dependent on illustrations to piece out his slight tales into the semblance of bona fide books, Cabell collected postcards of St. Augustine scenes for the illustrator. Marjorie Rawlings as dedicatee was unhappy that her dedication appeared on the copyright page; fortunately there was a second edition to rectify this lapse in etiquette. The critical reception of the work was tepid, and the Richmond *Times-Dispatch* (23 August 1946) in "Pro & Con Cabell" pointed up how the local celebrity was receiving ever more mixed reviews.

The summer of 1946 at Ophelia was a time of growing anguish for Cabell, with his wife's physical suffering unabated. He confided to Rawlings, "I lie awake at night grieving over her, but I have learned not to condole in the day time, because it merely upsets her into a seizure of self-pity, which otherwise she avoids dauntlessly." For distraction he revised the various essays tenuously associated with the Commonwealth of Virginia and gave them the title *Let Me Lie*. The chapter "Miss Glasgow of Virginia," is based on reviews of her works and his publicity squib for the Book-of-the-Month Club. He toned down considerably his facetious review of *A*

Certain Measure that had disrupted their friendship. This chapter is prefaced by a citation from Glasgow's last letter to him dated 22 August 1945, a letter that had not alluded to his review, perhaps a sign of forgiveness on her part. It was accorded a sentimental importance now that she was dead: "I feel that the war has killed so much more than armies and human beings, that it has, in a way, put all artistic impulses into a long sleep, or into a trance of futility. But I wish we could have again, on this perfect summer afternoon, one of our old talks on writing and the kind of writing that was worth while. Even if we did not agree, our talk would be with the old friendship and sympathy (230)."

The sentiment in this letter was surely her last reflection on their relationship. But unfortunately, it was not phrased so felicitously. Cabell was again "collaborating" with Glasgow. Her letter reads, "Even if we did not agree, the talk would be better than the endless complaints about points and rationing [during World War II] I have had to hear for the past several years." Her letter closes "With my love to the three of you [J. B. C., Percie Cabell, and Ballard], and with the old friendship and sympathy, Ellen." In joining her coda with a thought in the body of her letter, Cabell was indulging in more than esthetics, though his rewording does read better. His whole chapter on Ellen Glasgow in *Let Me Lie* (1947) is an *amende honorable* to a friend and fellow author whom he had wounded, knowingly or not. In this benign mood he wrote, "We were friends for some forty seven years, with an ever increasing intimacy." They were not on a first-name basis until 1926, when she was fifty-three and he forty-seven. He spoke of differences but added, "Yet we differed always without any rancor." Serious qualifications are in order here; this statement was a handsome wreath laid on a dead woman's grave. He, living, joined forces with her, dead, to present a harmonious front to society, in a sense a manifestation of the instinctive good taste of two Virginians unified to preserve a gracious public image. But judging critically, Miss Glasgow in her last letter and Cabell in his "apology" were nostalgically looking back to a relationship that was never quite the free-and-easy exchange they wished to remember. Romance was at work. And Cabell would once again have cause to reassess their relationship.

Another significant personal loss occurred for Cabell on 19 October 1946. His youngest brother, John, committed suicide in Savannah. Depressed by the attacks of an opponent in a political campaign for tax commissioner, an office he had held for years, John had suffered declining health. He left two sons, another Robert Gamble Cabell, a student at VMI, and an older son, John. The latter was to die four-and-a-half years later when he slipped on rocks while fishing and drowned. James Cabell had remained close in spirit to his brothers. It was John who was responsible for the first publication of an aspiring writer under his real name, in the *VMI Bomb* in 1901. He and John had been youthful companions and eligible young men at the Virginia summer resorts. John had been interested in his oldest brother's family research and in his heraldic renderings. Both James and Robert Cabell looked to John's sons to carry on their family's heritage.

Let Me Lie was scheduled for February 1947 publication, but review copies did not go out until late March and the trade edition not until April. With the Cabells in St. Augustine for the winter, Marjorie Rawlings planned a publication party at the Crescent Beach Cottage. On 21 February she wrote: "If Priscilla thinks she can manage it, and if you will allow me to make a gesture that would please me very much indeed, you will inform me of the proper date, and provide me with a guest list of your choosing, of approximately fifty people? By asking different groups of people for different hours, we should be able to manage a total of perhaps seventy-five." The party was followed by an intimate supper for close friends. Rawlings's warm acceptance of each of Cabell's works was in marked contrast to some of the coldest reviews. The New York Times (30 March) dismissed *Let Me Lie* as "a collection of stylistic devices designed to conceal the fact that the author has nothing in particular to say. It is an elegy for the elegist." *Commonweal* (18 April) deemed it "a tiresome swan song."

In contrast, Marjorie Rawlings's career continued at flood tide. She had spent a month in the mountains of North Carolina expanding a short story into a film script for MGM. She assured Cabell that he would loathe it, because it was "sweet." The *New Yorker* bought her stories. *The Yearling* had been filmed to popular acclaim. Cabell wrote her on 27 April: "It is a grief to me to report that as yet we have not seen The Yearling. It did not reach Richmond until after we had become marooned for the summer in Northumberland County; and indeed I question if in my now enfeebled state of health I could survive this picture. My stepdaughter tells us that in Richmond its patrons sobbed aloud like infants during its progress, and at its end had to be helped out of the theatre, in a tear-blinded condition, by the ushers. I cannot but think there is enough sorrow in most forms of social recreation without your adding to it thus ruthlessly."

As the capstone of her career, Marjorie Rawlings was planning a long, serious work based on her Grandfather Traphagen's life in Michigan in the decades following the Civil War. She was offered the use of a cottage outside Van Hornsville in upperstate New York where the countryside would serve as the setting of her novel. The day after her arrival, she was stunned by the death of Maxwell Perkins, an editor as close to her as Guy Holt had been to Cabell. At first tempted to give up her planned work, she was persuaded by Norton Baskin that Perkins should be honored by her perseverance. In July she fell in love with a pre-Revolutionary Greek Revival house nearby and set about its restoration. She had employed a New York decorator for the Crescent Beach cottage, and she again turned to Margaret Freeman for advice about furnishing the Van Hornsville house. Cabell had continued to hear of Margaret Freeman's activities over the years through Hunter Stagg. The latter had lived in Washington with his sister since early in the war, and Margaret had worked in the Stage Door Canteen there. She continued her close, confiding friendship with "poor Hunter" upon her return to decorating in New York. Marjorie Rawlings's contacts with Margaret helped recreate in Cabell's memory the positive, take-charge Miss Freeman who had raised the money for the *Reviewer* of happier days. In *Let Me Lie*, he had laid a handsome wreath on the memory of that publication, just as he had on that of Ellen Glasgow. The four editors had been thrilled to be remembered after a quarter century.

At Ophelia, where life moved slowly, three loose ends of the Biography continued to nag its author. *The Music from Behind the Moon* (1926), *The White Robe* (1928), and *The Way of Ecben* (1929) really should have been grouped together as a volume of the Storisende Edition. Inspired by Gabriella Moncure, an aging nympholept wanted to tidy up these brief allegories of the poetic spirit, making them into a small volume as a final unacknowledged tribute to the one who had placed him under a powerful enchantment when he was sixteen. His publisher was not keen to reissue these slight tales. Even Cabell realized that a jaded postwar America had little interest. He wrote John Farrar on 19 October 1947: "It seems better to accept the wholly revolting terms offered for the *Witch-Woman* trilogy than to leave it temporarily unpublished, because in the latter case I would continue to revise it interminably. So let us get ahead with it and thus at any rate start some republishing. Even though I shall not make any money out of the book, I incline to offset this bleak fact with the reflection that you will probably lose money on it, so that we may then all three pose as art's martyrs."

Back in St. Augustine, the Cabell ménage settled into its routines that were increasingly restrictive owing to Percie Cabell's rheumatism. The once-famous author corresponded gratefully with two academics interested in his career: Edward Wagenknecht and Julius Rothman. Wagenknecht's "Cabell: A Reconsideration" appeared in the February 1948 *College English,* so pleasing its subject that he requested more offprints to place advantageously. Marjorie Rawlings reported to Carl Van Vechten, "This spring [Cabell] followed a perfectly strange girl into a local book-shop just to find out what she bought." He had ambitious plans for a Lichfield-Fairhaven tetralogy, an omnibus volume containing his four early "contemporary" novels, thus refuting those critics who said he was socially irrelevant. On his birthday, Rawlings entertained him at a party with just their respective spouses. On the same day, he was interviewed in the St. Augustine *Record,* wherein he announced that reprints of his works were underway but that commercial second-thoughts by his publisher had wrecked these plans.

Back in Richmond, Cabell wrote Marjorie Rawlings on 27 April. Thanking her for his birthday party, he added:

> It was good to have you and Norton just by yourselves, for once anyhow. The longer I consider him, in passing, the finer person do I find him, and the deeper becomes my sympathy for his lot in being married to a writer.
>
> I have no news. We arrived in Richmond the evening of 22 April in an outworn condition and had to be lifted severally out of the car before being reanimated with alcohol. Since then we have pottered about feebly in an attempt at housecleaning, and we are planning tomorrow to visit Ophelia so as to find out if our cottage there still stands and is habitable for the summer.

The Witch-Woman was issued in May to unfavorable notices with the exception of Wagenknecht's in the Chicago *Sun Tribune Magazine of Books* (23 May). Fanny Butcher, who formerly had been positive in her reviews of his work, had commented two weeks earlier in the same publication that despite his skills Cabell was no longer "in vogue." Even so, Cabell was pleased and reported to Rawlings that he had expressed his appreciation "in terms which befitted a little gentleman." In the same letter (22 May), he continued: "Upon the same Monday that this should reach you, we are planning to leave for Ophelia, and to stay there, we hope, for the summer. Thus far, the continued cool and rainy weather has headed us off; but I am trusting now to settle down to a month or two of undisturbed slavery, so that I may finish the book at present in parturition. At any rate, do you forward the Wagenknecht anthology to me there at your convenience, and I will try to read at least some of it during the summer." The Wagenknecht anthology was *The Fireside Book of Romance* (1948), in which both Cabell and Rawlings had stories. The latter, not knowing she was represented in it, had borrowed the book from Cabell when it arrived in St. Augustine. The book in parturition was *The Devil's Own Dear Son*, first drafted in the first person but changed over to the third.

With Marjorie Rawlings at work on the house in Van Hornesville in the summer of 1948, she had interesting news for Cabell about two old friends (9 July).

> Margaret Waller Freeman has been helping me with the furnishing of the New York house, as she did with the beach cottage. She came to Van Hornesville and we had a gay time. When Norton joined me, and we went on to New York City, Margaret had everything ready for me to look at, and we decided on furniture, draperies, rugs and so on in short order. She will join me again in middle or late August to put things properly in place. She is a lovely person, and I rather imagine she has had hard sledding, but takes it in her stride.
>
> I am sure I knew, but had forgotten, that you were well acquainted. She is one of your greatest admirers, as you must know. She asked Norton and me to supper at her apartment in the city, and had Carl Van Vechten and his Fania there, too. I disgraced myself utterly. I tried to out-drink Cousin Carl (I shall explain that presently) and found too late it couldn't be done. Cousin Carl and I kept on drinking, and scarcely touching Margaret's superb food, and the last thing I remember is my answering him by saying, "I could be faithful to you, too." Norton was extremely cool for several days, and Fania, I am delighted to report, was in a tizzy. A large part of my seduction of Cousin Carl was because Fania annoyed me so. She nagged the poor man unmercifully.
>
> WELL, when Van Vechten asked me questions about my Northern abode, I told him the story of my family Bogardus portrait, and it seems he is descended from the Bogardus line, too.
>
> He has just sent me a copy of the Yale Gazette with his most engaging essay about James Branch Cabell. There was some material there, new to me, but I do think the Western professor's monograph on you had more to offer.

The Western professor was Wagenknecht, Cabell's new champion, and Rawlings wrote "Cousin Carl" thanking him for the *Yale Gazette*.

> Your essay on James Cabell is delightful. I suppose that during his life-time at least, none of us will dare hazard any public guesses as to the reasons for his "protective armor"—if reasons are ever necessary to account for what, after all, is any man's right to his own personality and character.

I am fascinated, too, by the photograph you made of him. I have never seen him so tousled! His gray hair lies as smooth these days as the feathers on the head of a swan. I wonder if the photograph drove him to what Priscilla insists is his vanity. She explains his daily walks (taken, I am sure, as an escape from Priscilla) as being for the sake of his figure. "James is vain, you know," she says. "He won't allow himself to become paunchy. He wants to be as trim as a young man."

Almost as an aside, Marjorie added, "His letters to me are delicious." So too are her letters to Cabell, but a subtle difference underlies their humor. She is as open as a person can be, sharing her subtlest thoughts unreservedly. Rawlings was that way in intimate social converse, although when the occasion demanded she could be a social hypocrite with the best. On the other hand, what Van Vechten and Rawlings referred to as Cabell's "protective armor" never allowed him to bare his soul to another. He came close in certain letters and in some of his confessionals, but even in these revelations small mendacities rearranged chronology or fact. Certain alterations of youthful memories were deliberate, and others might be attributed to psychic wounds imperfectly healed. Marjorie Rawlings continued her search for the real Cabell, but she learned not to sport with his pose of imperturbability.

At a theater party in St. Augustine, she slipped a silk stocking into Cabell's coat pocket so that a length of it dangled conspicuously. In animated conversation, he did not notice it while everyone else enjoyed the joke. His discovery was not accompanied with the good-humored sophistication that Rawlings expected. She wrote him the next day, 26 February 1949:

> From the cold glint in your eye at the theater last night, I got the dreadful conviction that my practical joke with the stocking had back-fired, and that you were anything but amused. I asked Norton if he thought you could possibly be seriously annoyed, and he said you might well be, that he considered my sense of humor quite misplaced and definitely un-funny.
>
> I simply followed a sudden and irresistible impulse. As I told Priscilla at the bridge party, I had the stocking in my coat pocket, to try to match in town, and it struck me that it would be hilarious to embarrass the most pornographic writer in the country, since his personal life was impeccable. Priscilla seemed to be amused, and I told her I should be most disappointed if she didn't tease you thoroughly.
>
> I shall be crushed if I have offended you. My long respect for you as an artist has so combined with my deep affection for you and yours, since I have

had the privilege of knowing you, that I shall go in sack-cloth ashes for as long
as you wish, if you share Norton's opinion of my conception of a jest.

Their friendship survived. His next opus, The Devil's Own Dear Son, scheduled for mid-April publication, was dedicated to Norton Baskin, and Rawlings planned to celebrate Cabell's birthday on 14 April. She invited the
president of the University of Florida as a prelude to the school's offering
some honor to Cabell. The Virginia writer was sensitive to the fact that,
unlike most of his literary friends, he had never been tendered an honorary doctorate. Priscilla Cabell died, however, on 29 March 1949. In As I
Remember It Cabell records the final days of his wife's illness and death in
harrowing detail, his protective armor laid aside in this baring of his most
intimate emotions. On Friday the 25th, a friend had driven James, Priscilla, and Ballard Cabell "across the Bridge of Lions, and then down Ana-
tasia Island, to Crescent Beach, where we paused to chat with Marjorie
Rawlings about how splendid it was that Priscilla was up and feeling all
right again." That evening she was stricken with heart failure.

On 1 April Priscilla Bradley Shepherd Cabell was interred in the Emmanuel Episcopal Church Cemetery, where Mr. Shepherd, father of her
first five children, was buried. She was survived by her two sons, Emmett
and Ballard, two daughters, Priscilla (Mrs. J. Hopkins Davis), and Virginia
(Mrs. Edward King Davis), and a bereft, nearly helpless spouse of over
thirty-five years' dependence. Priscilla Davis made arrangements to care
for her stepfather and half-brother at 3201 Monument, and Virginia Davis
made arrangements to bring her family down from Tuxedo Park, New
York, to spend part of the summer with them at Ophelia. Cabell was totally dependent on these two daughters for all household arrangements,
chauffeuring, employing servants, taking Ballard to church. Though Cabell
was grateful, he was a creature of habit, and any alteration of routine depressed him. Marjorie Rawlings wrote frequently and at length. She wrote
him on 13 April, the day before his birthday, and wired him on the 14th.
He responded, "Your telegram and your letter were very dear of you, and
displayed that better side of your nature which I have almost always believed you to possess."

It was at this traumatic time that The Devil's Own Dear Son appeared to
mock his grief. Published on his birthday, it provided reviewers the opportunity to proclaim, as did the Richmond Times-Dispatch, that "James
Branch Cabell, at 70, Produces 50th Book." The preface to the new book

was pure biography and appeared simultaneously in *Vogue* (15 April) as "A Note upon the Art of Being a Winter Resident." Catherine Mary in the opening chapters is patently a portrait modeled on Percie Cabell, and the author once again makes his metaphysical journey to Hell and Back. For part of his trip Diego chooses the silver stallion of Poictesme and is advised he has picked what "is nowadays an infirm and discredited animal." Norton Baskin professed gratitude that the work was dedicated to him, but it reads like a private joke between the author, a few jaded reviewers, and perhaps Marjorie Rawlings who chortled over the topical innuendos. In later years, Cabell scholar Joe Lee Davis accorded the work a charitable reading, but then Davis wanted to add the subtitle *A Comedy of Incorrigibility* to his *James Branch Cabell* in the Twayne series. That Cabell was the author of fifty books needs qualifying; "titles" would have been more accurate, in that some were reworkings of earlier publications.

John Farrar came to see Cabell at Ophelia, but a despondent Cabell felt he had written his last book. He tinkered with a bibliography of his writings for a graduate student, he corresponded with Edward Wagenknecht whom he liked. On 4 September he wrote "Pet Marjorie":

> Our summer was not wholly unhappy, but I did not enjoy it. I still do not enjoy anything, and I in particular do not enjoy being age-stricken. People keep on being excessively kind to and considerate of poor Ballard and me in our forlorn condition. Among such people, by the bye, I must rank Margaret Freeman, who drove in upon us one afternoon at Ophelia, so that we might weep upon each other's shoulders over our dead past. We did; and then cheered ourselves up by telling, over a couple of highballs, just exactly what we always really did think about a number of joint acquaintances during the said past. We dealt faithfully with almost every person whom we had ever known in common, and a viper would have envied us.
>
> I must add that after she had left, Ballard gravely suggested he would like to have me marry Margaret Freeman, because he was very fond of her, and she would not ever put up with any foolishness from me or from anybody else. I agreed, so far as went the fondness and his character sketch.

Rawlings replied on the 7th: "I was enchanted by Ballard's suggestion that you take on Margaret Freeman, and actually, it seems a most plausible idea. But he is quite mistaken—Margaret *would* stand for any amount of foolishness from you. She is most sensitive to the needs of others."

A month later he informed Rawlings that "only today did I find opportunity to send on Ballard's suggestion to Margaret Freeman, whose New York address I lacked. I shall await her reply with some natural interest, now that Ballard keeps on continuing to remind me that we really do need Margaret Freeman to keep house for us and to drive the car. I infer that he too has in him a streak of the Scot."

20

Antan

1949–1958

Margaret Waller Freeman was admirably qualified to care for Ballard Cabell. During World War I she had been trained in occupational and rehabilitative nursing, and her maternal bullying had made many of her patients fond of her. During her twenty-five years as a decorator in New York her business experience had taught her how to deal with employees in a no-nonsense manner, and she had become an excellent cook. In the mid-1920s Cabell had urged Hunter Stagg to propose to her, and ironically it was to inquire about dissolute Hunter that Cabell wrote Margaret Freeman on 20 November 1948, after Margaret had entertained Rawlings and Van Vechten. She sent news of Hunter, living in Washington and far-gone in alcoholism, and Cabell thanked her on New Year's Day 1949. Margaret had maintained literary friendships in New York; her visit to Ophelia in the fall was to a writer she had known in happier days. She had never been exposed to Ballard in social intercourse and could hardly have foreseen his immediate infatuation with her. Cabell's 6 October 1949 letter to their visitor simply repeated Ballard's suggestion without any comment of his own. Her response was to accept the suggestion as a light compliment. Back in St. Augustine, Cabell wrote on 9 November.

It would be well, I think, for you now to consider Ballard's notion with complete seriousness. For my part, I have already done so; and from my personal point of view, his notion appears excellent. The difficulty is that I of course do not know anything as to your point of view — nor for that matter, about your present-day commitments whether in New York or in Richmond. I know only that I, after all, have admired and have been fond of you now for some thirty years, and that I have in you complete faith.

So then, my dear, just how seriously can you consider our both doing what we can to make Ballard happy? With that settled, we can settle all other matters.

The idea of becoming Mrs. James Branch Cabell appealed to Margaret Freeman. After working for twenty-five years she managed to support herself, but her prospects of ever becoming affluent were dim. She would soon have to undergo an expensive operation for a goiter. As the wife of a once-famous writer, her niche in history would be assured; for her remaining years she could reign as a social leader in a Richmond that had patronized her. A businesswoman, she saw the proposal as a contract, and she determined to lay out all her liabilities to the man contracting for her services. She did not have a patient disposition, being quick to fly into indignant rages. As an antidote to her tantrums, he could rely on her "protective and maternal instinct." She had a nephew with mental problems who could be an embarrassment. She owed something to herself, and she could enjoy bossing Ballard and him. "He needs you, my dear," Cabell replied. "Last Thursday, after having returned—alone, if that requires saying—from divine worship, he who had been wholly cheerful all day broke down of a sudden because it was Thanksgiving and he had no mother to be thankful with. Then I did too, because I felt so very sorry for him, and I could not help him. You could have done so."

Margaret would consider the proposal seriously except that she was not a well woman; she needed an operation for the goiter and did not have the money for it. That was no problem, he wrote on 3 December; the operation would be his Christmas gift. While he was not wealthy, there was enough for the three of them to live on in fair comfort; his brother Robert attended to all such affairs. After the operation she could visit Marjorie Rawlings, who would help work out further details of the marriage contract. "The ring needs of course to wait until April. We cannot flout Mrs. Post." If she was faced with an operation, he too was not in the best of health, suffering from conjunctivitis and undergoing another of his chronic colds. Ballard also was writing Margaret charming letters, telling her how much she was needed. She had been raised a Methodist, had become an agnostic, but would consent to becoming an Episcopalian upon the groom-to-be's insistence.

Margaret arrived in Richmond from New York and scheduled her operation for 13 January. She did not want anyone in Richmond to know that she was contemplating matrimony with James Branch Cabell so soon after his first wife's death, so Cabell dutifully enclosed his letters to her in Marjorie Rawlings's envelopes. Now that they were engaged, albeit secretly, both were nervous about meeting again face to face. The operation went smoothly, but the trip to Florida was postponed owing to Marjorie Rawlings's over-indulgence. She wanted to give a cocktail party for the prospective bride and announce the engagement; Cabell found himself in the unlikely role of temperance lecturer. During her convalescence in Richmond, Margaret was taking driving lessons, a matter of vital import to Cabell.

On her trip south, Margaret first went to visit a friend in Miami before coming back to St. Augustine in early February. The meeting between the middle-aged spinster and the elderly widower went well, with Marjorie Rawlings on her better behavior, Margaret her talkative self, and Cabell relishing the presence of another domineering woman. By the time Margaret left, she had agreed to become Ballard's stepmother; she would return to Richmond in May and would learn to drive a car before the wedding in June. The nature of her relationship with the groom remained undefined, though both understood that she would continue as a decorator in New York on a part-time basis. He wrote her on 24 February: "Like you, I was in a dither about your visit. Either one of us, there was the chance, might prove unsatisfactory to the other, whereas Marjorie stayed wholly unpredictable. Then too I knew that for me to seem the least bit devoted in public would arouse gossip here. (I continue to remark, just casually, that you were a teacher at the first school I attended.) But in the outcome, to my finding, everything went beautifully. And my heart hungered to have you stay on longer, while discretion whispered— or shouted, to be rather more exact — that it wouldn't at all do."

While in St. Augustine, Margaret Freeman had continued to lay her cards on the table, confessing that she was technically a maiden and had not been promiscuous but was not an intact virgin. Suddenly in the seventy-year-old male's eyes she became romantically interesting. "Looking back: I had not thought seriously about any physical affection until we were left in Marjorie's car in front of ——'s house. Everything changed for me then and there." One of her lovers was a man he had known, one, indeed, two years older than he. That this plumpish, fifty-five-year-old, snub-nosed, round-faced woman had been an object of desire excited his libido. She could be more than Ballard's stepmother. But in his letter of 27 February, he made a mistake: he referred in writing to the former lover. The dedicatee (Virginia Randolph Ellett) of *Between Dawn and Sunrise*, he joked, should have been her, another female, as sharing the mutual affections of the editor and the edited. He had torn away the lady's self respect; the engagement was ended. Professions of contrition ensued. They needed to talk again, face to face. Cabell confessed "it was my blunder (such is my theory) to ignore the fact that we in social converse can discuss quite amicably, as your visit proved, matters which when typewritten about become, to your finding, high explosives. I shall not offend again in this fashion. And you in return must promise me not ever, out of a clear sky, to break off our engagement for a third time."

His letters from Florida to Margaret in Richmond and New York for March and April mostly concern business details, but they also include amorous allusions. Margaret stopped off in Washington to consult with Hunter Stagg about what a seventy-one-year-old spouse would expect in the way of conjugal relations. Having been commissioned to redecorate 3201 Monument Avenue, she proposed dividing it into two apartments, one upstairs for her and Ballard and one downstairs for an increasingly amorous groom. The latter was not keen for the arrangement. Ballard had no concept of sex nor, for that matter, of nudity. He was wholly affectionate. "Never has he referred verbally to what happened last year," Cabell wrote Margaret, "But upon the anniversary of his mother's death, very early in the morning he came over into my bed and put his arms around me and began to cry quietly. He did not say anything at all. I forewarn you that if ever in the future you should be unkind to Ballard you will find it the one offence I will not forgive, not upon any terms."

Cabell was concerned with breaking the news of his proposed marriage to his closest associates. His brother Robert, his financial advisor, saw it as a practical move for the comfort of two lonely males. Maude Cabell, Robert's wife, had reservations about Margaret Freeman; "a snob," the groom retorted. Wirt Marks, a step-son-in-law and Cabell's lawyer, approved of the arrangement and attended to the legalities of property and wills. Of the two daughters-in-law, Virginia was the more receptive. Priscilla did not care for Margaret's domineering, take-charge, "Now see here!" style, but she remained affable out of affection for her half-brother and stepfather. Emmett Shepherd was outside Cabell's affections and therefore outside consideration, although Emmett, his wife, and daughter Priscilla felt close to Ballard and visited Ophelia later in the summer. Before he left Florida at the end of April, Cabell arranged to have a black employee of the Buckingham Hotel work for him that summer as a chauffeur-chef.

When Hunter Stagg, the suitor rejected twenty-five years earlier, learned that Cabell himself had proposed to the strong-willed lady, he wrote to congratulate him. The letter reveals his usual candor and perception:

> . . . [Margaret] as long as you have known her, which is mighty nearly as long as I have known her, has persistently professed a notion that you held her in small regard. As steadily I have argued that the contrary was true, that you had a far higher opinion of her than of all the rest of us put together. This I always felt to be true — and I the things I feel are things I know far more certainly than anything I have tangible proof of. Not that this was all instinct. Back of it was all the reason and logic that for brevity I will sum up in the question Who wouldnt? She was certainly better and finer, etc., than all the rest of us put together. . . .
>
> . . . I finally reached the conclusion that, despite my having been clearly knocked for a loop by the news, and barely able to contain my excited enthusiasm even now, I was not really at all surprised that you and Margaret are going to marry each other. . . .
>
> At any rate, I do see it as fitting, beautifully fitting, and I am very happy for you both. Happy too for myself, since it is a merging of the two greatest interests I have in life. Any interest worthy of the name involves some emotional expenditure, and I grow economical, rejoicing that soon I will not be expending mine over so great a portion of the Atlantic Coast, from New York to Florida, but directing it all to one spot, for you will be one.
>
> But I do most hellishly itch to be in a number of places at once, myself, when this news is given out, or gets out if it doesnt wait to be given. I would like to be in several Richmond parlors and living rooms when it reaches them. But most of all I should dearly love to be in a certain Philadelphia house when it is heard there. There is in it one who, always jealous and envious, will be in a frenzy wonderful to see and hear, and I take it hard that, not having been on terms of communication there for years, I will never know anything about it. But I am convinced that, always basically naive, she will fret her life away trying to puzzle out WHY-WHY-WHY?
>
> Why what? Why you didnt ask her, of course, instead of Margaret. (16 May)

At the time Hunter wrote this letter, Emily Clark Balch was confined to her room in Philadelphia being nursed by her devoted and long-suffering stepmother, Alice Clark. It was Margaret, conscious of her elevated status, who wrote Alice Clark of the nuptials, after the ceremony.

Having agreed to an Episcopal marriage service at Emmanuel where Cabell was a member and Percie was buried, Margaret received instruction in church doctrine. The young minister there was not satisfied with her profession of faith, whereupon she was accepted by the less exigent Churchill Gibson, rector of St. James. She was not confirmed until long afterward. Much of May and the first part of June the bride-to-be spent in New York attending to her decorating business. The wedding was planned for Thursday, 15 June, at Emmanuel with Cabell's old school friend and former rector at Emmanuel officiating. Margaret arrived from New York late Wednesday, and upon meeting Cabell the next day found that their plans had to be altered. She wrote Hunter Stagg the following Sunday from Ophelia.

> I am writing on James's famous typewriter, and as you will have gathered, everything is now legal. As a matter of fact, the whole performance as we went through it, set Richmond on its ear. I got there late Wednesday night and found the next day that James had not yet spoken to the minister, and did not know that a three day wait was required in the Episcopal church. So although I got the medical certificate on Thursday morning, and he had his already, and we got the license that afternoon, his old friend and class mate—Mr. Carter Harrison told us we could not be married by him in Emmanual Church until yesterday morning. As it appeared to be necessary to sign a will — (a marriage invalidates all other wills in Virginia) and as James said Wirt Marks's literary style ran to 18 to 20 pages in triplicate, Mr. Harrison both agreed and advised that we have the civil service on Thursday afternoon. This we did, and nothing was known on Friday morning, but as I well knew reporters had gotten to the records and by the afternoon paper it was out. However we were married yesterday with ten or so people in attendance in the church, and as James says — and has been continuing to write to his friends all day — "so far the marriage has been not unhappy."

Cabell's will set up a trust of $75,000 for the care of Ballard; the remainder of his estate, amounting to approximately $50,000, he devised to Margaret along with his real estate holdings. Margaret had agreed verbally that she would remember Percie Cabell's three other living children in her will, as most of Cabell's assets had been inherited from his first wife. This pledge was not honored, nor, for that matter, were most of the provisions of the will she made late in life.

The marriage of Margaret Freeman and James Branch Cabell proved to be the practical arrangement that it was intended to be. A bath was added to the bedroom downstairs at 3201 Monument, but they abandoned the idea of separate apartments as an impractical monetary investment. Margaret learned to drive and became an accomplished gardener. But Cabell's fantasies for a late-blooming romantic liaison did not materialize. In later years Margaret confided to a friend that she had seen passion in James's eyes only once. "Of course, I felt nothing and I could not respond. I saw the light die, and I never saw it again." One or two of Cabell's letters to Margaret read otherwise, perhaps to mislead the prying eyes of posterity or to reproach an unresponsive wife; they may simply have been referring to affectionate intimacies that she did not define as passion. After Cabell's death, his widow destroyed several of the letters she had written him and heavily censored some of the letters he had written her.

With a semblance of order restored in the routine at Ophelia, the writer again gravitated to his typewriter, feeling the old urge to be at work on a manuscript. By September, Margaret was again in New York tending to her decorating business, of which Cabell grew increasingly resentful. As an added insult, he had to address his letters to Waller Freeman, her professional name. While in New York she consulted a gynecologist about a female problem, and an operation was advised. As a result, she returned to New York in October for a longer stay. The abandoned husband allowed himself a prohibited reference to his wife's former lovers. She may have asked why he harped on the dead lover that Cabell had known, resulting in a two-page typed response entitled "A Sermon Which is Left Unsigned for Obvious Reasons." Cabell had liked the man, but the latter's relationships with women had been based on a lie; he was therefore a cad. In a letter dated 30 October Cabell referred to his own inferiority complex as a failed lover. "I wish I could tell you, face to face, my wholly dear one, how much I love you. I could write you, of course (with revisions). . . . Verbally, I am inarticulate, and always have been. I regret the fact whenever I try to talk with you. But what with the ultimatums and the perambulatory monologues—!"

The Cabells did not return to the Buckingham Hotel in St. Augustine that winter but instead took a furnished apartment. It was one of the coldest winters on record. Margaret introduced Ballard to gouache, a technique of painting with opaque watercolors. Ballard took to the medium with enthusiasm and produced pictures that were considered non-representational to most observers but were representational to him. He gave them intriguing titles, such as *The Risen Curtain of Tosca*. That winter the

University of Florida, at Marjorie Rawlings's behest, commissioned the chair of the Fine Arts Department to sculpt a head of Cabell for its library at Gainesville. At the unveiling in St. Augustine, Margaret took the occasion to present a display of Ballard's works, prompting the local art association to give a one-man showing. The works excited favorable attention, and Margaret wrote Hunter that the artist's father was very pleased; she added that James also commended her for wearing "pretty well, and that the only time he has had any chance to do any talking is when Ballard and I simultaneously had laryngitis." That winter Cabell had worked on the small volume of essays that would be issued as Quiet, Please. The manuscript went to John Farrar on 10 April, for a critique and possible publication by Farrar & Straus, but silence ensued. After the University of Florida Press expressed interest, Cabell wrote Farrar on 26 May demanding the return of his typescript and apologizing "for ever having bothered you with it."

Back in Richmond, Margaret took off for New York on 10 May. Again complaining letters were addressed to Waller Freeman. Cabell's ire with "La Princesse Lointaine" allowed him to request a photograph of the dead lover; his nose was of interest. In early June the princess, through the encouragement of Adele Clark, entered three of Ballard's paintings in the outdoor show at the Carillon in Richmond, and Ballard received the prize for the best nonobjective painting. He rushed home and flung himself into his father's arms, crying out, "Father, I got the prize for unmentionable art."

In July Cabell wrote Rawlings about his University of Florida Press contract and took the occasion to comment on his year-old marriage to Waller Freeman. He thanked Marjorie for her role in bringing them together, with a proviso. "Of course, though, one never knows what may happen in the light of her so continuous obstreperating all over the place. So I type my gratefulness youward with my fingers crossed." Rawlings had a suggestion.

> Now once upon a time, as I recall, she lost her voice. Although she laid this to laryngitis or something of the sort, of course you and I know that she had only talked herself speechless. I give you that ray of hope to which to look forward, and suggest that you encourage it by slipping into her room after she is asleep, removing the coverlets from her throat (no, no, you misunderstand me) and turning an electric fan, played over a block of ice, on the columnar box that houses her all too warm vocal chords. Two or three nights of this treatment might bring at least temporary relief—to you.
>
> You would still have to face the fire in her pretty eyes, multiplied tenfold

by her frustration, so perhaps, unless you can induce her to become a Quaker or to study St. Paul, all is hopeless.

On November 10, Mary Dallas Street died. Emily Clark, another co-editor of the *Reviewer*, was in Richmond to retrieve her recently deceased stepmother's effects. Emily had become an alcoholic and was credited with worrying Alice Clark into her grave. Margaret Freeman Cabell wrote Hunter Stagg on the 14th: "As Kitty Guy says, after killing Alice Clark, she seems to be recovering. If I hear any more about her, I will let you know. I went to the funeral [Mary Street's] and she was not there. . . . I was really afraid Emily might come, and didn't know how many others would be there, and couldn't face the idea of meeting Emily over Mary's grave. I don't think she came."

Quiet, Please, the forthcoming small volume of biographical essays, was not a work over which Margaret could wax enthusiastic, and she refused to have it dedicated to her without revisions or deletions. It mocked the "reading public" of Virginia; Florida was "that haunt of the age-stricken"; writers who delighted Cabell's youth were now bores; and that as a writer himself he had utilized "nearly everyone of his acquaintances . . . under this or the other disguise, howsoever flimsy." He bragged of amorous conquests in his youth that Margaret may have felt were greatly exaggerated, and she positively refused to let him publish a tasteless episode in which he described an orgasm. She also insisted that he delete an attack on the honorary degrees accorded other writers. *Quiet, Please* appeared in February. Marjorie Rawlings, still in search of the man behind the mask, found the introduction, ostensibly by Marjorie Burke but touched up by Cabell, an excruciating bore, although its ironic references to his works do reveal an understanding of those works. Rawlings savored the rest of Cabell's confessions but was not misled by his evasions on Dorothy-la-Desirée. Here he had falsified the record, imposing traits derived from Norvell Harrison onto the persona of Gabriella Moncure as his age references underscore, nor did either of these women jilt him to marry another. "I could have taken a fraction less of your perfectly proper carping about Pulitzer Prizes and 'best-sellers,' and a great deal more of the intimate revelations. . . . Your 'Dorothy la Desiree' left me cold." *Quiet, Please* was the precursor of Cabell's next book in that Margaret insisted that he had to write about the people and things he liked; Marjorie considered *Quiet* a "teaser"—"You are committed to follow it through, telling 'all.'"

Margaret complained of a severe bout with bursitis in the spring of 1952 but even so planned a trip to New York on their return to Richmond. Cabell continued to be unhappy with Waller Freeman's business trips, but an external force soon altered her plans. Cabell wrote Marjorie Rawlings on 27 April, congratulating her on the long-delayed completion of a novel and explaining what happened:

> To begin with, there were the necessary trips down to our country mansion at Ophelia and back, to see about getting the place in order for the summer. Then without any warning fell the thunderbolt of Margaret's being requested by her landlord to vacate her apartment in New York. You can well imagine how that necessitated some impassioned days of long distance telephoning and of vivid declamation and of stern demands of heaven for information if ever before in all this world's history any other poor woman had been so consistently downtrodden. And I am afraid I was not sufficiently enraged and sympathetic about it. The fact was mentioned.
>
> Anyhow, she in the end decided to make her headquarters in Richmond henceforward, and I with a cowardly concealment am delighted. So at this instant she is in New York and is packing up between trips to the dentist, and Ballard and I have been scuffling through the last week as best we might.
>
> —Though he also, I must add, is habitually hilarious nowadays, if upon different grounds. You see, the picture which he exhibited in St. Augustine during March was bought by a hitherto unheard-of admirer from Alabama, who paid for it $50., and this windfall the gifted artist is now engaged in spending as fast as seems humanly possible.

In May Cabell was cheered by Edward Wagenknecht's handsome assessment of his career in The Cavalcade of the American Novel. Hunter Stagg was invited to Ophelia in July, and literary talk interspersed with gossip of writers they knew made his stay enjoyable for Margaret and James. Margaret drove to Sunny Bank for fresh seafood and to the best cake-baker in the neighborhood for walnut cakes; fresh produce came from her own garden. She explained to guests that James had never had a cold meal in his life; an uncooked garden salad as a meal was incomprehensible to him. On 1 July Cabell wrote Rawlings, "We lately celebrated the second anniversary of our wedding with many pleasant mutual compliments upon each other's superhuman powers of endurance." He was at work on the final testament entitled As I Remember It. Writing John Farrar on the occasion of his daughter's wedding, Cabell mentioned his own work: "But do not be alarmed. I am not going to bother you with it, after two rejections. Enough is, as they say, too much."

September brought the exciting news that Marjorie Rawlings had been

asked to write a biography of Ellen Glasgow. Rawlings had the approval
of Glasgow's sister Rebe Tutwiler and companion Anne Virginia Bennett.
Now she wanted Cabell's approval, for he was the "only proper person"
to write the biography. Aside from the fact that Irita Van Doren, Glasgow's
literary executor, did not like Cabell and had not asked him to write the
life, Rawlings knew she was dealing with a friend who had a proprietary
interest in Glasgow's biography. He was vitally curious about Glasgow's
comments concerning him in her memoir, and he planned a chapter on
her in his own forthcoming revelations. She had told him "with a grim
enjoyment" that he would not like her posthumous remarks, should he
outlive her. Her autobiography, *The Woman Within*, could not be published
while Henry Anderson, Glasgow's erstwhile fiancé, was alive, and that
gentleman, though seriously ill, still lived. Cabell wrote Marjorie Rawlings
that Glasgow's autobiography should be published before anyone attempted a definitive biography. She agreed but noted that a biographer
had to start now, while those who knew Glasgow were still alive; she
planned to devote five years to the task, and even then publication could
be delayed if necessary. She would approach cautiously the Richmonders
to be interviewed; she would take a house or apartment in Richmond,
becoming a neighbor worthy of confidences. She won Margaret over by
soliciting her help in finding a house. Margaret won James over, and they
both wrote that they would seduce the reticent Henry Anderson.

In November Cabell pocketed his pride and wrote John Farrar about
his work in progress. It was to be a pleasant book, reminiscences of persons whom he liked to remember and to whom he felt grateful. Nothing
obscene would blemish its pages. Margaret, with Cabell's concurrence,
decided to forego the annual winter pilgrimage to Florida. Because Cabell
had a heart condition and was subject to respiratory infections, he felt he
should stay close to his Richmond physicians. In an attempt to alleviate
Cabell's flu-like symptoms, his physicians administered the new "wonder
drugs" aureomycin and penicillin. Cabell had a severe allergic reaction,
one that further impaired his heart. The prescribed bed rest left him
bored and impatient. In mid-February, Marjorie wrote her husband from
Richmond:

> Margaret Cabell calls me two and three times a day. I don't know whether
> she thinks I am lonesome, or just wants to talk because she is so confined,
> with James' illness. Her hysteria is really overpowering when it goes on long
> enough. She has always been more or less that way, but it seems worse now.
> She had two women in to meet me yesterday afternoon, and one of them, a

good friend of Ellen, had some perfectly charming anecdotes. We are to meet again, and I think she will have a great deal of the lively sort of *harmless* personal stuff that gives a certain sparkle to a biography. . . .

Only Anne Virginia and the Colonel are holding me up.

Anne Virginia Bennett was receiving electric shock treatments for severe depression. The Colonel, Henry Anderson, not a well man, was every bit as reticent as James Cabell when it came to personal confessions. The teller of charming anecdotes was the ever-delightful Emma Gray Trigg, who had enchanted Joe Hergesheimer and Carl Van Vechten thirty years before.

A boost for Cabell's sagging spirits at this time was a letter from Frances J. Brewer of the Detroit Public Library proposing a bibliography of his works. Already interested in such a project, Cabell encouraged her, and a warm relationship developed between them for his remaining years. Another friendship was renewed when Grace Hegger Lewis wrote asking for Sinclair Lewis letters and permission to publish them. A charming woman who was Lewis's first wife, her visits and communications also warmed the winter of Cabell's discontent.

Despite John Farrar's previous rejections, Cabell sent him the typescript of *As I Remember It* for a critique. He was still on the list of invalids, Farrar was informed, a hint that this was his last book, but again Farrar's silence wounded his sensibilities. On 23 May he wrote: "This mainly is to ask that you forget, or at least condone, my blunder in sending you that typescript and asking for a candid opinion on it. I should, if but in the light of experience, have known far better."

Emily Clark Balch died in Philadelphia and was buried in Richmond on 10 July. The Cabells in Ophelia did not see the funeral notice in time to attend. Emily's money established the Balch prizes in American Literature at the University of Virginia. Hunter Stagg was again invited to Ophelia, for the Labor Day weekend. The summer had had its discontentments, owing in part to a tropical storm that toppled trees on Poynton Lodge. Marjorie Rawlings, who was beginning to feel optimistic about the Glasgow biography, paused in Richmond in late October and early November. She too was not in good health but drove herself with dogged determination to complete a nearly impossible task. Back at Crescent Beach with her husband, she was struck down by a cerebral hemorrhage on 18 December 1953. Cabell wrote Edward Wagenknecht on 2 January of the new year: "Our Christmas was deplorably saddened by the death of

Marjorie Kinnan Rawlings, who had visited us here but a few days earlier, in the best of health apparently, and whom my wife and I had both regarded with affection for numerous years. I had also a peculiar personal interest in her planned book upon Ellen Glasgow, for which she had assembled a huge bulk of data, but no word of which, alas, was yet written."

Henry Anderson died less than three weeks later, on 7 January, thus releasing Glasgow's autobiography for publication. Cabell was anxious to read Glasgow's assessment of their friendship, hoping to have the last word in his own memoirs. As he tells us midway through *As I Remember It*, Margaret Cabell was responsible for this final testament. Having disliked its predecessor, she prevailed upon him to record in a generous way his memories of those whom he had admired for various reasons. It resulted in some of his best writing and serves admirably as a capstone to his career. His memorial to his first wife, the beloved Percie, tempers his irony with affection, and the rest of his portraits are limned with humanizing compassion. In this final confession he achieved what his critics found most wanting in the corpus of his oeuvre, characters of flesh and blood and heart. By 14 June he boasted that he had found a publisher and that there would be no future books. "Those accursed antibiotics poisoned me . . . and have left me a permanent—or rather, a far too noticeably impermanent—invalid. I have to write nowadays with both legs propped in front of me on a stool, and I find this posture to be unfavorable to inspiration."

The Brewer bibliography occupied him. More and more people were interested in his correspondence with other writers. His oldest literary friend, Joseph Hergesheimer, died on 25 April, and Dorothy Hergesheimer wrote asking permission to sell the letters he had written to Joe. An agent for a collector, Clifton Waller Barrett, asked to buy his correspondence in bulk along with his library and typescripts. He was cooperating with Gracie Lewis on her memoir of Hal. He longed for an agent to handle business matters. Finally, through his appeal to Irita Van Doren, he was allowed to see the proof sheets of Glasgow's autobiography, scheduled for fall publication. He could round off his chapter on Glasgow with his final say on their relationship. At the same time he heard from John Farrar that *As I Remember It* was a publishable work. Cabell wrote Farrar on 1 October: "Well, and as I wrote you, I have had overtures, but I have delayed in tying up with anybody until after our return to Richmond about the middle of this month—mainly because I wanted first to see the Glasgow book. When, and if, anything is settled, and should forsaken Lear be taken in somewhere from out of the cold, then you shall be the first to hear of it."

Glasgow in *The Woman Within* touched on the "homosexual" episode in Williamsburg and the murder of John Scott in Richmond, which gossip had attributed to Cabell. She played the role of benign defender in recounting these episodes. In his "Speaks with Candor of a Great Lady," Cabell observed that "I did not ever encounter, of course, quite the personage whom she depicted in Ellen Glasgow's autobiography, that beautiful and wise volume which contains a large deal of her very best fiction." To Farrar, he wrote that "in dealing with matters which I happened to know about, she has touched up and suppressed the truth always improvingly, over and yet over again." He took full credit for conceiving the notion that her work constituted "a Social History of Virginia" and for getting *In This Our Life* into a final form so that it could be accorded the Pulitzer Prize, matters still questioned by literary scholars. In any event, *The Woman Within* did what even Ellen Glasgow's death had been unable to do: it freed Cabell to write of her with candor. He gives us a portrait that has a vitality lacking in her autobiography. What is even more significant is that Cabell's freedom from constraint allowed him to express a *genuine* admiration as opposed to the polite encomiums found in reviews or the nostalgic tenderness in *Let Me Lie*. There is no reason to doubt his seriousness when he states that he found in her an interesting, "a distinctive, nay, a gorgeous personality."

The fall of 1954 found Cabell corresponding with his old publisher, Robert McBride, who was interested in seeing the typescript of *As I Remember It*. Feeling optimistic for his literary legacy and gratitude for the future care of Ballard, Cabell penned a letter to Margaret in the waning hours of 1954. "You have cared for both Ballard and me with an incredible patience," he wrote, "and—that's the strange part—without your ever having been endowed with any patience." Perhaps as token of his appreciation, his assessment of Margaret's former lover in *As I Remember It* was almost totally generous, with just a few tiny ironies seeded therein for her irritated delectation. His last act of charity was to dedicate this final work to John Farrar, the publisher who had declined it and had objected to Cabell's allusion to Hugh Walpole's homosexual behavior; Walpole, Farrar stated firmly, had been a model of rectitude in their social intercourse.

In the spring of 1955 Cabell was stricken with a virus in early March that hung on for months owing to his inability to tolerate the drugs used to treat it. By July he was convalescent. The efficient Margaret took on the responsibilities of literary agent, a chore she rather enjoyed. Academe was awakening to a renewed interest in Cabell, inspired in part by Ellen Glasgow studies and a growing emphasis on southern literature in general. In October Cabell was cheered that the Bibliographical Society of the University of Virginia had contracted to publish Frances Brewer's bibliography of his works, and in November *As I Remember It* was published. Burton Rascoe's review in the Chicago *Sunday Tribune* led the encomiums. The personal and genial nature of the memoirs inspired a flurry of letters from old friends and acquaintances. It also led to calls for a reappraisal of the total Cabell oeuvre. Edmund Wilson in the *New Yorker* (21 April 1956) pointed the way with "The James Branch Cabell Case Reopened." Louis D. Rubin, Jr., added his voice with "The Prospects of a Cabell Revival" in the Richmond *News-Leader* (5 June 1956) and "James Branch Cabell Today" in the Baltimore *Evening Sun* (6 July 1956).

In February 1956, H. L. Mencken died after a lengthy and incapacitating illness. Cabell wrote John Farrar: "He was a great man, of whom, and with good cause, I was sincerely fond. And I find it a bit depressing to note that all of his generation—which by ill luck includes me—are wholly done for. But at least we had a fine time while it lasted." In May vivacious Grace Lewis Casanova visited the Cabell household in Richmond, to the delight of all three. Her charming memoir of Lewis, *With Love from Gracie*, was published in August. Cabell wrote her on the 23d: "Do you accept my heartfelt applause. And 'heartfelt' is the exact adjective. For you left me alike charmed and wistful and saddened, when I recalled 1918 at the Alum and the last time that I saw Hal in 1941. Moreover, you left me feeling incredibly old."

Cabell's reestablished liaison with his old publisher was of brief duration; in economic difficulties, the McBride Company was taken over by creditors. Robert McBride started another company, but Cabell's contract as well as the unsold copies of *As I Remember It* remained with the unknown owners of the old company. Wirt Marks, Cabell's lawyer, attempted to unravel the intricate legalities but with little success. Cabell's most successful work in decades disappeared from the publishing lists and bookstores. The publication of the bibliography was delayed by the request of the Bibliographical Society of the university that Cabell's works be subjected to scrutiny by a Hinman machine to determine variations of text. Both Brewer and Cabell were opposed, feeling that corrections in an edition did not constitute a new version. The *Bibliography* with a foreword by Cabell finally emerged in late 1957.

In March 1957, Burton Rascoe died. Cabell wrote Hazel Rascoe on the 23d: "In Burton I lost a valued and an invaluable friend of some forty years standing. I have never forgotten, and I can never forget, the so many good services and the pleasure which I got out of that friendship. To him and to Guy Holt, I feel, my books, such as they are, owe more than to any other men whom I have ever known." On 2 April Cabell wrote a forgiving letter to John Farrar, his last remaining confidant:

> It is a bit depressing nowadays to reflect that all my literary contemporaries are gone, and that I myself have become too old and too feeble to write. Still, I don't know what can be done about it.
>
> I hope that with you, as a callow youngster of sixty-one, affairs speed rather more cheerily. And I have almost succeeded in forgiving you for turning down my last two books, as was of course your duty to your firm, since by retaining me as an author they were losing money. I am having, by the bye, unlimited trouble with the so called McBride Company, in the way of collecting my modest royalties.

Cabell was grateful for greetings on his seventy-ninth birthday from Carl Van Vechten: "It is a matter in which I both need and like sympathy. . . . With Rascoe's death, you have become virtually the only author whom I know—or rather, used to know, inasmuch as we never see each other nowadays, nor seem likely ever to meet again upon this side of the Styx."

In September, a graduate student presented to Cabell a copy of his long, dull dissertation written in French, "Les Sources Etrangères du Roman Epique de James Branch Cabell." The subject whipped through the study in a matter of hours and wanted to discuss it. Yes, perhaps the Storisende Edition had been a mistake, as the student maintained, because it equated his best work with the inconsequential. True, it had not been an organic concept from 1901 as claimed. Which works, in the opinion of his guest, would survive the test of time? There was a bit of cautious hedging, but the author seemed pleased with the five titles suggested.

Also in September, Hunter Stagg, was committed as a chronic alcoholic to St. Elizabeth's Hospital in Washington, where he would remain with other distinguished guests until his death in December 1960. Cabell was a lonely relic of his era. With the exception of Van Vechten, his closest colleagues were all gone: Frances Newman and Elinor Wylie had died in 1928, Ellen Glasgow in 1945, Sinclair Lewis in 1951, Emily Clark and Marjorie Rawlings in 1953, Joe Hergesheimer in 1954, H. L. Mencken in 1956, and Burton Rascoe in 1957.

On 1 January 1958, Cabell asked Gracie Casanova to write another memoir, "and for my sake do you please be quick about it. In addition to old age, I am now dealing with, as they say, pretty much every known malady from aberrations to zymosis." He hoped to see Frances Brewer and her husband at Easter: "If at the time I happen to be in extreme dishabille, you will just have to put up with it. I haven't actually been dressed since the first week in last October. . . . I feel myself apt at any moment to be incommoded by having to wear a halo and trying to get used to it when I lie down." Cabell died at home of a cerebral hemorrhage on the evening of 5 May. He had recovered from a slight stroke in January 1957 and was feeling somewhat better. He was buried according to the rites of the Episcopal Church in Emmanuel Church Cemetery beside his beloved Percie, his wife for over thirty-five years.

But irony continued to intrude into the Cabell epos. Margaret, the widow, had second thoughts about Emmanuel. Ballard was to be buried next to his father. She was not a member of Emmanuel. Where did that leave her? Besides, all the "best" people were buried in Hollywood Cemetery. She prevailed upon the civic powers to sell her a choice plot in the older section of Hollywood. James and Percie Cabell were moved from Emmanuel where they lay side by side to Hollywood where they were separated by a space intended for Ballard. Thus Margaret made a place for herself next to the widower who had conferred upon her at age seventy-one such immortality as she was to know. Over the remains of her husband she erected a Renaissance-style tomb, embellished with a verse he had written on the death of Beverley Bland Munford. Priscilla Bradley Cabell is identified on her flat, eighteenth-century-style stone as "First wife of James Branch Cabell"; there is no mention of her being the wife of Emmett Shepherd and the mother of his five children. Ballard died in 1980, having long outlived early prognoses. He is memorialized as the "Beloved son and the joy of Priscilla Bradley Cabell and James Branch Cabell." Margaret died in 1983 in her ninetieth year; on her stone is engraved "Whom time has converted into a person even more dear."

Closer to the river in Hollywood Cemetery, Annie Cabell lies in the Branch section, near Martha Louise Patteson Branch. Also close to the river, Dr. Robert Gamble Cabell, Jr., lies with his parents and siblings in the Cabell section. In Woodstock, New York, Gabriella Brooke Moncure lies in the Artists' Cemetery. When in his late sixties Cabell returned to her in spirit in *The Witch-Woman*, he added "An Epilogue as to Other Wanderers." Horvendile and Ettarre, the doomed lovers, bring joy to others

347

but not to themselves, each following "after the derisive shadow of a love which the long years have not made real." In this epilogue Cabell wrote: "For all happiness must end with death, and all that which is human must die. But Horvendile and his Ettarre, they who are neither happy nor quite human, may not, so does their legend tell us, ever die; nor as yet have they parted from each other for the last time."

Bibliographical Notes

All references to Cabell's works are to the first edition, unless otherwise noted.

Chapter 1, "Ancestral Voices," is based on Alexander Brown, *The Cabells and Their Kin* (1895); James Branch Cabell, *Branchiana* (1907); various newspapers as noted; a memorandum by Margaret Freeman Cabell addressed to Emma Gray Trigg and Edgar MacDonald found in the Margaret Freeman Cabell Papers; and Cabell scrapbooks of the period, found in Special Collections of the Cabell Library.

Chapter 2, "Reflections in the Mirror," is based on Cabell's *Let Me Lie* (1947); *Quiet, Please* (1952); *As I Remember It* (1955); *First Gentleman of America* (1942); *There Were Two Pirates* (1946); and on his scrapbooks of the period; Perceval Reniers, *The Springs of Virginia* (1941); Charlotte Lou Atkins, "Rockbridge Alum Springs: A History of the Spa, 1790–1974"; Robert Beverley Munford, *Richmond Homes and Memories* (1936); Mary Wingfield Scott, *Old Richmond Neighborhoods* (1950–1974); Maurice Duke, "James Branch Cabell's Library: A Catalog"; Walter Russell Bowie, *Sunrise in the South* (1942); Richmond city directories; Chancery Court records as specified.

Chapter 3, "The Emerging Chrysalis," is based on John P. Little, *History of Richmond* (1933); Virginius Dabney, *Richmond: The Story of a City* (1976); *As I Remember It*; *Branchiana*; Munford; Chancery Court records; a memoir by James Ransom Branch as recorded by Melville C. Branch; Walter Russell Bowie, *Women of Light* (1963); Richmond newspapers; Mary Wingfield Scott, "James Branch Cabell and the 'Jack Scott Murder' and "Wild Branches I Have Known."

Chapter 4, "Severing the Cords," is based on the annual William and Mary College catalogs of the period; the *William and Mary College Monthly* as specified; letters to Alice Serpell; William Leigh Godshalk, "James Branch Cabell at William and Mary: The Education of a Novelist"; James M. Lundgren, "'Whatever is Un-Virginian is Wrong': The

APVA's Sense of the Old Dominion"; James M. Lundgren, "'For the Sake of Our Future': The Association for the Preservation of Virginia Antiquities and the Regeneration of Traditionalism"; interview with Mary Cary Moncure, half-sister of Gabriella Moncure, Williamsburg.

Chapter 5, "Palingenesis," is based on *W&M Monthly*; scrapbooks; Godshalk; James Branch Cabell, *Special Delivery* (1933); Cabell, "Cabell," a 5-page typed biographical sketch dated November 1917; Emmett Peter, Jr., "Cabell: The Making of a Rebel"; William and Mary Faculty Minutes; *History of the K.A. Fraternity and Its Institutions*; Ellen Glasgow, *The Woman Within* (1954).

Chapter 6, "Charles Washington Coleman and Gabriella Brooke Moncure," is based on the Tucker-Coleman Papers, Swem Library, W&M; Coleman's *In His Own Country* (1942); the interview with Mary Cary Moncure; several interviews with Mrs. William Ronson of Woodstock, N.Y., sister-in-law of Gabriella; Marion M. Duncan, *The House of Moncure Genealogy* (1967); Margaret Freeman Cabell first told me that Gabriella Moncure was the only woman that Cabell loved in a romantic sense.

Chapter 7, "Exile," is based on Richmond newspapers; Cabell's 1917 autobiographical sketch in the Alderman Library; the Henry Sydnor Harrison Papers, Manuscript Department, William R. Perkins Library, Duke University; Frank Durham, "Love as a Literary Exercise: Young James Branch Cabell Tries His Wings"; letter of Martha Patteson Bowie to Martha Patteson Branch that is in the possession of Mrs. Henry Converse, daughter of Martha Bowie.

Chapter 8, "Murder in Rue Franklin," is based on Cabell's 1917 autobiographical sketch; scrapbooks; the Mary Wingfield Scott memoranda; Glasgow's *Woman Within*; Richmond newspapers; Edgar MacDonald, "Cabell's Richmond Trial."

Chapter 9, "The Alchemist," is based on Isaac Frederick Marcosson, *Before I Forget: A Pilgrimage to the Past* (1969); Richmond newspapers; scrapbooks; 1905 letterbook of James Ransom Branch; the letters cited of Justus Miles Forman, Theodore Roosevelt, Robert Bacon, H. M. Alden, Walter Hines Page, R. H. Dana, William Loeb, H. L. Mencken, all found in the Cabell Papers of the Cabell Library.

Chapter 10, "The Skeleton in the Closet," is based on correspondence that was held by the firm of Scott & Stringfellow and passed on to the late Robert G. Cabell III, then to Robert G. Cabell V; scrapbooks; *Special Delivery*; Letter Book of James Ransom Branch; Cabell, "The Dream"; *The Certain Hour* (1916); *The Soul of Melicent* (1913); notebooks.

Chapter 11, "A Brown Woman," is based on *As I Remember It*; Richmond newspapers; scrapbooks; "The Lady of All Our Dreams"; *Townsend of Lichfield* (1930); notebooks; *The Cream of the Jest* (1917); *The Rivet in Grandfather's Neck* (1915); Cabell letters provided by Priscilla Harriss Cabell; Mary Wingfield Scott memoranda; Dorothy McInnis Scura, "Cabell and Holt: The Literary Connection"; Harrison, *Angela's Business* (1915).

Chapter 12, "Formulating a Creed," is based on Burton Rascoe, *Before I Forget* (1937); Vincent Starrett, *Born in a Bookshop: Chapters from the Chicago Renascence* (1965); H. L. Mencken, *New Mencken Letters* (1977), *Letters from Baltimore* (1982); Ellen Wilkins Tompkins, "A Day at Dower House"; Carl Van Vechten, "An Introduction with Candor and Some Little Truth," in *Between Friends: Letters of James Branch Cabell and Others* (1962). This biography makes increasing use of Cabell's published letters, those in the preceding title, edited by Padraic Colum and Margaret Freeman Cabell, and those in *The Letters of James Branch Cabell* (1975), edited by Edward Wagenknecht; however, original letters to Cabell in the James Branch Cabell Library have been used; Cabell's letters to Rascoe are housed in the University of Pennsylvania Library.

Chapter 13, "The Redeemed," is based on James Branch Cabell, *Preface to the Past* (1936); Grace Hegger Lewis, *With Love From Gracie* (1955); Ronald E. Martin, *The Fiction of Joseph Hergesheimer* (1965); Hansell Baugh, ed., *Frances Newman's Letters* (1929); Rupert Hart-Davis, *Hugh Walpole: A Biography* (1952); Mrs. John Lightfoot (Nan Maury Lightfoot), *A Few Minutes* (1923); Glasgow, *The Woman Within*; Hugh Walpole, *The Art of James Branch Cabell* (1920).

Chapter 14, "The High Place," is based on Burton Rascoe, *We Were Interrupted* (1947); Emily Clark, *Innocence Abroad* (1931); Marie Keane Dabney, *Mrs. T.N.T.* (1949); Gerald Langford, ed., *Ingénue Among the Lions: The Letters of Emily Clark to Joseph Hergesheimer* (1965); Newman letters; scrapbooks; Maurice Duke, *James Branch Cabell: A Reference Guide* (1979); Duke, "Ingenue Among the Richmonders: Of Emily Clark and Stuffed Peacocks"; Dorothy McInnis Scura, "Mary Dallas Street: Editor, Novelist, and Poet"; Edgar MacDonald, "Hunter Stagg: 'Over There in Paris with Gertrude Stein.'"; Lightfoot, *The Bookman* (1921).

Chapter 15, "The Magic Circle," is based on *As I Remember It*; specified issues of *Town Topics*; Ernest Boyd, *Portraits: Real and Imaginary* (1924); Bruce Kellner, *Carl Van Vechten and the Irreverent Decades* (1968); *Letters of Carl Van Vechten* (1987); Montgomery Evans Papers and diary, Special Collections, Morris Library, Southern Illinois University; Clark, *Ingénue Among the Lions*; James Branch Cabell, *These Restless Heads* (1932); *Innocence Abroad*; Stagg letters to Evans; Cabell to Holt; Van Vechten to Stagg; letters of Carl Van Vechten to Emma Gray Trigg are in the Alderman Library, University of Virginia.

Chapter 16, "Tea and Intrigue," is based on letters of Hunter Stagg; Charles Baldwin, *Men Who Make Our Novels* (1924); John Chipman Farrar, *The Literary Spotlight* (1924); Kellner, *Carl Van Vechten and the Irreverent Decades*; Clark; Richmond newspapers; Carl Van Doren, *James Branch Cabell* (1925); Van Vechten to Stagg; Bruccoli, *Notes on the Cabell Collection* (1957); Duke, *Guide* (1979).

Chapter 17, "Mispec Moor," is based on the Stagg, Van Vechten, and Newman letters; Cabell-Hergesheimer correspondence; Cabell-Holt correspondence; Cabell-Mencken correspondence; Hunter Stagg, "The Nationality of James Branch Cabell," *Richmond* (April 1929): 9, 28, 34; Warren A. McNeil, *Cabellian Harmonics* (1928); Dorothy Scura, "Glasgow and the Southern Renaissance: The Conference at Charlottesville"; Sally Wood, ed., *Southern Mandarins: The Letters of Caroline Gordon to Sally Wood, 1924–1937* (1984).

Chapter 18, "The Possessed," is based on Stagg letters; *These Restless Heads*; New York *Evening Post*; *As I Remember It*; Granville Hicks, *The Great Tradition* (1935); Ritchie D. Watson, "The Ellen Glasgow–Allen Tate Correspondence: Bridging the Southern Literary Generation Gap"; Bruce Kellner, "Ellen Glasgow and Gertrude Stein"; Henry Hazlett, *The Anatomy of Criticism: A Trialogue* (1933); Northrop Frye, *Anatomy of Criticism: Four Essays* (1957); Edgar MacDonald, "The Glasgow–Cabell Entente"; Gordon Bigelow, *Frontier Eden: The Literary Career of Marjorie Kinnan Rawlings* (1966); Tonette L. Bond, "'A Thrilling Sense of Friendship and Sympathy': The Correspondence of Ellen Glasgow and Marjorie Kinnan Rawlings"; Glasgow, *A Certain Measure* (1943); Joe Lee Davis, *James Branch Cabell* (1962); Stagg letters; Rascoe correspondence; John Farrar correspondence; Glasgow correspondence.

Chapter 19, "The Past Reclaimed," is based on *Selected Letters of Marjorie Kinnan Rawlings*, edited by Gordon E. Bigelow & Laura V. Monti (1983);

manuscript letters of Glasgow and Rawlings held by Special Collections, James Branch Cabell Library; Cabell letters in University of Florida Libraries. For the most part, letters cited are from *The Letters of James Branch Cabell*; Glasgow correspondence; Stagg letters; "The Glasgow-Cabell Entente"; *Frontier Eden*.

Chapter 20, "Antan," is based on Wagenknecht; Bigelow & Monti; manuscript letters in Cabell Library; correspondence of Margaret Freeman in Cabell Library; Stagg letters; Farrar correspondence; Davis, *James Branch Cabell*. The period covered by this chapter coincides with the biographer's friendship with the late Margaret Freeman Cabell.

Works Cited

Atkins, Charlotte Lou. "Rockbridge Alum Springs: A History of the Spa, 1790–1974." Master's thesis, Virginia Polytechnic Institute and State University, 1974.

Baldwin, Charles. *The Men Who Make Our Novels.* New York: Dodd, Mead & Co., 1924.

Bigelow, Gordon E. *Frontier Eden: The Literary Career of Marjorie Kinnan Rawlings.* Gainesville: University of Florida Press, 1966.

Bowie, Walter Russell. *Sunrise in the South.* Richmond, Va.: William Byrd Press, 1942.

———. *Women of Light.* New York: Harper & Row, 1963.

Boyd, Ernest. *Portraits: Real and Imaginary.* New York: George H. Doran, 1924.

Branch, James Ransom. Correspondence. James Branch Cabell Library, Virginia Commonwealth University, Richmond, Virginia.

Brewer, Joan Francis. *James Branch Cabell: A Bibliography of His Writings, Biography and Criticism.* Charlottesville: University of Virginia Press, 1957.

Brown, Alexander. *The Cabells and Their Kin.* Boston: Houghton, Mifflin Co., 1895.

Bruccoli, Matthew J. *James Branch Cabell: A Bibliography.* Part 2, *Notes on the Cabell Collections at the University of Virginia.* Charlottesville: University of Virginia Press, 1957.

Cabell, James Branch. *As I Remember It.* New York: McBride & Co., 1955.

———. *Between Friends: Letters of James Branch Cabell and Others.* Edited by Padraic Colum and Margaret Freeman Cabell. New York: Harcourt, Brace & World, 1962.

———. *Beyond Life.* New York: R. M. McBride & Co., 1919.

———. *Branchiana.* Richmond, Va.: Whittet & Shepperson, 1907.

———. *The Certain Hour.* New York: R. M. McBride & Co., 1916.

———. *The Cords of Vanity.* New York: Doubleday, Page, 1909.

———. *The Cream of the Jest.* New York: R. M. McBride & Co., 1917.

———. *Figures of Earth.* New York: R. M. McBride & Co., 1921.

———. *First Gentleman of America.* New York: Farrar & Rinehart, 1942.

————. *The High Place*. New York: R. M. McBride & Co., 1923.

————. *Jurgen*. New York: R. M. McBride & Co., 1919.

————. *Let Me Lie*. New York: Farrar, Straus & Co., 1947.

————. *The Letters of James Branch Cabell*. Edited by Edward Wagenknecht. Norman: University of Oklahoma Press, 1975.

————. Notebooks. James Branch Cabell Papers, Special Collections, James Branch Cabell Library, Virginia Commonwealth University, Richmond, Virginia.

————. *Preface to the Past*. New York: R. M. McBride & Co., 1936.

————. *Quiet, Please*. Gainesville: University of Florida Press, 1952.

————. *The Rivet in Grandfather's Neck*. New York: R. M. McBride, 1915.

————. Scrapbooks. James Branch Cabell Papers, Special Collections, James Branch Cabell Library. Virginia Commonwealth University, Richmond, Virginia.

————. *Some of Us*. New York: R. M. McBride & Co., 1930.

————. *Soul of Melicent*. New York: Frederick A. Stokes, 1913.

————. *Special Delivery*. New York: R. M. McBride & Co., 1933.

————. *There Were Two Pirates*. New York: Farrar, Straus & Co., 1946.

————. *These Restless Heads*. New York: R. M. McBride & Co., 1932.

————. *Townsend of Lichfield*. New York: R. M. McBride & Co., 1930.

————. *The Witch-Woman*. New York: Farrar, Straus & Co., 1948.

Clark, Emily. *Ingénue Among the Lions: The Letters of Emily Clark to Joseph Hergesheimer*. Edited by Gerald Langford. Austin: University of Texas Press, 1965.

————. *Innocence Abroad*. New York: Alfred A. Knopf, 1931.

Coleman, Charles Washington. *In His Own Country*. Richmond: Whittet & Shepperson, 1942.

Dabney, Marie Keane. *Mrs. T.N.T.* Richmond, Va.: Dietz Press, 1949.

Dabney, Virginius. *Richmond: The Story of a City*. Garden City: Doubleday, 1976.

Davis, Joe Lee. *James Branch Cabell*. New York: Twayne Publishers, 1962.

Duke, Maurice. "Ingenue Among the Richmonders: Of Emily Clark and *Stuffed Peacocks*." *Ellen Glasgow Newsletter*, 3 (October 1975): 5–9.

————. *James Branch Cabell: A Reference Guide*. Boston: G. K. Hall & Co., 1979.

————. "James Branch Cabell's Library: A Catalogue." Ph.D. diss., University of Iowa, 1968.

Duncan, Marion M. *The House of Moncure Genealogy*. Alexandria, Va.: n. p., 1967.

Durham, Frank. "Love as a Literary Exercise: Young James Branch Cabell Tries His Wings." *Mississippi Quarterly* 18 (Winter 1964): 26–37.

Farrar, John Chipman, ed. *The Literary Spotlight.* New York: George H. Doran, 1924.

Frye, Northrop. *The Anatomy of Criticism: Four Essays.* Princeton: Princeton University Press, 1957.

Glasgow, Ellen. *A Certain Measure.* New York: Harcourt, Brace & Co., 1943.

———. *The Woman Within.* New York: Harcourt, Brace & Co., 1954.

Godshalk, William Leigh. "James Branch Cabell at William and Mary: The Education of a Novelist." *William and Mary Review* 5 (Spring 1967): 1–10.

Gordon, Caroline. *Southern Mandarins: The Letters of Caroline Gordon to Sally Wood.* Edited by Andrew Lytle. Baton Rouge: Louisiana State University Press, 1984.

Hart-Davis, Rupert. *Hugh Walpole: A Biography.* New York: Macmillan, 1952.

Hazlitt, Henry. *The Anatomy of Criticism: A Trialogue.* New York: Simon & Schuster, 1933.

Hicks, Granville. *The Great Tradition.* New York: Macmillan, 1935.

Hobson, Fred. *Serpent in Eden: H. L. Mencken and the South.* Chapel Hill: University of North Carolina Press, 1974.

Inge, M. Thomas, and Edgar E. MacDonald, eds. *James Branch Cabell: Centennial Essays.* Baton Rouge: Louisiana State University Press, 1983.

James, Henry. *The American Scene.* London: Chapman & Hall, 1907.

Kellner, Bruce. *Carl Van Vechten and the Irreverent Decades.* Norman: University of Oklahoma Press, 1968.

———. "Ellen Glasgow and Gertrude Stein." *Ellen Glasgow Newsletter* 2 (March 1975): 13–16.

Lewis, Grace Hegger. *With Love from Gracie: Sinclair Lewis.* New York: Harcourt, Brace, 1955.

Lightfoot, Mrs. John. *A Few Minutes.* Richmond, Va.: n. p., 1923.

———. *The Bookman* (April 1921): 185–86.

Little, John P. *History of Richmond.* Richmond, Va.: Dietz Press, 1933.

Lundgren, James M. "'For the Sake of Our Future': The Association for the Preservation of Virginia Antiquities and the Regeneration of Traditionalism." *Virginia Magazine of History and Biography* 97 (January 1989): 47–74.

———. "'Whatever is Un-Virginian is Wrong': The APVA's Sense of the Old Dominion." *Virginia Cavalcade* 38 (Winter 1989): 112–23.

MacDonald, Edgar E. "Cabell in Love." In *James Branch Cabell: Centennial Es-*

says, edited by M. Thomas Inge and Edgar E. MacDonald. Baton Rouge: Louisiana State University Press, 1983: 17–39.

———. "Cabell's Richmond Trial." *Southern Literary Journal* 3 (Fall 1970): 47–71.

———. "The Glasgow–Cabell Entente." *American Literature* 41 (March 1969): 76–91.

———. "Hunter Stagg: 'Over There in Paris with Gertrude Stein.'" *Ellen Glasgow Newsletter* 15 (October 1981): 2–16.

McNeill, Warren A. *Cabellian Harmonics*. New York: Random House, 1928.

Marcosson, Isaac Frederick. *Before I Forget: A Pilgrimage to the Past*. New York: Dodd, Mead & Co., 1969.

Martin, Ronald E. *The Fiction of Joseph Hergesheimer*. Philadelphia: University of Pennsylvania Press, 1965.

Mencken, H. L. *Letters from Baltimore*. Edited by P. E. Cleator. London: Associated University Presses, 1982.

———. *Letters of H. L. Mencken: Selected and Annotated by Guy J. Forgue*. New York: Alfred A. Knopf, 1961.

———. *New Mencken Letters*. Edited by Carl Bode. New York: Dial Press, 1977.

Munford, Robert Beverley. *Richmond Homes and Memories*. Richmond, Va.: Garrett & Massie, 1936.

Newman, Frances. *Frances Newman's Letters*. Edited by Hansell Baugh. New York: Liveright, 1929.

Olson, Stanley. *Elinor Wylie: A Life Apart*. New York: Dial Press, 1978.

Peter, Emmett, Jr. "Cabell: The Making of a Rebel." *Carolina Quarterly* 14 (Spring 1962): 74–81.

Rascoe, Burton. *Before I Forget*. New York: Doubleday, Doran, 1937.

———. *We Were Interrupted*. New York: Doubleday, 1947.

Rawlings, Marjorie Kinnan. *Selected Letters of Marjorie Kinnan Rawlings*. Edited by Gordon E. Bigelow and Laura V. Monti. Gainesville: University of Florida Press, 1983.

Reniers, Perceval. *The Springs of Virginia: Life, Love and Death at the Waters*. Chapel Hill: University of North Carolina Press, 1941.

Rubin, Louis D., Jr. "A Virginian in Poictesme." In *James Branch Cabell: Centennial Essays*, edited by M. Thomas Inge and Edgar E. MacDonald. Baton Rouge: Louisiana State University Press, 1983: 1–16.

Scott, Mary Wingfield. "James Branch Cabell and the Jack Scott Murder." Mss7:1, C1115:1, Virginia Historical Society, Richmond, Va.

————. *Old Richmond Neighborhoods.* Richmond, Va.: William Byrd Press, 1950.

————. "Wild Branches I Have Known." Papers of Edgar E. MacDonald, James Branch Cabell Library, Virginia Commonwealth University, Richmond, Va.

Scura, Dorothy McInnis. "Cabell and Holt: The Literary Connection." In *James Branch Cabell's Centennial Essays*, edited by M. Thomas Inge and Edgar E. MacDonald. Baton Rouge: Louisiana State University Press, 1983: 40–64.

————. "Ellen Glasgow and James Branch Cabell: The Record of a Friendship." Ph.D. diss., University of North Carolina, 1973.

————. "Mary Dallas Street: Editor, Novelist, and Poet." *Ellen Glasgow Newsletter* 4 (March 1976): 3–8.

Stagg, Hunter Taylor. "The Absence of Mr. Cabell." *Brentano's Book Chat* (March—April 1925): 23–27.

————. "The Nationality of James Branch Cabell." *Richmond* (April 1929): 9, 28, 34.

Starrett, Vincent. *Born in a Bookshop: Chapters from the Chicago Renascence.* Norman: University of Oklahoma Press, 1965.

Tompkins, Ellen Wilkins. "A Day at Dower House." *Reviewer* 1 (June 1921): 236–38.

Van Vechten, Carl. "An Introduction with Candor and Some Little Truth." In *Between Friends: The Letters of James Branch Cabell and Others.* New York: Harcourt, Brace & World, 1962: ix–xvi.

————. *Letters of Carl Van Vechten.* Edited by Bruce Kellner. New Haven: Yale University Press, 1987.

Walpole, Hugh. *The Art of James Branch Cabell.* New York: R. M. McBride & Co., 1920.

Watson, Ritchie D., Jr. "A Bibliographical Essay." In *James Branch Cabell: Centennial Essays*, edited by M. Thomas Inge and Edgar E. MacDonald. Baton Rouge: Louisiana State University Press, 1983: 142–179.

————. "The Ellen Glasgow–Allen Tate Correspondence: Bridging the Southern Literary Generation Gap." *Ellen Glasgow Newsletter* 23 (October 1985): 3–24.

Yeats, W. B. *Essays and Introduction.* New York: Macmillan, 1961.

Index